DRYLONGSO

Also by John Langston Gwaltney

THE THRICE SHY

DRYLONGSO

A Self-Portrait of Black America

JOHN LANGSTON GWALTNEY

The New Press, New York

Published in the United States by The New Press, New York
Distributed by W.W. Norton & Company, Inc.
500 Fifth Avenue, New York, NY 10110

LIBRARY OF CONGRESS CATALOGING-IN-PUBLICATION

Drylongso : a self portrait of Black America / [edited by] John Langston
Gwaltney. —1st ed.
      p.   cm.
Originally published: New York : Random House, c1980.
ISBN 1-56584-080-1
    1. Afro-Americans—Social   conditions—1975-   2. Afro-
Americans—Civil rights. 3. United States—Race relations.
I. Gwaltney, John Langston.
E185.86.D77   1993
305.896'073—dc20   92-50839
                                                            CIP

                        9 8 7 6 5 4 3

Established in 1990 as a major alternative to the large, commercial publishing houses, The New Press is intended to be the first full-scale nonprofit
American book publisher outside of the university presses. The Press is
operated editorially in the public interest, rather than for private gain; it is
committed to publishing in innovative ways works of educational, cultural,
and community value, which, despite their intellectual merits, might not
normally be "commercially viable."

For Lucy
and all the other flowers in
Aunt Hagar's garden

Acknowledgments

I liked the idea of talking to you about my life, but you
want me to do that more than I want to do it. I am just
talking, but you are working, and if nobody will talk
to you, you will be out of work.

Edith Warren

I am grateful for a sabbatical leave from the Department of Anthropology
of Syracuse University and for a fellowship from the American Council of
Learned Societies which greatly facilitated the writing of this book. The
indispensable financial assistance of the National Endowment for the
Humanities, the American Philosophical Society and the Social Science
Research Council placed me on the scores of street corners in the black
towns where I listened. But the street corner is no place to consort with the
soul of a great and subtle people living under conquest conditions. It was
through the grace and generosity of the hundreds of black men and women
whose opinions inform this volume that I was permitted to leave the tangen-
tial vantage point of the street. Miss Edith Warren, a young bank clerk, is
the first of the contributors to this volume, and I am proud to acknowledge
a debt past calculation to the many people like her who shared their time,
hospitality and profundity with me. They asked no recompense other than
that their contributions draw a self-portrait of their black American commonwealth that is not foreign to their considered view of themselves.

The late Dr. Margaret Mead and Professors Morton Fried and Conrad
Arensberg, of Columbia University, were encouraging and helpful from the
earliest conception of the project. Dr. Mary L. McDonald, consultant to the
Health Planning Services of the Canadian federal government, and Professor John F. Szwed, director of the Center for Urban Ethnography at the
University of Pennsylvania, offered helpful and pertinent reactions to an
early version of the manuscript. I am grateful to Random House editor Mr.
Erroll McDonald for his crucial role in editing and preparing the manuscript for publication.

My daughter Karen and my friends Mrs. Moitsadi Moeti, Dr. Ana
Pujols, Ms. Nancy Rose Sparrow, Professor James Bartow, Messrs. Theo-
dore McKee, Kenneth Milligan and James Yohannan were all extremely

helpful in a variety of very important ways in the successful completion of this project. I wish to thank my cousins Florence Wilson, Clarence Gwaltney, Augustus Tucker and Tylor Wilson, my nieces Linda Fletcher, Robin Gwaltney and Laura Westry, and my nephew, Frank Westry, all of whom were of great assistance to me in the field.

Most special thanks are due and lovingly tendered my wife, Judy. Her proficiency in editing, her skill and patience in typing and her lively, diligent mind were all absolutely indispensable in the translation of these data into book form. It is no exaggeration or perfunctory domestic duty but a statement of plain fact to say that without her assistance it would not have seen the light of print.

My brother Robert's disinclination to be interviewed ("You know what I think") was more than compensated for by his never-failing material assistance in transportation, sustenance and lodging. His resourceful, tactful wife, Janet, was also unfailing in her support of the project.

My sister Lucy, to whom this book is dedicated, has been, from my earliest days, a constant source of inspiration and an exemplar of the core black way. There is no one to whom I am so deeply indebted for the profound satisfactions which proceed from the exercise of the mind and the imagination. She bore us both on wings of print to Troy and Thebes and Xanadu. Her command of the art of puppetry lent substance to many of the shadowy characters which have their being in the realms of books and art. She showed me what a campfire was by kindling one in a great iron pot in the center of our living room. She showed me how to make everything from exquisite cheese biscuits to perfume of dubious quality. But the success of those experiments has much less to do with their immediate product than with the habit of inquiry which she strove so patiently and graciously to inculcate in me. Lucy was a prime mover in my introduction to almost everything that is excellent in life and creditable in character.

To the scores of people who freely gave generous portions of precious days off, to those who put my name in the pot and their feet in my paths, and most of all, to those who accorded me the supreme privilege of insight into their minds, I am eternally grateful.

Contents

MORE THAN MERE SURVIVAL

"You got to live it the best you know how."
Cora Sumter

Glossary

apple puppies—fried apple fritters; dried apples.

Aunt Hagar—a mythical apical figure of the core black American nation.

beni—human excrement.

biffa—streetwalker.

big bell—the bell that rings out the terrestrial order and rings in Judgment Day.

black person of the blacks—a member of core black culture.

blow hair—hair that is "fine," straight enough to be easily disheveled.

boogie-joogie—nonsense, trickery.

boss—fine, good; a master of something.

brown-skin whitefolks—people who are publicly reckoned as white by Euro-Americans, but who are considered to be nonwhite by black people.

bukras—whites.

Cal'donia—a mythical folk representation of the black woman (the name does not apply to seniors).

call out of one's name—to insult.

carry oneself right—to conform to core black notions of propriety.

cathead—a kind of thick, crusty biscuit.

Chahlie (Charlie)—generalized Euro-American male.

cockleupwards—upside down.

color-struck—accepting Euro-American aesthetic and racial values.

cool—a wary presence of mind; a felicitous amalgam of equanimity and alertness.

days work—domestic labor done on a daily basis.

do-nothing-stool—buttocks.

dog bread—a low-prestige bread generally made with salt, water, and coarse corn meal.

doodleesqua'—nothing; less than nothing.

do something to death—to overdo; tasteless redundancy.

drag—a mild form of "sounding."

drylongso—ordinary.

feet to the fire—under extreme pressure.

'fending and proving—serious reasonable disputation, especially the art of slave clandestine theological exegesis.

Geechee—a southeastern United States littoral and insular black culture centered on the Sea Islands of Georgia and South Carolina.

git'n over—succeeding by Machiavellian half measures.

git-too—jocular folk rendering of "ghetto."

give advice—spiritual counseling dispensed by persons thought to be responsive to the supernatural.

grayboys—white men.

Guma Guma—one of a number of mythical, stereotyped "savage" tribes; a folk rendering of stereotypes of so-called darkest Africa.

heard the thunder—to be of advanced age.

he-said-she-said—gossip.

hinkdy—snobbish.

hoecake—a variety of griddle bread generally made with wheat or a wheat-corn mixture.

hoppin' John—a New Year's dish made of some kind of boiled legume, smoked pork and rice.

hummel, humble—a fruitless course; a misguided effort.

ig—to shun.

jackie—a strong alcoholic drink consumed especially at New Year's.

jackleg—bogus.

Jalapa—a very distant place; a celestial place in clandestine slave theology; sometimes Africa.

joogies—black people, a term which may or may not be derogatory, depending on who uses it and how.

knocking and kicking—the ancient martial art practiced by slave clergy and their followers.

light bread—yeast bread.

low stones—hell.

Mad Dog—a cheap wine.

meat men—ordinary people.

meats in turtles—complexity in human nature, roughly analogous to the ancient notion of humors. Derives from the seven different kinds of meats thought to be found in turtles.

Miss Anne—a mythical folk representation of all white women except very young ones.

mojo—originally a slave elder's rosary, now generally any magical charm, often worn around the neck.

the mojo and the sayso—the highest power.

Mose—an archetypal representation of the average "straight" black male.

munglas—any person or group reckoned as black by blacks but accorded an intermediate social/race status by whites.

napfrying—hair care.

nigger-rich—pseudo-rich.

ofay—white person.

outside—illegitimate.

over-sport—to overextend oneself beyond one's financial, emotional or physical resources.

paddy—a slightly negative term for a white person or white people taken collectively.

peck—a derogatory term for Southern white men.

peola—a pale black person.

the people—core black people.

Prophet Nat—Nat Turner, "Ung 'Thaniel."

put sport upon—to tastefully exceed requirements.

raised right—to be reared according to core black notions of appropriateness.

the reverend thing, revern'—the unalloyed, irreducible nub of things.

root doctor—a secular specialist in magic and healing.

Rumshumkrushafu—heaven of the old-time core black religion.

salty—angry.

scoff—food, eating.

sedidy—bourgeois young women seen as overly sedate.

see, to "see" things—to be gifted with supernatural sight.

shooting and cutting—noisy, non-violent disputation.

showing out—youthful exhibitionism.

simon cakes—salmon croquettes.

Sister Caroline—from poetry of James Weldon Johnson, "God's Trombones," an archetypal elderly black woman; stereotypical grandmother.

skosh—a little, a tiny bit; a short while.

slave—job.

sounding—a non-serious form of detraction employed primarily by children and young adults outside the family.

sport—to treat someone; to display something new or different.

stone—"reverend," the unalloyed, irreducible nub of things.

straight—correct, complying with acceptable core black standards of conduct.

street man—a person wise in the ways of the street.

strong food—traditional food thought to be possessed of the strength-giving elements, "substances."

switchy—nonalcoholic punch; originally just sugar water.

tally—Italian.

tole—to entice, to coax.

turkey—traditionally from "turkey buzzard," meaning white man, depending on age of speaker.

turkey treat the devil—the justifiable violation of one's pledged word.

turn—traditional civility, especially of children and very young adults; to show evidence in one's daily behavior of having been raised right.

two-cent slick—Pyrrhic perspicacity.

uku—many, a large number.

what-I-might-say—euphemism for a stronger term that might be considered indelicate.

what Satan do despise—the truth.

whiddledycut—six of one, half-dozen of the other.

whistle white—an element in the whistle code, employed most often by children, that means white people.

who-shot-John—circumlocution.

woofing—exaggerated, mildly menacing boasting or complaining, employed generally by young people outside the family.

Introduction

I think this anthropology is just another way to call me a nigger.

Othman Sullivan

Since I don't see myself or most people I know in most things I see or read about black people, I can't be bothered with that. I wish you could read something or see a movie that would show the people just, well, as my grandmother would say, drylongso. You know, like most of us really are most of the time—together enough to do what we have to do to be decent people.

Harriet Jones

Mr. Sullivan, a middle-aged industrial worker, is the first among equals in his men's civic club. The principal reason for the existence of this association is the diminution of the terror which demeans the neighborhoods in which these men must rear their children.

Harriet Jones was almost seventeen when she became one of my guides and assistants on this project. She is a model of promptness, diligence, endurance, imagination and tact.

This work owes a great deal to the sagacity and public-spiritedness of many people whose thoughts are but briefly represented in the following introduction. Although barely in her thirties, Miss Elva Noble enlisted the assistance of five senior women with long experience in the arduous environment of the laundry worker. Both she and her younger cousin, Mrs. Nannette Pryor, not only contributed their worthy reflections but facilitated that general air of conviviality so necessary to good talk by excellent gifts of traveling coconut cake and black-walnut fried chicken. Mrs. Lucy Ann Melton is a private person in the best sense of the term. Knowing her, I would not ask her to face a tape recorder, but we can still talk as freely and profoundly as we ever have, and she has been sharing her quiet wisdom and splendid cooking with me since I was a child. I am grateful to both Curtis Thornton and Marcus Tally for their generosity in offering me not only their opinions and entrée to their peers but transportation, shelter and sustenance. Mr. Thornton is a long-distance truckdriver with a deep aversion to the "top forty" who has spent much of his thirty-four years in serious consideration of the profoundest issues of national life. Marcus Tally is a man in his early thirties with a passion for basketball, chess and deep-sea fishing. The life of a long-distance truckdriver holds no charms for him; his principal goal is to be a gym teacher and to that end he is attending college part time. Iris McCrae is the youngest daughter of her large, cohesive family. "Equanimity" is the word which comes most readily to mind when I think about her role in the many discussions she organized. There is a basic sense of fairness and a quiet but formidable insistence on going to the root of questions which makes this young woman a judge with turn even among her seniors. Mrs. Ana Wright is in her early forties, and is charged with the responsibility of rearing four children ranging in age from five to nine. Three of these children are her nieces.

She finds time to scrub, without recompense, the urine-sullied halls of the building she lives in, enthrall a court-yard of young listeners with stories of her own devising and talk to at least one anthropologist.

I would also like to acknowledge many kindnesses. Maynard Brown, who gave me my first haircut decades ago, graciously put his barbershop at my disposal, and it was the scene of a number of first-rate folk seminars. Both Jonathan and Gloria Melton contributed personal documents, gave me the use of their home as an interview site, provided me with greatly appreciated transportation and fed me and the participants they recruited according to the highest standards of the old-time gastronomic tradition. Mrs. Surry made her home available to me for the recording of life histories, and when it appeared that there was the slightest possibility that her presence might be an inhibiting factor, she always remembered some shopping she had to do or some church activity that she just had to attend. And it always just happened that she happened to have some sage pork or yam pie or fried chicken which we were politely but firmly ordered to eat during her strategic absence. The term "key consultant informant" owes nothing at all to professional condescension or some kind of glorification of the funky folk, but is an accurate description of the role of the people who made this project work.

This book is the product of an anthropological field study conducted in the early 1970's in more than a dozen northeastern urban black American communities, and of my own experiences and observations as a member of such communities. It stems from my long-held view that traditional Euro-American anthropology has generally failed to produce ethnographers who are capable of assessing black American culture in terms other than romantic, and from my belief in the theory-building and analytic capacities of my people. In other words, I share the opinion commonly held by natives of my community that we have traditionally been misrepresented by standard social science.

This book is a self-portrait of what I call core black culture. It consists of personal narratives that were offered in contexts of amity, security and hospitality. All who contributed did so with the plain intent of presenting ourselves as we think we are. The people whose voices are heard in these pages are eminently capable of self-expression, and I have relied upon them to speak for themselves. They knew what they wanted to say and they had pronounced opinions about what I ought to be doing as a social scientist. "I'm not trying to tell you your job, but if you ever do write a book about us, then I hope you really do write about things the way they really are. I guess that depends on you to some extent but you know that there are more of us who are going to work every day than there are like the people who are git'n over" (Elva Noble). This is not, therefore, another collection of street-corner exotica but an explication of black culture as it is perceived by the vast majority of Afro-Americans who are working members of stable families in pursuit of much the same kinds of happinesses that preoccupy the rest of American society. Almost all of the men and women whose thoughts are represented in this volume think well of themselves and are well thought of by their relatives, friends and neighbors. Their feelings of personal and communal satisfaction are rooted in the astonishing reality of their civil, principled survival in spite of the weight of empire that rests upon their backs. In black culture, as in any other, there are those who can and those who cannot "get it together." *Drylongso* is the creation of those who can. Once elemental conditions of security and confidence were met, black men and women of consequence, on their own ground, steeped in their own core black tradition, dispensing monumental hospitality at a time of their own choosing, offered observations, assessments and musings on their lives and the life. My main intent is to be an acceptable vehicle for the transmission of their views.

The notion that black culture is some kind of backwater or tributary of an American "mainstream" is well established in much popular as well as standard social science literature. To the prudent black American masses, however, core black culture *is* the mainstream. The minority of black Americans who significantly depart from core black customs and values may pass, may become bourgeois in spirit as well as income, or swell the ranks of marginal drug and welfare cultures. But far more often than not, the primary status of a black person is that accorded by the people he or she lives among. It is based upon assessments of that person's fidelity to core black standards. The categories "real right" and "jackleg" cover the spectra of statuses, professions, occupations and character. There are doctors and doctors, clergymen and clergymen, cooks and cooks, professors and professors, and we know the difference. Exemplary heroes are rare in any culture, but most black people are well within the ordinary, acceptable, drylongso standards of core black culture. Most black people agree, on all levels of consciousness and in their overt actions, on what these specific standards are. And to that end Clinton Banks remembers the foreparents in rhyme, Porter Millington makes his jackie, pays his debts, and saves enough to make his getaway, Miss May Anna Madison makes up her own mind as to whether an anthropologist is a human being or an educated fool, and Miss Rosa Wakefield is led by the evidence of her senses and common sense to the same reservations about the concept of race shared by many anthropologists.

The men and women who kept my tape recorder, typewriter and brailler constantly employed occupy dwellings as diverse as castellated luxury apartment buildings and multistoried warrens that pass for public housing. Some people live in single family dwellings, and some few have no fixed abode at all. Some live in the environing suburbs of great metropolises, but most occupy the desolate, decadent, battle-scarred cores of central cities. Many have at least two jobs. Among them are domestic workers, industrial workers, teachers and the retired. Most could certainly not be called affluent or even comfortably well off. The vast majority consider themselves poor and are considered poor by their neighbors.

These people are my relatives, friends and acquaintances, and the relatives and friends of my relatives and friends. The key strands in this network of kinship and amity are the lines of regular interaction which have been maintained very often over a lifetime. The fact that some of the participants in this project had known me since the hour of my birth certainly did not prove to be a hindrance. In other cases I was checked and cross-checked by many before a decision was made to take part in the research. The opinion of a reputable member of the community was incalculably more valuable than purely professional credentials. Implicit in the decision to take part, of course, was the faith of most people in their ability to reveal only as much of themselves as they wish. "I know you must have sense enough to know that you can't make me tell you anything I mean to keep to myself" (Hannah Nelson).

A proper regard for security and reciprocity are vital to the establishment of rapport in core black enclaves. The prudent are wary and slow to bestow confidence. Rapport is, generally, merited grace that is accorded by people who, in their considered judgment, have decided that the would-be researcher is not just another jackleg educated fool. The force of a person's character and his public reputation, which is still transmitted with astounding fidelity by the same old goofered grapevine, determine that person's public esteem. If it is determined that a prospective field investigator is just another one of that phalanx of fatuous hucksters and junketing assessors who prey or groove upon us, he or she will be politely but effectively disregarded. Black American culture has as many ways of taking a stranger lightly as it has of saying maybe, and it is in need of them all.

People were motivated to participate in this research for a number of reasons, not the least of which was the desire to assist a native career. Ethnic solidarity is equated by blacks with civic responsibility, and one of the consequences of this deeply felt social motivation was a wish to set the record straight. As a blind ethnologist, I was usually assigned a place in that capacious, ambivalent category reserved for "the sick and afflicted." The injunction to assist the sick and afflicted is rooted in traditional notions of theology and fair play. Arbitrary disregard of this injunction, for some, carries the prospect of divine retribution. In this culture, doing this type of work, blindness often proved to be an asset rather than a handicap.

I made minimal use of questionnaires and none of psychological testing devices. "Talking like a man with a paper in his hand" is still a fairly common core black expression for talking nonsense or babbling. I wanted both the contexts and the venues of interviews and folk seminars to be as informal and removed from officialdom as possible. "I'll talk to you all day long, Lankie, but don't interview me" (Lucy Ann Melton).

Folk seminars were convened in locations as varied as churches and taverns. They were devoted to the exchange of views on recurrent themes in personal documents, the evaluation of some main premises of social science and the indigenous definition of core black culture. The complement of folk seminars ranged from three to twenty persons, who were, for the most part, well known to each other. Once I or some key consultant informant initially clarified the purpose for which we were assembled, discussion was free and almost invariably civil, with no reliance on formal rules of procedure. Almost all of these people have been told from infancy that "we can all sing at once, but we can't all talk at once." As core black culture carriers, they have been taught to scorn "showing out"—being more vociferous than the conventions of the culture demand. There is a common, ingrained proverbial assumption that "common courtesy is due a dog" and a detestation of being "loud, long and wrong." So folk seminars were well conducted forums where people met to take care of strictly anthropological business. The good talk produced by the seminars was generally inspired by good traditional food. (Miss Elaine Young cooked a half dozen complicated, time-consuming traditional meals for the largely student folk seminars she organized.) From folk seminars, interested, articulate men and women came forward as donors of the personal documents that are brought together in this book.

Core black culture has traditionally esteemed good talk and profound dialogue. It has sustained a variety of forms of oral discourse from 'fending and proving—the art of clandestine theological exegesis practiced by slaves —to non-veracious forms, such as woofing and sounding. Black culture proceeds upon the premise that "the truth is the light," but it is equally aware that "the truth is a razor," so people were at pains to render meticulous narratives. They were deeply concerned to distinguish clearly between reflections offered as the whole truth as they honestly understood it, and those offered as some variety of non-veracious discourse—"It wasn't told to me, I only heard." *Drylongso* is their truth which I heard because it was told to me. Most seminar members and donors of personal documents were plainly aware of the harm that might be done a native career by lying—"If I can't help you, I won't hurt you." The consistent striving for truth often occasioned chagrin, rueful reflection, and tears. Interpretive interjections were routine—"Now, that's what I said, but this is what I mean." "Now, I said that to say this." "If I'd a said what I meant, this is what I'd a said."

Those who were gracious enough to donate life histories took it for granted that proper understanding of the material is indispensable, and many quite specifically alluded to the danger of outsiders imposing their own meaning on their life histories. "I wouldn't want to talk to any anthropologist or sociologist or any of those others if they were white because whatever I said they would write down what they felt like, so I might just as well save my breath" (Nannette Pryor).

Most men and women established the formidable ramparts of their own intricate anonymity with great invention and meticulousness. A few were willing to have their real names used, some gave names which we both knew were false, but most left the orchestration of their anonymity to me. Many people warned me about the dangers of telling the truth as they see it. Many asked me if I wished them to modify their considered opinions because of my own lack of anonymity. Many reiterated Fats Waller's timeless admonition, "Don't give your right name, no, no, no!" In any case, despite what I recognize to be very good and well meant advice, mine is the only real name used in this book. Place names have also been changed for the protection of the innocent and guilty, living or dead.

My insistence on compensating people for their time demonstrated the seriousness of my intentions and the esteem in which I held participants. Because of the graciousness of many people, I was obliged to resort to various strategies of indirect compensation. Wise old Jackson Jordan, Jr., has stood politely but adamantly upon his dignity only once during our friendship of three decades, and that was when he refused money for his invaluable contributions to this book. We both share a monumental lack of interest in beauty contests and an unspoken understanding of why we both invested rather heavily in tickets which were being timidly sold by his favorite grandniece in aid of one of those romantic deceptions. Successful black native anthropologists will bear home in their field kits an extraordinary number of raffle chances, spiritualist tea tickets and sundry other mementos of the Pyrrhic campaign to keep remotely abreast of the generosity of their people. But the effort must be made, as the culture turns a disparaging eye toward cheapness. It is not concerned with instant quid pro quo but scorns as base and infantile those who do not show an adult grasp of its subtle canons of reciprocity. Being set down as having a "handful of gimme and a mouthful of much obliged" is fatal to rapport.

The narratives in this book are loosely arranged so as to illuminate main themes, but certain narratives overlap chapter headings because that's how people talk and think. However spontaneous these narratives may seem, they are never ad hoc or slapdash. The thinking which informs this volume proceeds from men and women of ripe judgment. Almost all the people I listened to have examined their lives, the life and the nature of humanity. Their contributions were informed by that discernment which has enabled them to survive with dignity in a caste-like conquest environment. Their reflections and observations were offered as statements in which theme and development are manifest. In ranging over the lesson-strewn panorama of their own lives, people may illustrate a personally held premise about color hierarchies by an example which may be drawn from childhood, work experience, or courting behavior.

People required extremely little, other than the most general clarification, to determine upon the course of their reflections. From that time on, the rhythm, sequence, and style was a matter of each person's own very particular spirit. Most of the people who appear in this volume are masters of a number of English speech forms. Under conditions of security and amity they move quite freely among them and this motion is reflected in the narratives through apparent inconsistencies of "standard" grammar and orthography.

From these narratives—these analyses of the heavens, nature and humanity—it is evident that black people are building theory on every conceivable level. An internally derived, representative impression of core black culture can serve as an anthropological link between private pain, indigenous communal expression and the national marketplace of issues and ideas. These people not only know the troubles they've seen, but have profound insight into the meaning of those vicissitudes.

Core black culture is more than ad hoc synchronic adaptive survival. Its values, systems of logic and world view are rooted in a lengthy peasant tradition and clandestine theology. It is the notion of sacrifice for kin, the belief in the natural sequence of cause and effect—"Don't nothin' go over the devil's back but don't bind him under the belly." It is a classical, restricted notion of the possible. It esteems the deed more than the wish, venerates the "natural man" over the sounding brass of machine technology and has the wit to know that "Everybody talking 'bout Heaven ain't going there."

The expectations and canons of core black culture are arbiters of black intra-communal status and style. Walking those walks, talking those talks, keeping that cool, showing that turn, are some of the salient items in the catalogue of qualities which go toward the making of a proper core black person. These people live, move and have their being in their particular variation on the human theme. They do so with the same minimal regard for the occurence of their traits in other societies as do people in other cultures. When Miss Young served me lamb stew with okra, I don't think she thought of it as a Middle Eastern dish. When Porter Millington cooked maws and chiddlins or cracklin' corn bread, he was aware that the French make the same use of pork, but he did not feel that his pork dish was anything but core black. When Mrs. Roberts got married and determined to rear her children non-romantically, she was doing what her parents and grandparents had done. She was not attempting to approximate any norms she didn't regard as core black any more than the Calabrians who sit down to a meal of pasta think that they are eating Annamese or Cantonese cuisine.

In black culture there is a durable, general tolerance, which is amazingly free of condescension, for the individual's right to follow the truth wherever it leads. Just as Mrs. Sumter's strong faith, cogent reasoning, and exquisite nut cake are personal variations of black thought about the supernatural, the truth and gastronomy, so are Mrs. Nelson's atheism, apt deductions, and superb nut cake. Neither lady's civil maintenance of her own position would excite any overt antagonism in the other. People of every conceivable human color, creed, political persuasion, income and level of education share the cramped confines of black towns. It is not regarded as particularly noteworthy when members of one family subscribe to different versions of Christianity and Islam. "I don't condemn anyone as long as they don't bother me. You never know what you may come to" (Gloria Melton). This spontaneous response to a television apology for lesbianism was offered by a strictly heterosexual, Baptist lady whose delightful seven-year-old has unimpeded access to the African Methodist Episcopal knees of her favorite paternal uncle and the Muslim lap of her paternal grandfather. Similarly, for most black people the Islam of Betty Shabazz's husband or the Judaism of Marian Anderson's grandfather are nobody's business but their own.

The sense of nationhood among blacks is as old as our abhorrence of slavery. Black nationhood is not rooted in territoriality so much as it is in a profound belief in the fitness of core black culture and in the solidarity born of a transgenerational detestation of our subordination. The tradition which is so vital in shaping black culture was founded and fostered by those slave foreparents who are so widely respected for their refusal to accept, in their hearts, the Euro-American definition of them as things. Rare is the black family without its proverbial charter for principled survival in the infinity of tight places occasioned by racist oppression. These charters were first graven in the living song, stories and daily courage of the foreparents whose lessons and traits are still very much remembered. Jonathan Melton and Howard Roundtree are both part owners of farms wrested from their families' former masters. Miss Carolyn Chase still teaches young children arithmetic with the slave counting game of Jack-in-the-Bush, and Mrs. Ruth Shays is a living link to bondage and is widely relied upon for her knowledge of slave pharmacopoeia and philosophy.

Almost all the contributors to this volume tend to judge their neighbors by the principles of cool handed down by those who survived in the crucible of slavery with free minds. The foreparents, their personal victories and defeats, their martyrdom and shame, are not so much formally commemorated as they are experienced on every level of awareness. Their names are in our New Year pots, contrapuntal clapping and intricate singing because our current existence differs only in degree from theirs.

White people loom large in the narratives because racist subordination is the ramified goad that black people must deal with. Given the negative conditioning of the Afro-American historical experience, it is astounding that so many black people are prepared to deal with white people as individuals. "If you are wrong, you are not right, I don't care what color you are. Should I not speak to some white person who is polite to me just because some other person that looks like that was nasty to me? All kinds of people have tried to make a fool of me, so if I went by that I wouldn't speak to anybody. I know it's hard to do, but I guess you just have to take people as you find them" (Iris McCrae).

Taken in the mass, white Americans are responsible for the inegalitarian social order which creates black power disadvantage. A hypothetical color-blind conqueror who reduced the whole earth to bondage would bulk large in the thinking of all of us. On both the personal and the societal level, it is cultural and natural nature for us to devote more than scant attention to the architects of so much of our misfortune.

The complex of crises surrounding the Watergate issue were fresh during the field phase of this project and they are still very much in the minds of black people. The topic may not prove to be as durable in core black memory as slavery, but as it is generally perceived of as part of the same conspiratorial process, Watergate will probably remain a lively issue for some time.

It is very difficult to define or describe one piece of the great American mosaic without reference to other pieces. "You can't be black *or* white, I guess, and not think about the differences between these two communities" (Marcus Tally). What kind of people are black Americans? How would you describe us to an extra-terrestrial being? What is unique about us in the way of gastronomy or philosophy or sexual conventions? Such questions quite naturally bring to mind the continuum or gradient of ranked ethnicities that comprise the great American hierarchy.

One of the salient features of transgenerational conquest hierarchies is the cultural and genetic blending of their components. In a very real sense there is sufficient white in the blackest of us and enough black in the whitest of us to justify Albert Murray's identification of the national character of the United States as omni-American. The paradox of being separate yet inseparable from the fabric of American life mandates the anomaly of forced inclusion in the Euro-American caste-like empire and arbitrary exclusion from a just share in its wealth and power. There is, quite naturally, a more intense double consciousness of this paradox among black people.

Core black ranking of other ethnicities of the American caste-like commonwealth is almost entirely an assessment of the degree to which those communities are involved in black power deprivation. There is no general, theoretical anti-Semitic or anti-Oriental tradition in core black social thought. To the extent that Igbos, Jews, Italians, Cubans or any other ethnic group is thought to be "git'n over on us," they will not stand high in core black esteem.

The reputation for sound-mindedness and responsibility enjoyed by the people I worked with is founded on the readily apparent integrity of their lives. The thinking of the authors of this book is more than crude data. Proceeding from the bedrock of their respective personal experiences, they speak about the climate of communal coexistence in terms which are plainly analytical. When Othman Sullivan, a man reckoned by his neighbors as deliberate, circumspect and wise, says upon reflection that anthropology is just another medium for the expression of racism, his remarks should not be summarily dismissed. That the eminent anthropologist Bronislaw Malinowski did think of the Melanesian field populations that were instrumental in his ethnographic prominence as "niggers" does lend some weight to Mr. Sullivan's view. Mr. Sullivan's premise is in no wise diminished by the various social scientific assessments of black American culture as "pathological," "distorted" and "criminal."

There is an a priori assumption among blacks that the prime preoccupation of social science ought to be race relations. Social science literature and much of the essay and biographical reading matter in the possession of most of the people I worked with pertained very directly to questions of race and color prejudice. But the people who opened their thoughts and homes to me do not expect social science to usher in the millennium and consider much of it to be simply a part of the general Euro-American caste-ordering establishment. It is important to note that the widespread opposition to and suspicion of such institutions as social science and the military are to the actual function they serve, not to their intrinsic value.

To the extent that the prudent masses of black people are interested in anthropology at all, that preoccupation is almost exclusively concerned with rectification of the record. The record, that is, what anything actually *is,* is infinitely more important than the *intent* of anything. Black Americans are, of course, capable of the same kind of abstract thinking that is practiced by all human cultures, but sane people in a conquest environment are necessarily preoccupied with the realities of social existence. "I understand why they [white people] don't want us to think they are prejudiced. But if most of them were not prejudiced, it wouldn't be a prejudiced country" (Curtis Thornton).

Porter Millington knows how he perceives the society at large and also has the acumen to see himself as others see him. He knows his place in society but does not accept that status as an objective index of his own very considerable capacities. He is not the first person to observe that the subordinate know the superordinate far better than the subordinate are known. His considered judgment that it is folly to reveal oneself to the powerful stranger is more than unprovoked xenophobia. The connection he makes between the general Euro-American presumption of core black ignorance and the difficulties he experienced in transmitting his own recipe for his own brandy is not, in the light of real experience, level mixing.

Principled survival in a familial and communal context, complicated by the iron inconsistencies of caste, is a preeminently analytical process. It demands a virtuosity at option sorting and general improvisation which places an often mortal premium on profound thought. It is this kind of indigenous analysis that I call "native anthropology." In the sense that Frantz Fanon used the term, "native" means subordinate, dark and poor. The consideration of perspectives, philosophies and systems of logic generated by populations which are usually expected to produce only unrefined data for the omniscient, powerful stranger to interpret could augment the vital elements of diversity and accuracy which are prime prerequisites of a truly post-colonial anthropology.

Anthropologists have often been the uninvited, boorish guests of the people they study. Some have gone so far as to deny the very existence of black American culture. Properly understood, native anthropology can be the beginning of the most fruitful exchange in the entire history of social science, for, in the broadest sense of the term, there is not one of us who is not a native somewhere. When significant attention is devoted to what any given people think of themselves, then the concepts "cross-cultural" and "relativity" will attain their most appropriate meanings. "No one can listen only to himself and stay sane" (Ana Wright).

A NATION
WITHIN A NATION

Black men have no country, but they are a country in their hearts.

Joseph Langstaff

I wish we had two countries, one for us and one for them so we wouldn't have to do every stupid thing they feel like doing. I am not worried about the Arabs or the Vietnamese or anybody else over there. It's these whites who are killing us.

Grace Holbein

Mr. Langstaff, a retired carpenter and mason, generously contributed extensive narratives and organized a number of folk seminars. At the age of seventy-three he is a quiet, profoundly knowledgeable traditionalist whose word and counsel have a force double that of any formal law for many of his neighbors.

Mrs. Holbein took time from her demanding managerial position in a local hospital to host, organize and participate in field seminars. Both she and Mr. Langstaff equate patriotism with communal responsibility, and in so doing are in harmony with an enduring core black tradition.

Hannah Nelson

We are a nation primarily because we think we are a
nation.

*Mrs. Nelson is a universal woman. I do not know anyone who has sustained
so many diverse interests with such intellectual vigor for so long a time as she
has. The splendid development of her mind is all the more remarkable as she
has had very little opportunity for formal instruction. The circumstances of
her life made the completion of even an elementary school education a highly
prized but unattainable luxury, but she has read and listened avidly and
systematically. She has supported herself for most of her life by the drudgery
of domestic service.*

*Her neighbors call her "Professor" because she gives piano lessons, but she
certainly has more than one legitimate claim to the best that that title implies.
Almost all the knowledge she has acquired through self-discipline and
sagacity was sought to satisfy a very private passion for learning. She has
taught herself languages, cuisines and art forms. The pursuit of her avoca-
tions has led Mrs. Nelson to the mastery of such practical skills as fine
historical sewing, manufacturing her own herbal paints, catering and piano
tuning.*

*She has endured three burglaries, one mugging in which she was stripped
in the street and two attempted muggings. Mrs. Nelson has not yielded to the
understandable temptation to become a recluse. She makes music for and
with her neighbors. As presiding elder in her church's black history and
culture club, she teaches those who wish to learn what she has learned about
black ecumeny. Her dealings with her neighbors and officialdom are characterized by a natural sobriety totally lacking in missionary zeal. She is the
kind of person who takes quiet pleasure in watching others enjoy themselves.
She is the kind of person whose presence is the indefinable but very real good
life of the party.*

I am a colored woman sixty-one years of age. I was born in Boston and
grew up right here. I came to Harlem when I was about six or seven and
I have always come back here, although I have lived in many other places.
I have never spent much time in the South, but I, like most of us, have

people there. I am a widow. My maiden name is Nelson and I married a man named Nelson too. Anyone who could see me would say, "There goes a colored woman in her early sixties who could afford to lose a few pounds." My hair is gray, but it was that color before I was thirty-five. That happens frequently in my family. But to look at me, you would not think there was anything special about me.

I don't like the term "colored" better than the term "black." It's just that that was what came into my head. You can call me anything but nigger, nigra or gal, and get along with me. I don't so much care what you call me as how you say it. My father used to say that some people could say "Goddamn" like a blessing. I remember he whipped my brother for saying "Thank you" like "Goddamn it." I don't get excited about things like that.

I remember this woman I used to work for for two years, and she called me Anna consistently. She knew my name was Hannah, but she didn't think my name was important enough to remember, I guess. I learned her name, which was much longer than mine. Most of her friends didn't pronounce her name correctly, but I did. Every so often she would catch herself and make much of the fact that she was not calling me by my correct name, but she never really would say Hannah for very long. She wasn't a stupid woman. She was, well, she was just burdened down with making the things she had to do fill the time she had to do them in. Now, she didn't have very much to do because I did most of the really hard work. Now, I knew how to do those things because I have done them for most of my life, off and on. Telling people how to do what they already know how to do doesn't really require a great deal of time. I know this and she knows it. Her husband knows it and doesn't know it, so, well, that leads to trouble because people are, well, kidding themselves. I guess it is that white people, like most people, like to feel that they are useful, you know, that their being alive means that life is made easier—or less complicated, anyway—for people they know and care about.

Now, since I am black, I think anybody who is living and not making life hard for anybody else is doing pretty much what they should be doing. White people are very interested in seeming to be of service, but it is very hard to really be of service, especially if you only want to be of service with just a part of yourself. Now, that's me and most people. I know this about myself and it doesn't bother me. All I really want, very often, is time to think about what is important to me. I don't feel that way, you know, twenty-four hours of every day, but I do feel that way very often. Since I have to work, I don't really have to worry about most of the things that most of the white women I have worked for are worrying about. And if these women did their own work, they would think just like I do—about this, anyway.

Well now, you must pardon me, we are leaving our subject far behind. I promised that I was going to tell you what I think about the national character of our people.

Well, from the start, it should be said that we are a nation. The best of us have said it and everybody feels it. I think it was Frederick Douglass who said we were a nation within a nation. I know that will probably bother your white readers, but it is nonetheless true that black people think of themselves as an entity. There are millions and millions of us and we are by no means a dying community. We have what is to us a national anthem, and I will sing it in a minute. The reason most black people won't sing it is that they don't know it any better than they know "The Star-Spangled Banner." Many do not know it as well, but most like it because it means more to us. And, quite frankly, "Lift Every Voice" is just a better song than that warmed-over drinking song. That's my professional opinion.

Seriously, though, what makes black people a nation has very little to do with formal things like anthems and flags and national days. Most of us are very uncomfortable with those things or completely indifferent to them. That's because they mean one thing to us and something else to white people. Most of the things I had to learn in school that were supposed to arouse national pride in me really made me feel anger, shame or indifference. I worked in Birmingham a little while and tried to convince myself that I was in love. I went to a football game with a young man I knew there and they played "The Star-Spangled Banner" and "Dixie," and my friend thought I was angry about them playing the Confederate anthem. He was wrong because "The Star-Spangled Banner" does not mean any more to me than "Dixie." I don't care what flag white people have, it gives me a headache to salute the Stars and Stripes or the Stars and Bars because I hate what both of them have really stood for. Now, everybody knows that black people feel this way. How would any rational people feel in our circumstances?

Most of the women I've worked for have asked me about my feelings, and most of them have not been able to understand that it is possible to love the land and hate sharing it with them. I think that is because most white people do not make a distinction between themselves and the land. When they say "America, love it or leave it," they really mean love *them*, agree with *them*, or go somewhere else. I love the ground I buried my mother in, and me and that land could go on very nicely if there were not a single person calling themselves white within a million miles of it.

We don't really agree with white people about anything important. If we were in power, we would do almost everything differently than they have. We are a nation primarily because we think we are a nation. This ground we have buried our dead in for so long is the only ground most of us have ever stood upon. Africa is mercifully remote to most of us and that is a good thing too. Most of our people are remarkably merciful to Africa, when you consider how Africa has used us.

It isn't just that we feel one way about the flag or the national hymn, or that we like our food cooked differently, or that our patriotism is for our group rather than for the United States. We are the kind of people we have to be. I believe that is true of every group of people in every culture. I think that ancient Egyptians put in the Georgia and Carolina lowlands under conditions of slavery would be Geechees. I think that German tribesmen under the conditions which produced Japanese or Zulus would be Japanese or Zulu. White people would be the same kind of people we are if they had had our historical portion. We would be the kind of people they are if we had had theirs. People with the same blood, by which I mean the same biological heritage, are living in different ways from us in Africa and Europe. So I think that our way of living is different because of what you could call historical reasons. But our history is our history and it makes us the kind of people we are. I have known children of the same father to grow up in different races and think of themselves as very different from each other.

I think the most important thing about black people is that they don't think that they can control anything except their own persons. So everything black people think and do has to be understood as very personal. Many of the women I have worked for have criticized most of the black people they had any dealings with as being too touchy or oversensitive. And in this they were probably correct. White people think of themselves as just a part of a great nation and a tradition. There is a feeling among whites that the police and the President and the governor and the priest and hundreds of other people and things are upholding them and caring for them.

One time in rural Georgia a white woman and I were stranded in a ditch in her car. When some policemen came and helped us, she was relieved to see them but I was frightened. Now, I know many other black women who have had experiences something like that, and most felt just like I did. I didn't know what those policemen might do, but the white woman with me felt quite certain that they would help us. Well, I knew they would help *her*, but I didn't really think they would help me. I was very glad that the white woman was there with me because she was the only protection I felt I had at that time. My safety had nothing to do with any respect for my person, you see. Those white men did not deal with me as they generally deal with young black women because there was a white woman of high standing there with me, and any disrespect to me personally would have been disrespect to that woman's nigger.

I'm sure she knew how I felt, but we never talked about anything like that. We were both bouncing up and down at opposite ends of a huge car and the seating arrangement was not accidental. She was the kind of person who made up for their dullness by a great show of pride, and she got every bit of her "Yes, ma'am, Miss Annes" from each and every body. Since she was that kind of person, I used to try to see if I could feed her enough of that to choke her, but she was just too well raised to refuse. I do not mean to do her any more injustice than she is due. She was, by white standards, a kind person, but by our standards she was not a person at all because there was no way of knowing what kind of person she was on her own. We never really talked about that whole business. If we had talked about it she would have had to face the truth about the thing. Most people who have worked in service have to learn how to talk at great length about nothing. I never have been very good at that, so I don't speak, normally, unless I am asked something. Some people I have worked for think I am slow-witted because I talk very little on the job.

I like talking about what you've been asking me. I will speak generally to our thinking about ourselves, but you know that it is Hannah Nelson speaking. I see by your face that it was not necessary for me to say that. There are just two of us here and if you are not speaking and I am not silent, who else could be speaking?

Now, that is a great difference between black and white people. Our speech is most directly personal, and every black person assumes that every other black person has a right to a personal opinion. In speaking of grave matters, your personal experience is considered very good evidence. With us, distant statistics are certainly not as important as the actual experience of a sober person. We are, by reason of the lives we have led, a suspicious people. We are the children of suspicious people, as were our grandparents and their grandparents. This has been so with us even back to those people most of us call foreparents. Now, if we were otherwise we would probably all be white or dead! Every reasonable black person thinks that most white people do not mean him well. Every reasonable black person knows that many other black people cannot afford to treat him fairly. Most black people believe that most other human beings will seek their own advantage at the expense of other people. We do not really think it has much to do with the justice of a situation. People will do what profits them. We think white people are the most unprincipled folks in the world, but everybody bears watching. I believe we are righter to think in this way than any other, considering our circumstances.

We do not just imagine that most people we have to live with are against us. We live with people who sold us for things and forced every kind of filth upon us. Life is still hard for us. I am a woman sixty-one years old and I was born into this world with some talent. But I have done the work that my grandmother's mother did. It is not through any failing of mine that this is so. The whites took my mother's mother's milk by force, and I have lived to hear a human creature of my sex try to force me by threat of hunger to give my milk to an able man. I have grown to womanhood in a world where the saner you are, the madder you are made to appear.

It is the greed and cruelty of white people which is at the root of all this business. The world runs to imperfection. If the whites were not killing everybody inch by inch a day at a time with their laws and their papers and their machines and their childishness, aches, age and foolishness would still carry us away. It is a terrible thing to say of a group of people, but the existence of white people has meant for many of us that it is sometimes hard to tell whether life is more to be desired than death.

Not all the time, but sometimes I feel like getting all the food I can afford and locking my door to everybody for the rest of my life. I am tired of standing in pointless lines and filling out the same papers for somebody to lose. I am tired of being governed by people who are not as considerate or intelligent as I am. Most black people feel that way. Most black people are intelligent enough to know that the trouble we have in getting value for our money and recompense for our wrongs is not accidental. Not that it would matter to most of us even if it was accidental. If I can't do my job so that it comes out right almost all the time, I am shown the door very quickly. I should be; why should anyone pay to be inconvenienced? Booker Washington and W.E.B. DuBois said that degradation was a ditch that the whites could not hope to keep us in without holding us there. That means that degradation is the common lot of whites *and* blacks. Is that what they really want?

I'm always being asked what black people want. I never answer the question, but I always think, "Anything worth having." I would like to know what white people really want. If it's that they want schools, neighborhoods, hospitals, armies, post offices, police forces of their own, fine! Whatever they have, they seem to want most of whatever we have and that is bad for both of us. If they really think that we are their inferiors, why do they wish to remain in union with us? If they really believe in States' rights, why don't they just let us take a part of what we have built and govern ourselves?

I used to be a waitress, and I can still remember how white people would leave a tip and then someone at the table, generally some white woman, would take some of the money. She would try to do it secretly, of course, but most waitresses have had this experience and, of course, they are often seen sneaking those quarters and dimes off the tables. That is something I have never done when I was being served in a restaurant. I can count on the fingers of one hand the number of black people I know who have done this. It is greed, wanting to have everything and still be known as a generous person.

We are interested in having all those things the whites have taken from everybody else—land and everything you can do with land. I don't know anybody who thinks you have to be with white people to enjoy all these things. It is being with white people which prevents us from enjoying these things. If, after all this time, white people have remained the same kind of people, it is dreaming to think the two of us can ever really share this land. White people will always take back a part of what is ours as long as they are strong enough to do it. When they are the weakest, we suffer least. When a foreign enemy threatens them, they give us a little more of the fortune we have earned. When their own Southern brothers threatened to become too greedy, they finally promised us freedom, but when they patched up that quarrel, the white people north and south took back that promise.

Now the whole matter is so mixed and complicated that nothing but a knife can put it anywhere near right. Each day that we live like this, with more responsibility than any other people and no authority at all, our people become more disorganized. TV, movies, drugs and school make our young men into walking disgraces, and we can do nothing about it so long as we live among white people. Do you think I would tolerate a school like that one Kwame goes to if I were running a school? Do you imagine I would create a welfare system which degrades women and children? What have I lost in Chile or Cuba or Southeast Asia?

Harriet Jones

Sometimes I wonder if there are any other Americans
besides us.

---

*Both Hannah Nelson and Grace Holbein said that Harriet is the kind of
young woman they would want as a daughter. Barbershop symposia, beauty-
parlor colloquia and neighborhood opinion all deem her a good girl without
a trace of condescension. The people buy the excellent pastry she makes,
employ her as a baby-sitter, and admit her to their homes to perfect her piano
technique because most of them wish to do what they can to see that she
becomes a good woman. Most of them are motivated by that same amalgam
of sympathy and ethnic solidarity that prompted them to contribute to this
popular anthology. Although many people help Harriet, the bulk of the credit
for her civil, principled survival in the face of maddening provocation most
certainly belongs to her.*

*Harriet's gravity is understandable in the light of the trials she endures.
The multistoried warren that she, her alcoholic mother and hundreds of other
black people call home is less than three quarters of a mile from the palatial
residence of her father and half sister, who alternate between white and
non-white status. There is more than a little of the siege in Harriet's existence.
"I'm always ready to run," she said. Schoolmates, policemen and Superfly-
bemused young men have attempted to extort everything from lunch money
to sexual favor from her. These confrontations have made her discrete and
wary, but not desperate. She finds solace in the flute and in eighteenth-
century English essays, and joy in her vision of the country life she would like
to have.*

I have lived sixteen bad years, but I am a good person. Because my life
has been hard, I am very tired. It isn't just being a good person that has
made me tired, but being any kind of person at all. No matter how good
most of the people I know live, their lives are hard. A lot of people feel that
their lives will be short. Miss Edla thinks something terrible must be waiting
for her because she has had two years of very good luck. Mr. Banks feels
that he is going to be killed by somebody trying to kill someone else. My
father thinks that some white people will kill him because he has not given

them some money or they think that he has not given them all of the money that he owes them. Right now I think I am a good person and the people here say, "Harriet is a good girl," but I feel very old. No matter how you try to live your life, you have to pay something for trying to live that way. Even if you say, "Well, I'll just go along with things and not fight it," you still will be worn down and out. I mean that life is sad enough anyway without the things that people do to make it worse than it actually has to be.

Once my father came to live with us. My mother says I can't really remember much about that, but I can remember all of it. My mother cooked him everything she even *thought* he wanted. I know now that nothing we could have done would have been enough to make him stay, because he wouldn't have stayed even if he had wanted to if he thought he would have made us happy by staying. My father likes to hurt my mother, that is the truth. I didn't want to believe that and for a long time I just wouldn't see that. That is sick and nasty, I think.

Some things in my life are so hard for me to bear, and it makes me feel better to know that you feel sorry about those things and would change them if you could. My father would not change these things and he caused many of them just because he was able to do that. He would make himself sad to make us unhappy. He used to lead my mother to think that he wanted something, you know, a kind of biscuit or a pie, and then when she went to the time and trouble to make it the very best she knew how, he would go hungry rather than give her the pleasure of seeing him enjoy that thing she had made especially for him. When my mother is sober she could cook for God, and she was sober all the time then.

I really think that is the way the whole country is. I think white people would wreck everything if they thought the only way that they could save the country was to be as nice to us as we have been to them. I said this to Junior and Ace and they got very angry. They said their fathers were not white and a lot of junk like that. They are angry all the time, so they didn't really hear what I said—I mean, they didn't hear the meaning of what I said. And they didn't think about how it hurt me to have to say it. But they think like they live. Junior says, "I stay mad to keep from getting mad." I know what he means and I know why he does that. I mean, white people have done really terrible things to him, you know—I mean, some white people have—and he doesn't know what the others would do. He knows that these bad things happened to him and he knows that he didn't do anything to deserve these bad things.

I stay away from my father. The only time I see him is when he comes looking for me, and then he doesn't see me a lot of times if I see him first. I don't know why my father wants to see me unless it is to do something that he knows is going to make me feel bad. I think it is the same way between white and black people. We keep doing all the things America stands for, and the better Americans we are, the bigger suckers we are. But we are doing what we think we should do, not what white people say we should do, but I still feel like a sucker. I mean, white people could not care less about the Declaration of Independence or the Constitution or the flag, and they have everything. If being an American is so great, why aren't the people who *always* knew that slavery and lynching and massacre were low things, why aren't black people having a better time in this world?

I feel sometimes that I'm the only person in my building who really cares about the project. I know that most people in there don't mess it up, but we can't stop the people from doing these things that make it bad for all the rest. Some of the people who mess it up don't mess it up all the time. Mr. Kingsley is very nice when he is not drunk. He calls me "Daughter" and asks me to baby-sit for his sister, but last Friday he took out his penis and peed on all the buttons of the elevator. I was the same person I always am, but he didn't have any respect for me because he was drunk. I mean, he didn't have any respect for himself, so he didn't have any for anything or anybody. Now, what can I do about that? He is old enough to be my grandfather, I guess, and I like him some of the time, but I have to watch him *all* the time. Well, to me the thing about being an American is a bigger thing, but it is the same thing. I feel that most black people I know are like me. We are not angels, but we do what we are supposed to do most of the time.

Now, I don't really know any white people in the way that I know some black people—I mean, to know someone like I know you or you know me. I see white people every day and they see me, but that doesn't really mean anything. There was a white boy who used to throw a note at me in that insane study hall. And there was an Italian girl that Peaches was going to beat up because of the fire. Mr. Kingsley made Peaches leave that girl alone. I helped this girl—somebody took her books and her money. So, for a while it was so we could find out whether we liked each other or not. But we were not dealing for ourselves—I mean, I was, but she wasn't. I went to her house once and that was it, and she wouldn't even come to my house and I don't blame her. She knows why I wouldn't go to her house again, too. Sometimes she used to call me and we would go through that small-talk number, but we both know how it is. Peaches drags me about that sometimes. But when she saw that bothered me, she said she was sorry and wouldn't do it any more, and she doesn't. But I feel foolish and, I guess, ashamed of helping that girl, but I still think that I was right to help her. I think that's what people are supposed to do for each other. Marie thinks so too, but she's not sure that she would have tried to help me or Peaches or Mr. Kingsley over there.

I guess I feel the same way about patriotism, or whatever you might call it. I would like for everybody to get along—you know, no impossible number, just get along. But it isn't that way and I really don't think that it is our fault that it isn't. Sometimes Italian women look at me as if they wanted to kill me. Now, I really don't know why they should want to give me a hard time. I really don't know why most white people want to give me a hard time. I really have not done anything to them. I would like you to go to one of their neighborhoods and try to find out what they think we ever did to them. I don't really mean that you should risk your life to find this out; I guess you would have to risk your life. I would like to know what the Polish people or the Jews or the Chinese think black people did to them. I don't think it would change things much, anyway. I really don't think we did anything to all these other groups or nations or whatever.

I think we probably take this American thing more seriously than any of the others. I mean, somebody like Mr. Kingsley—he didn't want to see Peaches beat up that girl because he didn't think it would be right. A lot of black people feel that way and would try to do something about something they thought was wrong. For example, that guard at the Watergate —he didn't have to blow the whistle, but he was the only one in that whole business who tried to do what should be done and he is suffering for that now. All through history, I think, it has been like that. Lincoln freed the slaves because he had to do that, but Harriet Tubman freed them by risking her own personal life because she knew that it was the right thing to do. Sometimes I wonder if there are any other Americans besides us.

I guess I feel the same way about patriotism that I do about anything in my personal life. You know that I would like to have a real family, but you know that I don't really have one and that I can't help anyone so much that I mess myself up. I don't mean that I have to be selfish. It's just that I can't let anybody, not even my own mother, mess me up. Well, my mother means more to me than any flag or constitution, and if I'm ready to put her down if I have to do that, you know that these other things will have to go too if they are going to mess me up. I mean, I have to take care of myself— you know, not at anybody's expense, but I can't let these things kill me. I think it is a kind of suicide to like anything that hates you. If we are the only people who really want to be Americans, what is the point? I don't mean jumping up and down on certain days and making a lot of noise, but doing what everybody knows is right and not doing things you know have got to be wrong.

As long as white people have been running this country, they have done everything the exact opposite way that we all know that things should be done, but they have not paid for that yet. I would just like to say, "Forget all that stuff that happened before. Let's just do what we know we should from now on," but my grandmother would never agree to that and I understand why she can't do that. But Marie can't agree to that either, and her grandmother was born in Italy and so was her mother. I don't know any white people who would really agree to that.

John Oliver

That man has got his country and we are our country.

*Mr. Oliver describes himself as "a man with one foot still in the country."
Decades have passed since he left the rural South, but his values and life style
still have a strong black peasant component. He prepared a meal for me that
was an impressionistic summary of the fusion of urban and peasant traditions
in his life. He drove six miles on a Friday evening to the supermarket to
purchase frozen rabbits, which he fried with green onions, thinly sliced turnips
and salt pork. He served the game in a cream sassafras gravy. On one trip
to the supermarket in quest of his beloved game, Mr. Oliver's car failed him,
so he pushed it into a garage for repairs and walked the remaining five miles
home.*

*He still has a countryman's legs and a countryman's direct, exacting
critical faculty, which is sometimes mistaken for simplicity. "If it look like
fish, swim like fish and tas' like fish, you can believe it ain' buzzard." Neither
Bibles nor Korans nor princes nor presidents nor professors are able to convince Mr. Oliver that the evidence of his own experience and perception is
grossly misleading. He is willing to entertain almost any alternate view of
almost anything, but his personal experience is far and away his most cogent
reality. Although he has reasonable facility with the written tradition and
speaks its "standard official" dialect, at home with black friends he generally
speaks one or another of the common black vernaculars. He scorns hunting
in the North as indiscriminate and dangerous "horseplay and homicide."*

*Mr. Oliver's formal church connections are minimal, but he meets many
of his neighbors in the lively informal symposium of the barbershop. Despite
his indifferent church attendance, he is the treasurer of two church associations because he is known to be a trustworthy person. He did not seek either
of these offices and plainly warned the members of both associations that "I
am not no paper man. I keep my books in my head."*

*Mr. Oliver has successfully defended himself against two attempts at mug-
ging and foiled one of four burglary attempts in less than a year.*

*He spends less time in the social club of his local tavern since he witnessed
the severing of the right hand of one of the youths who plague night life with*

vandalism and robbery. But many of his talking and drinking companions now meet in one another's homes with the same gusto that used to characterize sociability in the bars.

Mr. Oliver sings fine, grace-note-rich falsetto tenor and profound baritone with the Olijambra, a quartet deriving its name from the first three letters of the surnames of the three men who formed it. (In black culture the word "quartet" also means vocal ensemble. Such groups often have four members, but may also consist of five or three.) He goes deep-sea fishing with members of his Sportsmen's Club and devotes most of his considerable catch to the unassuming but effective enhancement of his reputation as a generous, judicious person who merits the generosity and respect of others.

You can say what you willormay, but I can do anything that any white man can do. I don't want to sound like I'm bragging on myself, but I can do almost anything I can think of better than most white men I know. And if you think about it, you know that when it comes to most things, we are really better than they are. They think so too; that's why they have to go through so many changes to see that we don't get that even break. They know that we can outdo them; that's what they say themselves. They think we are stronger than they are and they are right. They think we can raise more hell between the sheets and I think they might be right about that. If I want something done I try like hell to find a black man I know to do it because I know it will be done as well as I could do it myself then. Now, I can paint much better than some—no, I'll say most—of the white guys I know in the union, but they don't want me in the union because I can do my job better than they can.

Now, I don't want no black lawyer, because he is not going to be able to do no business with no judge because his face is just not the right color. Now, he might know more than the Jew, but he don't know *who* the Jew knows. When it comes to dealing with the man, you better get one of his relatives because you could be as smart as you want to, but that man is going to listen to a fool his color before he would hear Jesus Christ himself!

It seems to me that the only thing they do that we don't do is getting together on what the whole group wants to do and doing that. Mose is not good at that because he feel that if he cannot be the bell cow, he is not going to gallop with the gang. See, white people get together and they choose one white man who is just like the others and they say, "Let so-and-so be the President." Then they all act like this President is better than they are, but they know that he wasn't shit before they made him the President. That's why they made this dude Nixon the President. They like his trickiness. You see, the whole thing is built on tricks, so naturally they want somebody who can trick other people.

You know all that shit about "a cleaner New York is up to you"? I do not mess up this city! I cannot stop some other dude who don't care how he lives from messing up this city! Now, that is where it is. It is not my fault that I can hardly afford hamburger or beans. I did not tell these crackers to go over there and mess with those Arabs and Vietnam people! If a black man was President, all that shit would not have gone down, because that cat would have to be righter than right. Those crackers would be watching him all the time. He couldn't get away with a dime, because he wouldn't have no relatives on newspapers or in courthouses or banks to cover up what he did wrong.

Black people are just not as common as white people. If you could see, you could just look at people in the street and see what I mean. White people are so damn ordinary it is a shame. Black people don't look like every other black person walking down the street. My grandmother used to say that blackfolks are like a well-cooked dish of rice—every grain is standing for itself. Now, white people are like jello or mashed potatoes. You can't tell where one stop and the other start. Now, I'm trying to tell you in a way so that you will understand. My daughter says that white people are just "blah." She means that they don't have no twang to them. She's into this awareness thing and that's all right. It's just the same old thing that some blackfolks was into when I was a boy. Even way back there in the slavery days there was some folks that would Tom for another peck of meal and some folks that would kick this Tom dead in his do-nothing-stool if they caught the dog away from his master. King Solomon said it and I believe it: "There is no new thing under the sun." You told me to talk and that's what I'm doing. What I'm saying make sense to me, so I'll tell you what I think.

It is like I told you. Black people think that white people can just get things together much better than we can. Now, you know that the people say that all the time. How many times have you heard somebody get real pissed off because a few whitefolks can come into a place and cool out a whole passel of joogies! Well, that's just saying the first thing in another way. See, everybody knows that Charlie's boys will back him up because they can see that if they don't put color ahead of everything else, all the rest will catch the same hell that one white cat would catch if he came out here and started dealing man-to-man. You see that whenever old Mose get Chahlie out here by his lonesome, Chahlie gets wasted. Look at your sports —your boxing or baseball or football! You give Mose half a chance and he will take over because he is just a better man than Chahlie ever dared to be. Chahlie knows that just as well as we do; that's why he keep changing the rules.

Now, Chahlie will rule you to death. He love to sit on his ass and figure. If he didn't win he gon' show you how he should have, and if he don't like the way something went down, he will try to just run that deal and keep rubbing it out until he come up the winner. Now, Chahlie know that he is wrong as two rabbits when he do things like that, so naturally he don't want to hear about these things.

Now, when you say that they can get it together, you don't mean the same thing all the time. There is nobody in this world who can make more out of practically nothing than we can. See, our rule is, you got to work with what you got to work with. On New Year's Eve or Christmas Eve or just about any other time we can get free to have a party, blackfolks will stone *paar-dee*! Now, you know that's the truth! Everybody knows what a good party is and most folks just go and do something that will make a good party. On my job some dude wanted to set up a committee to give this retirement party for some dude who didn't even speak to us most of the time. Now, you know that had to fall dead on its ass because nobody gave a damn about it anyway. Whitefolks are lazy and they are strictly out for themselves, so when they give a party they just throw some mess together and call it a party, and then all these dudes who really want to be somewhere else just hang around. Black people would tell you right down front, "No, I don't want to pretend to have no party! If we gon' do it, let's do it."

A lot of whitefolks will tell you that we don't do nothin' but play. They save their money because they got some to save. I save as much money as I can, but I sure am not raising a bit of hell in the bank. Now, my car is just as nice as most other people's cars that I see. I'm sixty-five years old and I have two daughters that are still on me. I don't mind that a bit, because they are doing what we all agreed that they should do. Education is still the way to make it. But I can't see just getting into books, because that's the kind of thing these white folks are going to take all for themselves when old need starts to nudge 'em. I know—I have seen it too often. I want them to also have something that they can do that whitefolks think they can't do. Let 'em learn a little napfrying or dietician's work too to go along with that high-class diploma so they can help themselves when times get tight as Dick's hatband again. Don't think we left hard times behind. I know this man, and I know he is going to run it into the ground again because he still doing that same kind of hooray-for-me-and-to-hell-with-everybody-else thing that he always do.

You take welfare. Any fool knows that if you are on your ass, what you need is lots of money and a way to *make* some money. It is no big thing —everybody knows that is the way to make it. I mean, in them old fairy stories the way the poor man made it was, the king would lay a lot of loot or half the kingdom on the dude. Or maybe some good fairy would show the cat how he could get some food or some silver and gold. But any fool knows that if I am poor, and God knows I am, what I need is money! But this man runs welfare like he runs everything else. See, to begin with, he don't really want to do it, so naturally he is going to fix it like he fix everything else. He gon' do it and not do it at the same time, and you know that you can't do a damn thing that way. The man is actually using welfare to put the people down even lower. When they help their own they give them the money and say, "Here you are, my man. Go for yourself." But with us they just figured a way so their young boys could try for some black pussy and so their snotty little bitches can look big in front of a whole line of black women. If I had said to you, "Here, dog, have one of these ham sandwiches and some of this sweet bread," you would have known right away that I was white and I'll bet you a funky monkey and two old maids you would have told me what I could do with this food. Anyway, I hope you would. Now, welfare ain't shit. It just helps you to git over. And you got to take shit to get this shit, so I can't see it.

My grandmother was a tailor back there in slavery days, and she used to make the fancy dresses that those chicks up there at the big house wore. They used to show her things in the ladies' magazines and Grandma Yula would whip it right up for them. So they took her north so she could look at the dresses in the big stores and whip them up for these crackers. Well, she made two trips for them, but that third trip she made for us. All those other times she would be getting to know what was what, and when she figured she could make it for herself, she shook! Now, if welfare taught you something you could use to earn a good living, then it would be doing something. Now, when Grandma Yula came up here the first time and went back, that must have got to her, but she didn't let the man know a thing about that. He didn't know that she was going to treat him like that turkey treat the big devil.

Now, when I was coming along, if a black person wanted to do something, if he didn't do that thing it wasn't because he didn't try like hell to find a way. That's what gets to some white people about us. They ask me, "John, how do you people get these big cars and all that?" I say, "What big car? You ought to see what my wife is driving!" See, they do everything they can to keep us down, and still we got things they think we ain' got no business with! So they wonder what they would have to do to keep us all the way down there where they want to see us. They keep thinning this soup and we keep coming up with chicken fricassee!

Now, they just cannot get to that. It's like that thing in the Bible where they made these slaves make bricks without straw and they made these bricks anyway. That got to the masters because they thought they were really laying it on these slaves. I mean, suppose I have the power and I send you out here and tell you to bring me back a whole barbecued hog in two hours after I have taken every hog and every match in the country into my farm. Now, if you cool in here with two barbecued hogs and a yam puddin', what the hell am I supposed to say? I mean, that would really get to me. Here I fixed everything so you couldn't do what I told you to do and then you went out here and did more.

You notice that whenever they have some program about us, they always have some tongue-tied cat or some Tom up there that nobody would choose to speak for us? They love to get some educated fool up there who is just out to make rep for him, and don't care whether the man knows how we feel or not. I'm not no Muslim or Jew or anything like that. Most of us are just drylongso black people just like me, but I don't see a soul on that tube that looks like me and think like I know most blackfolks out here do. You see, the man don't want to hear that. It don't surprise me, you understand, because it is the same old stuff. White people have always been crying over us half the time and telling us we should be proud to be Americans the rest of the time. I don't care what they do. I just wish they wouldn't go around braggin' about doing things which they never did and never will do until we can make 'em.

I get tired of that one-nation-under-God boogie-joogie. We are ourselves. We are our *own* nation or country or whatever you want to call it. We are not no one tenth of some white something! That man has got his country and we *are* our country. Maybe we might get to that one nation, but we sure won't make it the way we're going now! If the Lord took every white ass away this afternoon it wouldn't change me any. We don't need them to do what we do. They need us more than we need them. How many black people have you ever heard come on with that one-nation stuff? You know damned well that Nixon is the President of the whites, who put him in there. If it had been left to us, that dude would still be sweetening transmissions and putting junk cars together for the chumps to buy.

I'd be a fool if I thought that army was our army. If it's my army and guard and navy and all that, will you tell me why it was shooting at me here a few years ago? If anybody can be the President, why all them dudes look like they do? If you could see the money, you would see that there just are none of us on it! It's their money, just like it's their country and their damned army and their damned post office and their damned everything else. Ain't nothing ours but us and they tried to say we didn't even own ourself. You know what gets to me? Why do they have to go through all these lying changes? We all know how it is, so why do we have to pretend all this home-of-the-brave and land-of-the-free bullshit? Paddies can't stand us and we don't think a hell of a lot of them. Now, that's where it really is.

It's all a bullshit game, but I can't figure out why they have to play it all the time. If I had what they have, look like to me it would be enough just to have that. I mean, if I was doing what they are doing, I would say, "Okay, I'm a rotten cat, but I get what I want and I like getting what I want better than I would like to be known as a good cat. I know I'm gon' pay for what I'm getting, but that's all right. I'll whale while I'm whalin'." That's what they are doing, so why don't they just kick ass while they can and get theirs kicked when it's payback time? That's what we have to do. If I do something out here that has "jail" written on it, that's my tiddy and I will nurse it. I am not going out here and shoot babies and I am not going out here and do every ugly thing I can think of doing and expect the cats I just fucked over to give me a damned medal. That's one big difference between us and them. No matter what Chahlie do, he want his mama to pat him on the head and tell him how cute he is. Well, maybe his mama will do that because she gets part of what he gets, but I am not his mama, so I don't feel like telling this man that he is good when I know that he is a asshole from the git. If I was to go for bad, I know I would have to go for bad things too. That is the only way you can get anybody to give you all they got. You got to get out here and make them get up off it. Who is going to work hard and say, "Here, take my pay"? Who is going to say, "Here, let me get down here with these rats and roaches and you take that good house"? Chahlie won't get with that.

You know, there was this Czechoslovakian guy on my job, and people used to feel so sorry for him because those Russians almost got his ass. Now, he comes over here, bumps a black man off his job and is then going to stand up in the cafeteria and tell me in broken English why "the colored people are pushing too fast for their rights." I told him that I was sorry that the Russians or the Germans or some damn body didn't waste his ass over there on his side of the water. You know, that sucker actually cried. Whitefolks didn't speak to me for days, but that didn't bother me at all. I also told him that if it had been left up to us, his ass would have been wasted before he could dry his feet because he is just another Nazi as far as I am concerned. These whitefolks told them fools to get out there and throw stones and sticks at tanks, and then when they got wasted behind that, Sam just igged 'em. Now, you and I both know that these crackers were not going to go over there and help them. If they had any sense they should have known that too. Now, if anybody should get up off their jobs for these refugees, it should be those paddies that told them to break bad with the Bear to begin with. I didn't have no nickel in that dime, so why should we have to get bumped off our jobs for some dude who is going to come over here and try to do to me just what was done to him over there on his side of the water? That man got here because he was white, not because he was right.

You don't hear Sam telling these Africans that are still under slavery in South Africa to throw no stones at those cracker tanks. They got better sense, anyway. But when they get shot up and messed up, do you think any white cats are going to tell them to come over here and get one of their jobs? Everybody is bugging the Bear to let these Jews leave there. Do you ever hear anybody but some black cat saying that they should let some of those Africans come out of that South African slavery and come over here? If those Africans get out it's because they made it on their own, just like black people have to do everywhere! I can't call his name right now, but I saw this senator telling everybody that if the Russians don't let the Jews leave Russia, then we should stop selling things to them. Okay, that's fine, but I'd like to see that same man say, "Let's not sell anything to those South African crackers, too, until they let some of our people go." I'd like to hear that same dude say, "We don't want no more crackers in this country, and if those folks that the Russians let go are going to come over here and bump black people, then let them stay the hell over there where they are." Now, you are not ever going to hear anything like that because this country ain't nothing but a group of little countries.

Just like we are our own nation, the whites have their own nations and the Jews and the Irish and the Italians and all them little white nations do what's good for them first. I see it every day! The Italians and Irish are always up in my face talking about the Jew, and the Jew is always telling me what a good friend he is of mine and how the white man hates him worse than he do me. But when I say, "Ruby, you mean you ain't a white man?", that dude does not want to hear that! The Irishman is looking down on the Italian and the Italian is looking down on the Jew, but you can believe that they all are looking down on you!

You know, I hate it when somebody who is dumber than me tries to trick me. I just listen to all that bullshit, and I don't side with any of them because I know that they are all together against me. That's just more of that I'm-bad-but-I-want-everybody-to-say-I'm-good shit. My brother went for bad, you know that, but he was bad and he knew that was wrong and he knew that nobody was going to thank him for being bad. Now, we know that you can't be good and bad at the same time, but Chahlie don't know that because his mama done told him that he can do anything he feel like doing, so that's how he sees things. See, they figure if nobody blows the whistle, then nothing wrong has gone down. As long as they can make somebody say that rough is smooth, they are happy. Like that place they shot up over there in Vietnam—the first thing they want to do is to prove that those dudes didn't mean to do what everybody know they did. What difference does it make whether the dude meant to do it; he did it, didn't he? Now, how that really was is these gray dudes went over there and couldn't make these Vietnam people do what they wanted to make them do, so they treated them like roaches. They lynched those people because they was mad with them, and if they had not been black, then they would not have treated them that way. Did you ever hear of whitefolks dropping napalm or atomic bombs on other whitefolks? You have *not* heard of that and you are not going to hear of it, either! Like I told you, whitefolks don't care nothing about what the truth is. It's like when you lie but so much you don't know what the truth is. This man thinks the truth is what is good for him and a lie is anything that is good for us.

I wish you would write a book about that. Why do whitefolks have to be bad and good at the same time? If they get what they want, why can't they just go with that? You know what they used to say about street angels and house devils? This dude don't want to admit that there is anything wrong with him. This devil that is handing out more hell than anybody wants everybody to think that he is an angel. You could whip head till hell freeze over, but hell is still hell and you can't *be* decent and *do* rotten things.

Sometimes I really do think that there is something wrong with this man's wig. I mean, they really do act kind of simple. All the black cats I know who go for bad do that because they kind of like being bad. They want you to know that they are bad asses! If a black bad cat gets half a chance, he'll tell you, "I'm bad, don't mess with me!" Everybody knows what a man like that will do. Now, with white people half of what they do just don't match the other half of what they do. I mean, they will shoot uku people who were just minding their own business, and then work like hell to get them to the hospital sometimes. Now, I cannot get to that. Why didn't they just leave those people alone to begin with?

When I used to live in the projects, a whole gang of cops came down there looking for some boy that they said was a sniper. Well now, I'm coming home from work and it has been a long time since I was a boy. But six of these guinea cops start beating on me. Now, if you know why, I know why! They took my pay and beat and kicked me like I was the worst criminal in this world. Now, after they beat me for nothing, one of them says, "Let the nigger go." Now, the others say, "We have to get this man to the hospital." Now, I didn't want to go to the hospital, because if the cops will half kill you, the doctors might finish you. But, do you know, they made me go to the hospital anyhow? I had not done a damned thing! I never did get my money and I had to pay $109.50 to the hospital. Now, what kind of sense does that make, will you tell me? I knew these cops wanted my money, so I told them what I had and where it was. But they had to beat me anyway. It wasn't just me—they were beating anybody and everybody they saw, women and little kids! Now, they found this so-called sniper and he was a white high school kid, but they didn't beat his ass and they didn't even put him in jail. The only person he shot was a black woman. Now, I don't understand what those cops were trying to prove. They hurt more people than the sniper and they stole people's money and stripped grown men and women in the street.

Now, these junkies out here are doing the same thing with the permission of the cops. But if I show my black face in certain places, every cop in creation is right there. "What is your business here?" "Keep moving, nigger." "Do you work for some white family around here?" Shit, this might just as soon be South Africa. See, that's so these junkies they are making down here don't go up there and sock it to those big pushers up there living in those fine castles.

They do everybody that is not their color that way. I mean, they will bomb the shit out of some little country that never did anything to them, and then pat theirself on the back because they sent some Band-Aids and a jackleg doctor over there to patch up these kids that would have been fine if they had left them alone. I think it would make more sense to give them Vietnamese some planes and ships so they could stop crazy people from bombing them. I mean, it's like this nut that was going around killing women and writing on the walls, "Stop me before I kill again." It's the same thing! You know, they can just act like the truth is whatever they feel like it is.

I see these damn commercials telling me to "see America first." Now, how do I know that my family can go where these white people are going? I'm not going to spend my money to have some dude spit in my soup. I can cook, so I don't need to pay for a hard time from Howard Johnson or any of them other places. Now, if they tell me that black people are just as welcome as anybody else, that don't mean a damn thing either, because I have been asked to go to places by whitefolks who almost had a shit fit when I got there. You can't believe nothing the man says. If I go to a place and check it out, then I know what is going down—that day, anyway. A white woman is going to find a hell of a lot more gracious living than I am in most of those places. Even if she wasn't welcome in there, they are not going to go upside her head or put her in jail, like they would you or me. That's one of the worst things about the whole country. Half of everything you have to know about doing anything here is left out. If you ain't in the know, you are in danger!

THE LEGACY OF SLAVERY

I'm not saying "Yessir" to no damn cracker.
Jonathan Melton

I've heard my grandfather tell many a time about how his father killed his master and took his silver and his horse. My aunt still has some of that silver. But that was a long time ago and should have nothing to do with now.
Iris McCrae

When Jonathan Melton's wife refers to him jokingly as "everybody's husband," she is echoing his neighbors' appreciation of his willingness to assist others in everything from repairing oil burners to lending an ear in times of family crisis.

Iris McCrae is a member of a large extended family that was of incalculable assistance to me. Although in the midst of planning for her wedding, she gave generously of her time and, with energy and unerring appropriateness, suggested prospective narrative contributors. At her family's insistence, Iris acquired both practical and academic training. She holds a bachelor's degree and is also a skilled hairdresser in great demand.

Ruth Shays

When you don't know when you have been spit on, it
does not matter too much what else you think you
know.

*Miss Shays was accorded a splendid constitution and nimble mind in the
great genetic lottery. She is interested in an astounding variety of things and
knows an astounding number of people. When I first met her she was giving
up her apartment to enter a residence for senior citizens. Among the possessions she was obliged to discard or give away were lovingly preserved record-
ings of the Fisk Jubilee Singers, Alma Gluck and Enrico Caruso, many
albums containing her own watercolors, a collection of fans, the* Authorized
History of the War of the Rebellion *and the libretti for* The Gondoliers *and*
The Magic Flute.

*She is the kind of principled, practical person who assists people in their
descent from extreme positions of ego. I first talked at length with her less
than two weeks after her bloody and successful defense of her person in the
streets. I was not really surprised to learn that Miss Shays not only had cut
her would-be assailant, but had given him first aid as well.*

I think there is more talking *around* what black people are than there is
talking *about* what we are. I can't do that. Well, I could do it, but I spend
so much time talking around things at work that I wouldn't want to waste
my time that way with you. I mean, I am the kind of person who doesn't
have a lot of education, but both my mother and my father had good
common sense. Now, I think that's all you need. I might not know how to
use thirty-four words where three would do, but that does not mean that
I don't know what I'm talking about. You must know that because you are
over here in this little barn of mine listening to me and I know you must
be a busy man.

Now, in explaining about the Aunt's children, the first thing to say is
that we are not Africans or whitened-up blackfolks or anything else but
what we are. When they sent us over here, that's when we stopped being
Africans of Africa. Now, we learned whatsoever language that the whitefolks made us learn, but that didn't make us no kind of English people.

We are what we are and the whites are what they are.

Your black man is generally a poor, clean person. Now, that is not to say that all black people are that way. There are some black people who have heaps of money and there are some black people that I wouldn't eat with. But generally your black person is cleaner than your average white person because he has to spend more time cleaning. That's because if the food you love takes more cleaning to make it fit for folks to eat, you will have to spend more time cleaning it. I don't care what anybody will tell you, you have got to put much time in washing chiddlins, maws, greens of whatsoever kinds and all such stuff as that. If you have fewer dresses or blouses or stockings or whatsoever, you must wash them more than somebody who can change their clothes often because they got these closetsful or maybe have somebody to take care of their things for them. Like I say, your average black man or woman or child is clean and poor.

Your average black person is more interested in hisself than anything else. Now, that is a good thing and a bad thing at the same time, like most big things. I'm going to try to explain that. You see, your average black person would not care if you told him that the king of this or that place was standing on the corner. I was in that barbershop down there by the tavern. They sent a boy to the tavern for something to eat, and the boy came back there and said that the President was out there. Well, most folks didn't move a peg because it didn't mean anything to them. What excites the white man does not move most of us. Now, partly that is because most of us don't want white people to know when something does move us, but generally the black people don't like the way that white people are running the country, so we don't want to have anything to do with their big muck-demucks who are making all these little white people out here behave the way they do.

One thing about your average black man, he does know what is going on. Now, I am not what you might call one of these great-minded women, like Mrs. Bethune or Mrs. Roosevelt, but I have good common sense, so I don't sit here like a fool and believe everything I see on this TV. You know, you can say whatsoever you willormay, but there is the just plain, ordinary common sense of a thing and that is what I go by and that is what most of us black people go by. You hear people out here saying, "Believe nothing you hear and only half of what you see." Now, when a black person says that, he means pay that paper no mind because what happened is what *could* happen, not what some white man told you happened.

Now, when they told us that this little country most folks didn't know thing one about had jumped up in these crackers' faces, no blackfolks believed that because it didn't make sense for a thing like that to happen. Now, if they went over there and bothered those Vietnam people like they do us and those people just wouldn't take low, then I could understand why we had to go over there to back up what these white people had done to the Vietnam people. But there is no way in Christ that a little country is going to bother a country this big unless these white people go over there and mess with them. Now, they say that they sunk or shot at one of these whitefolks' boats. Now, will you tell me what that boat was doing over there close enough to these other people's land so they could attack it? If anybody just comes in here off the street and tries to use my bathroom or my kitchen without my sayso, Ruth is going to war! You can believe that! And I am going to shoot, cut, hit and just generally damage every piece of that nervy devil until he gets his what-I-might-say back where he pays rent. Now, that's what those Vietnam people are doing and I for one don't fault them a bit.

Almost everything I hear on the radio sounds just like a lie to me. I listen to it because that's all there is to listen to. I don't know many people out here that pay much attention to what they read or hear. Like most black-folks, I look for the big lies that have got to be under there when they tell the little lies. What these politicians do is admit to some little thing they did to cover up the big things they are always doing. My grandfather used to say, "When you tell on yourself, you don't tell much." Now, I believe that thing! I got to say this like I got to say it, you know.

Now, you know that everybody is used to his own dirt. If somebody else has just come out of that bathroom, then it is hard for me to go right in there behind them, just like it is hard for them to use it after I have just come out of there. I don't know why that is true, but it is—we all know that. I mean, it is the very same with the body in general. You can't just go putting parts from one body into another body, because every person is, what you might say, more at home with itself. I was reading about this heart-transplant number. Sometimes one body just won't live with a strange heart. Now, something like that is going on with the truth. It will not kill people to hear the truth, but they don't like it and they would much rather hear it from one of their own than from a stranger. Now, to white people your colored person is always a stranger. Not only that, we are supposed to be dumb strangers, so we can't tell them anything! Now, you know that I'm right about that. They won't tell each other the truth, and the lies they tell each other sound better to them than the truth from our mouths. They like their dirt better than cleanness from you or me or their own kind.

Now, you take this mess with the President. I can tell you that you will never know how big that lie is. And I will bet you that that white man is not gon' spend day one in jail. And they are gon' let him pick the next one to get in there. Now, if I steal my club money there is no way in Christ that these women are going to say, "Ruth, you got to go, but you can have the sayso about who gets the sayso after you go." Now, will you tell me what kind of sense that makes? If we did that the first thing most whitefolks would say is, "Look at those niggers making a thief be their judge. Hee, hee, hee, ain't that just like a nigger?" But because they are doing this wrong number, it is all right and they won' spend too much time looking at what they are really doing. They'll *write* around it and talk around it, but when it comes down to really looking at that number, they are not going to let themselves do nothing in this world like that. Now, that is why it is rough and wrong out here. Your big white men, they are the cause of most of that. Just like the law don't mean what-I-won't-say to the President, it don't signify much to the rest of these big white men and their friends. I understand that. If you got the sayso you want to keep it, whether you are right or wrong. That's why they have to keep changing the laws—so they don't unbenefit any of these big white men. All my life I have seen them do that. The law is whatever they feel like saying it should be. If I did half of the things this sorry President did, they would put me under the jail and send every key to the moon. They have the little punishments for the big men and the heavy chastisement for the poor.

Now, you could tell them that, and they would say "Uhn-huhn" and go right on doing what they felt like doing. They would even tell you that you was right, but still just go on like you had never opened your mouth. Now, if you kept on telling them the truth, even if they asked you what you thought, they would find some nasty thing to do to you for having the nerve to tell them what they knew anyway. You see, if you tell them the truth —well now, to them that means you fear God more than you do them, and they do not like that because they want all the sayso.

You remember in the war they used to say that God was on their side? When Joe Louis said he was on God's side, the woman I was working for laughed and said, "There's a lot of tongue-tied among the colored." Now, I know she wanted to say "niggers," not "colored," but, you see, these Japanese and Germans was threatening to cut their toenails too short to walk, so she called herself being friendly by not using that word "nigger" because she knows I hate and despise it. Whenever they get a little scared they try to act like they might be decent, but when that war was over you didn't hear much about freedom and the equal rights, and what you heard didn't have much to do with what was going on.

I still don't know where I can eat, where I can travel or live when I leave here. I have visited France and Spain and Sweden, too, and I still felt better about asking for a room or getting on a train to someplace I didn't know than I would feel here about going to a strange place. Never mind about *strange* places! Right here in this city I do not know—I mean, I don't feel like I can just walk into anyplace where I can afford to eat and eat there. Now, I am a neat, clean woman and I have not spent my first day in jail, but here in the only country I and my foreparents have ever known I never feel like I was just folks like anybody else here. That is not my imagination. I do have good common sense and I do know when somebody is trying to insult me.

Now, most of us feel the same way. Most of us are tired of trying to figure out what whitefolks mean by what they said. I would rather have a little something to call my own where I know where I stand than all this great big America-the-beautiful that a black person has got to tip around in, hat in hand. If we can't get along together, then let's divide up this place before this kingdom gets torn down. You know, I really do believe that most black people feel that way.

Never mind all this feeling sorry for me. I can do as much with a dollar as any white woman I ever knew, and if they don't make it no harder for me than it would be just naturally out here, I will do all right for myself. I lived in spite of their numbers and I could live much better if I didn't have their stumbling stones to worry about. That's one thing we don' have to worry about—they cannot do anything any better than we know how to do it. That's really what bothers them. They may have more of what everybody wants than we do, but, you see, there are more of them. Now, they don't have anything down here completely to themselves—there is nothing that they know how to do that we can't do just as well.

Now, you know my father was a slave—my *father*, not my grandfather —and my mother was a slave too. Now, I mention that because they felt the same way I feel. I know it has changed some, but we still feel the same way because it has not really changed anything like enough. My mother was a knee-baby when Lee surrendered, but my father was a boy big enough to go to the swamps. It just has not changed all that much. Whitefolks are great for making things look different. Like the war didn't make all that much of a difference, well, it's like that now. We keep having these wars and these civil rights. Well, if they really changed things, we wouldn't need all of that now, would we?

When it comes to those old times, you can' go to books and courthouses because most of our foreparents had sense enough not to spill their in-gut to whitefolks, or blackfolks, either, if they didn' know them. Now, they— I mean the cracker—say they was simple back there. Now, I think they had more common sense than most whitefolks or blackfolks got in these times. They had sense enough to know they had to get free. They just kept everything to themself. They didn't pay much attention to all this, if and or but. What folks really did was what they went by. They didn' care about what you thought you did or what you wanted to do. They used to do what they wanted to do whenever they could do that, because they knew what they wanted to do and they didn't have all this foolishness about good folks doing wrong and bad folks doing the right thing. They said Paul was a liar and a snare to the true believer. I have heard my father say that many a time. They didn't carry everything to the white man, either, because they had understanding of their lot. They knew that to the crackers it didn' make no difference about the truth of the thing.

When I first came up here (that was when they was fighting that First World War), Elder Tucker told me not to be running to these courts because the guilty are corrupt judges. A woman whose name I won' call because she is dead and in the devil's hands said I taken some dishes and pans and two pounds of meal and sugar from her house. Now, she was very well liked by these white people we both worked for, so she brought them into this thing. They told her that she should go to court if I didn't pay her for these things. Elder Tucker, who was elder in this church we went to then, told us not to go to court. I said, "Elder Tucker, I am willing to put it in your hands." So then he asked her if she wanted to put it in his hands. She said that she knew what happened and didn' need to put it in nobody's hands. So then the white woman, who didn't know thing one about the whole business, started paying some of my money to this woman. And she said she would keep doing that until twelve dollars of my money was paid to this woman that said I stole her things. Well, I couldn't do anything about that, so I just let her do that. Andrella Mobley, who was as good as any human woman can be, came to me and put every cent I had lost into my hand. Now, she was first cousin to the woman who told that lie on me, but she loved the truth. Now, that's the kind of folks the best blackfolks are. They do despise a lie and a liar. Now, this woman's man would not uphold her in her lie because he had sense enough to know the truth. The white woman was just playing big. She didn't know or care what had happened, but she took my money and gave it to this other woman. Now, she called herself watching me, I guess, to see that I wouldn't take anything from her, but she was watching the wrong person and never did find out what a fool she was.

Now, you ask me about the foreparents—they would find the lie if it took them a year, just like my parents or your parents would find it. The white-folks most likely wouldn't know a thing about it. Those slavery elders didn' ask you if you wanted to put something in their hands. They was the Lord's watchmen just like they people was their watchmen. Now, if you see wickedness and snares and you are any kind of a watchman at all, you will remove it. You won' waste everybody's time asking this one or that one if they want that snare taken up or left there where it is. The foreparents found the truth because they listened and they made people tell their part many times. Most often you can hear a lie. I see you doing the same thing. I do it too. If you are dealing in the truth you will tell just about the same tale just about the same way. Now, sometime they would let sassafras find the lie. They had good common sense, so they knew whose word was light. Those old people was everywhere and knew the truth of many disputes. They believed that a liar should suffer the pain of his lies, and they had all kinds of ways of bringing liars to judgment.

My father's mother told him that they made one liar suffer by the hand of the white man. There was this woman, a black woman on this big rice farm, and she was a snare to any black person on this farm. So one Christmas time this devil told the people, "None of you can stan' me, but you are all eating my dirt." Then she let it get back to the row that she put a gourd of her filth into the molasses that the whitefolks gave the people during the Christmas time. So the elders decided to make that lie turn back on her.

Now, the mistress was a fool about these china dolls, and the young mistress with her. So they took two of those dolls and the whites searched the row to find them. They taken them to the swamp so they couldn't find them. Now, since this devil was always up under them half the time, it looked like she was the one that could have taken those dolls. The white folks didn't want to believe that she was the one that took them, but they felt funny about her after that. Then they cut up the mistress's ball dress that she got from across the water, and that did it. There was no way in Christ after that you could show that white woman anything good about that black devil. They sold her somewhere in Virginia after a while, they said. This rice farm was in South Carolina. Now, some folks know where one of those dolls is to this day, but I know your mother must have told you what mine told me: "The tongue is steel, but a closed mouth is a shield."

You know, I said that to that child and she got out her little book and wrote it down. I like that child because she's what I was when I was young. I don' mean I looked like her. The truth is, son, I have never been the kind of person people would turn around and look at in the street. I'm just, well, what you might say drylongso. Neither ugly nor pretty, just drylongso. It does my heart and soul good to see a young woman like that. Now, there are no flies whatsoever on her, but her looks won' be a snare unto her or anybody out here. I see what's going on out here and she carries herself like she thought something of herself. A young woman like that can start a lot of mess in this world.

Now, this thing you asked Rose about, about the women. I have been wanting to speak my piece about that for a long time, but I don' waste my time. I am going to tell you how I feel about that because I believe you want to know. Now, most times I wouldn't talk about something like that because most people already know how *they* feel about it and that's all they feel like listening to. You know, if I think this way or that way about a thing, I don' much care who agrees with me or whosoever might not agree with me on that thing.

Now, I will say this because I believe it and I think I can help you by saying it: Your woman and your man, being flesh, are pretty much the same when they come here. It is the living of this life that makes the most difference. That is what makes the color and the sex whatsoever a cross it might be in this world. Now, son, there are things about being a woman that are a cross to women and you should know that by now and I know you must. First, now, this bleeding every month is a pure-dee pain where me and the chair come together. I put up with that for longer than you have breathed in this world. I have known very few men that understand as much as they could about that. Now, just suppose that a headache and upset stomach was to work on you for days every month that God sends for years and years of your life. Now, the least somebody who did not have to put up with that number should do for you is to sympathize with you. My father said that back in the slavery times they made those ladies pick up their hoes if they could crawl. Now, you hear talk about sharecroppin'. Well, I know that white men would whip a woman to the field when she was just about ready to birth a child, so you know they didn't care nothing at all about the period. I know what I'm talking about because I'm talking about myself. I'm talking about what I have lived. The mind of the man and the mind of the woman is the same. But this business of living makes women use their minds in ways that men don' even have to think about. Like I told you, it is life that makes all these differences, not nature.

Both your man and your woman are pleasant creatures to look at, though each one thinks the other one is more pleasant to see, and that is natural. Now, I am one woman that could never understand men loving men or women loving other women. But all I ever had to worry about was what I did about this natural burning. I don't care what grown folks do on their own time in their own room. But I do believe that whatsoever that might be should not be put in the streets. Now, me, I don' want to know what anybody else is doing in their house. I don' want to tell no lie. There is in me, like I think there is in most folks, a desire to mind other people's business, but I know that that is the child in me, not the woman in me. So because I am a woman, not a child, I manage to deal with that. I still have to fight to keep my ear away from some walls and my nose to myself. I do believe that women are nosier about some things than men, but then, your average man is nosier about some other things that most women wouldn't go 'cross the hall to see.

Now, people see women doing certain things and they say, "Well, that's women's work." Now, me, I cook, but it was my father who had the patience to teach me how to cook. My mother was a woman who could get something done while most people were still sitting there thinking about doing that thing. She didn't have much patience and she knew that abou⁺ herself. Most folks would say she was a very calm woman, but she just wouldn' do the things that bothered her if she could help it. I'm that way too. I think work is work and whatsoever kind of work you can do is your work. Now, you know that our people can't do the kind of work they want to do anyway, so one kind of job is like another. I wanted to be a doctor and then I thought that I would like to be an architect, but that was just something to let run through your mind and forget if you were black and poor. I didn't feel like cooking half the things I was told to cook, but you got to give people what they pay you to give them.

I worked for a woman in Chattanooga in nineteen and twenty-one, and the finest person in that family was this old woman. Now, the doctor had told this woman's granddaughter just what she should eat and that same doctor told me the very same thing. Now, I had done that kind of cooking before and I have been nursing folks all my life, so I knew what was supposed to be done. But that young white woman in her wickedness thought her grandmother was a cross. Now, she was getting the old lady's money and she would have got most of it when God decided to take her away, but that wasn't enough for her. She killed that old lady just as sure as if she shot her. She just killed her with food instead of shells, that's all.

I worked for them about a year and a half. Everything I did was all right. Nobody found fault with what I did. They bragged on my cooking like it might have been theirs. But when the old lady first got down and they had the doctor to see to her, then I couldn't do a thing right around there. Every time that doctor would leave there with a smile on his face, that white woman would find something I did to pick at. I was feeding that old lady what she should eat and I did her little exercises and things with her. I believe her granddaughter thought I was trying to get something out of the old lady. The old soul said something about remembering me in her will. Now, I told her not to say that. She asked me why and I told her 'twas foolish to hurry your life away. Now, how was I going to tell that old lady that her granddaughter wanted every cent she had and wasn't above throwing dirt in her face to get it? Well, that old soul just went on singing my praises and digging her grave.

Now, that young white woman was just as lazy as any three people ever wanted to be, but she started taking the meals I cooked for her grandmother upstairs. I saw her put salt into some veal soup I made. When the old lady said 'twas a little salty, I didn't say a word. Well, then we had it. Nothing was said, but we had it just the same. Now, it was her house, but she didn't know much about the kitchen. The fact is, she didn't want to know anything about it. She wasn't supposed to know anything but how to tell me what she wanted done. She wasn't that smart a woman, so it wasn't much of a job to stay ahead of her.

One day her husband asked me to explain something I had never heard anything about. He said that some things were on his accounts at the butcher's that his wife didn't know anything about, and could I explain that? I asked what these things were, and he got mad and said that I owed them six dollars. Well, that was a lot of money back then. They had just paid me, and he said next time he was going to take the six dollars they said I owed them out of my pay. Well, I knew what all that really meant, so I gave my notice. The husband said, "You are a smart gal. Why don't you go up north? They say the colored can do very well up there for themselves." I finished out my two weeks, and not a day went by that that white woman didn't ask me why I didn't think about going to Chicago or Detroit. She told me not to tell her grandmother that I was leaving. She said she'd see about letting me have my full pay and a little extra if I didn't upset the old lady. Well, I couldn' see what good it would do to tell the old lady anything, so I never breathed a word of the whole business to her.

Well, anyway, about three days before my time was up, the old lady told me, "Ruth, I hear that you are going north." I knew then that her granddaughter had told her that. I had not told a soul that I was going anywhere because I hadn't made up my mind about what I was going to do or wheresoever I might go to do it. So, I saw that she really did want all the money, even what she owed me. Sure enough, the doorknob of the old lady's room had just barely bumped me in the back when that worthless grandchild was up in my face pretending to be angry with me for telling her grandmother that I was leaving. I knew that meant that I had just worked two weeks for nothing and the little money, whatever it was, that the old lady had just said she was going to give me to help me when I went north —well, if you spent that money, I did! I know her husband must have put all that devilment together. He was just as smart as his wife was simple and greedy. Now, I could have thought of how such a rotten business could be done, but I would never have done more than think about it and I would have been ashamed just thinking. Now, I believe that your average black person or your average white person in their natural self would be ashamed to do a wicked trick like that. But life gets hold of you as soon as you leave your mother. That is what makes the difference between the whites and the blacks, just like it separates the men and the women.

Now, if you have nothing but yourself, you have to prize whatsoever it is you have. Most blackfolks have got their self and not too much else that cannot be taken away from them. So the average black person will think twice before he dirties himself. Now, a lot think twice and go on and mess on themselves anyway, but most blackfolks will not make fools of themselves as quick as most whitefolks will.

When the white man—I mean the big whitefolks that are telling everybody, white and black, what to do—when they say something, howsoever foolish it might be, blackfolks remember that this man is a liar from his heart, but whitefolks remember that he is their man, that he looks like their husband or their uncle or their whatsoever. Now, there are all kinds of white and black folks in this world. That big white man might look like my cousin or whosoever's uncle, but even then you think, "Well, that devil is passing, and if he would deny his brothers and sisters, can anything but a lie be found in him?" I am the treasurer for my club and my church circle because I am known not to be light-fingered. Now, I would not be trusted if I had not been worthy of that trust. If everybody in that church was a cousin of mine, you could not get that many black people to let a person they knew was light-fingered handle their money. They wouldn't care what you looked like.

Now, white people are just subject to different temptations. Their big men keep telling them that they can be big, too, if they keeps us little enough, and that's all they need to hear. I have lived in South Carolina, Georgia, Tennessee, Michigan, New York and plenty of other places, and I have not been anywhere where there were not some white people who were just as poor as most of the black people in those places. I have known some white women that carried themselves like they thought something of themselves. I have had a white woman walk off the job because I was being walked on, but most whitefolks have just enough to make them think that they can get what these big shots have. That is why so many of them can be fooled.

A person whose name I will not call but who is just as black as some of my cousins because he *is* one of my cousins has a job, and has had it for twenty-five years, that a black person can't get. Now, why does he have this job? Because white people can look at this black man and see a white person in front of them if they read somewhere or get told by one of those big shots that such-and-such black people are really white. Now, you can't do that with black people. They might say "Uh-huh" and "Yessir," but you know they are thinking, "If he's white I will eat him without salt." Now, you know that we have some colored people like that, but there are a heap more who have to pretend to believe every fool thing they hear than there are who really do believe what these big white folks tell them. Your black man is the hardest person to figure behind that God ever let breathe.

Now, most of your whitefolks don' think that they have to worry about whatsoever might come out of their mouths. They say, "I'm free, white and twenty-one." They used to say that thing at the dropping of any old hat. Now, to them that meant that they could say or do anything they might want to do and it was all right. Now, blackfolks don' have no such saying as that. You might hear a black person say, "I'm grown, ain't I?" That means that that person thinks that he is big enough and black enough to do whatsoever he is big enough to do. Now, he don't think that the President or the police or his cousin or anybody but his revern' self is going to help him do this thing that he thinks he is bad enough to do. Now, as a black woman—no, let me say me—I know and always have known that I have to do for myself just like any other grown person out here. I say "grown person," but I was doing the work of grown people since I was a little child because I had to do that. I think more black women know this than white women because poor white people have a little bit more than poor black people, you know, for the most part. But like I say, it does not always work that way.

I hear people talking about the poor: "Oh, the poor this and the poor that." Now, there ain't a thing that is to be known about being poor that I don' know. I scrape along on what I saved and help from my folks, and sometimes I can help someone. But, son, the poor is mostly in need of money. Now, if I could get my hands on money, I know what to do with it. Black people already get twice the good out of these funny dollars than anybody else gets. I am grown, so nobody has to tell me that I have to keep a roof over my head, clothes on my back and something in my stomach. When they take this little money I have, they don' say, "Now, Miss Shays, how much do you want to go to the Jews or the Arabs or the Spanish people?" They don' ask me if I want to make some bomb and drop it on somebody I never heard of. Now, they might say, "Well, Ruth, you know you don't pay much taxes." Now, I figured this thing out and I shouldn't be paying any. That's how I feel. But now, howsoever little I pay, they think it is big enough to put me in jail if I was to decide not to pay it.

If you give somebody something, you got to get your hands off that thing. Now, that walnut pie, for an instance—if I wanted to eat it all more than I wanted to let you have a piece of it, you would never have known that it was in this world because I wouldn't tell you about it. But now, when I cut you a piece of this pie and give it to you, then I can't tell you how to eat it. Now, you decided to eat it in your hands—all right, I understand why and I do that sometimes, but generally I use a fork. Howsoever you show respect to my pie is all right with me. Now, when times was really hard out here, when you wasn't nothing but a leelittle boy, a man asked me to help him. I did not know this man, but I do know those missing-meal cramps. So I took half of the pot roast I had and made him two sandwiches. Now, he wanted money, so he threw my sandwiches in my face and cursed me. That was the first and the last time down here in this world that I would raise my finger to help him. Now, I said that to say this: If you give somebody something, then you got to let go of it and that could turn out good or bad, but you can' give and keep at the same time. But now, if you're grown you got to be careful both ways.

There are some things I will not take, you know. There are some things I shouldn't have to ask for and some things I should be ashamed to ask for. Whitefolks never can get these things straight. Now, if I'm selling pie and milk, you will know what it costs and you can figure out if you want any. But if I give you this little something to eat and then after it has gone down your little red lane I start pestering you for money or anything else, you are going to think some bad thoughts about Ruth Shays, just like Ruth would think about you if you did such a white trick.

I have been poor enough to be on any kind of welfare they have out here, but I know you have got to be a better person than most of these big white folks to really give me some money. Now, I see what some of these women have to pay for that little git-over money they give them. Now, Esau sold his birthright just because he was hungry, but I still think more of him than I do his brother. What kind of brother would do a thing like that? Any fool could think of doing something like that, but doing it is a rotten thing.

Suppose you had sugar and you took too much insulin—should I sell you orange juice? Now, that happened to a friend of mine. The woman was going into shock, but this white man wouldn't part with a glass of his orange juice until he was sure he was going to get his thirty cents. Now, your average black person wouldn' behave that way to anybody, white or black. I don' know how many white people would do what that dog did, but I do know I never saw a colored person do anything like that. Most of that man's trade was black people, but he'll never get another dime out of Ruth Shays! There is nothing a person like that can give me. Now, people my age and your age understand how I feel. I told that child about that and she walked out of there. But you see so many of these young fools nodding and talking their lives away in there. When you don't know when you have been spit on, it does not matter too much what else you think you know.

Grant Smith

In many ways I was more of a slave than most of my
black ancestors.

*Mr. Smith is a tall, tense man in his thirties. His neighbors defensively dismiss
him as "color-struck," "hinkdy," "vain" and "nigger-rich." These negative
assessments persist because it is very difficult for people to get to know what
kind of person he is. Mr. Smith consciously strives to keep it that way. He
apologized for being quite rude in the initial stages of an interview which he
requested of me.*

*He is a man of obvious capacity, a scarred genius who is thrice shy and
trebly wary lest life treat him as it did for so long. The written tradition,
imported beer,* haute cuisine, *drawing-room civilities—all that is meant by
that shotgun, catch-all category of "the finer things of life"—are, and probably ever shall be, new wine for him. He told me that photography was his only
"way of creativity." He has a darkroom and has invested heavily in photo-
graphic equipment. His primary link with his neighbors is through free-lance
photography, and many agree that he is very good at that profession.*

*During the course of our second interview, we discussed his neighborhood
business, and he lamented the tardiness of many of his customers. As a case
in point, he predicted that the Emersons would never pay promptly. That
family had a well-deserved reputation as scrupulous observers of their obliga-
tions, so I was mildly surprised at his prediction. "You are an anthropologist,
but you don't even know your own people," he said. About fifteen minutes
later, an hour and a half before the appointed time, the Emersons' thirteen-
year-old knocked timidly upon Mr. Smith's door. The girl apologized for
being early, but explained that she was attempting to coordinate her errands.
Mr. Smith was halfway through his meticulously couched harangue about
"Negro irresponsibility" before the absurdity of the situation became apparent to him. He gave the girl the pictures and initially refused to take the
money. The girl asked to use the telephone to check with her parents about
this new development. Her mother advised her in tones urgent and audible
to everyone in the room to leave the pictures if Mr. Smith wouldn't take their
money, but in any event to get out of there as rapidly as possible. The puzzled
youngster translated these orders into immediate action and made more than*

deliberate speed for the bosom of her family. About twenty minutes later, a delegation of grim and formidable Emersons knocked somewhat less timidly upon Mr. Smith's door in hot pursuit of a satisfactory explanation. As this was a not altogether unexpected denouement, I was seriously weighing the benefits of a discreet and premature termination of the interview, for as my brother always says, "When you study long, you study wrong."

Mr. Smith lands himself in impossible and ridiculous situations sometimes because he often scrutinizes the world around him with overly stereotypic glasses. If he were not so often tempted to put on the whole armor of the finer things of life, and if his neighbors would expend upon him some of that unpremeditated open-mindedness they extend to religious, ethnic and sexual dissent, Mr. Smith could be a friend to more people. But his neighbors cannot pity him for dangers they do not know he has passed.

I work as an X-ray technician. I don't like this job, not because of the danger of radiation, which is a part of the work, but because I don't really like most people. I never have liked most people I have known. Maybe that's because I always felt better than most people I have had to depend on. Sometimes I was right and sometimes I was just stupid to think like that! I know that now, for example, I do more than I am paid for, but I can't do anything about that right now. I don't mean that I'm going to just accept this situation. When I can, I will try to better my condition. Anyway, I know that I am worth much more than I get. I think I could be a doctor or do any kind of medical work. I was once a male nurse, but I gave up that profession because I couldn't stand the kinds of things some people said about my doing that kind of work.

Well, I'm losing the thread, as they say. Well, to tell you the truth—and that's what I'm going to tell you; otherwise I would be wasting your time and mine and if you didn't want to hear that, then you should not have asked me!—to begin with, I knew my father, but he pretended not to know me. If you could see me you might not believe I am a black man. My mother looked white and my father was white. You might find it hard to believe, but I am a Southerner by birth. I was born in southwest Georgia. My mother was one of six daughters of an old hypocrite I used to call grandmother. My mother was always sick. I know that now, but I didn't really understand that then. She and many other people in my family were epileptics of one kind or another. I don't think any of us really understood what that meant. I think we always had the idea that a person could control their physical reactions much more than is really possible. We thought that way about many things.

I remember one time I got a job taking watermelons to a little town in north Florida. Well, the truck broke down and the white man took a bus back home, but I had no money, so I walked. It was a great distance, but it had to be done, so I did it and it never occurred to me that that walk was beyond the capacity of a young boy. I did it because I had to and having to do things was the chief reason we did anything. Do you understand?

Somebody would say "Do something" and no matter how impossible that thing was physically, if you were told that the proper authority said you had to do that thing, then you would try to find the energy to do it. People would make jokes about that, but they really felt that way. They told an old man, I remember, that his mule could not die because white people had ordered it to live. Well, they laughed about that—the Negroes, I mean—but they really did try to do things which now strike me as physically impossible, simply because someone in authority had said it had to be done! They would say, "So-and-so is not going to die" or get sick or feel better because one or another of the Smith family had said he couldn't do any of those natural things.

The Smiths owned the land many of us worked on and possessed our bodies pretty much at will—in the twentieth century, mind you! Thomas Smith was my father. When he and many of his relatives had nothing else to do, they would impregnate black women in his cabins or his fields or his big house. All his black children could look forward to was a little credit in his store and an incestuous attention if they were pretty or just happened to strike his fancy. James Smith was the father of my sister. My father was the kind of person who never should have been born! I think my mother was about thirteen when I was born. My mother was often sick, but sometimes my grandmother would accuse her of laziness or willfulness. My grandmother would sometimes beat her because she wanted her to go to the fields or cook for those who had gone. But sometimes everyone had to go to the fields. My mother was sometimes forced to disrobe because my grandmother said she wasn't going to wear out her clothes with the peach branch she used to beat us with. One day while she was beating my mother for not going to the fields, Thomas Smith came. He dismissed my grandmother and I was probably conceived sometime that day. This was not in Noah's time, I am not a senior citizen, and the same thing is probably going on right now as I talk to you!

Work and church are the things I remember most about childhood. I have always worked at something. Long before I was four, I was expected to work at washing dishes or shelling peas or carrying wood. The difference between work and play was the terrible consequences if you failed to finish your task or do it with meticulous care!

My grandmother always talked a great deal about love and Jesus and she could be very kind, but she was also vicious and sadistic and thoroughly dishonest. She made her daughters that way also. Most of them, anyway. They were bribed or beaten or frightened into her service. I am not talking about sister Caroline or anybody's grandmother but mine. But you and I both know very well that there are more than a few like my grandmother was. My aunts should have run from our worn-out, sick county as soon as they could. They should have gone to some healthy place. My grandmother should have gone before they were born. For all her dishonesty and sadism, she was still one of the most intelligent people I have ever known. She would have lived well in a place that was not so rotten. I don't just mean she would have made money and had nice things; I mean she would have been able to help people and do worthwhile things for herself and her children and her friends. But she stayed and lived to make everyone else stay in that rotten place!

It was staying in that sinkhole which ruined all of us; I mean, it decayed our brains before we even knew we *had* brains! It reduced us to polite, hypocritical opossums. The whites feed on us and we feed on each other! I was beaten by all those frustrated women, but it was my grandmother who was especially ingenious at figuring out excuses for chastisement. I was beaten for things I did and things I was imagined to have done. I was often not beaten for things I thought I should have been beaten for. My mother was the only adult who would not beat me with a peach switch or a strap or a stick. But when I became conscious of what was going on, just looking at her was a kind of beating, just as thinking about her often is, even now. She died in childbirth when I was about thirteen.

Death was a kind of part of life, I guess. Someone was always dying or threatening some dependent with their death. I never hated my grandmother when I lived with her. I needed all the adults I lived with too much to really wish they were dead. But my grandmother would ask me even when I was a little child what I would do when my laziness and lack of attention to her would kill her. Of course I had no answer and I was very much afraid. You see, I knew when I was very young that I wasn't able to take care of myself. I knew that I had to be taken care of if I were to live. For some reason I wanted to live and I thought I needed my grandmother and everyone else to a lesser degree. Not only that, I firmly believed that if I caused someone's death, they would come as a ghost and make me pay for having been responsible for their death. Even when I was no longer a very young child, I simply never thought to drag these fears out and really think about them logically. You see, you get locked into a kind of mindlessness in which the assumptions which move you are so apparent that it never occurs to you to do anything but act on them. I never asked why I was doing anything or why I wasn't doing something. I just did whatever it was I was doing at the time. I don't mean that everyone was like that; I think most people were, though. The Bible was "the Good Book" because it was the Good Book. People died because they died. I should do whatever my grandmother said because she said I should. Everything was like that. That is a kind of death too, you know. Everything has been decided and you just have to go along, and you don't even know that you are just going along because you don't really know that there is anything else to do. You don't even think to wonder about anything else.

People hardly ever talked about the birth of Jesus, but they never tired of talking and singing and reveling in His death. You know, I think the most inhuman thing black people do is to bury each other the way they do! One of the worst hallmarks of our people is the cheap extravagance of our death shows. As a very young child I can remember watching people lie and sweat and shriek and generally degrade themselves for hours and hours. I was about four when my mother's sister, my Aunt Sadie, died. I was taken to the funeral. She was kinder to me, or I remember her as being kinder. I was very sorry she had died. Her funeral lasted for hours and hours, and that terrible ceremony made her into a ghost, or a "hant," as I used to call them. So I feared even to think about her and I was a grown man before I lost my superstitious fear! For me the air was filled with the spirits of dead people and animals. I wasted years of my life degraded by this shameful fear of the dead.

Even after I lost my fear—I mean, when I understood intellectually what death was—there is still the emotional fear which still attacks me. It was the funerals which made me afraid of the dead, you understand. There was so much noise and it lasted until the last ounce of restraint was wrung from the living victims. The corpse was always displayed. People would fling themselves on the coffins or even into the grave! I don't go to funerals. When my grandmother died I did not go to her funeral. My aunt found me and asked me to go home to bury her, but I told her I would never go to another funeral. She said there was one I would *have* to go to! But I said I didn't want a funeral. And she said she would give me one whether I wanted it or not if she lived longer than I did. You see how deeply this thing is ingrained in our people? She means it, you know. Knowing that a funeral is the last thing I would endure if I were conscious, she would impose a funeral upon me anyway. She is a good woman, and I owe her more than I could ever pay her, but she is like most black people. If you don't share their important beliefs, you are simply insane as far as they are concerned. She doesn't argue about it, she doesn't even like to talk about it, but you can bet your life that nothing could ever make her change her mind about funerals or any other thing she really believes in.

In spite of the fondness I feel for my aunt, her certainty really angers me so much that I frequently cannot stand to be in her presence. You see, I've come a long way since I was a frightened boy back there and she helped me, so it really bothers me to see her still thinking some of those old crippling thoughts. I believe in a clean break. I am not moved by any of this "soul" nostalgia! To me, my past is almost all bad. In many ways I was more of a slave than most of my black ancestors. At least they knew they were slaves, and it was only their physical bodies and actions that their enemies could even try to control. They helped each other and they were merciless to their enemies, no matter who they were.

I used to hear the old people talking about that in whispers generations after what they used to call the Yankee war or the silver war; generations after that they were still afraid and secretive! They still are, you know. There were a number of families with traditions which were really kinds of carry-overs from slavery. The best root doctor was the son of a man who had been a greatly feared root doctor before him, and that family had been root doctors for as long as anybody could remember. And black people and white people were afraid of them. But my life was ruined by many people who didn't even know they were my enemies! I did the same thing. I hurt many people without even knowing that I was hurting them. Things hardly ever happened in a clear-cut way so that I could say, "Oh, that's what is happening" or "That's what I am doing!" I don't know whether it was that people didn't talk about what was really on their minds. They didn't do that very often. It seems to me now that there just wasn't anything on their minds very often. We just sort of lived without very much planning. Things just happened to you and you didn't know how important they were.

My grandmother's friend whom we called Aunt Sis used to take care of us small children sometimes. We would all sleep in her big bed. Sometimes on these occasions when the smaller children were all sleeping, Aunt Sis would put her hand inside my night clothes and play with my organ. She was doing this thing to me, yet I was somehow afraid that she would tell someone or that she would punish me for something. I would generally lie perfectly still as if nothing were happening, and on those few occasions when I did try to touch her, all she had to do was to push my hand away and speak sharply to me. You see, our blind respect for our elders was so strong that even when they were wrong we always gave in to them.

You know, they used to tell a story about my Aunt Velma. She followed my Aunt Betsy to the North, but found it very hard to get used to. She was very worried about getting arrested. She would not take a chance on eating in a restaurant if she saw any white people around. So she got very weak during job hunting. One day she told my Aunt Betsy that she felt she was going to faint. My Aunt Betsy told her that it was against the law for black people to faint in Boston, so she didn't! You see, many of us had no idea what our most natural rights were. Fear was always with us, so much so that we took it for granted. It made clever people seem dull and stupid. When I was a child and an adult molested me, sexually or in hundreds of other ways, I never resisted because I didn't have any idea that I had some rights over my own body.

When I was fourteen my father's wife degraded me in the same way and I just stood there like a fool. She *ordered* me to stand still and put my hands down by my side, and then she masturbated me! She would do this whenever she felt it was safe. Sometimes I would become excited and move my hands from my side, and she would slap me as hard as she could. As a young man even, I had no idea what responsibilities went with anything except work. But the truth is, people were handling my *mind* without my permission! Not only without my permission! The worst thing was that they were manipulating me without my *knowledge*—sometimes even without their own knowledge!

My father never talked to me without trying to manipulate me. That is a terrible thing to have to say, but it is true! The only real conversations we ever had were about sexual things. I was always afraid I would say something I shouldn't, so I generally didn't do anything but grin or giggle or do something else equally as stupid. He would joke with me about some gal, as he called them. All black women were some kind of "gal" or other —you know, little black gals, fresh-assed little black gals, fine, big-tiddied little black gals. He would say, "I bet you git'n some of that!" I would just laugh. Sometimes I would deny that I knew anything about the girl at first. We would laugh about it and then I would lie about it. You see, I generally didn't have anything to do with most of those girls. But I knew what he wanted me to say. I don't want to give you the impression that I was innocent. I had done some of the things he kidded me about, but nobody could have done all of them. In an odd way, I guess, he thought he was patting me on the back and I was just too afraid not to tell him what I knew he wanted to hear. I guess he just wanted to prove to himself that he could make me do anything, even make me lie when he wanted to.

You see, white people want black people to do whatever white people want them to do at that time. They just don't want black people to have a mind of their own, or anyway, they want to be sure that we won't show it. My father regarded my mind as an enemy and he had to suppress it to assure himself that he was in control of my body. In that respect he was like all white men I have ever known. Many whites do not know this about themselves, and it is a completely dangerous waste of time to try to explain this to them. I don't think I could face that if I were a white man. That's where real friendship between the races breaks down. You simply cannot be honest with white people.

A father should tell you right from wrong. But the most important thing about me to my father was that I was black, although he was darker than I am. Even though I was his own child, he only wanted to cheapen and degrade and deceive me. Everything he ever said to me or did for me was at the expense of my dignity, and the worst habits I ever acquired were all encouraged or put in my mind by the very person who should have helped me to be a better person. When he would talk to me about girls, I would become so excited that I was ready to do things I hadn't really thought of before. He used to tease me about a schoolteacher who was old enough to be my mother. The more I denied any interest in the woman, the more he teased me. He told me I was a fool and that I was stupid not to try her. He said I should expose myself and ask her. He kept teasing me about that. One night I half did what he said I should and was astounded by my success. When my father teased me about it the next time, I told him what had happened. He slapped me on the back and said he knew I could "get it." He said that he knew it wouldn't bother me if she had said no, because I lived in a house full of "pretty yella gals." I don't know why, but I didn't really take offense at this. He teased me about that a lot, but I would never say anything. One day he asked me if I had ever slept with my Aunt Pearl, whom he called Madison's gal. I don't know why, but this idea really shocked me. I told him that, but he just kept on teasing me about other girls.

I liked my Aunt Pearl. She was nicer to me than the others and she was younger. She had been north, where she had married my Uncle Madison. I liked both of them, but I can't honestly say I had never thought of her in a sexual way. But she was my aunt and was an authority over me. She was my friend in a way, but she was my aunt and you could never forget that! She did things that an older person should do. She used to give me a little change for Saturday trips into town. And her husband would send me clothing and other necessities which made life much easier for me. But we had a very friendly relationship. When I gathered berries, especially blackberries, she would make pies of them, which were the things I liked best in the world then! As I told you, I did used to think about her sexually, but I was always too afraid or too ashamed to actually approach her. I guess I really thought failure would be, well, fatal. You know that we all hated white people, but sometimes that hatred can be used for bad purposes. I started a conversation with her about my father. I criticized him to her, but I really did that to see what she would do when I mentioned the subject of sex with her. She was not fooled for a minute! She wasn't angry, either. She told me exactly what I was thinking and said that nobody could be blamed for what they thought. She said we were going to talk about this thing once and then everyone could think whatever they wanted, but that we were going to *do* right!

She sat me down and we talked about my feelings from all angles. You see, nobody had ever made me do that before. She didn't preach at me at all. And you know, she wasn't angry—I really don't think she was! Her husband, Madison, had been nice to me. He sent me the first new coat I ever owned! She pointed out that Madison had done many thoughtful things for me and that he hadn't had to do any of them and that it would be pretty poor gratitude to sleep with his wife. She told me that Madison could have used the money he spent on me for himself and that she knew that he was nice to me partly because he knew it made her happy. She said she would be a pretty poor wife to repay her husband's kindness to her and me by sleeping with someone else. She said that she and Madison had promised each other not to sleep with anyone else when they were married and that she wouldn't have made that promise if she had not meant to keep it. I asked her how she knew Madison would not sleep with someone else. She told me that the devil had put that question into my head. She said that she thought that Madison could do anything she could do and that even if he didn't keep his part of the bargain, that was no reason for her to do wrong and especially to do wrong with her own sister's child!

My Uncle Madison was working in Philadelphia and my Aunt Pearl was saving money with him. They were doing something for something. They had a goal they were working toward. This made them special in my eyes. I think most people around there felt that way also about them. That talk with my aunt was probably the beginning of my humanity. I don't mean I was bad before as much as just thoughtless, I guess. I think what I really mean is that that was the beginning of my real consciousness—you know, the beginning of being or trying to be a thinking person instead of just acting and accepting everything without thinking. For much of my life, all I had to know about a thing was whether or not I wanted to do that thing. If I felt like doing it and I could, I did it. I didn't think about consequences much, and I hardly ever thought about whether the thing I felt like doing was harmful to anyone, even myself! You might say that talk was a small thing, but in my life things that might appear insignificant to others have been very important to me. I think that talk changed my life because it made me think. It's as if I was ready to listen then, so I paid attention.

I heard a country preacher talk about the power of an idea whose time has come, but I don't think it really works that way. It is that people are ready to listen and really think at some points in their lives, and they are not ready at other times. I have to admit that my grandmother often gave me sound advice and so did many others. But it was just that what they said simply did not register. I heard them and I didn't hear them at the same time. I was never rude to any adult—I knew better—but still, nothing most people said really meant anything to me. I think I can tell now when people are really listening to me, and generally they don't. Generally most people don't listen to anyone else. I know that I hardly ever listen to what anyone else has to say, even now!

It scares me sometimes when I think of the kind of person I was and the kind of person I might have become. I mean, some of the things I used to take pride in now make me sick! Most of the people I exploited and, I think, most of the people who exploited me never really were conscious. I fathered four children before I was sixteen and might have fathered others, for all I know. Most of the women and girls who risked pregnancy for me did so for the stupidest reasons. As you can imagine, it was not my fine character but my "good hair" and my pale skin which made many women take a sexual interest in me. I was proud of my father's natural gifts to me without ever thinking of the terrible price my mother had to pay for them. Even now, I haven't gotten that right. I suppose you must have figured that out by now.

I've had a great deal of trouble with black people. I know that some of it is my own fault, but not all of it. You know, everybody talks about discrimination as if it were always light-skinned people rejecting darker people, but it isn't always that way. The truth is really unknown about that. My aunt thinks I make my own trouble. She says she never has any trouble. She married my Uncle Madison, who is very dark. I think my Aunt Pearl is the best person I have ever known. Madison is certainly as fine a person. He has the typical black male weakness for gambling and sexual slipping around, but he is hard-working and keeps his foolishness in check and is basically a person you really have to respect. Neither of them have very much formal education, but they are astonishingly well read and think a great deal about what they experience. They gave me a home when I came north and were far better to me than anyone else has ever been. I left Georgia because I was more frightened of staying there than I was of leaving.

I remember that I was punished as a child for things I had not even thought of doing, and then sometimes I would do something which I thought I should be punished for and get away with it. A girl I had a fight with told a lie on me and that's really why I had to leave. She told a man that I had been sleeping with his wife. This was not true, but the man was a root doctor and he disliked me. I know he had great contempt for me because of my color. He poisoned his wife, but nobody could ever prove it, even if they had wanted to. I knew he would kill me too. He didn't seem angry—he never seemed angry—but I knew he was and I knew that he would kill me if I stayed there. I still think these are very dangerous people. I used to fear them for superstitious reasons, but they are very ruthless people! He never threatened me and was always polite, but I know that he would have killed me. I wasn't certain that he could not kill me no matter where I was, but I wanted to be as far from him as possible.

My grandmother and my Aunt Pearl gave me money enough to go to my Aunt Matty's in Baltimore for a little while. I said it would be for a little while, but I knew my fear would never let me go back there. Somehow it seemed to me that it would be better to die here by any means, even drowning, than to go back and be killed by Mingo. The weeks it took to get the money and to arrange things with my Aunt Matty were terrible! Mingo was more cordial to me than ever. He never failed to smile and address me politely. But his wife's death was a warning to me and I have never been that afraid before or since! I felt sick and I vomited every time I ate and often soiled my trousers. Just thinking about what Mingo might do when he decided to act caused me to lose control of my bowels sometimes!

My Aunt Matty's husband, Nick, was the darkest man I have ever known. I have never seen anyone, even Africans, who were any darker than he is! I feel certain that he hated me; I know I was afraid of him. He never did anything to me directly. As a matter of fact, he was fair to me, I suppose, but I know he resented my being there. When I asked him, he said he did. But that is one difference between me and everyone else in my family. I speak as I think about a thing. All the others won't do that. Nick, my Aunt Matty's husband, would never have expressed his feelings to me, but something made me express my anxiety about his feelings to him. Mingo and Nick were not related, but they looked very much alike. Nick was devoted to my Aunt Matty, but I don't think that he respects most people of our complexion. His father killed a white man and ran away with Nick and some of his other people. Nick's father was a root doctor and he became very rich here. When my Aunt Matty died only about a year after I came, I lived with Nick for a while and then went to live with Madison and my Aunt Pearl in Philadelphia.

You know, people's minds are always delivered after their bodies. I was born consciously—I mean, my mind was really born—when I went to stay with them. I learned to be a human being in those years. It may seem odd, but whenever I have tried to help someone, something very important has happened to me. I don't mean that I am a do-gooder or anything like that. Sometimes my helping someone has been a selfish thing. Often I knew that by helping someone I would be assisting myself far more.

An elderly blind boarder stayed in my Aunt Pearl's house also. In a way he was really my father because he was responsible for the birth of my consciousness, or mind, or whatever you want to call it. Even at his advanced age, he was very erect and tall. There was something about his whole presence which said to everyone with any sense at all, "This man deserves respect." He was the first really dark man I can remember who did not frighten me. He did frighten me at first because I was afraid of blind people and because he was very, very dark. But I eventually loved and respected him as I never loved anyone. He gave violin and piano lessons when he wished to, and I learned everything I know about music and those instruments from him. We all used to sing and play together. We played old dance tunes, hymns, popular songs—everything from Handy to Handel!

That was a good time. It was the best time of my life. Maybe I owe Mingo, the root doctor, something after all. It was my terrible fear of him that would not permit me to go into the streets by myself. I only had to think of him back there plotting my destruction and I was immune to every pleasure the streets could tempt a young man with. I stayed in at first because I was afraid to go out, but soon I came to prefer the quiet and sanctuary of our house for other reasons.

My formal schooling had been neglected. The education of black children in much of rural Georgia was really dictated by the whims and agricultural needs of the whites who control our schools. They closed our wretched schools whenever it suited their purposes, and I am ashamed that I often regarded this privation as a blessing because I used to prefer field labor to school. My aunt and uncle and Mr. Jackson made me read and spend the money I earned or was given on worthwhile things. To us, reading was a magical thing and we read everything we could get hold of. I read to Mr. Jackson. You know that I can read well, but books and reading were once very foreign things to me. Mr. Jackson, even with his insufficient command of Braille, could read faster than I could at first. My aunt was not really a good reader, but she and I learned really together. Madison taught us. He was a good reader, and he and Mr. Jackson taught us how to read phonetically and also taught us what to read.

I spent almost all my time with them. Even when I went out, it was generally with Mr. Jackson. He was a wonderfully unselfish person. He could do something for you and it might be months later before you realized he had done it or that he had done it for you. I know now that much of the things he had me read to him were really designed for my benefit. He was the kind of person who was just serious enough. He would come to the grocer's where I worked simply to assure me that I was not alone with my fear. That was quite a sacrifice, I felt, because I never thought much of his ability to get around by himself. Now I know he was much more mobile than I thought he was at the time. I know now that much of his complaining about the difficulty of reaching the store was to show me how much trouble he would go to for me. I needed that support then and I needed to feel indispensable to someone I respected. He was the first real gentleman I ever met. My Uncle Madison was a fine person, but he lacked the refinement and sensitivity which were quite natural to Mr. Jackson.

Most blind people I have known have been beggars. I hope this doesn't offend you, but it is very important to me. One day I was guiding Mr. Jackson when a white lady thrust a half dollar into his hand. Without changing his pace or his expression, he handed her two quarters and thanked her for allowing him to be of some service to her. I can still see the awe and stupefaction on her face!

He carried a gold-handled cane with strange faces carved on it which he had made himself. He taught me how to carve flowers and animals out of wood. I used to try to do that with my eyes closed, but only succeeded in cutting myself. He taught me to value my life and the lives of others. He taught me manliness. He taught me how an English sentence should sound. He taught me how big the world was. He taught me Latin and subtle cooking and what I know of style and grace. If I am not the man I want to be, neither Mr. Jackson nor my aunt or uncle have anything to reproach themselves about. At least I know what kind of person I should be and I really do try to be that kind of person most of the time. But that is very hard because my old ways keep intruding and because sometimes people just won't let you be the kind of person you would like to be.

Carolyn Chase

Many people say our people are unpredictable.

Born in rural Arkansas, Miss Carolyn Chase is in her early thirties. She was prompted to contribute her narrative by Iris McCrae and by her attendance at a number of folk seminars. She is a cautious, open-minded, hospitable leader of the fight for security and cleanliness in the large housing project in which she lives. She is a keen student of current affairs with a comprehensive knowledge of Latin America. She is justly proud of her fluency in Mexican Spanish, her skill at chess and mastery of three great cuisines—Provençal, Mexican and southeastern black American.

Miss Chase is an unpaid but thoroughly effective leader with the confidence and respect of two language communities. Her organizing ability is manifest in activities as varied as a children's puppetry class and a senior citizens' current-events group. Her accomplishments are all the more remarkable as she suffers from a chronic disability which frequently makes walking painful and difficult for her.

I have sugar. Many of my people had it and some have it now. I have also a swelling of the legs. I'm just a little heavy in the place where "our girls" are heavy. I guess I have what they used to call the hourglass figure. I'm dark brown, about your color. I'm a black woman, so you know I'm curious and will show it. So, if you don't mind, I'm going to ask you some questions: How should I refer to you? Do you resent the word "blind"? Would you rather be called "sightless"? I've heard "visually handicapped" but wouldn't use it here because some of these girls in my building are very quick to scream "educated fool" or "Miss Anne" at you. So unless we are talking race or religion, I limit my syllable output.

But sometimes you can get into an awful lot of trouble by trying to break things down too. Mrs. Marshall in 3B is still very active and alert, although we celebrated her eighty-ninth birthday just two weeks ago. You should really try to talk to her. When I first met her I was trying to explain some silly thing about the tenants' union to her. My girl friend Gladys, whom you should also interview, had told me that Mrs. Marshall was going to be eighty-nine soon, so naturally I tried to break my message down. Well, in the process I garbled everything and confused even myself! It has been quite some time now before I just start automatically breaking things down without carefully looking over the situation. That old lady just sat there, and when I was just about as hung up as it's possible for one human being to get, she cleared her throat and said, "Dear. You have accomplished prodigies in the vineyard of oversimplification. But perhaps the end of genuine communication might be more efficaciously facilitated were you to couch your explanation in standard English, a dialect with which I have a more than casual acquaintance." We both fell out! She says you should talk to everyone in his own tongue and if you listen to them, you'll find out which tongue they prefer.

When I lived in California with an aunt of my father, there was a blind man boarding there too. You know, many of the girls would permit him to touch them when they would not let men who could see do anything like that under those circumstances. On his birthday one lady I know slept for him, or with him, however you want to say it. I know that this is often the custom and I have often wondered how it got started with us. I think our people like to make people who are down feel good. I think that's why we accuse very poor people of having a great deal of money. I don't want to offend you, but I do think many sightless people must find it more difficult to find sexual partners. So much of this mating game depends upon being able to see. If you could see the way different women dress, you might have some idea of your chances. Then, too, because almost all women talk more nicely to a man with a handicap, it must be very easy to get the wrong idea about your chances. But then, maybe sighted people get as much or more out of this than the sightless do.

Mr. Ramos was kidding me about your being here. That was an excuse for him to raise the subject of *that talk* with me. He has asked me to go out with him several times and one time I did. Then I started getting some very evil looks from one of the Spanish girls I used to help. So I cornered her one day and asked her right there what was wrong. She said she liked me, but was angry because I was trying to take her sister's husband. I told Neva that somebody was lying and that we should get to the bottom of this mess. I said she could come to my house or I would go to her house or her sister's house. We finally went to our friend Ana's house, and Ana said she knew I was a decent woman and Ruth said she thought so too.

Then both Ana and I asked Neva to go and bring her sister. But she didn't want to do that, so we called her sister. Her sister's child was sick, so she was not able to come to Ana's, but we asked if we could come there. She hesitated, but Ruth persuaded her, so we went over there. She said she didn't want any trouble, but she didn't like people taking bread out of her kids' mouths and sleeping with her man. So I said that I would certainly not like anyone to do that to me if I had a husband and a family, and that was why I would never do that to another woman. Then I got up and went right over to that lady and told her the truth, which is that I do not go out with married men! She looked at me and said that she believed me. Then

Ana said that she had known me a very long time and had always respected me.

Then her husband, Mr. Ramos, came in and saw us all there, but I still didn't know he was her husband. So I said, "Hello, Mr. Diaz." He just looked at me and said, "My name is Ramos." Then everybody knew I was telling the truth; they could tell just by looking at the look on his face. I asked him to tell Mrs. Ramos what he had told me about himself. He said I was crazy and that he was in a hurry because he had to meet someone. He said, "I'm not going to stand around here arguing with a bunch of crazy women!" He practically flew out of that apartment! So I told Mrs. Ramos that I was sorry for the misunderstanding, but that I had not known that Mr. Diaz was her husband. We sent Mrs. Ramos' oldest boy for some pizza and chicken and made a sangría and had a regular party! And we have been good friends since then.

I like to cook and if you could see me you would know I like to eat. Well, anyway, I like to cook, especially the traditional dishes people are now calling soul food. I don't know whether you know it or not, but traditional black cooking is probably the least well known of all the great cuisines of the world. I just can't eat in most of these so-called soul-food restaurants! Don't get me going on food or you'll be stuck here for weeks! I had the pizza and sangría in their house, so I invited all the Ramos family and Ruth to have dinner here and, do you know, they came, even Mr. Ramos! He's very careful with me now, but he still sort of halfway tries. So maybe his kidding me about your being here was a sort of way of raising the great forbidden subject. Who knows? I guess I don't trust most men very much.

Did you know Mr. Ramos was teasing me about you? Frankly, I didn't know whether you understood us or not. Your face didn't indicate anything. It's really not fair, is it, that we should be able to judge you by looking at you and you can't do that with us. You have to be very careful, don't you? But then, can't you judge sighted people's emotions by their voices very often? I guess we all have to be very careful.

I guess I wondered whether you understood us because most black people don't accept first impressions. We are a very suspicious people and I'm sure we lose a lot that way. My aunt used to say, "A heap see, but a few know," and I guess it's quite natural for us to think that way. The white systems we have to deal with have hidden their real workings from us. We have never been able to act honestly with the white people who run and own these big agencies. We compete with each other for the favor of these systems, so there are many areas in which we cannot be honest with each other. The whole thing is very mixed up. For example, you know, white prejudice completely reverses the truth! It was the slaves and their children who had to be devious, subtle and complicated. Masters and their children kind of had to be simple people. If you can *make* people do things, you don't have to persuade or trick them into doing what you want them to do.

When I was under my aunt and she wanted me to do something, she would tell me to do that thing, and if I didn't she would beat me. I guess she did that because she was tired and that was the quickest way for her to get done whatever it was she wanted done. My aunt's husband never even *threatened* to beat me, but he could get me to do almost anything very quickly. He was the most wonderful person I have ever met. My aunt loved me, but she was always angry about something and she would do terrible things to everyone, which she would be sorry about after. But she never would say she was sorry. She might cook something she knew you liked especially, or give up several days' pay to buy you something she knew you liked, but she could never just say she was sorry for something she had done to you. In some ways it used to seem to me that talking with my aunt was like talking with a friend of mine who had difficulty hearing. Sometimes, you know, she would be very angry just because it took a long time for people to understand her. I guess she was angry because she stammered and couldn't hear very well. I told you we had a blind boarder and he would be angry sometimes if he had to wait on a strange street for someone to help him cross. I've always wondered why people get so angry and I have always been afraid of getting that angry. If my life had been different, that's what I would have tried to study. I haven't had very much formal education. But I read a lot and I think about what I read and what I see.

I'm the kind of person who misses out on many exciting things, but I have never made some of the big mistakes some people I know have made. My life is quiet and I prefer it that way. I never married and I don't plan to. I'm one of the many people who should live by themselves and I know it! For some reason I don't understand, the good people seem to get matched up with the bad and that's one set of opposites which should not attract, but I think somehow they do. They really do. You know, I have hardly ever seen a good marriage! I grew up with my aunt because my mother and father separated. They separated violently, I'm afraid, and my aunt should have married almost anybody except my uncle. I really do think my aunt loved me, but she was very often angry with everybody and was frequently very mean to me especially. My uncle wasn't anything like her or most other people. I would like to think I'm a lot like him. He was a man who had no enemies.

No one really knew what he thought about anything, but many people thought that they did. I know he loved me and expected a great deal of me, and I would have tried to do anything in the world to please him! I could always tell when I pleased him. He was the person who introduced me to everything I ever found lasting satisfaction in—reading and thinking and cooking and music, everything! He was a very difficult person to argue with. Even his anger was cool and generally designed to prove a point. I never ate very much as a child, and for a whole week one time my uncle made me drink a whole quart of milk every time I sat down at the table. He never threatened me; he would just bring the milk and say, "Drink that." I was used to him being my ally in my fight to avoid eating, so I couldn't understand why he was making me drink all that milk. I asked him why I had to drink it and he said he was trying to help me to get white as fast as possible, since that was what I seemed to want. I cried and swore I didn't want to be white. Then he asked me very calmly why I didn't want to drink coffee and why I would not let him drink his in peace. When I lived in the country my people didn't want me to have coffee. They didn't say coffee costs too much to waste it on children or that something in coffee was not good for children; they told me that coffee would make you black. On his birthday my uncle had a coffee cake with coffee ice cream and iced coffee. I now know that he was not very fond of iced coffee, but for years it was a thing I did for him, making iced coffee with chocolate ice cream. To this day I am practically addicted to coffee. That was the way to teach me how silly and sick I was being. If you love or respect your teacher, his lessons will last.

When she was very angry my aunt used to say that I should have married her husband. One time I got angry too and told her that I wished that I had because I would not spend my life thinking of ways to make his life miserable! I was fifteen then, but she beat me with an ironing cord until I fell down. And when I fell down she kicked my head until Mr. Rodriquez made her stop. We lived with Mexicans and Koreans and blacks and many other groups. We had an elderly German doctor who taught me German as a part of my pay for tidying up his office. They called him because I was hurt by my aunt and I had rheumatic fever. When he came he got so angry that he struck my aunt! My aunt said she was going to call the police. Dr. Fischer said, "Good, Mrs. Butler, you call them, because there is something rotten going on here they should know about." My uncle came in and found out all about it. He told Dr. Fischer not to slap my aunt again and asked him not to call the police. Then he told my aunt that if she ever touched me again he would have her committed to a mental hospital. He didn't shout, but everybody knew he meant every word he had said.

I had rheumatic fever as a child and some other complaints, so I missed quite a lot of school. In the country my people didn't seem to worry much about school or education. My people didn't, but many other people worked very hard to educate their children. When we went to California I missed a lot of school, but I learned a lot anyway. My aunt's husband taught me many things and recommended many things to read and see. And since it pleased him to have me read, I read with a vengeance! And then reading pleased me. He taught me to learn what I could from the people who lived around us. So, to please him I learned Spanish from the Mexican people and learned to cook their dishes. To please him I carried myself like a lady and that was not easy for me! That was hard for me because though I am a cool-minded person, I guess I have what the Victorians called a passionate nature. But to please my aunt's husband, I did obey my aunt's half-hearted orders to keep my pants up and my dress down. I knew then that my aunt wanted me to become pregnant.

You know how you sometimes do just the opposite thing white people expect you to do, just to frustrate their stereotypes? For example, sometimes when I go into a good record store one of these fresh little Jewish salesmen will start handing you what he knows you have to want. Then I like to blast his little ego by asking him for something I don't think he would think I know anything about. Do you understand, I say "Jewish salesmen" because they are the most offensive to me, and I can give you all the chapter and verse you need! Well, I guess I liked to frustrate my aunt like that also, and because I knew her husband was proud of me, I did not get involved with boys. I knew that the men in the barbershop and the pool parlor talked approvingly about my virtue. I was one of the good girls of the neighborhood, and because my aunt's husband delighted in his coolness, I guess I did the same. So I tried very hard not to make much of my behaving myself or criticize any one of the good-doing girls. And that's still how I am trying to get through life now. Also, you know some of our people think they are doing a dark girl a favor just to be seen with her. A lot of the boys and men I might have gone out with made it very obvious very quickly what they expected me to do. I let *them* know just as quickly that I'm not excited by pale skin!

I've seen too much pain and stupid, unnecessary suffering to believe that any moral, sane power is running things. Ask yourself if a fine person like you would be sightless if a well-trained dog were running the universe. There is a song called "Why Should the Beautiful Die?" Carol Brice reduces me to tears with that song! I have been asking myself that question ever since I found out what death does to living things. When I saw the chickens hanging for Sunday dinner when I was a child in Arkansas, I thought it was a terrible and revolting thing for us to feed on each other. And yet, even then I felt that it would be fatal to talk about my terror and revulsion to the wrong person. I kept it all to myself. I loved everything, but in a kind of vague way. I guess you'll find this hard to believe, but as a child I hardly ever spoke when I lived in the country, and I'm sure many of my people thought that there was something mentally wrong with me. I think I thought so too. I don't mean that I thought I was insane; I guess I thought that I couldn't do anything right or that whatever I might do would start a great deal of trouble. It was as if I were carrying or holding a lot of hatboxes with pretty eggs in them and I just had to stay very still or they would all fall and break. I used to dream that when I was a child.

When I was a little girl a white man came to our house and made love to my mother. I saw that! I was in the same bed! And what I thought was really bad about that at the time was the way he hypnotized her with his penis. He really didn't say much of anything. My mother told him to leave, but he just kept walking slowly toward her holding his penis in his left hand. This was in our living room, where our biggest bed was. My mother kept looking around the room, but she would always look back at his penis. I had never seen my mother helpless or very silent. She always seemed to know what she should do and what other people should do too. She backed across the living room until she stood with her back to our big bed, and he pushed her, just a little push, and she sat down. He picked up her legs and placed them on the bed and my mother started to shake. He said, "Come on, Martha." He suckled her. She asked him to stop, but she did not strike him or push him. Then he pulled up her nightgown and he pushed her down on our big bed and mounted her. I remember every detail of that morning. My mother didn't have to ask me not to tell my father. Whenever the white man came it was always the same. Sometimes my mother would just stand up in the middle of the floor and shake and wring her hands, but we never talked about it or anything else important. I think she was afraid that everything would fall down if she did the wrong thing or if she did anything at all. I really don't think my mother wanted to sleep with Mr. Gilford. I think most people just don't know what they should do most of the time.

My father bought a secondhand piano for me when I lived in the country. He bought and paid for that piano. He bought it from a white man and we had it for three weeks. Then the white man who sold it to us came and said it was an antique, so he had to have more money or he would have to take it back. My father told him that a deal was a deal and that he had paid the price the white man had asked and that as far as he was concerned he was going to keep that piano. The white man who sold my father the piano said he would give my father another if he would give back the first. My father agreed and some men came to take it, but my father would not give them the first piano until they gave him the second. Then the sheriff came and took legal possession of the first piano and made my father and some other men move it back to the white man who had sold it. We never got our money back or any piano, either! My father always hated that, but he couldn't get his brothers to help him against the sheriff, and although he had risked death about the piano at least three times before, he was helpless the last time. Even when we know what we should do, we can't always do it.

Many people say our people are unpredictable. I think it is that we have to put up with so much that you can never tell when some black person has just had all he or she can stand! We are better than any people should have to be for a long time, and then we just get tired of taking it and we get to the point where we don't mind dying if only we can get out from under all that undeserved weight! When my father refused to give back that piano, both friends and relatives and people from nearby communities came and begged him not to start any trouble by keeping it. Everybody, black and white, knew about that piano and most people urged him to avoid trouble.

My father took me to California and that was good for me, but it was probably very bad for him. My brother Milton was not my father's child. He still stays with my mother's people. I haven't really seen any of them since I was about nine. My father and I went to stay with my aunt in California. My father died on my eleventh birthday. He was carrying some gifts for me. I still have the doll, which I keep on my bed. He was bringing me some rock candy and some chunk chocolate. A man shot him because he thought he was someone else. I remember the long, barbarous funeral, which was true to our worst traditions. I remember every loud, cheap, dishonest second of it! My aunt's husband helped me as he always did. He said, "Tinai"—he always called me Tinai—"cry if you want to, but don't worry about Hubert. He doesn't see or hear or feel any of this. When you get ready we'll leave these good sisters to their marathon lamentations. He is earth now and, Tinai, the earth belongs to the living." It wasn't just what he said but the way he said it and his calmness when everyone else seemed out of his mind. He acted like my father would have acted if he had been alive.

When my aunt's husband died I came here, but I don't think I am going to continue to live here. I'd really like to live in some tranquil place where I could hear birds and running water and eat good wholesome food. I'm a diabetic, so you know what my greatest weakness is—I worship the joys of the bakery! If I ever needed a reminder that I'm no better than the rest, I get one every time I try to walk quickly past a good baker's window! I am five foot seven and weigh 160 pounds, so you know I don't win the good fight often enough.

I hope I have been able to help you some with my wandering reflections. I wish you every success in your project. But if I can offer some entirely unprofessional advice, please describe us as we are. We will still emerge as good as any other people. It's like making a cake, I guess. Some things cannot be enjoyed by themselves, but taken all together they make a good thing which is just as good as any other good thing. Only a fool would try to prove that black-walnut cake was better than Baltimore cake.

I've tried to tell you the whole truth and I've told you things I've never told anyone before. You may find it hard to believe, but I am not normally a very talkative person. I know I'm not always the easiest person to get along with. After all, a thirty-two-year-old black virgin with a crush on a dead hero can, like everyone else, be a pain where she sits down. I started not to talk to you at all. And quite frankly, if you had not been blind, I don't think I would have.

Howard Roundtree

There is nothing on this earth as low and lazy and
cowardly as a cracker.

Howard Roundtree is a tall, heavy man in his fifties. He was born in Virginia.
He has done everything from coal mining to string playing for a living. He
thoughtfully converted a weekly gathering of friends into a folk seminar. The
group gathers in private homes for the conviviality which neighborhood tav-
erns used to provide. He lost his only child as a result of federal suppression
of black urban insurgency, and feels that his wife's death was a consequence
of that tragedy.

Man, we could sit there till Lincoln came back and we still couldn't think
of nothing in this world no lower than a white man! Now, that is what God
loves if anybody ever heard it. Whitefolks have done me every kind of dirt
they could think of doing. There is just nothing else you can do but hate
them suckers! Even they got sense enough not to like each other. They can't
stand me, either, but that's because I am a man. Every time they see me
they know what they are trying to do to me, and that gets to them. I don't
have to say a word for them to get salty with me. I mean, they are some
hateful things! Just thinking about them makes me feel like I have swallowed shit. I mean, a rat or a maggot is better than the best white cat who
ever drew breath. Just looking at those things makes me want to spit up.
Everything they do is rotten. I hate to even touch them or be around them,
and they are always shoving their dead hands at people. I can't go with all
that Muslim deal, but they are right about one thing: Whitefolks *can't* do
right even if there was one who wanted to. I think it must have something
to do with their blood too. They are so damn greedy and cheap that it even
hurts them to *try* to do right! And they didn't just get that way, either. They
have been that way ever since they have been here.

The slavery-time people had it right. My grandfather said that back then,
if they wanted to say that some crackers were around they would make a
noise like a turkey buzzard or they would draw a buzzard on a tree.
Sometime they would just do like a buzzard. Sometime they would whistle
white. In my home we used to call pecks turkeys, and that meant turkey

buzzards. We used to call these tough young fellows that would try you in a minute turks. I remember there was this sorry little cracker that we used to call Turk. He got the grandest kick out of that. He thought he was something because his father was one of those big crackers. We called this poor little cracker Turk and he really did like that! He didn't know that when we were talking about him, "turk" was short for turkey buzzard. We used to laugh about that a lot.

Now, he could go around doing anything he felt like doing because his boys would back him up. Now, you can believe that any colored man could have kicked his ass in a fair fight. As a matter of actual fact, I can't think of anybody, man, woman or child, who could not have done the same thing. But don't say nothing about a fair fight to no peck. He don't want to hear nothing about a fight unless the people he is going to fight are tied up and don't even have a stick or a brick to their name. Even then he is going to need the air force and the army and the cops. No, Cracker don't like to take no chances. But you take all that shit away from him and he is the sorriest cat on this earth. I have kicked more white ass than I can remember, and I have never lost to one of them and I never heard of a colored man who ever did. Cracker don't even think he can beat us in a fair fight or in any other fight where it's one of us with one of them or ten of us with ten of them. Paddy will git that big edge on you and if he can't have that, then his ass is wasted from the git. The way Paddy sees it is, he don't mind fighting, but he don't believe in getting hurt! Now, if he can get his machine to fight you or get some black cats to go in there and get you, then he's all for that. I will take ten from them to give them one because I know that will be the ball game. That sucker is soft and he think so much of his pretty ugly face that he don't want to get out here like I do. He'll tell you in a minute, "Niggers don't feel pain." Shit, I wouldn't let that bastard know *what* I felt! I tell all these grayboys, "Never mind how you feel, just get out here and deal. That's what we have to do."

Now, that is the big difference between us and them—that is, we don't play. I mean, our feet is evermore to the fire, Jack. We can't play no games out here because we have to make it twenty times as well just to hang in. I have to do my job. I can't expect no check if I don't. I can't call up the man that owns the joint and cop no kind of plea. I didn't get this little shit slave because I was the friend of the friend of the man. But they don't say, "I got this or that because of *who* I know." That dude lies to me and him and tells me he's over me because of *what* he knows. Old Cracker will tell you real quick, "Whar thar's a will, thar's a way." Now, what he *should* say and what he really mean is, "If I can fix one thing, why the hell can't I fix everything?" Well, he can't fix my fist and I do love to lay it on him!

When I was just a kid this cracker I told you about that we used to call Turk was actually paying colored boys to let him beat them in these fights he used to like to have to show those other buzzards how bad he was supposed to be. All those young crackers used to jump up in our face so they would look good an' bad in front of their women or their old men. I don't know anybody who couldn't waste his ass, but some people would take him up on it and stand there and let him go through his bad number. Most people who got into that didn't do it for the money. You see, you could never tell what his father would do if you told this little son of a bitch what to do with his braggedy little self. Now, if I had a son that rotten, I'd put his ass out with my own two feet. But that white man couldn't see a damned thing wrong with the way his son behaved. Not only did he uphold him in every rotten thing he did, but he tried to buy him anything he wanted.

Old Turk, short for turkey buzzard, got in behind this really nice colored girl from my home. Now, she wasn't a tramp, so you know she didn't want to go with him. Peggy's father was an undertaker, so he didn't need a damn thing the white man had, and like a sensible man he appreciated a good daughter. Everybody looked up to Peggy because there wasn't anything else a sensible person could do. She carried herself right. She was a really nice-looking and nice-acting colored girl. Old Turk was evermore trying to get next to her. He got his father to try to get Undertaker Hays to let Peggy come up there and do a little house cleaning. Old Man Hays told him right to his face that Peggy had to clean her own house.

Some old sorry niggers—I call them that because that is what they had to be—some of them put their nose in the thing and told Mr. Hays that he should let Peggy go up there. They said that if she didn't go up there, there might be some trouble. Well, Old Man Hays was as stout as they come, and he told everybody there that there sure God would be plenty of trouble if he found his daughter anywhere she didn't want to be. Now, when he said that, he had his shotgun on his knees and every one of his brothers and cousins were there and they were just as ready as he was and that was just about as ready as you can get! Everybody gave him a lot of credit for that. You know that there are always a few niggers who are just about as low as some crackers. Peggy stayed right there in her father's house until she came up here to go to school. She didn't go over there to clean no cracker's house, either. But can you see upholding your son in a rotten deal like that? Now, that was a common thing for any cracker who was big enough to try to get away with.

You been south, so I don't have to tell you a thing because you know what I mean. I'm just telling you what you got to know already. There is nothing on this earth as low and lazy and cowardly as a cracker. I have seen a grown man beat a woman who was just about to birth a child because she wouldn't get out there in his damn fields and work just like there was nothing wrong with her! I couldn't count on my two hands the white men that have killed people and burned people out and robbed them and raped little girls. Now, they have done all these rotten things and they have not done a day in jail for doing them! If I was anywhere near that rotten, I know I couldn't stand myself. The only thing a peck cares about is, "Can I get away with it?" I have to work with these devils because I don't have a job of my own. They are always trying to tell me how I can save some money if I let them rob me. I stay away from all of them as much as I can. They talk about each other like dogs and tell you every fart they let and are simple enough to think I'm going to do the same thing. They think I'm sick half the time. They don't know that I'm just sick of them.

There is this one little nigger—that's just what that little shit-colored bastard is—he's always up in their face. He's always handing out some bullshit about everybody being of the one blood. He'll tell you about his cracker brother in the Lord right away, whether you want to hear this shit or not! He is not trying to get something back, if you know what I mean. He is playing with something I know should not be messed with. I knew that little faggot when he was a stone Muslim. He told me that I was going to lose my white head just because I helped a blind white girl to cross Lexington Avenue. But now! He just loves whitefolks! Now! He would eat a dozen yards of their shit and ask a white doctor if a dozen more would hurt him! I cannot stand niggers and he is a nigger if there ever was one, and when the big bell sounds his ass should be the first to go! He thought he was playing with me and them.

Tuesday when I was trying to eat my lunch, nothing he must do but come over there and bother me with another one of his white brothers in the Lord. Well, I wasn't feeling but so good, so I asked him why he put the Muslims down and what color did he think God was now. You know, that dude lied by notes. He told me that I must be mistaken. He hadn't even *heard* of Elijah! He told me it didn't matter what color the Lord was. I asked him how many images God had. I asked him if God was his color or did He look like that Italian girl he is slipping around with? Well! That was all she wrote! Now, you can believe that his paddy brother in the Lord did not want to hear that! These tallies swear that they are just as white as all those other crackers, so his so-called brother in Christ was stone salty when I laid that on him. That little jackleg faggot couldn't talk fast enough that time! Now his white brothers don't have too much to do with him, and those white sisters in Christ ig him whenever they can because they don't want those white cats to think that he is getting next to them! I'll say one thing for that jackleg, he's a nervy ass! He is still stone hanging in. He is still grinning in their face all the time and they don't know what to do about him. I didn't want to blow the whistle on the dude, but he caught me wrong. I told him to cool it, but he oversported his hand and that was it! He tried to be two-cent slick, so his ass had to go. He tried to bad-mouth me with the people, but everybody knew what was going down. Everybody told him to take that noise somewhere else.

What do you mean, why did I help that blind girl? I didn't know her, no—I had never seen that girl before. I just helped her because that was the human thing to do. I'm not white! I don't say, "Well, chick, because you look like you do, you can just stand there in the rain or go on out there and get yourself smashed up by a bus or a car or something." I do not mess with the sick and afflicted! She was having a hard time and she hadn't done anything to me as far as I know. If I was a cracker I might say, "Hell with her. She's not my color, so pump her!" You know a cracker is steady looking out for himself all the way. He might have looked at her and said, "Oom, she don't look but so bad. Maybe I'll see what she has to offer." Whatever a cracker does, he does it first because of what is in doing that thing for him. I just did that because I thought it would help her—you know, just like any other black person would. It was no big thing. I didn't have to go too far out of my way.

You know, you never know when you will need help because you never can tell what will happen to you. I'm not one of these people that are always jumping up and down in church, but I do have ordinary common sense to know that the Lord don't like ugly. I don't like it myself. I get along perfectly fine with people that are worth getting along with. Now, see, that is the biggest difference between us and them. We believe in live and let live. I don't go out here looking for no trouble. I pay my debts. I go to work. And I do my level best to help anybody who asks me to help them if they are worth helping.

I would like to know why you asked me about that. Do white people ever help you to cross streets? If I didn't have my sight, I'll be damned if I'd let them get near me! You can never tell what people like that might do. Well, if that girl had felt that way about me—well, I didn't take her anywhere but where she said she had to go. She couldn't see, but she could hear, so she had to know that I was black. Because she was blind didn't mean that she couldn't think like everybody else. If she had any sense at all, she had to know that she was safer with me than she would be with one of her own rotten kind. If she didn't want me to help her, all she had to do was say so and she wouldn't have to worry about Howard Roundtree!

Mabel Lincoln

I am a hard woman because I have had a hard time out
here.

*Mrs. Lincoln is a shrewd, direct, slender person who is generally reckoned
"hard but fair" by her neighbors. I am deeply in her debt for her kindness
in introducing me and my project to several other senior ladies whose saga-
cious, poignant reflections were invaluable. She told me that experience had
taught her to expect the worst of most people most of the time, but she added,
with the same wry chuckle which accompanies most of her thinking about life,
"When I go, son, it won't be pleasant surprises that carry me away."*

I'll tell you *what* I think, but you know how I think, just like I know how
you think. Now, I wouldn't know where to start if I had to explain black
folks to anybody who was not one of the people. This is not an easy thing
to try to do. At first I thought, "Well, I'll start with me." But that's not
all that easy to do, either. If you could see me you would know some things
about me, but they wouldn't be the most important things that there is to
know about Mabel Lincoln. What do you know about the way I look? Now,
son, I wanted to see how you answer questions and I see that you are trying
to be nice. I know that you know that I have a limp, but you didn't mention
that. You say I'm small, but you know that a heap of folks would say I look
like a very flat ironing board. You kept it to looks and that's what you
should have done, because that's what I asked you to do. But you know,
there are more folks out here who think I am mean than don't, and my
father was the only person I ever knew who thought I was sweet. But be
that as it willormay, I am going to tell you what kind of person I know I
am and what kind of people I think we are.

Now, I never had much of what you might call education, but I have
heard the thunder more than once and I have not slept too much in this
world. The fact that I'm sitting here talking to you is the best proof of that.
Now, you know that isn't my doing, but it is mostly my doing. Of course,
you can do howsoever you will and still get carried away from here because
of something somebody did that was not known to you or anybody you
know. Anyway, I am going to tell you about me and us like I know how

to tell things, without any who-shot-John or he-said-she-said.

Marva Johns Selby Lincoln breathed her first breath on December the eighth in nineteen and three in a little place I wouldn't call a house now in a little place in South Carolina that most Geechees never heard of. My mother died a day after she birthed me, and my father and my mother's sisters brought me up and they brought me up hard and I am glad of it to this day. My father was a blind man, and he made as much of a living as he could by carving decoys, teaching people how to play stringed instruments like the guitar and banjo and the piano, too. My mother's sisters were hard women, so they didn't like some of the things my father did because he wasn't what you might call a practical kind of person. Anyway, the crackers killed him. Ran him down beside our house. A carload of young crackers from somewhere ran him down in front of our house. They were just playing with him, but when he didn't run, the one at the wheel got mad and ran right over him. He didn't die for a week, but he was out of his head. I was twenty-one. He died on my birthday. I left there then and came here to work, and work is what I have done and work is what I am doing and will do until they throw dirt in my face.

Now, if you want to know one thing black people are known by, it is working. You can smell my house, so you know that it is wholesome. If you could see this house you would know that you could eat off the floor. Now, that's another thing about blackfolks—they will clean theyself if they possibly can. They are fussy about what goes into their stomachs. When I first went to Detroit, there was this black man working in the restaurant I used to work in. I cooked and waited and washed and did some of everything you should do in a restaurant. Pretty soon they was buying so much food that they got another man to sort of manage this place, and he was a devil. He didn't do much but tell folks who already knew what to do and when to do it some fool something that just slowed things down. Well, this fool didn't like me, so he used to do things that he thought would bother me. Now, he didn't know me, so most of the times he couldn't bother me, but one thing he did used to bother me no end. He would say, "Mabel, I'm glad you liked the beef stew, but I just spit in it." Well, that would make me sick and he would laugh and say how foolish blackfolks were to him.

So one day James Selby brought him some corn-clam chowder, which he was a fool about. He ate two bowls of it and said to Jeems, who was doing all the cooking then, "Will, that's good, but it's a little salty." And Jeems said, "Right, Mr. Simon. That's because I pissed in it." Now, that's how I lost that job, because when he got rid of Jim I took my apron off the hook and was out the door before anybody. And that's how I come to live in Chicago with my half sister.

Now, I did not forget what I'm supposed to be telling you. I'm trying to show you why I am the kind of person I am. I am a hard woman because I have had a hard time out here. I mean, I do whatever I have to do to take care of myself in such a way that I don't feel low or nothing or dirty because of my own weakness or greediness. If somebody takes advantage of me because of something I didn't know or couldn't help, well, all right, they got me. But I didn't help them to do me. But if I get hung because I helped somebody who wouldn't help me, if I lose money trying to get your money, well, then I feel like dirt and I would rather take a whipping than feel that way.

I have had to tell my own half sister's child, "You got yourself into jail, now get yourself out!" Now, that hurt me to my heart, but right is right and it don't wrong nobody that should not be wronged. Now, that's hard right there! In the Book of Proverbs in the eleventh chapter and the twenty-ninth verse, it says that "the fool shall be servant to the wise." To me that means if you don't look out for yourself, somebody will have you looking out for them.

Now, you remember that I told you that whether you can see me or not wouldn't help you to know my mind. What I think is more important than what I look like. Now, that is not just because I am an old lady that don't worry none about looks. I still worry about my looks, although the truth is I never really had any. Now, that don't mean that I haven't had all the trash talked at me that any other woman would have to listen to. I even liked hearing some of those lies, but I always knew they was lies. Some slick men got mad with me because I had the nerve, black and plain as I was, not to let them make a fool out of me after a little sweet talk. I hope them words about black and ugly are not out of turn, but that is how it is with a lot of people out here. Now, you are a dark man, son, and I know you have to know what I'm talking about and that is one of the things about our people that some would like to hide. But I do not believe in that. If all I can do for you is tell some more lies about blackfolks, then we might as well just say any old thing or, better yet, don't say nothing at all. I would rather be what I am than anything I know anything about. But I'm not going to sit here and try to convince anybody that I'm perfect. I'm all right, but I have done and will do some things that don't make much sense to me and some things that I know are wrong while I'm doing them.

Now, that's the way it is with my people or any other people. Too many blackfolks are fools about color and hair. That is probably the most mixed-up thing in this world. Now, me, like a fool, would not marry Jeems Selby for five years because he was a red-headed man. He lost his job over me and did everything a good man could to please a simple woman, but I would not marry him because, thinking as I did then, that the color was every-thing, I couldn't figure out why Jeems wanted to marry me. Jeems' sister Nancy was the best woman friend I have ever had, but I wouldn't trust her for years because she looked whiter than most whitefolks I ever saw. Now, that is another thing that most black people do that they should not do. I can understand feeling that way about most white people, but I know that's not right, thinking that way about black people who look white. It took me a long time to get that as straight as I managed to get it. I've been telling you about wrong things about myself and my folks, but there is much more right about us than there is wrong.

At May Anna's I didn't say much, but I was thinking a lot. There are so many blackfolks of so many kinds who know they are black that it is a hard thing to say what makes them all black. There are so many of us who don't want to be known, and a few who keep jumping up telling anybody who will pay them some mind that blackfolks are whatever this leelittle passel of loud mouths say we are, that it must be hard for a foreigner to know anything about us. Now, that's all right, you know, because most of us don't want foreigners knowing but so much about our business no way. Now, I have told you what you know is the most important thing about us: we are very private people. And most of the time the more anybody tells you about his business, the less you really know about that person. I know because I am that way myself and most black people I know are that way too. Now, if I didn't think you was that way I wouldn't say anything to you. I wouldn't lie to you, because that would be putting a stumbling block before the blind. I know that you are not going to put my business in the street so it will come back on me. I don't want my truth to be a snare to me, so generally I don't say much about anything to anybody. The old lady don't trust any and everybody out here; now, that's the blackness in her, you understand.

One thing that is very important to most black people is that you should call them by whatsoever name their mamas saw fit to call them. There are not too many of us that don't have more nicknames than Carter got pills, and some folks can use some of them and some can't, and you have to know the person to know what you can call him. But above all, don't give me some damn name and call me by it like you had been knowing me as long as my mama. If it's not worth the trouble to you to find out what I want to be called, then don't bother to call me at all. If you are going to call me Will when you know my name is James, you might as well call me dog or dirt or any other thing I am not. Like most of us, I feel very strongly on that, but I know that if you are the kind of person who would call me what you want to call me instead of what I should be called, well, I couldn't explain anything to you if that's the kind of person you are. Most white people— anyway, all the white people I know—are people you wouldn't want to explain anything to. I don't think it is in the color because I have known and still know black people who are the same color but who think like I think.

I can't tell you about how many of us there are and how much we make and things of that kind. I just know there are a lot of us and that I have never been anywhere where there were not some black people there before I got there. I have been a waitress, laundress, cook, cannery worker, and I have worked in service for more than twenty-seven years. I thought it was hard for me on the farm in my home, but that was because I was young then. It was hard because being poor is hard and even if your people take advantage of you, they are cursing you to bless you. They know that their time may be short and they know that when they are gone you must scuffle for yourself. My father took a few pennies out of every quarter he made and kept it. He said that he was keeping it for a new suit to bury him in. He took money I earned too, and that was the only thing I ever disliked that he did. When I was just learning to write, he made me write a note: "This is for Marva." And when they buried him, you know, they were going to put his money together to help with the funeral, but they found my note in the cigar box with $146. I left home with that money; he knew I would want to.

But now, when you are working for folks that, as they say, "ain't folks," now then, you will suck sorrow! I am talking about what I know. Now, if you are a woman slinging somebody else's hash and busting somebody else's suds or doing whatsoever you might do to keep yourself from being a tramp or a willing slave, you will be called out of your name and asked out of your clothes. In this world most people will take whatever they think you can give. It don't matter whether they want it or not, whether they need it or not, or how wrong it is for them to ask for it. Most people figure, "If I can get it out of you, then I am going to take it." Now, that's why I have to be hard and that's why my people are the same way.

Now, life is hard and it is whitefolks that make it harder than it has to be for me. Now, they are a people that will bless you to curse you. Last Sunday my elder preached on welfare, and he took his text from Job, the thirtieth chapter, the fifteenth verse: "My welfare passeth as a cloud." Now, he preached welfare's funeral! And somebody like me can look at him and still listen to him. He has not got more money on his back than I will see in a year and he knows how to work just like I do. He don't take no vacation in some place I couldn't find on a fifty-dollar map and expect me and folks that work as hard as I do to send him there. Now, while we are at it we might as well kill that chicken too. Some blackfolks worship their ministers more than they do their God, and that is a great sin and foolishness. I used to be as guilty of it as anybody, so I can and will speak of it. When I married Arthur Lincoln I was taken sick and could not work for a solid year! Now, the doctor used to come to see me and this little red minister used to come too. That doctor would wait for his money, but Reverend Summers was always hinting about my empty envelope. Fool-like, I borrowed some money from Nancy Selby to help my South Carolina Club Diamond Circle. She lent me the money, but she opened my eyes to the truth. I got me some good food and paid the rent and my doctor. Now, Nancy was a good friend because she gave you good advice and whatever else she had that you needed and ought to have. She didn't loud-talk you, but told you softly and honestly when she thought you was wrong. Now, that is the kind of friendship most black people appreciate.

To black people like me, a fool is funny—you know, people who love to break bad, people you can't tell anything to, folks that would take a shotgun to a roach. Now, I can help myself some and help anybody that really wants to be helped a little. That's all I have time for. If I have to run you down or put up with uku lip from you to do you some good, then I will go on my way and you can do the same. Schoolboy was over here last Thursday telling me what I thought when he was supposed to be finding out what I thought. Now, I just don't have time for that. So I just let him drink Arthur's beers until he went to sleep and called Roland to come and get him. That's how blackfolks are. They say a thousand maybes for every yes or no to anybody they don't know and the foreigner walks away happy. Nobody in this world can say "Uhn-huhn" like we can. Now, no matter how we say it, it is a way of not saying anything if we don't trust you, and we don't trust most black people, so you know how we feel about the rest. There are more meats in blackfolks than there is in turtles!

But most of us try to be cool. That is what we respect the most in ourselves and look for in other people. That means being a person of sober, quiet judgment. My middle name, and the name that anybody back home would call me, is Dorcas because my father, who named me, wanted me to be a wise, sober, upright woman. He told me why he called me that and I tried hard to live up to that name. Now, that was some use to me because it was trying to live up to that name that kept me from making a fool of myself in the corn rows or just saying any old thing that came into my head. I don' have to tell you that in the Book of Proverbs, in the twenty-ninth chapter in the eleventh verse, it says that "a fool uttereth all his mind." Out in the street people say "Be cool" when they mean look out for something or somebody, but being cool is a more weighty thing than that. My father used to say, "Laugh with your friends, but smile with strangers." When I was coming up, you didn't frown with anybody.

THE MANY
SHADES OF BLACK

Too many blackfolks are fools about color and hair.

Mabel Lincoln

I am black! I was too black for my father's people.
Would you believe I wasted my time hating dirt like
that? But that's all right. I have one child and I know
who his father was and he was a good black man and
he was lighter than my father. I have a good job and
I married the father of my child before he could swear
that I was a woman. It's not color in this world that
gets it—it's the honesty of people.

Johnetta Mills

Mrs. Mills' regard for her seven-year-old son and for the elderly woman who unofficially adopted her when desperation drove her out of the foster-home shuttle is the engine of her existence. Her home is a kind of shrine fiercely dedicated to the people and things which have not betrayed her astounding capacity and need for devotion and loyalty. The saints, whom she feels failed her, are absent, but large pictures of her late husband are in every room of her pleasant apartment. Events almost entirely beyond her orchestration have conspired to make Mrs. Mills a sober, watchful widow well before her thirtieth birthday. I remember the fervor and dedication in her voice when she told me, "I had to be an outside child, but I will never be an outside woman!"

Erica Allen

He looks as white as any white person, but you'd better
not tell him that unless you are ready to go to war.

*Miss Erica Allen displays a surface placidity poised precariously above an
essentially impish good nature. She likes being unbound by schedules of
reciprocity except her own, but she earns her reputation for stealthy generosity. She is twenty-five and lives in her own large apartment. Domesticity is
still not high on her list of priorities—a fact that she unconsciously demonstrated by reducing three frozen dinners to charcoal during our initial interview. She felt harried by family and work pressure, so we ended that day by
going to an excellent Greek restaurant. Miss Allen is fond of most things
Hellenic, having spent "some of my most cool days" in Greece. One subse-
quent Saturday she invited me to interview her and served a fine traditional
meal of fish-stuffed potatoes, green gumbo, hoecakes with carrot-pineapple
preserves, egg pie and banana pudding. This interview metamorphosed spon-
taneously into a seminar as Miss Allen called friends to share the meal, which
she prepared as she talked. She told me that most of her relatives would think
that she was going about the task of preparing that complicated meal "cockleupwards." But she did contribute an eloquent and moving life history and
made a very good meal.*

*Miss Allen is fond of "well-raised kids," but doesn't think that marriage
and motherhood are for her. "Will you tell me who is going to put up with
a nut who likes sweet gherkins with her vanilla ice cream?" Her nuttiness is
more apparent than real. She understands that all life styles fall short of
perfection and exact their own particular tax of pain, frustration and chagrin.
But all things considered, she has plainly elected to cultivate often close, but
always elastic, ties with a great many people rather than total commitment
to any one person.*

My uncle is a preacher and he says that white people are born evil.
He'll tell you in a minute that the Bible says that the wicked are estranged
from the womb. Now, as far as he is concerned, when you say "the
wicked," you have said "the white race." He cannot stand white people,

and although he is a man with good common sense most of the time, you
cannot make him see reason about this race thing. He looks as white as
any white person, but you'd better not tell him that unless you are ready
to go to war. He won't even call them men. He says, "The beni did this"
or "The beni have said so-and-so." He was more like my father than my
uncle because he helped my mother to bring me and all the others up
right. He was every bit as good to us as he was to his own children. And
he has never once thrown that up in any of our faces. Believe me, he is
one in a million. That's why it's hard for me to go against him, but now
we don't agree about this race thing, so we can't agree about much. He is
hard about that.

His daughter married a white boy about five years ago. They have two
nice kids and are getting along fine, but Uncle Josiah acts like they're dead.
She was—I mean, she is—his only girl and they were very close, so it's hard
for everybody. It's been about five years now and you could count the weeks
on the fingers of your hand that Felicity has not come to see him. He just
won't have anything to do with her. She said that she'd keep coming to see
him, and I guess she will because she's just as stubborn as he is.

You know, it's really weird. When I got out of the army, my family gave
a party for me. They really put on pots of all sizes, and every Allen or Grove
or Smallwood in the world was there. One well-raised little Grove girl asked
my uncle how Felicity was, and that man said, "My daughter is dead."
Felicity is the straightest woman God ever put on this earth, so you know
I insisted that she had to be at my party. Well, when that little Grove child
was introduced to Felicity, she kept her cool, but you could see she was
really shook! Felicity is the boss of buttermilk-custard pie and Uncle Josiah
is the champion destroyer of that goody, but he wouldn't touch that and
I could see that Felicity felt bad about that.

Look, I know how my uncle feels—in a way I do. I felt bad when Felicity
married a white person because she is a choice girl. Now I get along with
both of them, but at first I really didn't like that white guy just on general
principles. Now, personally I was never impolite to him, but I just didn't
like him. I mean, why should this ordinary white boy walk in here and take
a queen? That's what her brother said. Felicity is the kind of girl, I guess,
that every boy wishes they had married. A lot of us were angry in our own
way about it. But now everybody except my uncle really knows it was none
of our business. I mean, they were living together, not with us. I like Ted,
and he's not really very ordinary, anyway; he just looks that way. You'd
have to be a real clown not to like Felicity, and if she saw something in him
—I mean, if she saw enough in him to marry—that's their thing. They've
raised their kids just like you or I would, so you can't really find any fault
unless you're just out to find fault. My uncle is losing his sight now and I
guess he's getting along, but my Aunt Felicity is really holding up remarkably well. All of us visit my cousin, she visits us, her mother goes to see her,
but Uncle Josiah won't, and when Felicity comes to see him he just won't

talk to her. I guess she wouldn't do that if he hadn't been such a good father. I guess she thinks she can wear him down, but I don't know. I don't think so. He is very strong in his opinions, and he will not change unless someone can show him that he is wrong.

Angela McArthur

One reason the whole thing is so hard to deal with is
that nobody really talks about it.

*At twenty, Angela McArthur is even less reconciled to not being able to take
the world on faith than most black people I know. Her shyness and suspicious-
ness are consequently more readily detectable. When a doctor told her that
she was made to bear children, she promptly switched physicians. That was
a year ago and she still occasionally wonders if she acted justly with the first
medical man. Her neighbors' judgment is that she is a good, sensible, pretty
girl who is prone to take too much time with people who "can't mean anyone
else any good because they are messing themselves up." The last impression
Miss McArthur would want to leave almost anyone with is contempt or
callousness on her part. She does not wish anyone to think her vain because
she is very pretty or pompous because she is formally well educated. So she
tends to keep silent, even suffering the unmerited abuse of fools and opportu-
nists.*

*Miss McArthur is a capable amateur viola player who generally underesti-
mates both her technical capacity and her familiarity with the score. Her
sister, Deborah, says, "Angela just lets people and things get to her too much."
"Sometimes I wish I had one of those hearts like a rock cast in the sea," Miss
McArthur told me once, after having sustained one of her sister's exhortations
to toughness. Her most discerning neighbors know, however, that her heart
is everything it ought to be and in the right place. A woman who later became
a major contributor and participant in this research warned Miss McArthur
to think long and well before granting me an interview in her home. In a
world where would-be burglars are posing as salesmen, repairmen and census
takers, in communities where the ringing of the phone may be a prelude to
breaking and entering, this admonition is entirely understandable. All three
of us laughed about this later, but it is a kind of insurance to be the sort of
person who will hear and weigh the counsel of discreet and discerning people.
Miss McArthur is that kind of person.*

I have never been asked to pass an opinion on anything by anybody! I
wouldn't mind giving my opinions. I guess I would really like to do this,

but nobody ever asked me. I would like to see if people felt the same way about things that I do, but I guess I'd be afraid to go up to somebody and ask them how they feel about something. I guess we're all suspicious. It's too bad that it's like that. Miss Lula is a different kind of person. She will tell you what she thinks if you ask her and sometimes even if you don't! But she's not mean and she has good sense. You know how I met her? She just came up to me one day and said, "I don't know your name, daughter, and what I'm going to tell you you might say is none of my business if you're a fool, but I'm going to tell you what I have to say anyway because if you were my granddaughter I would hope somebody would have sense enough to tell you." Now, she was right about the things she told me and I thanked her because she went out of her way to try to help me.

I didn't do anything wrong or anything like that. You see, I was going out with this man and I thought he was one kind of person and he was really not like I thought he was at all. Miss Lula told me the truth about him and some other people I kind of half knew around here. Now, I thank her for that because I was not trying to get in with those people. I really didn't know that they were doing things that could get them in bad trouble and me with them if I had not found out about them. Sometimes I'm not too smart about that kind of thing. I mean, I just used to take people for what they said they were if everything seemed to match—I mean, if they looked like what they said they were. I tried—I guess I still do try—to be friendly with people. You know how people can just look at you and say, "I know where he's coming from," or "I know her type." Well, I never liked that. I always was taught that you should be nice to any person who was nice to you. This man told me that he was a student and he dressed and talked like I thought a student might and he had this white friend who was also like what I guess I thought a student should be like. They did a lot of things that I didn't approve of. But, you see, I didn't know that they were doing these things. They were selling dope and they were taking things from people's apartments, but I didn't know that until Miss Lula told me about that. I liked to listen to them talk.

One day Kasavubu told me that he really liked me and he gave me a big transistor, so I asked him how much it was because I didn't want to take a thing like that from any man. He wouldn't tell me and said it was a gift because he liked me very much. I think he really did. I know I did like him, but I didn't like the things Miss Lula said he was doing. So I asked him if he really did do those things. He said no, but I could tell that he was lying. He said that I was just trying to put him down because he was black—I mean, dark. That didn't make any difference to me and I think he knew that, but I'm not really sure about that. But I hate to be accused of something like that because I know that there are people like that and I really hate it. I never did anything like that because I never thought that way. I'm really not that kind of person.

That's not a very nice thing about us, is it? It's true that most of us don't take dope and are not muggers and go to work all the time, I mean every day, but there are some things we do—I mean some ways that we think or that some of us think—you can't really say how many of us think this way, but a lot of people do think in a very wrong way about color. Now, I don't know if you want people to talk about that, but it is there. I think there are more black people who are not thinking right about color than there are who are taking or selling dope.

You know, when I was a little girl we would be reading about the Egyptians or some other people and I would wonder what it would be like to be that kind of person way back then. So I would pretend to be an Egyptian girl. I'll be twenty-one on the fifth of June and I still do that sometimes. I have five sisters and I pretended to have a brother for so long that I almost think I do have one sometimes. I used to pretend to have a brother, but I could never get so far out as to pretend to *be* a brother. I never could pretend that I was something really very different than I am. If I pretended to be an Egyptian, I could only pretend to be an Egyptian girl. Or if I was in typing class I might think—you know, pretend—that I was a girl astronaut or maybe a cowgirl. But I could never pretend to be white or male or something without life, like a machine. I used to watch little boys making noises like they were trucks or tanks or something, and that always used to seem very funny.

My sister, Debbie, tried to make me pretend that I was a dead patient. My mother was a nurse, so we always played these hospital and doctor and scientist games. Debbie tried to make me pretend to be a dead person and it just was too much for me. That was the only time I ever fought with my sister, Debbie, or any of the others. You just have to know Debbie! She is one of these people who will not take no for an answer! I tried to do it, but it really did scare me, so I told her no good. But she said she was going to make me do it and then she would do it. But I didn't care who else did it, I just thought it was crazy to pretend to be dead, so I wouldn't lie down, and she pushed me down and I guess that was it. I was the youngest, so they pretty generally let me have my way, but we were like stairsteps, so none of us really had much more sense than the others.

Anyway, we all beat up Debbie because of that and my mother got the word from her friend Miss Chapple, who had a hard time minding her own business. Miss Emily told us to stop. Miss Emily Chapple was one of the ladies who sort of looked out for us. But Debbie wouldn't play anything else and the thing just kept starting up again. Debbie said it was my fault and that she was going to kill me. She said this under her breath, but my father asked her to say it so he could hear what she had said and, Debbie-like, she repeated it. So my mother, who was ironing her uniform, said, "All right, you want to kill something, do you, miss? I'll shore God see that you get a chance!"

So my mother didn't go to the supermarket to get the chicken we generally had on weekends. She took Debbie with her to this chicken market and brought back this turkey and it was alive. So my mother said, "All right, Miss Dracula, do your thing!" Well, you see, Debbie didn't even know how to begin to kill this turkey, and when my mother said she was going to untie the turkey and let Debbie deal with it, well, Debbie just couldn't stand that. So she ran out of the house and we tried to stop her, but my father said, "Leave her alone." Debbie came back after about an hour and my mother said, "The turkey is right where you left it. Now, Bad Bertha, you choose: Either you kill *it* or I am going to half kill you!" Debbie didn't kill the turkey, so my mother was as good as her word and beat Debbie.

But Debbie was still mad at me, you know. She was the kind of person who always held a grudge the longest. I guess Debbie is what people would call evil. She was always very different from the rest of us. I don't mean that she looked different; she didn't, because we all look pretty much alike. Debbie is a twin, but she is probably most different from Marva. Actually, Debbie likes to fight with people, and she is the only one of us who is really like that.

But getting back to this color thing, I think it is the most important thing that we have to fight. You know that you said that your ideas about color might not be like—well, it might not be how people who can see think about colors. Well, I think you should know—I mean, if you don't know—that people who see colors don't always see them as they really are. When you said that about pinkish skin that people think of as white, you were really close to the truth. If I tell white people who are darker than I am that I am black, they will see me as being darker than I am and darker than they are. I heard what Mr. Chester said about you and I guess he wanted to see what you would do if he said that. He likes to shock people sometimes, maybe because he has been shocked so much himself. But you should know that your skin is not really black. I mean, there would be nothing wrong if it were, but really, it isn't. I mean, your skin is dark, but it isn't the color of anything that people would really call black. My skin is not really the color of anything that any sensible person would really think was white. I mean that my skin doesn't look anything like snow or milk and your skin doesn't look like my coat. So I just want to start by making it clear. It isn't that one color is not as nice as another, not only that, but that we don't even see straight when we talk about colors and we say things that we don't really mean. Each color looks different depending on what it is coloring. It's like you said about the textures and temperatures of things that you feel. I used to work in a hospital, and a lady there who was my supervisor liked me until she found out that I was not white. She used to tell me that she envied me my complexion. She called me her peaches-and-cream girl. Well, that's just something people say. Nobody really looks exactly like a shortcake! It's just something people say about a kind of mixture of pinks that you see in some skin.

Sometimes we all take turns spoiling Manman, my cousin, because he's such a nice kid and it really doesn't take much to give him a good time. Then, too, I guess all of us girls like to play mother or something. Anyway, one time Debbie and Marva and I took him to Quebec City, and a little girl ran up to us and said that Manman was a "little gingerbread boy." Well, that's the same thing, you see. Colors remind people of things that have something like the same colors or of ideas, you know, that people have about colors. I think it would be much better if people could start all over again. See, people have gotten colors all mixed up with ideas about what is good or bad or nasty or clean. I mean, people can just look at me and right away they have made up their minds about me. That's why I was surprised—pleasantly, I mean—when you told me that my hand made you think of the color green. I really like that because so many other people have gone through so many changes not to shake hands with me. You know what they say about white people having dead hands or fish hands. You know, my mother said that a lot of her own relatives did not want to eat her cooking because her skin was light. I mean, a lot of people think that light people are all—well, that they are not clean cooks. It works both ways—not the same thing, but every group has these stupid things about color.

My mother used to tell me about the blue veins, and when I was in high school some girls were really interested in that. If the skin is—well, if it is less dark you can see your veins. And this small thing was made so big that it split up friendships and made people hate and envy each other. My father told me about those paper-bag tests and comb tests that you had to pass to get into some of the clubs that they used to have in Louisiana—that's where he came from. I've never been there so that I can remember it, so I don't know if they are still doing this stupid thing now, but I don't think so. They used to put a brown paper bag in the bend of your arm, and if your skin was the same color or lighter, then you could join. Or maybe you could come in and eat or do whatever they did in those clubs. Sometimes there would be a man who would run a comb through your hair, and if it went through easily—you know, if your hair wasn't too curly—then you could get in.

You know the hospital job I told you about? Well, when a girl I knew in high school saw me there, she came up to me and started speaking the way black people from the South speak to me. Well, that's not the way I talk and that's not the way Princess talks, either, but she wanted everybody to know that I was black too. Well, I never told anybody that I *wasn't* black. I got the job because a black lady recommended me for it, and I never tried to be anything but what I am. I never have tried to pass or anything like that. I am the kind of person who speaks to anybody who speaks to me, and Princess should have known that. After all, we lived on the same street for half of our lives and I never did anything like that and Princess knew that, but still she did that! I asked her why and told her when she was going through her act that every girl at that table knew I was black and proud of it, so I asked her what she was trying to prove and she just walked away. Now, she knew that she was wrong about that.

There is another girl, a friend of mine—we went to school together for a long time. Her name was Virginia, but everybody called her Peaches. I don't know how people get that nickname. Anyway, Peaches had—I mean, living in their house was a boy there. They used to say he was a state kid. He lived with them. I mean, Ginny's mother kept these children and the state gave her money to take care of them. This boy, Roy, was very dark and Peaches was not very dark. His real name was Royal, but nobody ever called him that except me. One day he asked me to go to the movies. I went and a couple of days later Peaches and some other girls were teasing me about that. You know, we were just beginning to go out like that, and Peaches said, "Girl, I didn't know you dealt in coal." Well, I felt bad that she said that. Royal found out about it and he got mad with me, I guess. He never spoke to me after that. Now, I had not done anything to him. I liked him because he was very nice. I would never have said anything like that. I'm sure he liked me too. We used to do homework in the library and at my house. He told me how he felt about things, and he wasn't one of these boys who were always fresh. I really thought a great deal of him, but after that thing happened he never spoke to me. I tried to explain what happened, but he just stood there and when I finished he just left; he never opened his mouth. People used to say that he was "too smart"—I mean, that he had too many brains, you know what they say. My mother asked why he didn't come after school any more and I told her.

Some junkies cut him and I went to the hospital to see him, but he wouldn't talk to me. I never knew what he thought. In a way it's very silly, but it was very important to me.

My Uncle Matt used to say this little saying: "Black is evil, yallah so low-down, look here, honey, ain't you glad you brown?" I guess people think that way. I just wouldn't like them to think that way about me. I know that a lot of people feel that way. My Uncle Matt was brown, but I wasn't and I used to feel funny about that. But I'm sure he wasn't trying to make me feel bad. I guess I'm a kind of soft person in a way. I know that my feelings are easily hurt, but really, there are a lot of people who want to hurt —who like to hurt—my feelings. You might say, "Who does she think she is that people should be trying to hurt her feelings all the time?"

One reason the whole thing is so hard to deal with is that nobody really talks about it. Once there was this sort of program—I guess you could call it a kind of forum—and we were talking about some of the major problems in the country between the black people and the white people, and they asked me to point out one and I didn't say anything because I didn't know whether to mention the one that is very important to me. There were a lot of white people there, and some of the black people would have thought that it was wrong to talk about that when there were white people there too. We should really do something about it ourselves.

We should treat everybody well if they treat us well, no matter what color they are. People like Peaches and Princess should be shown up when they do wrong things like that. People should judge me by what I do to them. I think we should break up this business of light people marrying only light people and dark people marrying dark people. People just worry too much about color, and if it's wrong for white people to do it—I mean, make people's lives miserable for such an unimportant cause—then it's just as wrong for our people to behave like that.

Celia Delaney

It's sex and color that present the most difficulty, right?

Miss Celia Delaney is not yet forty, but her life seems fixed in such a way as to suggest early retirement. I have known her for more than half her life. I have never known a less frantic person than she is now. Her current reputation is that of a cool person who has come by that status the hard way. She extracted wisdom from the hectic crash course of the black revolution of fashion, which almost destroyed her. "I guess I sought my roots everywhere but where they are—in me," she reflected. "I think awareness made me a kind of prodigal daughter," she mused while driving me to an interview with an elderly retired teacher.

Miss Delaney too is a teacher. She teaches in an exclusively white school and derives satisfaction from her profession, but still regrets the failure of her perilous attempt to instruct children in a school in a black town. She has learned, at great cost to herself, that all things have their natural limitations. She has come to expect very little of other people and to doubt that anyone is much better than she is at her best. She counts it an extraordinary stroke of good fortune to be alive and unencumbered, and means to remain that way.

It's sex and color that present the most difficulty, right? I know I don't *have* to talk about anything. Just eat your gorgeous, gorgeous cake and listen to Celia, and she will give you cold milk and good advice. First, if people want to tell you something, let them. If they didn't trust you, they would be the first to know.

My mother and father were both Geechees. I say that now, I knew it then, so I suppose that makes me a Geechee, but the only Geechee trait I have is rice cooking. I inherited that via my very sedate grandmother and her sisters. My mother was very pretty, and I am told that she and her brother, my reverend Uncle Isaiah, died in a fight with some white men who were bent on raping my mother. The truth is, we never talked much about my mother, but dwelt at great length on my uncle. Most of the four sisters who sacrificed so much for me are mildly disappointed in me. Some of the values they tried so hard to instill in me are still with me; others I have let go. I grew up in Charleston and Boston and Queens. I was, I suppose, what you would call a sedidy. I was properly finished at Spellman and Radcliffe. I have been a teacher and a social worker. Even without a turban I have some trouble sometimes establishing my charter right with some blacks. That's because it was my particular luck to draw greenish-blue eyes, sort of yellowish hair, and the kind of light-pinkish skin which people mistakenly call white. During my thirty-six years I have been alternately proud, ashamed, reconciled and contented with my physical appearance.

When I was a very young child I remember that the good "mulatto" ladies who took such good care of me placed a high value on low spirits. I was inordinately starched and mercilessly scrubbed and subdued with great vigor. I had to wear wide hats to keep the sun off. I call my aunts mulattoes not because they would ever have called themselves mulattoes but to emphasize that they thought of themselves as members of what they would, and still do (however privately), refer to as the "better-class-of-colored-people." Members of the better-class-of-colored-people are fond of their blow hair, their fine features, their soft voices and their yearning for the finer things of life. I took piano and violin lessons because they were among the finer things of life—in spite of my astounding unmusicality. I was always dressed as if I were going to a party, but it was not until much later in my life that I experienced the feeling of having gone to a party and come home and taken my shoes off. As a child I always had the feeling of having gone to a great deal of trouble to do something which I had no great desire to do. I don't mean that I was especially unhappy; it's just that I was always expecting something more exciting to happen.

I always thought that food should taste a little bit better than it did to me. I can remember that ice water was one of the few things which did not disappoint me. On those rare occasions on which this genteel child was permitted the luxury of working up a sweat, ice water always tasted exactly as I wanted it to taste. If ice water failed to meet my expectations, I always knew why, and remembering to cover a strong-smelling food I had left uncovered or filling the water bottle earlier the next time would always restore ice water to its sparkling best. As a very young girl I can remember wishing that people could be understood and restored as easily.

Everything in our house was quiet and deliberate. Moving fast or randomly or being late were things I could just barely imagine. Looking back on it, I don't think there was a tremendous difference between me and my starched, carefully posed dolls, which I never liked much anyway. My aunts regarded spontaneity, full enjoyment and virtuosity as foreign to the character of the better-class-of-colored-people. Although they lived by these things, just like all the rest of us did, in a kind of subdued fashion they discouraged this in me. A dark-brown skin, bad hair and coarse—you understand, "coarse" means African—features were also things which the better-class-of-colored-people would do well to avoid. But these serious handicaps could be overlooked if the unfortunate offenders, or victims (we were never sure about that), had money and behavior. There were several dark-brown clergymen and medical types who established regular and grateful relations with the poorer female members of the better-class-of-colored-people.

I don't know how I was being fashioned or even that I was being molded. Assumptions which I now blush at were once taken for self-evident gospel. Like most everybody I know, I never thought much about my life. I was a terrible phony, but I didn't know it. I can remember having certain friends whose principal use—that's right, use—was as velvet against which I could display my better-class-of-colored-people hair and skin. My friend Astrid's dark-brown better-class father made up for his physical shortcomings by giving his daughter a name which was as white as he wished he could have made her. Astrid needed me because she needed someone to amuse and astonish, and I needed her because the jewel I then imagined myself to be required an Ethiop's ear. Now, when I say that I blush at my past behavior, I mean just that. But there was a time when I was shamefully exultant at being able to rattle off such phrases as "Was my face red" and "I blushed all over." I thought of myself as precious for all the wrong reasons, and most people I knew seemed to share my opinion of my purely external merits.

I really don't think most black people are much saner than I was. The insanity takes different forms, but color is something most of us are quite irrational about. It's hopelessly confused with sexuality and God knows what else.

I don't know how valid a physical anthropological observation it is, but it seems to me that pale black girls mature later. Anyway, I can remember the anxiety expressed by my aunts about my breasts, or the absence of those vital organs. I was rubbed with everything from coconut oil to goose grease and lard, with the general aim of bringing out my breasts. That is what they called it—"bringing out the breasts." Now it seems to me that one of those home stimulators came very close to overdoing it, but even at fifteen I can remember saying, deep inside myself, of course, "Maybe I'm flat, but I'm yellow." You see, I knew I was not white. I called myself yellow because I could not bring myself to say "yaller," even to myself.

I distinguished between us and them. Most white people I know are darker than I am. Even when I was most firm in my allegiance to my better-class-of-colored-people values, there was still the black-versus-white thing. I was far from a black nationalist then. My aunts had taught me that the better-class-of-colored-people had a responsibility to lead the less fortunate of our race. They didn't only mean poor black people, but darker black people, who, despite their unfortunate dark-brownness, had many things going for them—they were honest, clean, resourceful and strong. Actually, we lived among people of all colors. We told each other jokes about white people and black people, but I can't remember any jokes about yellow people versus dark brown people. These crazy things I and my relatives thought about dark brown people then was a part of the whole thing.

You know that dark brown people have their insanities also. Astrid

Haley's dark brown father would resort to almost any stratagem to avoid eating any food in the house of the most proper members of the better-class-of-colored-people. He shared the prejudice which so many dark people have about paler black people—you know, "Yaller's so low-down," as they say in the street. Both Astrid and I were under strict orders not to play with certain black kids. This off-limits group were, of course, the people we were most interested in. This group consisted of all kinds of black people. Some of those who were out looked like Astrid and some like me.

Astrid has married a German and her father will not have anything to do with her. Her father will not have anything to do with his grandchildren. Now, it is important to remember that these grandchildren look just like he would have liked Astrid to look. He says he considers his daughter to be dead, and he has acted as if she had died for eight years now. Astrid's husband is darker than I am, but her father is my most faithful correspondent! Astrid's little sister used to call both Astrid and me black whenever she was sufficiently provoked, and we spent a lot of time provoking her because she was a little sister.

Color is just one thing we blacks are unreasonable about. I call this mishmash crazy, but it is not the kind of madness which prevents us from being saner than any other people I know. Black people in America really have no choice about sticking together. Much of my own insanity about color was a part of my own provincialism, like many other prejudices of mine. For all our color hang-ups, we are a great deal saner than white people about it. We don't kill each other about color, although we have much more color diversity than white people do. I don't think color in itself is very important; it's only when it gets to be the formal excuse for other things that we think much about it. When you ask me what color something is, especially in comparison with something else, it is very difficult to give anything like an objective answer. Color is not objectively important; it's very important to ordinary daily behavior, though.

Rosa Wakefield

I don't trust anybody who would deny their color like
that.

*Florida-born, Miss Rosa Wakefield has known me practically all my life, and
I have always thought of her as a worthy senior with so much dignity that
the last thing she needs to think about is standing upon it. She is seventy-eight
and hale and preeminently sound-minded. Her buttermilk pies and watermelon pork are as fine as they were when I was a fifth-grader puzzling with
her over a text which asserted confidently that the Nigerian Hausa were not
black. I do not know anyone who has done more people more good with less
noise than Miz Wakefield.*

You understand that I am not an educated person. I was born with good
sense and I read everything I can get to read. At least I know that I don't
know very much. Now, if you still think I can help you, I'll be very glad
to answer any question I can for you. I can't answer for nobody but myself.
I will tell you what I think and why I happen to think that way. I was never
the first person you heard when you came to my father's house or a party,
but that never meant that I wasn't thinking as fast as some of these loud
folks was talking.

Now, this first question is something I have thought about a great deal
ever since I was a little girl. I think that I think more about anything I might
think about than most people. That's because I was my father's oldest
daughter and my mother died early, so I always had to think for more than
one person. And that is a responsibility. It's bad enough when you make
a mistake for one person, but when you make a mistake for more than one
person—you know, when you make a mistake that's going to hurt somebody who can't think for herself or hisself—then you really feel that more
than you would if you had just hurt yourself. I always thought about that.
My father and I sort of brought the others up. Now, I don't want to brag
on myself, but I guess we didn't do but so bad. Now, the truth is that I think
we did a good job.

But now, right there you have one of the big differences between blackfolks, or colored folks, or whatsoever you might call us, and whitefolks. We

don't like to spell things out but so much. We know what we mean, like you knew what I meant. You know that I don't really mean that I think we did a pretty good job in raising all those children. You know that I mean that it was very hard to do and we did it right.

White people are some writing folks! They will write! They write everything. Now, they do that because they don't trust each other. Also, they are the kind of people who think that you can think about everything, about whatever you are going to do, before you do that thing. Now, that's bad for them because you cannot do that without wings. I think that maybe you can't even do that *with* wings. They say that God's brightest angel fell. Now, ask yourself! Do you think God would have made this brightest angel if He knew that this angel was going to turn against Him? Now, it don't make one bit of sense to think that He would have done that. If He knew this brightest angel was going to ape up, what would He want to go and make this angel for? Now, if the Lord can be surprised, who are we to think that we can think about everything before it happens? All you can do is do what you know has got to be done as right as you know how to do that thing. Now, white people don't seem to know that.

I worked hard to put the others through school, and now they help me so the old lady can stir up a little sweet bread and talk to nice people like you. But, you see, there is hard work behind everything we do. You know that this sweet bread didn't make itself. I was telling you about my trips. You know that trip to Africa and that trip to Norway didn't pay for themselves! But, you see, if you eats these dinners and don't cook 'em, if you wears these clothes and don't buy or iron them, then you might start thinking that the good fairy or some spirit did all that. They asked a little white girl in this family I used to work for who made her cake at one of her little tea parties. She said she made it and then she hid her face and said the good fairies made it. Well, you are looking at that good fairy.

Blackfolks don't have no time to be thinking like that. If I thought like that, I'd burn cakes and scorch skirts. But when you don't have anything else to do, you can think like that. It's bad for your mind, though. See, if you think about what is really happening, you will know why these things are happening. When I get these cards on my birthday or Easter, I know that's because I sent my younger brother to school as clean as I could send him and made him get some sense into his head by seeing that he did what that teacher told him to do. They all send me a card on Mother's Day because they say that I was a mother to them. Now, they know that I am living all these other days, too, and they see to it that I don't want for anything I really need and a lot of things the old lady might just want. Rosa has washed her dishes and a lot of other folks' dishes for a long time, so she doesn't really need any machine to wash dishes, but she got one sitting right there in that kitchen! Now, Rosa didn't buy it and she didn't tell anybody to buy it, but it was bought. Now, my youngest brother is a professor too, but if he comes in here and sees something that has to be done, from washing dishes to scrubbing that floor, the next thing you know he just goes on and does it like anybody else. I never married, but any niece or nephew I got will come here if they *think* I need something and go wherever I want to send them.

Now, our children are more mannerable, but now so many of our children are trying to act like white children that it's hard to tell the difference just by the way they act these days. Some of these sorry things passing for young men and ladies that you see in the streets these days are enough to make you hang your head in shame! But so far, praise God, all our children have kept level heads and are doing just fine. In the summer we get together more and they tell me some things that are really hard to believe. I tell them to be nice to everybody that is nice to them and not to do every fool thing that they see being done. Little Rosa, my niece, brought a girl from Nigeria and a girl from Sweden. Now, that pleased me because I have read about those places and I have seen those countries and people there were nice to me, so I was glad to be nice to one of their girls.

We are revern' colored folks! We don't all have the same color skin, but we all have a strong family resemblance. My niece's mother is a German woman, and a finer lady you will never meet. But all you have to do is take one look at my niece and you will know that she is my niece. We all have a very strong family resemblance and we are a family that helps each other. If you know one of us, you know us all. We try to look out for each other. I told my brother about you and those mules and he said you looked just like a Wakefield. All you got to do to look just like a Wakefield is be black and do something good. But he's right this time—you do look a lot like us. You're quiet like we are, too. I guess in your work you have to be quiet because once you get us blackfolks talking, you won't get much of a chance to make much noise! But once a lady was out here, and she couldn't pay for her taxi because the driver had charged her way too much. We helped her and she swore that I looked just like her. Now, I'm a brown woman and this lady I'm telling you about looked as white as any white woman you will ever see. People like to claim kin with people they like. White people do that much more than we do, though. They can' stand the idea of anything good being black. If a black person does something good, they say he did that because of the white in him.

My father was sickly, but he worked hard all his life. He taught me and I tried to help teach the others. People have to go to school now, but they wouldn't have to do that if they would take up time with one another. I went to one college course to learn about the Negro. I'm sorry I did that now because all they did was to sit there and tell each other how they felt—I mean, how it felt to be black. Shoot! I have been feeling black all my life because I am not white! Now, what I wanted to know was not how they felt, because I already knew that; I wanted to know something about our great people and where we came from and how we kept on being folks all through slavery time.

My church and my folks got together and sent the old lady to Spain and Morocco. Everywhere I went I saw some of us. There was colored everywhere I set my foot. Now, I couldn't understand them, but I was looking at them and if I'm black, and we both know I am, there is nothing else in God's world for them to be but black too. There was all kinds of colors! Some of them were white like the people that call themselves white over here. Some of them looked mighty Wakefield. Now, I saw that in Spain and I saw that in Africa. In Morocco some of those people could have been your brother or mine. Some of them had kinky hair and some of them had straight hair and some had wavy hair. Some of them looked like Jews and Italians, but there was all kinds of folks. Most of those people looked like what we used to call munglas. I have read that the Moroccans are white and I know that Americans are supposed to be white, but it looks to me like they are just as mixed up as we are over here. Half of these whitefolks I see out here look like they are passing to me. That's the same way it is in Cuba and Puerto Rico. I have seen those countries and I know that most of those people are colored, just like most of those people in Morocco. I'm telling you what I saw, not what somebody told me. A lot of these people from those foreign countries may not speak English, but you can look at them and see that they are Aun' Hagi's children. A lot of them don't want to admit their color because they are afraid that these whitefolks over here would give them a hard time. Now, they are right about that.

I have been a cook and a maid and a housekeeper, and I have worked in hospitals. I still do every now and then, but I was in the hospital not long ago and I met this doctor that they said was an Arab. Well, he was darker than many people in my own family. I was proud to see one of the race better hisself. But, you know, that devil didn't want to hear a thing about his color! They had a lot of doctors from India and Jordan working there too. Now, a lot of the colored people didn't want to have anything to do with them because they said if they will pass like that, maybe they are not really doctors, either. I know folks that pass, but these doctors were just plain fools about it! I know people who pass to get a job that they should be able to get anyway, but they don't try to act like them all the time. There was this young Iraqian doctor there and he was darker than me, but he sure did everything he could think of and then some to show how white he was supposed to be. I don't trust anybody who would deny their color like that. And if Rosa Wakefield can't put her trust in you, you will never get your hands on her blood pressure or her diabetis or anything else!

Clinton Banks

I think that is rotten of them to lie to a blind man like that!

Clinton Banks is a walking repository of folk verse and rhyme, a modern bard of incredible virtuosity. He says that work and the street have been his only school, but schoolchildren and sober matrons urged me to talk with him. By common estimation, Red (a nickname frequently applied to persons with a certain reddish-brown cast of skin color) is a clever and essentially principled "street man." He is a migratory man of indeterminate age who says, "Sometimes I'm twenty and sometimes I'm eighty." Most people think that he is close to sixty.

I was a sailuh, and Jack! I sailed a while! I have seen all types of drunks. But a word high is a mess and hard to clean. Once in Alexandria, Egypt, I seen some nigguhs take a man apart just 'cause some preachuhs worked 'em up to doin' that! An' in Madras, India, I seen some more nigguhs do the very same thing for the very same reason. I seen some crackuhs do the same numbah behin' some stone signifyin' and damn lyin' of one of them jackleg peck preachuhs.

(I asked him if he thought of the Egyptians and South Indians he had seen as black.)

Why you asks me that? You know they ain' nothin' but blackfolks!

(I told him that most anthropologists thought of them as white.)

Well then, most of them anthropologists ain' never been to Alexandria, Egypt, or Madras, India, 'cause, Jack! let me tell you, they got some stone black citizens in both of them towns, not to mention the places in between 'em! Hell, no, they ain' white, an' if you could see 'em you sho' wouldn't be askin' no question like that. A whole heap of folks I saw in Alexandria and other places in Egypt was just as black or blacka den me and mo' than a few was blacka den you, and Jack! that is black enough! Now, that is where it is. If they white I'm white, and I know damn well what my coluh is.

Now, I don't know what they *think* they is, but I can tell you dis for a fact: the people in them countries ain' nothin' like their people who come over here to this country. America spoil everybody. The first thing one of them black people from over there try to do when he get here is to see how much white ass he can lick! But over there it is not like that. When they gits over here they play brown-skin whitefolks, but over there in they ownt nations, they know what the crackuhs are doin' to everybody and they don' even pretend to like it. Now, you know, they speech is not the same as ours. They eats some things I wouldn't let pass my chops, but ain' no way in Chris' you could look at them people and really think they was white, not an' be in yo' right min'! Them white folks in your school try to tell you them folks over there was white?

(I told him that most physical anthropology texts and most anthropologists say as much.)

Lawd! Lawd! I think that is rotten of them to lie to a blind man like that! But you was right to ask somebody who was black an' had been there and seen them people. I wouldn't lie to you. Man, if them people in Madras, India, is white, you a crackuh too, an' I'm tellin' you what Satan do despise!

THE MOJO
AND THE SAYSO

The business of white men is to rule.

Jackson Jordan, Jr.

These three astronauts were in this ship which was overloaded. There was a black one, a Jew, and an Italian. So the command told them that they would have to throw out as much as they could. Well, they did that and it still wasn't enough, so the command told them they had to answer a question and the one who couldn't get his question was going to have to be put out to lighten the load enough. So the command asked the Italian, "Who discovered America and when?" So the Italian said, "Christopher Columbus in 1492." The command said, "Good, you can stay." Then they asked the Jew, "What was the name of a famous ship that got in a little trouble?" So he said, "That would be the *Titanic,* sir. They had eighteen thousand people aboard. Sixteen thousand people were saved and two thousand people drowned." So they said, "Good, you can stay too!" Then they looked at the colored fellow and said, "Give me the first and last names of the two thousand people who were drowned."

Gloria Melton

Jackson Jordan Jr. still gives occasional lessons and demonstrations in the old-time slave-derived martial art of knocking and kicking.

Gloria Melton's banana pudding, good sense, passion for garage sales and boundless joke repertoire make her not only "the wife of everybody's husband," but everybody's raconteur and good companion.

Jackson Jordan, Jr.

The white man must pretend to know more than he
does, but we must always show less than we know.

*Close to ninety years old, North Carolina–born, urbane, wise Jackson Jordan,
Jr., sees life in terms of a few recurrent themes. Mr. Jordan was teaching
biology, classics, and scientific agriculture, and preaching the old-time religion before I was dreamed of. Three weeks after our final interview, Mr.
Jordan set out "to measure the civility" of his native city to discover if it is
"a fit place for an old black gentleman biologist to make his century in." He
is concerned for his safety, having been the victim of two burglaries. He says
he would like to retard the mechanical pace of life and accelerate the cerebral
pace. Mr. Jordan is aware of the awe and respect that his excellent health
and unpretentious erudition excite in his neighbors. "I used to be forgetful
of things I didn't particularly need to remember when I was eighteen," he
said. "I just try not to be so monumental that people will be reluctant to tell
me if I forget something."*

If what I have to say will help you, I'll be very glad to have you write
it down. My name is Jackson Jordan, Jr. My father was named Jackson
Jordan. I was born in 1886. My father was twenty years old when Lee
surrendered. I have seen our people come a great way in some ways, and
I have seen them lose ground and go backwards in some other ways. You
asked me what kind of people I thought we were and how we are different
from white people. First, let's get the subject clarified. I am going to be
talking about all the people I know of who used to call themselves Negroes,
blacks and/or colored people. Now, that is important to remember because
there's a sort of style in names for anything. Now, I was born a black man
and that's what I always called myself and that's what my father called
himself. Now, in any crowd you will find people who know what they are
about and people who just exist. Some colored people, or black people, call
themselves niggers. My mother said, "Only a nigger would do that," and
you know what she meant. From now on, I'm going to call our race what
I always did call it and what people with any sense always called it: I mean
to refer to this people as black.

Now, you must understand that this is just a name we have. I am not black and you are not black either, if you go by the evidence of your eyes. Mind now, black is a color, like any other color. It is no better or worse than all those other colors. If you can see, you are just used to seeing certain things certain colors and you think that's the only way it should be, but that's generally because you haven't seen much. To me, white chocolate is somehow wrong, just like black milk would be wrong to me because I have never seen it. I have seen white chocolate and I don't think much of it, but that's my particular prejudice. My grandniece doesn't care what color chocolate is and she is righter than I to think in that way. My grandniece is about the color I am used to seeing chocolate. Now, that to me is a very attractive color. I'm another color altogether and my skin looks about the same color as an onion—I mean a yellow onion. But all that is to tell you that color is a very hard thing to describe and it's not really worth wasting too much time on. Anyway, black people are all colors. White people don't all look the same way, but there are many more different kinds of us than there are of them. Then too, there is a certain stage at which you cannot tell who is white and who is black. Many of the people I see who are thought of as black could just as well be white in their appearance. Many of the white people I see are black as far as I can tell by the way they look. Now, that's it for looks. Looks don't mean much. The thing that makes us different is how we think. What we believe is important, the ways we look at life. Each one can do anything that the other one can do. Some people are smarter than other people, but that has nothing to do with their color. I have known stupid people of all colors. There seems to be more stupid white people because they talk more about everything than anyone else does. They are a bold people when they act together.

I have known backwoods simpletons to try to match wits with professors! Now, your average black person would not do that. A part of it is this master-race business. White people are not supposed to be stupid, so they tend to think that they are intelligent, no matter how stupidly they are behaving. This gives their more intelligent people much annoyance. At one meeting I went to, some white men were improperly dressed, which was pardonable because they did not have the means to come by appropriate clothing, but to make matters worse they started to pick their teeth and refurbish their nostrils. Now, this bothered their better classes. Now, we blacks were secretly amused by this because we thought to ourselves, "Here is the best proof of their superiority." No one said a thing, but we all knew what everyone was thinking. Now, it's important that you understand that white men of low intelligence say to themselves, "Hell, I'm white and my nose itches!" Their important men spoke to them and they finally struck a more decorous posture. Now, by the time a black person is old enough to feel pain he has been taught that you don't clean your nose or teeth publicly. Now, even if a black man didn't learn this elementary lesson, he is cautious enough generally not to be the only one in a place to be doing a thing.

I have taught music to white people and black people. White people find it much harder to learn to play with a group than black people do, by and large. White people are bolder because they think they are supposed to know everything anyhow. I have been a carpenter and it is common for white people to insist that you do something which is unsound, but they will not concede that they are paying me to do this job because they cannot do it themselves. They do not know enough about it to know what is sound or not. If they did know how to do my job, why pay me to do it?

Then too, white people have the power. After all, they have the mojo and the sayso, as my father used to say. They are supposed to know what they are about. But it is not hard to tell that they don't really know everything, and this knowledge makes us think that because they don't know some things, they must not really know anything. The simplest black man I've ever met was firmly convinced that he knew more than the wisest white man who ever lived. He sees the feet of clay and is convinced that the whole body is the same.

White people support their simpler brethren. They feel they must, so that makes our people say, "Well, if he supported him in that, then he must be just as stupid." So we feel a kind of contempt for them. But we admire their single-mindedness in helping their great personages. You would never get a group of black people to do that kind of thing. We try to do for ourselves and the few people we are close to what white people do for their race. Now, they are able to do that because they are sure that inasmuch as they do it unto them that are the greatest of them, they have done it unto themselves. We do not think that way at all. We probably think the opposite. That is why they will stand for leaders who are obviously lying to them and cheating them. They hope that their sons might rise to such a place of wealth, and they know that their power comes from deceit and force and know that it can only be maintained by massive reliance upon deception and force. It would be a matter of great concern to them if they thought they had put an honest man in charge of their business. Every now and then they make this mistake, but they are quick to kill off that man before he can really do something decent. You see, this country is basically an immoral enterprise. If an honest woman accidentally found employment in a bordello, they would either have to kill her, corrupt her or change the business of the house.

Pretending to know everything or just pretending to be better than you know you are must be a terrible strain on anybody. But that's the kind of life that makes people bold on the outside but weak on the inside. Numbers runners and other people who live by their wits are that way too. It has nothing to do with color, but all depends on the kind of life you lead. I don't think I am much worse than the best people I have known. I am conscious of my weaknesses and I have to drive myself to do what I know I should do. I also have to drive myself not to be petty and mean-hearted. I used to think that something would happen to me so that doing what I know is right and not doing what I know is wrong would just come automatically to me. The truth is, I used to think that virtue was a kind of habit which you could acquire if you kept on doing right. This is a great misconception which is responsible for much needless worry for young people and much foolish pride among old people. The truth is that every temptation is just as green as any other temptation. In spite of what they say, it's just as hard for you to resist anything that tempts you at eighty as it is at twenty. Doing what you think is right is more often than not an act of will. You could make a mistake because you thought something was right that really wasn't correct. But that's not what brings most fellows, young or old, to grief. It's when we do something we know we shouldn't do or talk ourselves out of what we know is what we should really do that we do wrong, and that's not a mistake.

The old people used to say that a certain thing had fallen within their net and that's why they had to do their duty, even when that duty was hard. I don't know whether there are really more people now who say duty be damned, but I notice them more now, anyway. But then, my father thought we were not the men his father was. But to be honest with you, I do believe that black youngsters are beginning to think more like white people than they should. I don't know how many are doing this.

So far in my family I can understand what my grandnieces and nephews say to me. I think they can understand me on a certain level, although they think of me sometimes as something that should be in a glass case. I try to tell them that you are alive as long as you think you are living. You wouldn't have had to explain that to a black youngster when I was seventeen or eighteen. I don't like much of the music they say they like, but I have heard it, so I do have a right to an opinion. They listen to the music I like with half an ear, and they don't know enough about it to know whether they like it or not. We don't argue about that. Ah, but one of them is a treasure. She loves me, so she loves anything I tell her is good. That's a great responsibility and a joy to me. My eyes are not as good as they used to be, so she reads to me sometimes and she listens to my records and I listen to hers. She has turn, which is what every black youngster had when I was a young man and what no white youngster ever had. She is a beautiful child and she's very pretty into the bargain. That's how a black child is supposed to be. We like a child to be quiet and inquisitive and ahead of his time, but not jarringly so. We like that because we know that is the way black people should live when they become men and women.

The business of white men is to rule. I did not make it so, but it is so now. They want their children to rule, even to rule them. It pleases them, no matter what they say, when their children are rude and overbearing, because that is a sign to them that those children are getting ready to rule as their parents have ruled. Now, our children must bear the rule of rude, weak, uncivil people, so they must always keep themselves to themselves. The white man must pretend to know more than he does, but we must always show less than we know. Fighting is the easiest thing for anybody to do. As a young man I used to teach knocking and kicking. All the young men in the country knew that then. But if you were good at that, you could very easily give yourself a bad reputation. Strength is a great responsibility. White men would have been better advised not to make people hate them because of their strength.

But this is a lesson people always learn when they are past profiting from it. You have heard people say, "If I knew then what I know now . . ." Well, that's the same thing they are talking about. But it probably works out the same anyway. I could have been a wiser man if I had been able to just do one thing at a time and turn off every part of my body except the part required to do this one thing I was trying to concentrate on. But I couldn't do that and anyone who says that he can is lying to someone. So all our efforts are imperfect because we are always thinking and feeling other ways about whatever we do.

This is the major part of the differences between the races. One set of people have got to bluff it out as rulers and the others have got to keep ahead of these rulers, who are always unsure of themselves. That brings me to another very important difference between white and black people: white people are very unsure of themselves. They cannot say they don't know what they are about—sometimes they don't even know this. But this is true anyway. Every white person likes to think that he is what you used to hear people refer to as "a self-made man." We used to read about all these poor orphans who rose to be great men. Now, the reason they were able to better themselves was that there was no huge weight of color prejudice holding them down. But we were supposed to think that it was their natural gifts which made them great. Now, back then, great meant rich. People—white people, anyway—worshiped money then. Rich men were supposed to be philosophers and great at everything else because they had managed to get a great deal of money. We were supposed to look up to the Mellons and the Morgans and people like that. Now, white people, I think, did but we didn't, or we didn't in the same way they did. For one thing, we knew that we would not be able to be the kind of rich men that they were. We also knew that no matter how much money we had, we would still have to be careful. That was Booker Washington's great mistake. He didn't know what the average black in the streets knew. My father could write and read, but he learned that secretly.

Well, I guess we've gotten a little off the subject. I guess I would have to say that the biggest difference is in how we think. White people are hard outside and soft inside, and black people are hard inside and tough outside, too, because we have to be. That's what my uncle used to say. White men look up to their leaders more than we do and they are not much good without their leaders. White people don't really know how they feel about anything until they consult their leaders or a book or other things outside themselves. Black people don't really have any leaders, I think, and that's too bad. Whites don't know how they really feel about anything, it seems to me. That's because they don't depend on mother wit and ordinary common sense like we do. You know that old street story about the white master who misplaced his member and asked his body servant where it was generally kept when not in use? Well, there is a lot in that. White people like to have books for everything. Don't you find it amazing that the Watergate people wrote down everything they did and even went so far as to record their unlawfulness? I really can't understand that kind of mind. You couldn't pay black criminals to do that.

You see, in a very real sense white men never grow up. They make everything into schoolboy games. X has always got to mark the spot for them. The average white man is Dr. Watson and the leaders are all supposed to be the great Sherlock. That's the way the average white man looks at his leaders. When I was a boy I used to think that only Southern white men did this, but now I know that it is a general habit with most of them. They are always waiting for orders. What they don't know is that their leaders are men just like themselves. There really are no people who know what to do without orders. Black people know this and make up their orders as they go along if they possibly can. When we can't, then all we have to do is wait for white people to make up their minds what they think they want to do. White men think that they can hide the fact that they generally do not know what they are doing. They think that because we don't tell them that, we don't know that they are meat men like all the rest. We don't tell them because we know that they are trying to convince themselves that they are what they would like to be. And so it proceeds. Of course, it is the rifle and the dollar which keep this game going.

White men are different from us because they have to live different kinds of lives. If we had to live their lives, then we would be the kind of people they are. If they were living our lives, then they would have to be careful what they say. They would have to depend upon themselves. They would have to be ready to do three or four or more things, depending on how we felt. When we have as much power as they have now, we will have to be the kind of people they are now. Our real hearts will be the treasure of our power. We will fear losing that treasure more than we will fear the loss of our self-respect or the good opinion of heaven itself! We will curse ourselves for being the kinds of people we will have to be to be powerful, but we will not surrender it. We will half do things and christen those tasks well done. We don't have to do this in the sense that there is something in our human natures which will not permit us to do otherwise. I might be wrong; I hope that I am. But from what I can see after a number of years of looking, most people are weak and greedy. Now, that means that they are going to use power over others in such a way that they will be pulled down by the weight of their short-sighted greed. Those early white men were selfish, and now even the best of their grandchildren live in fear of justice. Black people love justice because it is denied them. White men say they love justice, which they fear worse than hell. If I were a good white man, I don't know what I would do. I would not want to see my children braggarts and cheats, but I would know that justice would be fatal for them.

I would like to be able to talk to white men as I am talking to you, and I can tell by looking at some of them that they feel the same way as individuals, but it won't happen because the commonality of white men will not have it so. I am glad that I will not see our people come to that. White men, like Samson, may pull the whole green earth and everything that is in it to ruin. Black people might have another turn at ruling; I don't know what will happen. The generality of black men is better than the generality of white men because the blacks do not have to deny their civil natures. The best white men have told their brothers that they were wrong to live as they do. We know that they are. The decision to do wrong is a kind of chain too. They are prisoners and jailers too. To me, the knowledge that I am morally superior to white men is important. No one has to mention it. I don't recall ever saying that to anyone but you in all my life. But I know it and they know it and there is nothing they can do—even improving themselves—which can change that fact. During all our history here we have been right and they have been wrong and the only man who cannot see that is a fool or a liar. The white man's rule is ending because he is weak and selfish. But I cannot swear that we wouldn't have been just as weak and selfish if power had been ours.

I have never been a rich or powerful man, so to me, of course, the responsibilities of being rich and powerful are nothing, and the white man thinks that living under their rule is easy. They think it makes us carefree simpletons who scratch our heads and beat our feet on the Mississippi mud. I suppose that's their way of thinking, that they are making it easy for us. When I was a boy, I thought it would be the grandest thing in the world to be grown up because then you could be a mother or a father and cut the pie and dole out the chicken. My mother told me that cutting the pies was nothing compared to making them and getting something to make them out of. She said, "Fool, all you have to do is eat this pie!"

That's it, you see. If we could ever produce a generation of rulers like that, the world would be a fine place to live in no matter what color the rulers were. I don't want you to think that I am in anywise tired of things down here. I've had my share of years, but I can use all they send me. I have told you what I think. You know that I didn't make the world. If I had, it would be different for everybody. Things are not all bad. I still get a good dinner and a good enough bottle and a conversation that makes sense every now and then. I am not a hopeful man or a hopeless man. I just go 'long drylongso, as they used to say. I understand your position about the money, but you must understand mine. I've long since reached that stage where I'm supposed to be too old to be reasonable, so suppose we do it my way this time.

Porter Millington

Whitefolks are *how* folks and blackfolks are *what* folks.

Porter Millington is in his seventies now, a man of substance and judgment whose skill with and respect for food and music have made his life an introspective odyssey. He is a meticulous and imaginative carver of birds, from juncos to Eastern wild turkeys.

During the last of the three burglaries he has suffered, disappointed thieves damaged many of his carvings and books and slashed his furniture with systematic maliciousness. Although he is the possessor of a paid-up insurance policy, at least a year of negotiations with the company has failed to produce anything like even unjust compensation. When I last met him, Mr. Millington was crating his tools, paints, books and carvings. This was the first step in his plan to return to his native rural Missouri.

We know whitefolks, but they do not know us, and that's just how the Lord planned that thing. That is a hell of a thing to think about, you know. Now, I have thought about that thing all my life, but nobody ever came over here and asked to hear what I think about that.

First, you got to understand that it is not in the color but the thinking, how you might say, the attitude. And it's not in *your* attitude, but in the attitudes of all the people that growed you and of the people that you seen and heard about. A heap of those people are dead and their bones done rotted long ago, but that don' signify a damn thing because they still work on you anyway. Now, I know that and you know that, but one big difference between us and the cracker, or the white man, whatever you might want to call him, is, he don' know that we know this. He don't really think you know a damn thing. They don't believe that we got any sense at all. If you act like you ain't as dumb as he think you got to be, that will worry the hell out of him.

Now, they are great ones for begging you to tell them what you really think. But only a fool would really do that. Because whites don't give a damn about what something is really. I once tried to show a white man how to make this jackie. I gave up on that. My mother's father told me this thing and I remember it: He used to say, "Whitefolks are *how* folks and black-folks are *what* folks." He was a slave, so you know he really knew them. He was right about that.

Now, if a white man was to come over here and ask me anything, I wouldn't break bad with him. He could sit right there where you are in my best chair. If I felt flushed I might even lay a brew on him too. But I have got sense enough not to tell that dude anything but what he thinks I think. Now, that, you might say, is a shame because you know I would have to lie to him. I have heard the thunder a few times, and I know that the man is not going to thank me if I tell him the truth about anything. I found out the hard way! I lost jobs and almost did time behind that, so I know what I am talking about.

You can see what I'm telling you in the news. I am not no prophet, neither do I see things, but I can tell you right here and now that them same whitefolks that made that crook the President are gon' give him more money than you and me will ever see and a big house and pat him on the head and say, "Take it easy down there in Florida." That dude will not see what the inside of the jail looks like, but if whitefolks was worth a damn, he would be *under* the jail right now. No! No! He will not do a day! They took me down because I had a gun. Now, I needed this piece! I have been mugged five times.

You know, when I was just twelve me and my sister took some melons from a white man name MacDonald's field. Now, when my mother found out about this, she took the melons and didn't let us eat that day, but she whipped my sister because she was the oldest. If a little man does something wrong, he should pay, but if a big man does something wrong, he should be punished more because he wasn't poor, he wasn't hungry, he didn't need to break the law. But that's just like what I told you about whitefolks. They ain't worried about *what* he did, they just want to find out *how* they can make it look like he didn't do what you and me and he and them all know that he *did* do.

It's like I told you about that jackie. Now, if you or almost any other colored person I know came to me and said, "Porter, how do you make your jackie?" I would tell you how I do that. I would tell you to get your peaches and your cherries and your blackberries and your sugar and your crock—you know, all the things you would need. Now, I would be telling you what you need to do this. Now, if you was raised right, you would thank me and go on about your business. That's how we see things. I was working in Connecticut and I had me a little New Year's there, so I made me some peas—you know, I had to have my hoppin' John and a little jackie and yams for my luck. Well, these white people I worked for then just had to have some too. They really liked my jackie and wanted to know how to make it. But *they* told *me* how to make my jackie. That's really where the thing got to. They argued with me about how to make my own drink!

Now, I said that to say this: Don't never tell whitefolks that they are wrong. I know that they are wrong most of the time, but you will save yourself a kick in the ass if you just go on like you thought they knew what they was talking about. Like I told you, they are how folks. They want to know how you can make everything be like they would want it to be. Don't tell them *what* anything is. They do not want to hear it and they will give you a hard time.

Alberta Roberts

The biggest difference between us and white people is that we know when we are playing.

In their early forties, Mrs. Roberts and her husband, Sam, have four children and live in a suburban house. Having the entire house to themselves is very important to them. I have known them for most of the eighteen years they worked for this autonomy. Mrs. Roberts' first thirteen years were spent in rural Virginia, and something in that life made her an indefatigable foe of apartment dwelling. "It's all right for those who think it's all right, but I don't want anybody living overtop of me and I don't want to live overtop of anybody."

The Roberts' home is their castle. There the rule of politeness is strictly observed. Mrs. Roberts invited a former employer of hers, who is now her friend, to a barbecue Sam gave. Her younger brother objected to the presence of the white woman. Mrs. Roberts settled the nascent controversy with tranquil dispatch by telling the younger man, "Bobby, this is my house and I am a grown woman, so my friends are my friends." She commands attention without bluff and bluster because everybody knows she means what she says.

I think all people are born the same; then they get to be different as they live different lives. I believe it is what they learn from their different mothers that makes them different. If you think about it, you can see that it has to be the women that make the differences because they are the only ones who really care. A man only cares about one thing and that's having a good time. Men would rather play than eat. They even play at eating. You see how Sam and Maynard play around out here in the yard doing something I would have done two times as fast as they can get it done. I'd just take those steaks and broil them in the kitchen, and nobody would know the difference. Now, Ann and Hattie and Ruby and all of us women know that. The men are just playing at cooking. I am prepared to feed the kids until they get finished with that mess.

Now, the biggest difference between us and white people is that we *know* when we are playing. Now, all those men out there cooking and playing at cooking are going to dig in their pockets and send these kids to the store for some little treats to keep the children happy while they play with all that steer meat. They are out there playing superchef, but this is just something they do after work; and because they have worked to put food in their kids' mouths and do for them what grown people should do for their children, it's all right for them to play around out here. When this weekend is over we'll all get with the slave thing again. I'm playing a little bit too—don't get me wrong. But white people want to play all the time, and they won't admit that they are playing.

Now, you ask any white woman and she will tell you the same, because, as quiet as it's kept, there is the same thing under both our dresses and women know more about this than men do because they have to.

When it comes to playing, your white man wrote the book. Look at this Watergate mess. Now, that is nothing but men playing and not being able to see that that is precisely what they are doing. That is *all* they are doing. If I ran my house like they run the government, they would declare me an unfit mother. If a woman had done something like that, I mean that Watergate mess, she wouldn't have been childish enough to sit down and write and record her mess. That would be like a woman deciding to cut out on her husband and then hiring photographers to preserve her sin in glorious living Technicolor. Play is pretending that what's out here is not really out here. If you are black you just cannot make it like that because we can't buy our way out of things or make somebody say that square is round.

Now, that all starts with what these men learn from their mothers. I have worked for white people and I have worked with them, and I think it is a sin and a shame the way they treat their children, especially the boys. White women treat their sons like they should treat their husbands or brothers. That's where it really is. You can't spoil a good man because he's old enough to know how it is out here. Now, you can hear out that window how I'm spoiling mine. He can play out there eight hours and I will not bother him, but I don't want to tell this thing one-sided. When I get together in here and do my he-said-she-said thing, he will not bother me if I should be in here all day. He will not starve because he can do just as much in this kitchen as I can. If it comes right down to it, he can do some things I can't do, but that's because his mother didn't treat him like some little gold doll, but made him get in there and pull it too. What sense does it make to spoil a boy who doesn't know that it is a two-way street? I have seen white women, and some black women too, practically bow down to their sons and then get mad when those kids start treating them like dirt. You can't do that if you are like most black women because you know you might die and then who is going to put up with some brat with no turn whatsoever?

It really bothers me to see a lot of our women doing that now. That's why you can't correct a child in the street. They'll tell you in a minute, "You ain't none of my mother!" They'll tell you that in a minute. One told me that and I whipped his ass anyway. If you big enough to make off with Alberta's family groceries, you are big enough to have your behind smart for it. My Booker had the nerve to give Mrs. Simmons one of those short answers, but I bet you he won't do that again. I have seen to that! And I took him over there so that he could show Mrs. Simmons that I don't put that devilment into his head. Now, he was as nice and mannerable as he should be. I thought she was going to kill him with all that cake and soda she stuffed him with, but he got the message.

I love a mannerable child and everybody can tell when a child has been brought up right. I don't tell my children to do anything they can't do. And I do for them what a mother is supposed to do for her children. They better do what they are supposed to do—that's why I had *them* instead of them having me.

I have gone the way that they must go, and if they listen to me I can make their path easier. I didn't have a mother to do for me, so I know how much a child needs someone who will show them the way and keep them in it. You will never do that by making your children think that they are something they are not. Don't let them win every game they play. Show them *how* they can win. Now, you should listen to your children, but teach them how to get people to listen to them.

A white woman I worked for gave her daughter, who is not as old as my James, a live baby duck. She was one of those people who are always trying to draw you out, but I didn't say anything about it one way or the other. She kept asking me if I wanted her to get one for James. I used to bring James with me sometimes and she tried to interest him in it, and she did. She said, "Ask your mommy if you can have one." He did and I said no. Well, she tried to give him one, but of course he wouldn't take it after I had told him he couldn't. She told me in front of my child and hers that I was mean not to let James have that little duck, because he loved it. I told her that he would love that little thing to death because he wasn't old enough to take proper care of himself yet, so you know he couldn't take care of something as delicate as that little duck. Her daughter killed that little thing, and it doesn't matter that her mother just says the duck died. It died because someone who was responsible for it couldn't tell the difference between it and a doll or a set of jacks. You shouldn't teach children to play with everything. Now, that child's grandmother got her another duck and I think that was a sin, but that's how white children get started in this world.

Now, somewhere there might be some white people who would not have done that trick. I'm talking about the people I know, and I know some people. By the time we have to deal with these spoiled children, they are just *grown* spoiled children. Like children, white people who should know better will ask you for anything you have that they want. Now, I didn't ask you over here to lie to you. Three white women I have worked for have had the nerve to ask me to go to bed with their sons, and one, bless God, even had the nerve to ask me to take off my clothes for her husband. These were all fully grown women with children of their own. Now, can you imagine a black woman doing a thing like that? Hattie or Rena or Nancy, anyone out here, will tell you something like that. To white people your feelings just don't count for nothing. Nothing counts to them except what they want.

They teach their children to urinate in the same glasses that they drink out of. Now, this I have seen with my own eyes! They walk around with just as much clothes as they had on when their mothers birthed them, in front of their children. They put those children into the same bathtub together when they can hardly get one in there, and then expect them to respect each other and their childish parents.

Sims Patrick

There are two kinds of whitefolks. A few live like they
want to and the rest try to live like their big boss
leaders.

*Approaching his seventies, Top Chef, as Mr. Patrick is known, was born in
Alabama. He is an affable joiner; rare is the benevolent and protective order
he has not sampled. He has been a sailor and stills enjoys small sail craft.
He has cooked on ocean-going vessels and in domestic service. He knows how
to cook game so that people who thought they would never like such dishes
consume them with gusto. Mr. Patrick also does cold-hammered iron and
steel sculpture.*

*Perhaps because they have no children, Mr. and Mrs. Patrick are especially
interested in many of the children in their neighborhood. Each directs an
informal club for neighborhood boys and girls. Mr. Patrick and a number
of other neighborhood men rent a barbershop that failed as an economic
proposition, and still gather there for the kind of animated discussion they
had when barbershops were in their heyday. Mr. Patrick pays three shares in
support of the club. "Why not?" he told me. "I haven't got as much on me
now as some of the others." He is seen by his neighbors as a shrewd, hail fellow
who can take care of himself.*

John! This question is my meat! I have worked for and with them for half
a hundred years, so I know them suckuhs better than they know themselves!
Now, that is the truth. I've done farming and gardening and chauffeuring
and sailing and cooking and bartending! You name it and if a colored man
can do it, I have done it! I figure since you want my view, I'm gon' tell you
what I think like I would anyway.

Everybody knows that we are like them in some ways. I can just go out
here on the street and I can see white people that look like black people I
know. I can see black people that look like white people I know. You know
what I mean! A lot of things the both of us like, but we just like them
different ways.

I used to cook for white families and I would half cook their food because
that was the way they paid me to cook it, but now, you couldn't get a black

person to eat his food that way. Now, if you give a black person half a chance he will get himself some pork and he will cook it slow and he will eat yams with it if he possibly can. Whitefolks want to cook everything fast and they do not like to mix things together that we think should be mixed together. Now, a part of that is that whitefolks are always in a great hurry, so they mess up three times as much as we do. You can skate along if you're paddy, for the most part. But with us it's the reverend thing or your behind. We don't have but one chance at anything we do and then half the time we will not make it.

John, let's face it, git'n over is git'n over. You just can' make it like that without having it get to you in the end! Everybody thinks that it is us that are shuckin' the most. Now, that is a fancy lie because the average black person is shuckin' when he can't do anything else. You know yourself half of us who are into something wrong are doing that because that's the easiest thing or the only thing they can get into. Now, me, I didn't have to get into anything like that, so I didn't, but I do know people who were into something wrong because there wasn't too much else they could do. I know that there are rotten cats out here too. I don't know any black people who are half as wrong as these paddies that everybody looks up to. No, I can tell you that with the whitefolks that count, Fats Waller was right: "It ain' what you do, it's the way that you do it." These people hide their dirt or make everybody lie and say their dirt is not dirt or they lie to us about their dirt. I know that these are the rottenest people on God's earth and they know it too. But as long as they can get folks to say that shit is shinola, they would rather deal in shit any day.

The way they see things, there are the chumps like you and me and then there's them. You and me are supposed to do what they say do and they are supposed to do what they feel like doing. That's how this country, and the world too, really runs. The average person does not know this and half the time he don' want to know it, either. Now, you know what you know. You know what your people told you and then because that's the only thing you know, you get to thinking that that is the only thing you should know. That is blackfolks' thinking. But whitefolks do not think like that. There are two kinds of whitefolks: A few live like they want to and the rest try to live like their big boss leaders. Now, there is not one thing in this world that a white person who has money would not do to keep on having money and sayso. Now, they know that they can't do this by themselves, so they make believe that they made these laws and bibles for everybody, but they really just made them for the poor crackuh and the blacks. Things that would worry the average black person don't make them no nevermind whatsoever!

I used to work for these people and they had two kids, a girl and a boy that was twins. One afternoon this young boy had taken off every stitch of his sister's clothes. They were in this little shed, and when I walked in on him that dude had the nerve, scared as he was, to ask me if I knew how to knock on a door. Now, that is how they think. There was no way in this world for that young boy to be wronger than he was, but he couldn't see it or wouldn't see it. Now, that little dude was his father's son and neither one of them gave a damn about anything but git'n over. That dude was almost fourteen, so he—hell, both of them—had to know what they were into, but the only thing that worried either one was, could they get away with it? But even if you were going to do something like that, it was really simple to do it the way they were. They wanted to do it, so they just saw that shed as the right place to get it on. Now, if they had wanted somebody to catch them, that was just what they should have done. But they didn't want anybody to catch them. They just decided that they wanted that to be the cool way for them to do this thing, and wouldn't think of all the reasons why it was a pretty simple trick.

Now, say, for an instance, your average colored person—if he got caught wrong, he might break bad too, but he would have sense enough to know that he was wrong. He would know he was wrong and he'd feel bad about that. But the big shot, he don't give a damn about anything out here but not being able to do whatever he might want to do. You and me want to do a thing because we want to get something done; they want to do things because they want to be able to say, "You see there—I made them do what I wanted them to do." I don't see that at all. That's how kids think! I don't want it, I just want to see if I can make you give it to me. I have never known a white man who wouldn't go to as much trouble to get something that he wasn't interested in as he would to get something he really wanted. You know that everybody dreams of doing whatever they want to do. Well, to you and me that's just something we don't pay much mind to. But white people think they are supposed to do that. You can't, but they don't feel like admitting this, so they run things into the ground. The man knows better than anybody out here how wrong he is, but as long as he can make people shut up about it, he says, "Well, nobody didn't say nothing about it, so they must not have a damned thing to say." Now, because he don't care about what's really going down, that's all right with him.

When that dude say, "Sam, what do the colored people want?"—if you black, you heard some crackuh ask you that. If you say you don't know, that's all he needs to hear! Now, he know and you know that what we want is what he took. But off goes your head and a big chunk out your ass if you say anything like that! I was working for this gray dude with more money than you and me ever counted in our dreams. He got half-drunk around there at this party and got next to his nephew's wife. Now, he didn't go out of his way to hide much. Everybody knew what went down. But wouldn't a soul talk about it. This dude and his nephew couldn't stand each other, but the little nephew was too scared to bring his uncle down front. Everybody knew what was wrong. That old man would dare the little dude to say what was on his mind, but as far as I know they never did get to the revern' thing. See, that's just what's going down between us and them. They keep after you to see if you will mention the wrong thing. They don't have much cool. I know when I'm bad I got to show more cool. They would like to be the type of cat who can just get mad whenever he feels like doing that. Because some white people really are bad enough to do that, all white people feel that they should be able to do that too. Now, I feel like that too sometimes, but I do have ordinary, plain common sense enough to know that I can't.

A white cat will tell you right away, "I'm free, white and twenty-one!" Now, to him that means that he should be able to do any damn thing he feels like doing. When I was living in Boston I was working for this family. It was the first job I got there. I was chauffeuring then. I made me this goose-grease cake and the kids had to have some, so I let them take some. Well, they had this little girl staying with them, and she came in there and we were all eating cake. Now, she opened her mouth and the first thing that came out was, "Am I black?" What she meant was, Why didn't you tell me about the cake too? In other words, if you are denied anything, you got to be black! That's the way they think!

I used to work for this old devil who was as nice to me as he could be to anybody, I guess. His name was the reverse of my name. He used to call hisself joking me along, but I never get into that with them because the minute we get too tight this dude might call me out of my name and then I might not have cool enough to keep from hemmin' him up. Late one Sunday everything went to hell. They needed a plumber and an electrician, but they couldn't get one. Now, I was living in at the time, so I told this dude when he asked me that I knew a little about it. It was no big thing and when everything was straight, here come these plumbers. Well, that just tickled the boss and he told these plumbers what they could do for showing up so late, and when they left he said he was really glad that I had got the thing straight. And just like I'm sitting here talking to you, that old devil looked right at me and said, "Well, I guess we fixed their nigger wagons!" I could tell by looking at his eyes that he had opened his mouth before he thought, but do you think he was sorry or shook behind that? If he was he didn't show it much! Now, in his own way he liked me. He paid me for the extra work I did just what he would have had to pay them. He tried to help me in other ways, but like most white people he thought that to be his equal I had to be white, so after a while, even though he was looking right at me, he forgot that I wasn't white. If he had not forgot that, I don't think he would have said that.

I like for everybody to know where everything is and who everybody is. That way we don't have no trouble. I can't stand this buddy-for-a-minute shit. With me it is strictly business! Pay me what you owe me and goodbye, Chahlie! You can run yourself up on some tough snags if you really think whitefolks know what they are doing. A white man will grin in your face in the morning, and at night he's ready to give you the hardest time he can think of. I don't have no more to do with people like that than I have to. They try to watch everybody, so they can't watch anybody. They ain' nothin' out of the ordinary, as they say in the country; they ain' nothin' but meat men too. But to git over they pretend that they can do more than anybody else can. Now, they know that's a lie—I mean, the big shots know that's a lie. Now, that big white man don't deny hisself a damn thing. Like I told you, if he think he want it he's out there after it, and with all he got going for him, he don't lose much. So he'll be the baddest ass for a while and then somebody else will get the mojo and the sayso. But in the meantime whatsoever he think he want to do, he will do. You and me, we believe what our people that raised us up tell us. True, we know right from wrong just like whitefolks do, but we was taught to do right. When I'm wrong I hate that thing because I feel low to the person who is right. But it is not in white people to feel that way. He has been taught that wrong is all right as long as he don't do it to a white man.

When I was living down south in Florence, white parents used to sit right there and watch their kids throwing garbage at black people. My Cousin Floyd slapped one of the little cracker bastards twisted. Now, if that had been my kid I would have said, "You're wrong," and I would have warmed his behind for doing that. But the whites got in behind Floyd about that, so that he had to come up here. That's what I'm trying to tell you! They can't be decent and teach their kids decency and still cheat people and rob people. Like it says, no man can serve two masters. You can't be decent and rotten at the same time. The man has to make up his mind what he wants to be, and it look like to me that he did that a long time ago! He done been like this for so long that he is too greedy and scared to be any other way. But he'll kill you if you tell him that.

Bernard Vanderstell

The power to do one thing is never the power to do all things.

I had the good fortune to meet Bernard Vanderstell at a Y.M.H.A. Dylan Thomas reading many years ago. Easygoing, he is always open to different views and human types. "I was born in Guyana, but I guess I grew up all over the world." As a member of a dispersed international family and as a seaman and master machinist, he has traveled widely and observed profoundly. He speaks five languages at least as well as English, makes fine stringed instruments and is a serious naval historian. He and his wife, Greta, keep generous and tasteful open house for civil people of every human variety. How like them to have remembered my passion for proper fish hash and banana-mocha cake. Like the Patricks, the Vanderstells seem pleasantly suspended in a green middle age, although they are in their late sixties.

I thought about your questions and I guess I still feel the same way I always did. There are many kinds of black people and many kinds of white people, but they have certain things in common and they differ from each other profoundly, too. In spite of what we think about each other, we are all human. Both American whites and blacks are Westerners. But we have had very different histories, so we are very different kinds of Westerners. I get along pretty well with almost any kind of person, as you know. I'm far from the place I was born and I have seen many places and I'm probably a little strange to most people, white or black, here. To a large degree, people are what they have to do or what they think they have to do.

Every people or every generation of every people finds that what they are supposed to do has already been decided by the generations which came before us. You can make fun of those who came before or pretend not to care or know about them, but that's not going to change the fact that they were there and they left you a way of talking and thinking and eating and believing and making love and doing all the things that people do. Sometimes they leave you money and land, and it is the business of the people who are standing on those dead generations to place the feet of their children on their heads, just as their fathers gave them their heads to stand upon. Now, you can decide that you want to stand alone, but you must have eaten and thought and grown to be an adult before you could do that. Since you cannot do this by yourself, it stands to reason that you are whatever you have learned from the various people who made you a man or a woman. I'm trying to say that I think that there is no such thing as a person who is not in some ways a part of several ways of life. That's what I said in the beginning in a different way. If the ways of life that your people are born into are different, they will make the people different.

Now, black people everywhere have been born into a different way of life than white people, so we differ from white men. It doesn't matter that you and I were speaking different languages when we were children or that we went to different churches. The one fact that we were the children of slaves and that the word "nigger" meant the same things to both of us is very important. It isn't even that we were poor or rich; it is that we were poor or rich children of slavery that is important. It is how people think that makes them different. I have a brother who is white and he, as you know, doesn't think as I do. He hasn't had to be as careful as I have, so he isn't. He thinks that he can do more about life than I do, and he can. But he thinks that because he can do something to alter something, he can change more than he can. Now, in this respect he is like most white people. Black people think that they are at the mercy of life or that they must teach their children to be ready to stand whatever life brings. White people think they can be victors, even in death, and this no black person of the blacks can understand.

I lived in the rural Florida where it was a fairly common sight to see white men firing their weapons at the sky to make it rain or to stop it from raining. I never saw a black man do that, because the weather and the Boss of the weather cannot be threatened or bullied. White men are firmly convinced that everything can be bullied or bought. Now, I don't want to say that every white man who ever lived thinks like that, but most of them do.

You value things you can master. Whatever white men have permitted us to do we have mastered. So we are much more sure of ourselves than they are because we can do whatever we get half a chance to do. White men are never really sure what they can do as individuals and what they are doing because of their superior privileges. The failure of one white man is the failure of all white men, and the success of some white men is the success of the rest. That is the way they think. Now, with the common run of blacks, the failure of any black person is the fault of the white people. This means that the average black man does not have to take the blame as an individual for his shortcomings. Now, we are right to think in this way sometimes, indeed most of the times, but not all of the times. There are some things which white men are just not strong enough to prevent black people from doing, but that means that white men must bear the credit and the blame that comes with running anything.

Also remember that men are just half of the world. We used to be the white men's slaves. Now some men make their wives their slaves. We black men cannot do that here. Although I have seen places in the world where women did the same field labor we used to do for them, white men have their wives for house slaves and that is a part of what their grandfathers left them. I mean to say that they have the habit of having someone to serve them and they do not feel comfortable without this or the hope of it.

To realize the value of anything, you must have some idea of how hard it is to do that thing. It used to be that everybody who had anything to do with a job could do it sensibly, even if that person were just telling someone else to do it. I mean to say that I could not tell an organist how to do his job because I don't know his instrument. But, you see, I know that I don't know anything about that, so I never would try to write an organ piece.

White men have inherited a position of command and that means that they cannot admit that anything is beyond them, so they must pretend to capabilities they do not possess. The more one pretends to know, the more one must do to convince oneself and others that these capacities are really there. People can't go on like that for very long, and soon the whole structure must come down on everybody's head. I know that working with machines is a great responsibility. I know that the more the machine can do, the more careful I must be in using it. Power must be handled with care, but there is a kind of disregard which fills the minds of ordinary people because they will not take the time to think about what their power means. The power to do one thing is never the power to do all things. The power to do anything is lessened if there are people or circumstances which can make you use that power. You see, power diminishes each time it is used. If I am not powerful enough to prevent you from questioning my power, then I am not powerful enough.

Now, that is what all strong men and nations have always tried to find, but that is not something that any nation or person can have. And that is because any nation can learn anything that any other one can. If people can oblige you to use your power they can learn about it, and if they can learn about it they can use it too. I think that is what history is all about. I have learned not to threaten people because I had to pay a high price for doing that. A person might learn this, but I think it is too much to expect a large group of powerful people to learn this. I learned this in many little ways, and although I am not stupid, it took me years to make sense of it, although my life often depended on this knowledge.

Now, white men are under no such urgency to learn this. That is to say, they do not know that they must—that is, they should—have learned this lesson. Like most people they forget that some power is not all power. I'm sure that there is nothing racial about their inability to see that. It is that they are very ordinary people for the most part, and this is a fact which is not obvious, so it is missed by most people.

I can't tell you how I started to learn this, but I remember when I was first aware of it. I had a big tire and I used to float in it and my uncle tried to take it from me because, he said, it was dangerous. My mother and my aunts indulged me in this, so I kept my tire and did not learn to swim. One morning I went beyond the swimmers, and if it had not been for my uncle I might still be beyond them. Now, I was a boy then. I was seven years old, but I was beaten very severely by my uncle. He was the kind of man who would hurt you a little to keep you from hurting yourself a lot. When he had punished me he reminded me of what he had said about that tire. When I learned how to swim well enough to suit him and had learned how and when to use that tire, he bought me a kite.

When I got my first gun my uncle told me, "Look here, I know what you have bought, but do you know?" Well, I thought about that because he was the kind of person who said very little and whatever he said was worth paying attention to. Like most young men, I liked to make a little noise, you know. I used to go to dances and I suppose I wanted to be numbered among the bad. My uncle asked me not to go to this dance and out of respect for him I did not go. I lent my gun to Peter Wellington, who was my best friend. He challenged a man with a machete about a girl, and that gun wouldn't fire and the man with the machete killed Peter. Perhaps I might have been killed if I had been there. Perhaps I might have killed someone else, and then I would have to leave or go to jail or try to kill to stay out of jail or maybe the family of the man I might have killed would have tried to kill me. Well, you have heard people say, "Lord, if you will forgive me this time, I will never do thus-and-so again." Well, that's how I felt about that.

Now, I try to think about whatever power I have, whether it is the power to do something or not to do something. I know other people who think like I do, and they are almost all black and there are not many of them. No matter how you choose to live, there are risks because people are not content just to mind their own business. I choose to live quietly. Some people think that means that I am weak, and if they are of unmanly character they think that means that they can push me. Some people say, "Well, if he is quiet it is because he has hidden power and is looking for an excuse to use it."

You know how I am. I used to be very different, though. I once itched to show people when they were wrong. I listen to people now, or pretend to listen to them. I see people doing the same foolishnesses I used to do myself. I know that I can't stop them now. Most of the stupidity and ignorance I run into every day could only be changed by going way back, sometimes generations. It is too large for me or anybody to do anything about. A man wanted to bet me that if he put two horse's hairs in a glass of milk they would turn into a snake in two days. I had a little disagreement with a woman who thinks that a man's organ has a bone in it and that this bone can be broken, rendering the man impotent. So, you see, I just go along with the public. Here people of sense come and we talk and drink. I never had a formal education, so it is an honor for me to have friends who have. I have learned that many people are spoiled by their educations. It was a pleasure to be able to tell you what I think, and I would really like to thank you for the books.

THE WELFARE SIEGE

You cannot walk the streets without running into
something bad.

Maynard Brown

I am married to the only man I sleep with and I take
care of my children! You will never hear anybody say
that they saw mine running around some supermarket
when they should be in bed! I took a course at community college and all you could hear was this "black
awareness" junk. Anytime you are not aware enough
to give your child a name, you can stay away from me!

Jane Small

Iron times was just one of the innumerable subjects that occupied the shifting membership of Maynard Brown's barbershop colloquium. There was something very appropriate about the use of Maynard's shop as a polling place, something in keeping with the unofficial but consequential civic importance of men like Maynard. It is a matter of profound personal regret and civic tragedy that courage and nobility of spirit were insufficient allies in Maynard's gallant fight for life. Borne down by a sea of physical and economic troubles, he left this world the poorer for his death.

Mrs. Small is a thirty-two-year-old Pittsburgh-born "homemaker." She is doing a splendid job in the training of her five-year-old daughter, Jane, and her eight-year-old son, Ralph. Ralph Small, Sr., described his domestic hierarchy this way: "I'm not stupid, but I know Jane is smarter, so as long as she doesn't drag me about that, she does a lot of the heavy thinking around here." Mrs. Small is also rearing the twin infants of her sister, who died shortly after giving birth to them. Mrs. Small and her husband, Ralph, are both good amateur cornetists and puppet makers. She has spent two brief, honorable terms in prison, which attests to her civic commitment. Her antipathy to the revolution of fashion is understandable in the light of her life. She has been the victim of a half-dozen burglaries and two muggings.

Janet McCrae

We need to get *up*, not just get over.

Janet McCrae, whose "conversational interview" appears below, called our meetings reunion time. She was born in rural Pennsylvania and is in her late thirties. I have never heard a finer contralto voice than Janet's. I have had the pleasure and privilege of her friendship for more than twenty years. For much of that time her father lived in a veterans hospital, and her mother and slightly older brother were responsible for the sustenance and training of Janet and her three younger sisters. Even now, people tend to think of the McCraes as a single entity. "Being an aunt is one of my biggest numbers," Janet reflected. She thinks this will be the case for the rest of her life, no matter where she chooses to live. Her personal talent for putting people at their ease and proceeding civilly but inexorably to the real heart of any matter has earned her the respect of all kinds of sensible people.

I'm the kind of person who goes to sleep if I have to talk very long about something that doesn't interest me. I really do and I'm also, I guess, well, not a self-centered person, but I'm interested in people I know and I'm interested in things that I think are important and not very interested in things that somebody comes along and tells me that I have to be interested in. I'm the kind of person who wouldn't go across the street to see somebody just because their face was plastered all over the papers or the TV. I'm the kind of person who would come four hundred miles to see a very important friend of mine graduate from college and not tell her that I was there. That's the way I am. I'm still a country person, I guess, so I don't really care very much for what I see on the streets or the TV screen. Radio is more and more a total loss, so I don't pay any attention to it, either.

As for my time, you shouldn't worry about that. We never used to. I work and come home, that's about all I do. Everything else is just too much trouble. Everybody we used to know is very hard to know now. Everybody is working two jobs and getting very serious about things we all used to laugh at. It isn't just that we are all older. A lot of them don't seem to have grown any older, to hear them tell it. Every now and then I run into some people I used to see every day and sometimes we try to act like we all used to, but they are into other things, mostly aimless things, if you know what I mean.

I try to have a goal. You know I always was that kind of person. I really like traveling and I guess that's what I save for. You know, more black people than ever before are going to places that you would never think black people could afford to go to. I've been to Spain and Morocco twice. I went with my Aunt Isabel.

My mother is thinking of going to Jerusalem and Bethlehem, but we told her we wouldn't let her. We were just pretending in a way, but in another way it's a bad thing for her to do because she might get hurt over there. I don't want to go anywhere where the people don't want me to be there. I can stay home and just not work for a while and catch up on my reading or maybe visit somebody I like. I have been mugged here, so why should I go somewhere else to be mugged too? I'm sure she won't go and that's a great load off all our minds. I'm thirty-eight, so you know she should start thinking about taking it kind of easy. She said she'd go wherever she felt like going, but Jimmy just picked her up and said, "Look here, young lady, don't you think you're getting just a little bit too fresh for your age?" That was pretty funny, and she couldn't pretend to be mad with him; she never could. Jimmy, being the only boy, has always been able to, well, you know, talk to her. She'll listen to him before she will most people. We tried to explain how we felt and she could see it. She doesn't know it yet, but she's going with Jimmy and Candace and me to Morocco, Algiers, Tunis, and Paris and maybe Portugal. We're working on it, just like we had all the money we need. Together like this we can get it together much sooner. We mentioned something about the West Indies. She was born in Jamaica, but I really don't think she wants to go back there very much. She was very young when she came here, so this is all she knows and she doesn't get along but so well with most of that side. I've been to St. Thomas and Port of Spain, but I never really wanted to go to Jamaica, I guess, because I had it in mind that I would like to do that with her, and since she never seemed very anxious to go, I just never decided to go. Jimmy has been to the Islands, though.

Jimmy's into the same old nutty stuff. Did you know that he's soon going to be a lawyer? All that night school and day school and truck driving paid off, or I guess it will pay off. I really admire Jimmy. You know, he is the kind of brother that sisters dream of having and he always has been that kind of person. Most people let things go to their heads; he always had great strength, but he didn't push people around. I used to make him pretty mad sometimes because I used to like to live dangerously, but he would always look out for all of us. He'd always try to talk sense to you if he cared about you, and he would do it in such a way that you wouldn't feel embarrassed for yourself, but for him. Somebody should write a book about Jim. He's the kind of person that keeps everything going. Most people don't really give people like Jimmy much credit, especially if they are black.

You never really hear about black people like you or Jimmy or me. Not that there is anything so special about me, but everything I read about us is sick, or—yes, I guess I do mean sick in one way or another. I'm an ordinary black person. I have never spent a day in jail. I'm polite to everybody who is polite to me. I don't take drugs and I can save my money. I can say three sentences without "man" and "like" and "you know." I am not on welfare and am not about to get on welfare as long as I can work.

Look, the idea of welfare is good, but what happens to this idea when they actually start doing something with it? The same thing that happens with every good idea that you leave to bad white men to carry out! I have worked and paid taxes since I was seventeen, so I think that the country should help me if I can't get work or if I can't work. That's what a decent country should do for everybody in the country! But I don't have to tell you what really happens. It's just like everything here. Poor people get the leftovers and that's how it is with the welfare program too. It's just poisoning black people, men and women. We need to get *up,* not just get over, John! We'll never do that on this welfare system. If they thought there was any chance, they would cancel welfare yesterday. It's just more reconstruction!

Go to the supermarket or just walk down any street around here if you want to see how welfare is destroying people. I'm talking about my own relatives! I have seen a seven-year-old try to kick a baby out of his mother's stomach! Every day I see wild children stealing and terrorizing old people and younger people too. John, I know how to use a gun and I have had to more than once and I know that I'm going to have to use one again. I don't go out of my way to find trouble, you know that. But if I didn't have a gun I might be scarred, pregnant or dead by now, and that is the truth if ever I told it!

Drugs are the heaviest thing that we have to bear. I don't know very many people who are into drugs and there probably are not many, but there are enough to make life hell for everybody. We might as well be in jail, John. I do everything I have to do before dark and then I generally stay here, locked in, just like you found me. Jimmy was sent to the hospital by two people he went to school with! I've been robbed. John! my mother was mugged! They broke her glasses and took everything she had—carfare, rent, church envelope, everything she had. One of them said, "We ought to stripe this old chick a little." But the other one said, "No, she didn't give us any trouble, so what you want to stripe her for?" They work in twos so that when you think you're getting away from one, you run into the other one. They don't want to do anything about it because it doesn't get to them. Their answer to addiction is to give you another drug. Now just as many people are freaking out with methadone as with anything else! That's drug welfare and welfare is money drugs!

If I see someone who hasn't got enough to make it, I know that just giving them a couple of dollars is not going to help them to better themselves. Julia got into A.A. and they told her she had to stop drinking. Now, what kind of sense does it make to tell someone who is hooked, "Here, you take this drug instead of that drug"? Then you let these same people do all kinds of weird things with methadone, so that they are just as freakish as ever! If that's all they were going to do, why didn't they say, "Here, just take what you're taking"? I mean, if they would give them methadone, why wouldn't they give them any other drug they wanted? They want to decide what you can be hooked on and how far you can generally get in life.

If I were running these programs, first, John, I would run them honestly. If you are an addict, you shouldn't be, so I wouldn't let you be hooked on anything. I would bring down the price of all drugs so the people who really make a lot of money couldn't make it that way. I would get rid of those dope-fare workers. I think this is a big problem, so you couldn't cure it with a spoon. I would shoot anybody who sold drugs. I'd have it just like food stamps, only they would be drug stamps and you could have them if you wanted them. Then if you just had to be a junkie, you could just nod away and not mug old ladies or slash people's faces. Then if anybody got any drugs, you would know where they got them from. And if anybody committed any crimes under the influence of drugs, no ifs, ands or buts, the government would have to pay the victims. If there was a death, then the government would have to give the nearest next of kin to that victim one million dollars, on which they would not have to pay any taxes forever! That would make these people really enforce the law. I really don't think that you can make people give up drugs altogether. But you can stop people from getting rich on drugs and you can stop addicts from pushing everybody else around!

If I were running welfare—well, it's the same thing. You have to start right! Remember how we used to put our money together to buy some food or cook a meal? Well, that was slightly different because we all knew and trusted each other and we could agree on what we wanted to have. But that's how this welfare thing should be done. We have these standards, you know. A family of so many people should have so much money. Well, if they should have that, why not give that to them if they can't get it themselves? Most people I know on welfare are living just like the government admits they shouldn't have to live. I would start there. Nobody should be but so poor. Now, when you and I and Elizabeth and Jimmy and all of us chipped in to have a meal, you never said to me, "Well, Janet, you can only have one fifteenth of this or that because you didn't put in as much as you could if you sold your books or records." Nobody else sold their stuff to do this, so why should I?

It isn't just not having enough money that makes life bad for people, although that is the most important reason, I think. I don't think it's only a question of what you need to live with, but also *how* you live that's important. Almost everybody I know is living in a way that I don't think people were ever meant to live. People need space and they were never meant to be jammed on top of each other. Do you know any architect who would want to live in these projects? I wouldn't let people live like this, and I would give them money and a chance to live like people instead of ants! It's very hard for us because so many of us come from the country to begin with. I think it's very hard on old people. Some people think they are lucky because they have indoor plumbing and things like that, but I was born in the country and we had indoor plumbing and enough room to breathe, and everybody who wants that should have it. If you make people live like rabbits, they will have to act that way.

I guess I just wouldn't make it possible for people to live in a way that I would think was too degrading for me. But I know that that might mean that some people who are living better than they should would have to have a little less. I wouldn't just give people any old thing and say that I was helping them. These tarts are made with frozen blackberries. Well, if I didn't think that they were a lot better than no tarts, I wouldn't have given you any. Now, we all know that they would be better if they were made with the fresh berries. Well, that's what I mean. Maybe some people might have to give up the fresh blackberries so that we could all have the next best thing together. But it's not right that some of us should have fresh blackberries whenever we want and the rest have imitation blackberries that are not fit for people to eat.

You know, I used to think that there was a great deal to everything. I used to think that I couldn't do much by myself because I didn't know enough to do these important things that had to be done. I think that's a trick now—you know, a trick done by the people who run things. They have to make everything look like it's much more complicated than it is. I used to think the same way about what my mother did when we were all children, only she wanted us to learn how to do these things, so we all learned. What you want to do is more important than how you do anything. I know that now, but it's too late. It's too late for all just average people. It is not really that big a thing, John. It really isn't. If something is so big—I mean, if how to do something is so big that ordinary sensible people can't do it—then maybe we have no business doing it.

People hate to admit that they don't know something, but that's not the worst thing. People like to think that nobody else can learn what they have learned. Now, that's just not true, but you can make it true by making it hard for people who don't know how to do a thing to learn how that thing is done. Jimmy taught me how to drive, but a lot of other people couldn't or wouldn't because in one way they wanted to make it into a big thing. Sometimes the only thing that they could do that I couldn't was driving, so they resented my learning that. More men are like that than women, I think. I think most white men are like that. Not knowing how to do what you want to do makes you feel stupid. People feel stupider than somebody else. So all these people who know how to do things think they are smarter or act like they thought they were smarter than most of the people who just know what they want.

The trouble with welfare is that there are a lot of people who run it who think that there is a way that you can do what you want to do, even if you don't have what you need to do it with. I've seen these kids with their Mr. Clean degrees and several thousand dollars to spend on themselves alone telling a family of five or more that they should be able to make it on less than workers have for themselves. They really think that there is a way to do anything. There are probably ways to do a lot of things if you start right.

I had an argument with one of those workers at Sandra's house. He came and I didn't want to see him, so I went to the bathroom and, you know, he insisted on knowing who was in there, so I came out and he started his pitch, but I told him no good. We got into a discussion or argument or whatever about this same thing. It was a really stupid thing. He asked me to tell him something I thought could not be done. So I said it was impossible to make the ice cubes on the table into a pie. But, do you know, he couldn't see that. He said that just because we couldn't do it didn't mean that it was impossible to do. Sandra is still mad with me because she has a thing going with this clown and she didn't want me to make him mad and I guess she didn't like his talking to me so much.

A black person wouldn't think like that, and that is one of the big differences between us. Most black people don't think in such a far-out way. My mother says pigtails are pork. I'm not sure how to put this, but it is something you feel about us. Jocelyn says we still know where it's at. We're just not that interested in these games white people like to play.

Melvin Gabriel Wilmot

These whitefolks is evermore giving people things they
cannot use or do not want.

*Mr. Wilmot is a small blind man with very large, swift hands. Alienation and
suspicion are the master motifs of his life. His estrangement is from the world
systemic, from agencies and institutions and insolent offices. He is in his fifties
now and has forsaken all routines save his own whenever possible. He has
developed effective strategies for the maintenance of his cleanliness, which is
important to him because it is proof that he is not alienated from black life
generally. His caution is a more intense form of an endemic wariness that
pervades core black culture.*

*He is a Louisiana man who initially claimed Miami, Dallas and Jalapa
as his birthplace. He examined my hands meticulously before deciding to
accord me the courtesy of the truth as he sees it. "Hooks do not deceive me,
and you got hands that only Aunt Haga' hands out, my man." Before he
elected to assist me, he gave his name alternately as Rocktop and Joe Baker.
His choice of these dozens heroes, sexual supermen, reflects his dominant
impression of himself. Mr. Wilmot sees himself as a hot, principled, streetwise
race man. He sings, dances and versifies extemporaneously for the everchang-
ing audience of the streets. He is an astonishing repository of street verse. Such
is the intensity of his willful, conscious withdrawal from regulated, conven-
tional life that the fixed abode is for him a dimly remembered, unlamented
thing of his remote past.*

My mama named me Melvin for a brother of hers that would have been
a preacher if it wasn't for those Louisiana crackers. My father named me
Gabr'l for one of them slavery-time prophets, and you better believe there
is some power in that name. Now, Melvin Gabr'l Wilmot, being a dark man
born of a dark woman, has seen him some dark days in this damn white
man's world! Now, it may be long, but it won' be long always. One day this
man and his time gon' die! God said in His Book of Revelations, by and
through the mouth of His servant, our prophet John, "We shall not all sleep,
but we shall all be changed at the last trumpet in a moment." He said, "In
the twinkling of an eye!" Now, I believe that thing!

What the Book mean is that the last shall then be first, and then the last which shall be made God's first shall then put on His immortality, never to cast it off again. Now, that wicked race that was first before we received glory shall be moved. It is the white man's time that soon shall be consumed, and in that day that shall follow his last day there shall be no whiteness, for the worm-colored people shall perish utterly. In that latter day even the color of corruption shall be no more. Now, you know whitefolks don't want to hear this truth and that is why they are always lying on us to us. Now, whitefolks and black will lie, but you know that whitefolks are the biggest liars ever shit 'hine a shoe heel.

Black people lies for a reason, but whitefolks just lies to be lying. They tell them *outrageous* lies! Whitefolks lie so much that they can' tell the difference now between a lie and the truth. Now, that is because they are livin' a lie. Everything they do they must lie about!

Now, you just take this helpin'-the-blind business. Now, if ol' Mose was runnin' that, he would say to hisself, "A blind man is poor, so he need everything a rich man need." So right away Mose would give that blin' man some money. Now, Mose know he ain't no God, neither no spurit, so the very nex' thing he gon' do is to ask that blind man or that blind woman what special things or advice they needs. Now, you know Mose don't give nobody shit and baptize it sugar. But these whitefolks is evermore giving people things they cannot use or do not want. If whitefolks do give you something you do want or can use, they makes sure to take it back. If they don't take it back, they fix it so they get more out of helpin' you than you get helped.

Now, for an instance you take this shit-assed travel number. Let's say you poor and I'm gon' try to help you get back up on your feet. So I say, "Here, my man, I'm gon' spote you to a trip to Chicago." Now, I like that fine, but I find out just as I get on this bus or train or whatsoever it might be that I got to take your cousin with me to Chicago. Now, what kind of help is that? Suppose I got things in Chicago that are none of your cousin's business? Suppose I want to go by myself? Where am I going to put this cousin of yours? Suppose I can't get nobody who wants to go where I wants to go? Why should I have to worry about this with all these other things I got to worry about? Any blind man or woman could have told them that that was a chicken-shit way to do that. That's why they didn't ask us, because they were just figurin' another way for them to use us to git over. That is the way they do everything they do. They got more than anybody out here and will spend a thousand to keep you or me from enjoyin' a dime. They are the sorriest things that call themself people I ever heard anything of. I mean, I wouldn't be that cheap and let anybody know it to save my soul. Now, that is the biggest difference between us and them. Poor as we are, damn it, we ain' cheap.

That's Mose for you, but whitefolks take back fifty cent out of every quarter they run you down to lay on you because they can't get up off nothin'. Your white man think he is part of his country and they helps each other in that. Now, your black man know that he is the only country that he has, so he got to help hisself.

I keeps myself clean and show some turn to folks that treat me like they was raised right. I'm not gon' say I'm proud of everything I have done down here, but there are some things you and nobody else could pay me to have anything to do with. I wants what everybody else wants out here, but I'll be damn if I'll make a fool out of myself to get something I think I want. I have tended some bar and scrubbed me some floor and cooked other folks' meals an' grew their food. Now, I was a seaman and I sailed some, Jack! And when I was seeing, I saw something and I could never see me enough of the world. I have seen Tokyo and Casablanca and I have seen Sydney and Stockholm. I got ol', I guess, but I don' feel ol'. I never cared much for anything but goin' from one place to some other place I wanted to know about. I make music in the street sometime now because that is the easiest thing that I can do that people will let me do. I still like these streets because something is still going on out here.

Hattie Lanarck

I thank God that I don't need anything from the white
man.

*The Lanarcks, Hattie and Gilbert—born in Texas and Delaware, respectively
—were members of the formidable company of prospective-interview donors
suggested by Janet McCrae well before I began my field research. I first met
them in the tiny, pleasant restaurant which Mrs. Lanarck and her friend Mrs.
Shields own. On any given day their customers must decide between two main
dishes and three desserts. "We can't do any more than that and do it right,"
Miz Hattie explained. Mrs. Lanarck's assessment of herself as "a person who
will do the right thing if I know what it is" is borne out by her life. "I'm not
no Muslim, but when I stopped eating pork I felt better. When I stopped
eating all meat I felt even better, and when I stopped eating sweets I felt like
a new woman!" She is a small, laconic woman with a well-earned reputation
for getting things done while most people are still talking about them.*

*Mr. Wilmot occasionally washes dishes for Mrs. Lanarck and Mrs.
Shields, who are his models for "straight women." He told me that "One of
them git-over boys ate six thirds of one of Miz Hattie's fish dinna's and stone
refused to pay and swore he would run if she called the man! Miz Hattie said,
'Well, son, if you think you faster than this hot grease, run on.' Jim, that dude
paid and shook!"*

I thank God that I don't need anything from the white man. Nothing he
has will do us any good and if you take anything from him, then you will
be as sorry as he is. White people were not always so, but they have made
themselves so by living sorry lives and now they are making us the same
way. But I will say that they don't put a gun to your head and make you
take this welfare. I warned my sister not to get on it, but nothing she must
do but get on welfare. The first thing that white man told her to do was to
take off her dress. Now, she had sense enough after that to get off that mess,
but a lot of these women didn't get off it and they are paying for it and you
and I are paying right along with them. All these half-raised children
running around everywhere but home, and all these sorry half what-I-
might-say men taking their hens down there while Farmer Brown throws

them their corn. All these half-raised children growing into half-raised so-called men who will cut my throat or yours for whatever they can get from us. All these grown women out here having their own little United Nations of families with no more husbands than a yard dog has shoes. You can call it whatever you want to, but it is just commonness and nothing else. I never thought that I would live to see black women with high school educations living like common barnyard dogs and trying to pretend that they thought that they was right to live like that! I am telling you this because I can see you are a decent black man, but I would be ashamed to tell a white man this. Too ashamed and mad.

I broke my back in the laundry and in the white man's kitchen to give my daughter everything I never had, and she was doing fine and then she said, "Mama, I can go to college free." But I said, "No, you can't. If the white man is giving you anything, it is not for your good." Oh, she was mad because I wouldn't let her get into the opportunity program. I told her, "We will save our money and buy our education just like we have paid for everything else we got that is worth bringing home." I told her to get the same kind of education that the white students get because they will not dilute their own milk if they can help it. Now, she heard me—sometimes her lip was stuck out, but she heard me. I told her, "You are bigger than me now, so I can't roll that lip up for you, but you listen to this old fool's advice for a year, and then if I'm wrong I'll let you roll up mine." Well, she will tell you that I was right.

Gilbert Lanarck

You can't just take anything this man hands out, because he has a hundred different kinds of chains.

Gilbert Lanarck is a fifty-five-year-old railroad worker, his wife's junior by one year. "I love to grow things," he told me as he showed me the trailing house plants and tubbed trees which render curtains superfluous for purposes of privacy in the Lanarck home. Mr. Lanarck doesn't really regret his inability to finish elementary school. "In school, they never would go far into what I'm interested in—I mean, the history of the black man here and everywhere else."

Reflecting upon his decision to assist me, he said, "I'm not blind, but I've done a little begging in my time and that's no way to make it. I really admire you for not sitting on your ass. If there's any way I can help you, just let me know." I am deeply indebted to both the Lanarcks for good advice, fine food and excellent personal documents.

When I was a kid I had to scuffle and I did any kind of work I could find and I didn't say anything about my demands or desires. When I was twelve a cracker woman worked me two days as hard as you would work any grown man for half a dollar. She promised me two dollars, but as she was counting out that money it went through her mind that she didn't really have to give me anything if she didn't want to. So she just renegotiated our contract right then and there! She remembered that moldy dog bread and watered-down watery sorghum syrup she threw at me and that headache pill she gave me when the sun got to me in her melon patch and a lot of other things, like a pair of raggedy ladies' draws she gave me for some reason, and she proceeded to do some fancy deduction right there in front of me and her husband. He was cracking his sides! Deep inside them, all whites are like that that I have ever known. The only white American that I ever could stand was John Brown, and they lynched him when my grandfather was fourteen years old. Now, he must have been a good man —I mean, a great man—because he was doing what was right even if he had to fight his own people. Now, that's the kind of man I would like to be.

Over there in the park some black kids were beating up this little Jew, and I got into it and made them stop because they were behaving just like crackers. I'd rather see our people dead than be like them. You know, those kids tried to whip my behind too! Now, I know that times have changed, but sometimes I don't know whether it's getting better or worse. All these little black kids I see out here got better clothes on their backs than the little white kids I see, but I sure don't like what they are putting in their heads. You hardly ever see a black child with his books, even on the way to school or coming from school. I think it comes too easy for many of us now. You can't just take anything this man hands out, because he has a hundred different kinds of chains, and before you know what happened to you, you could be the worst kind of slave in the world—I mean the kind that beg for their chains. I thank God that neither chick or child is on my back. I wouldn't mind helping a child of mine to do anything right, but when I see what's happening to so many of our young girls who are doing that state whore thing they call welfare and all these young men putting death in their arms and up their noses, I'm glad I never had a family!

When I was a child I was poor in ways that a lot of black people can't even understand now. The state should have helped me to help myself, but it should not have paid me to mess up myself and kids who never asked to come into this world! My mother died when I was ten years old. I was her fourteenth child and I am one of two of us. My mother told me that that thing between my legs was a great responsibility and a dangerous weapon if you don't use it right. She was right.

Kenneth Simmons

You push enough for the white man and you get a
Cadillac out of his small change.

Kenneth Simmons is a neighborhood handyman. He has mastered many trades and is in great demand as a painter, plumber, carpenter and mason. Families of greatest discretion seek his services. His neighbors are aware that he was in jail but attribute his incarceration to pardonable economic desperation.

I figure that anybody out here could be a prisoner. It depends on what a man has to go through. If he is pushed or driven the wrong way, he could do something that would get him sent to prison. It depends on the hardships and struggles that he has to go through.

Now, I've seen men come in who were doctors. They had money, but they just were not satisfied. They just were greedy to the extent that they just wanted too much. I saw another man come in who didn't have anything. He just tried to get something to feed his family. I think that any man who has any get-up about him is not going to see his family go hungry if there is anything he can do about it. If he's forced to steal, he'll go to jail. But this man who has everything already, I really don't understand why he would do something that would get him in jail. He's got position, he's got money, he comes from a well-to-do family—what more could he possibly ask for? Now, here's a poor man and he has nothing but ninety-nine kids with their noses running and their stomachs cramped and he can't get a job and can't get on welfare. I don't blame him if he goes out here and takes something. Now, I mean takes something to feed his kids—he doesn't go out there to hurt a soul, he just wants to feed his kids. Now, if he is caught they give that poor man ten to fifteen, but that rich man who is stealing from everybody, they give him two to three! Now, I would like to know why this man who has all and steals gets less time than a man who steals because he had nothing!

There's making a living and just living after you make that living. Now, white people will look out for their own people before they would do anything for me or you. A white man coming out of prison will be accepted quicker than the black man when it comes to making a living. I went through my little ordeal, and when I came out I had recommendations to go to jobs. I asked my parole officer to help me find employment. They would tell me, "We can't find you anything." Now, I'd be sitting right there in that office and see and hear white boys tell that same parole officer that they couldn't find a job, and, you know, they would tell that white boy, "Be down here tomorrow at this time and we'll have a job for you!" They figure that whatever a black could scrounge up is good enough for him. But now, a white man can walk in there and say, "I can't make it off a hundred dollars a week." They will find him something that gives him a hundred and fifty dollars a week or they will send him down to the welfare board for supplemental assistance. Now, me, if I'm making a hundred dollars a week and it's not enough to feed my family, I can't go down there and tell them, "That's not enough to feed my kids." You know the first thing they will say to me: "Well, I'm sorry, we can't help you." One time I went to domestic court before me and my first wife separated. I said, "Judge, Your Honor, I have a job and I am going to pay." So he asked me, "What is your salary?" I said, "I make something like eighty to ninety dollars a week take-home pay." "That's all you make?" he said. "When they come to paint my house, it costs me fifteen to sixteen hundred dollars!" Well, I just told him, I said, "Judge, Your Honor, you got to consider, you have a white painter painting your house." I said, "If I came to paint your house, would you give me fifteen or sixteen hundred dollars?" He looked at me and said, "What are you trying to be? Smart?" You see what I mean? They'll look out for their kind, but they are not going to look out for me.

There was a white fellow who gave me a card right down there at the medical center. So I went to join the union. I went up there to see the union man to see if I could get in. Now, right away that man told me that I would have to have three hundred dollars in cash. Now, I never heard of anybody paying no more than two hundred dollars, but *I* have got to pay three hundred! This is recently I am talking about. They think a black man is just supposed to make it out here no matter what. He can, too, if he's willing to crawl. But I have been crawling for a long time and I am pretty sick of that now!

Most black people, if they are in a position to help you, will do that. When I came home I can truthfully say I had the same friends out here that I left out here when I went in. These people were looking for me to offer me what jobs they knew about. All up and down the street it was the same. "Hey, man, come back to painting with us," they would say. These were black people. Some of them said, "Man, I would have come to visit you, but I didn't know whether you had my name down on the visitors' list." Some said, "Man, I gave your wife a little piece of money to get in there to you." And it was the truth. My friend the funeral director, he went before the board and told them, "You can give him a parole because one thing you don't have to worry about is how he will make it in the street because he has a job and a place to stay whenever he gets out." This is a big man and he stuck by me. Negroes who are in a position to do something for you, if they think anything at all about you, they will help you. It depends on you. If you come out here with the attitude that you don't want to do this and you don't want to do that, well then, the next thing you know people wouldn't want to be bothered with me.

Now, it also depends on what you were in there for. Like that crime that happened here about a year ago. Some young boy took a young girl up there and raped her and killed her over there in the park, and left her out there in the woods two or three days. Now, I didn't see no sense in that. She was a young child, about ten or eleven years old. Things like this I do not understand. Now, when I see him walking down the street, I don't want him to say a thing to me! I don't want him to even open his mouth to me because I say he is nothing but an animal! She was nothing but a baby, and anybody who would do something like that is nothing but an animal! Now, I wouldn't feel that way about a man who did something just because he flew off the handle and was sorry for it later, you know. I don't have anything against that man, because everybody gets hot sometime. If it is something you could say, "Well, I might have done that too," well, you can understand that. But I can't see taking no little kid to the woods and raping her and covering her up with leaves and knowing all the time that her family is looking for her. Now, I look at a bunch of dogs. Sometime they'll be fighting over a female, but you'll never see one of those dogs try to hurt that female dog. So you look at nature and you don't see what that cat did. I ask myself why a man would want to do a thing like that.

Now, as I said, I can understand a man going to jail for some things, but the way things are out here in these streets, I cannot understand why a man would go to jail for rape. Now, murder, well, he might be pushed into that or he might be trying to protect his own life and accidentally kill somebody. In some court cases they talk about a moment of insanity. That could happen. A man might be so mad he wouldn't know what he was doing, but he regrets it later. This is something I can understand. But these people who just stand out here cold-bloodedly and tell you, "Give me your money," and when you give it they shoot you—no, that is a hard criminal! Or these people that plan to do something they know they shouldn't do that they don't have to do, like these people out here pushing methadone and goof-balls and all that stuff.

I knew better than to get hooked up with that drug mess out in the street. You see, I saw what it did to a lot of fellows. From what I can see, it is just as bad to take methadone as it is to take the real thing. There are people out here in the street hitting each other over the head behind methadone, too. It's nothing but a drug. It might not be as powerful as the real stuff, but very few poor blacks buy the pure stuff anyhow. And we don't know, methadone might be just as potent as that five-dollar bag. How do we know? People are doing everything with methadone that they ever did with heroin.

If I were governor I would bring capital punishment back right now! Because I figure the younger people are really getting outrageous now because they know that no matter what they do they can't give them any more than a life sentence. And after fifteen years that life sentence is up. From what I could see in prison, the majority of prisoners believe that the death penalty would cut down crime, because you would know that if you go out there and take a life and you go before the judge and they are going to take yours, I believe most people would stop. I'm quite sure we didn't have as much murder when we had capital punishment. Before they stopped this capital punishment they were not killing these cops in New York like they are killing them now. Before, when you knew that if you stood trial you might go to the chair for murder, people cooled it. But now all you got to do is say the wrong word and somebody is going to want to kill you! If I was governor I'd bring it back. People who committed brutal murders would have to face that chair—I mean, like those people who took a man down here. Now, he gave those fellows the money and still they turned around and blew his brains out! Now, does that make any sense? Down there at the liquor store the man told them, "Go ahead, take the money," and they turned around and shot him anyhow! Now, what kind of sense does that make? Look at Mr. Goldman. They killed Goldman. Wasn't he a nice man? I used to go in there sometime and say, "Mr. Goldman, I'm a little short of money right now, but I need a little coffee to take with me to the hospital." He would say, "I know you're good for it. You come in here practically every morning and get a dozen coffees to take to the hospital." He liked kids and he would stand out in front of his shop and talk to the kids. They blew him away!

If I was the governor I would stone bring it back and I would make a habitual addict serve life without parole also. A pusher caught two or three times selling to these kids out here—put him in there and forget about him! Give him some time and hang the key up. Don't even go back there to see if he's all right! Because he is the one who is really killing the youngsters out here today. Drugs are messing up the streets. You can't go out here on the avenue before some jive drug addict come trying to snatch you off that corner! Now, if you are standing there by yourself, you will end up being hurt. If it was up to me I'd make a law that would make it mandatory for all kids of a certain age to be off the streets, and I'd stop that law which lets these eighteen-year-olds go into bars. That is one law I would break up. Twenty-one, all right, but eighteen-year-olds should not be served or even allowed in a bar. They have run most people out of the taverns, these eighteen-year-olds! They come in there and ask you for a nickel or a dime to buy a bottle of beer, and if you don't have it they want to knock you in the head. Remember how crowded that tavern down the street used to be? You couldn't get in the door, but them days are long gone! People don't even go to the movies anymore unless they go in pairs; you stand a better chance in a group. They don't know who is the cop these days. Because they don't know who is who, they'll back up off you. They'd rather mug a single person. They're afraid the other one might hollah if they only grab one. They'll grab you and make you turn your pockets inside out. They use any weapon, from their foot and fist to a stick, knife or gun. Most of these young boys out here will have a knife, but they very seldom carry a gun unless they are planning something really big.

The majority of these business people out there today are going to keep a gun and I do not blame them! Over there where I was staying they killed a butcher. They robbed a bank over there. They ran the wnite meat market out of business over there! Now that the Negroes have taken it over, all those blackfolks got guns up under those counters. And if they shoot somebody who is coming in there to rip them off, they should dismiss the charges. Now, that is not what is happening. Things are really crazy because they are giving people time for protecting themselves! He's getting time for having the pistol, but yet and still, that man has worked eight hours in his store trying to feed his family. And here comes somebody who don't want to work even if you give him a job, but he's going to come and collect what this man worked for. He should be ripped off! And that storekeeper should not do a day for ripping him off; he is supposed to take that dude's life. Now, you offer that cat something, try to help him, and still he's going to come back and try to take all you have and maybe shoot you, too. No, he needs to die! Now, you have to think like they think. Anytime a man comes in there and says, "Give me your money," you should go to shooting! A lot of people are doing that because if they don't they might lose their money and their lives, too!

These streets are very unsafe. Don't you be out there by yourself after the sun goes down. If you don't have people to help you, it is rough. I know practically everyone I run into out there. If I don't know them by name, I know them by sight. I don't walk close to nobody's alleyway. When I leave here tonight I'll get in the middle of the street and walk. That way, if you want me you will have to come to me to get me. I get right out there in the middle so I can see the scene. The bus is not safe after certain hours. Yeah, let me tell you, things are bad out here. The stores and almost everything else close at five o'clock.

And these young people and a lot of the older ones are all Cadillac crazy and money-struck! Now, the average colored boy or Negro girl out here don't talk about anything accept maxi coats and Cadillacs and pocketfuls of fifty-dollar bills, and the only way they can get it is to handle the dope. If they are not into heroin, they are trying to move five pounds of reefer. These are the same cats that are out here talking all that revolutionary junk and pushing that stuff for the white man. You can believe that's who they are working for. The white man brings it in here and they push it onto black kids. That's where it is! You push enough for the white man and you get a Cadillac out of his small change, which he will lay on you. That's the deal!

If you go out there right now, I'll bet you every corner is loaded—no grownups, nothing but young kids out around the projects. They are all in the hallways. You can walk in those hallways and the smell of reefer is so strong you can cut it with a fork! And those that ain't smoking are shooting! All out in the parking lots, everywhere. You go out there the next morning and you'll find half of those cars have lost wheels. These kids have stolen them and sold them to buy drugs. People are afraid even to park their cars! To clean this up, you would have to lock up a hell of a lot of people!

SEX
AND WORK

Hard work don't have a thing between its legs.
Nancy White

There is a woman's understanding and there is a man's understanding. And there is wisdom.
Yula Moses

Nancy White is known to many of her neighbors by the principal nickname Miss Scrappy, but her persistence is always couched with the requisite degree of turn. Mrs. Moses is generally described as a "righteous" or "holy" woman. Some of her neighbors still rely upon her knowledge of the black folk herbal tradition and her profound familiarity with the Bible for medical and spiritual aid. She says, "The street is a pit," but does not appear in the least daunted by her responsibility for guiding her daughter through that perilous labyrinth.

Nancy White

When you lose control of your body, you have just
about lost all you have in this world!

*Miss White is an agile, cheerful cricket of a woman from Tennessee whose
amiability, vivacity and level-headedness have won her an enviable place in
the esteem of her discerning neighbors. The youthful quality of her clear
mezzo voice and the constant motion of her diminutive person produce an
impression of youth. She holds what she calls weekly tavern court in her house
when she and the eleven members of her gospel-singing society meet, generally
on Fridays. Then her passion for cold ale, sage barbecue and lucid, often
humorous reminiscence illumines the small hours of the morning. Her ability
to remain politely but resolutely on the right side of the often tenuous line
separating jollity and grossness has made her popular as well as respected
among her neighbors. She is the exemplar* par excellence *of the highest status
that core black culture can accord—that of the cool, dealing individual. She
is an able, affable princess of good fellowship who may be relied upon to make
every effort to give as good as she is given.*

My father was one of these people that always had a little saying for
everything, and he used to say that the only two people who were really free
was the white man and the black woman. He used to say that all the time.
When I got up some size I used to think about some of the things he said
—you know, I would try to figure out what he was trying to say by saying
those things. Some of these things were just funny to me. I didn't think that
they were true, but I wondered why my father thought that they were true.
He was wrong about that, you know—the only people that are free in this
world are the people that can tell other people what to do and how they
have to do it.

Now, I am a black woman and I am not free and I don't know any black
woman that is, nor any black man, either. White women are not free, either,
but most of them think they are and that is because that white man pats
them wherever he feels like patting them and throws all that moonlight
boogie-joogie on them and they eat it up! It's killing them, but they eat it
up and beg their doctor for a prescription so they can get more.

Now, you could ask yourself why that was—I mean, why my father, who was together most of the time, why did he think such a stupid thing? He could see me busting the white man's suds and mopping the white man's floors and minding the white man's kids, and he knew damn well that I didn't want to do any of these things! He was out here working all types of hours and taking all types of stuff from the same white man, not because he wanted to but because he had to. One day I just asked him why he said that thing. And he told me that when I was a little older I would understand, but that was nowhere near good enough for me.

You see, I have worked for money since I was nine years old. I am seventy-three years old and I still can't say what I want to do and do that and I still have to do a little days work, you know, because I am poor. I am lucky in my health and if you could see me you would be surprised that I am seventy-three, but I am and I am not one of these "old Miss Young" people to hide my age. I told you that because you couldn't see me. But you know that my voice is very young-sounding too. My hands are the oldest-looking thing about me. My hands and feet.

When I was just a little girl I used to wonder about things that people would say. That's how they tried to teach you then. They'd show you what they could and teach you what they showed you. Now, I think I learned that way better than I did in school. Now, I didn't have very much schooling because we were all poor and had to work whenever the man would let us lug it. I'm going to tell you the way it really was because I can remember it! I mean, right is right and it don't wrong nobody wrong and I think we ought to tell this thing like it really is out here! That life in the country wasn't so such-a-much. I know because I have lived in the country and in towns and cities, and I know!

At the bottom of most of the trouble in this world is that white man. Now, he makes living anywhere as near hell as the devil wants to get. That is near enough, right? Now, I know this and I am not ashamed to say it. The fact about that is that I *want* to say that. Now, if that man was my brother and owned me, I might not want to say that. If that man was bringing me pretty hats and nice shoes and getting somebody like me to look after his children, now, if he was doing all those things and I was too lazy to get up off my do-nothing-stool and content myself with what I could do for myself and my children, well, if that was the kind of person I was, I'd just bite my lip and shut my mouth. Now, *that* is your white woman. She can come into that kitchen and tell me to do twice as much work as she ever dreamed of doing in a bad dream. But, you know, those slavery foreparents in a way were freer than Miss Anne in her kitchen or in her fancy bedroom with the nice lamps and the little tables and the fancy phones. See, what I mean to say is that the slave didn't need no master, but the master couldn't no way make it without his slaves. See, those masters put those plantations on paper. They still do that in this slavery of today.

Every time you look around, this man got some kind of report. Now, I used to buy these reports, you see. Right over there on my shelf you could see them. That Warren thing and that Kerner report. I have little pamphlets about the government land and about everything I hear about that I want to find out more about. Now, I spent four, almost five years in school. I don't want to tell no lie, it was just about four years in school. Then they thought much more of the white man's crops than they did of keeping the schools open. You didn't go to no school if they needed you in the fields. It was the white man that decided all about that. I love to learn things, but like I say, I don't put much trust in paper, but I like to have those books. They look pretty and they smell pretty to me.

My father was a carpenter and all those people, white and black, got him to work for them because he knew what he was doing. That's how it worked with that plantation. Now, if I come in here and give you a map or a book that shows you how you should do something, that don't mean a thing until somebody does something with that map or book. Did you ever think that all these beautiful old houses was built by these slaves that wasn't supposed to know doodleesqua'? Now, how did they do that? Well, they must have known more than their masters tell us that they knew. Now, that black slave and his brothers that had to go out there and pull stumps and plant trees and gardens and build houses, they were doing what the white man dreamed about but was too lazy to do hisself!

Now, when you make bread or a cake or something like that, sometimes it just won't go the way those books say it will go. So then you have to do a little trick with that food to make it come out right. To do that, you got to be smarter than the person that wrote that book. Now, I have followed some of these receipts exactly and they did not come out right. I'm a grown woman, so I don't play. When I tell you I followed that thing, you can believe that I followed that thing! I did just what it say do, just like it said to do it, but it still didn't come out right.

One time, me and my madam (that's what they used to call the white women we worked for. They used to love to hear you call them that. You had to call these little prissy white boys master this and master that and give them long, fancy handles to their rotten names), me and this white woman had to make this light bread that was very special. This lady married a Southern cracker, but she was from someplace in Massachusetts, so she would get right in there and show you how to do something you didn't know how to do. She was prejudiced, too, but she just didn't come right out with it like your Southern whites do. I heard her husband tell her to call me a nigger because that's what I was used to. She called me Mrs. Tucker—that was my name then. But the others told her not to do that. Anyway, we had to make this bread and the fool stuff just wouldn't come out right. Now, she just kept on making it the same way and every time it would come out the same. I figured that if she wanted to do that, it was her kitchen. Now, I went home and made this dern bread and it came out right. The book was wrong! To make that bread with what we had, you just had to do other things and you had to know something about bread. Now, this Frenchman might be right in France—maybe they have different kinds of flour—but it didn't make any sense to just keep on making this bread just like the book said if the bread didn't come out right. Now, I knew I did what that Frenchman said I should do, and if I did that right and it came out wrong, then the Frenchman and not me had to be wrong. Now, am I right or wrong?

Well, you know why that makes sense to you? You know that a book can be wrong, but most white people don't know that. Those whitefolks just gave up on that light bread and made something else. They wanted to make it for the old lady, Mrs. Miller's mother. She had lived across the water and when she came back there they wanted her to have this bread. So Mrs. Miller told her how hard we had worked on this bread and it didn't come out right no matter how hard we tried. And do you know, that old devil looked at me and said, "Nancy knows how to do it." Mrs. Miller told her that we had both tried and it didn't work and if we couldn't do it together, she knowed I couldn't do it. But then old Mrs. Devil looks me dead in the eye and said, "You can do it, can't you, Nancy?" I said no, but she said, "Nancy, that's a lie and you are a liar." Well, when they cleared the table Mrs. Miller came out to the kitchen and asked me about the bread, and I said I thought I knew how to but I wasn't sure. So she said, "Let's try to make it Tuesday," and we did and it came out fine that time and every other time we ever made it, and we made it a lot because everybody liked that light bread. I made some today and if you don't think I'll kill you, I'd like for you to try some. I haven't buried nobody yet from my pots!

But now, I told you that to show you what I am going to teach you. Now, I wouldn't say that to a white man because he think I can't teach him a thing. When my father used to say that thing about the black woman and the white man being free, he was generally mad. White men were always messing with black girls. Sometime a black woman would have to move to someplace way away from there just so some white man or boy couldn't get his hands on her. Now, the white women saw this and they didn't like it, but they knew better than to stand up in Old Cracker's face and tell him that he was wrong. Now, he wasn't simple, so he knew that he wasn't right, but he figured like this: "If I want to do it and you can't stop me, well then, sad on you!" My father would go round the house with his lip poked out just like a child whenever something like that would happen. Now, he did that because he was as helpless as a child when it came to something like that. Lots of people didn't have money to be sending their daughters places. Lots of folks didn't have no place to send them to and couldn't send them nowhere because they needed them at home so bad. I am not telling you no fairy story. I saw these things happen and they happened to me. One of my best girl friends got sick from the falling-out sickness and the doctor that was supposed to cure her gave her a baby. He was a devil when it came to that kind of carrying on. A lot of those white men would get after these young black girls and those girls just didn't know what they should do. Now, I have worked for some nice people and some rotten ones. I've had to ask some hands off me and I've had to just give up some jobs if they got too hot behind me. Now, I have lost some money that way, but that's all right. When you lose control of your body, you have just about lost all you have in this world!

In one job I had I could see this young boy who was just able to pee straight making up his mind whether he was going to try me. I told the woman some lie and got my money and got out of there fast! Now, this woman's sight and her hearing was fine, just as good as mine, so she had to see what that young boy was up to! But do you think she tried to correct him? No, she just saw it and didn't see it. She knew why I left, but she didn't do anything. Now, she was all right as whitefolks go, but she couldn't do anything about that because she had spoiled that little fool boy of hers, and her husband wouldn't do anything but side with the boy. He might *say* thus-and-so, but everybody knew what he would *do*. All those young boys that was always bothering us had fathers and mothers and sisters, too.

When you come right down to it, white women just *think* they are free. Black women *know* they ain't free. Now, that is the most important difference between the two. White men are free to tell everybody else what to do. But now, they are too lazy to see it get done, so they ain't but so free, neither, but they are a hell of a lot freer than anybody else out here! The white women would be all right if they would just stop paying any attention to them sorry menfolks of theirs. This white man is tricking all the women and beating half of them.

Now, when I was under my parents I did what they said do. Most of that was what I could see that I should do. But you know how people are. Every now and then you want to do something when *you* want to do it and not when you are *told* to do it. Now, you might be wrong, but you still feel like doing it when you know they don't want you to do it. Now, in the old days they would tell you nice once and then they would warm your behind if you didn't do it. I used to think that was hard because I was a fool then. I told you that we didn't have much, so we all had to work and we put our little money together and tried to spell able. But that was hard and my parents had to see that that little bit got stretched as far as you could stretch it. I could see that, but sometime I would just get unnecessary, as the old folks say, and show out for myself. I knew that my father and my mother were denying themselves more than anybody, but I just would not see the truth sometimes. It was there for me to see, but I just turned my back on it!

The first job I had I had to clean and take care of some little children. Well, I guess I tried to act like the oldest girl I was taking care of. Her name was Nancy too, but she was white. She would break real bad with her daddy and stomp her foot and just get all out of hand. Well, I didn't do that because I wanted to still go on living, but I would ask for things I had no business with and couldn't afford. My father tried to get some of the things I wanted, like soft candy—wasn't nothing hard candy could do for me then! But my mother warmed my bottom and she was a bottom-warmer from her heart! Then she told me that we was doing the best we could and not to do "every fool thing you see Nancy Cole do!" And when she showed me she taught me. That's how I started to know what I know now.

My mother used to say that the black woman is the white man's mule and the white woman is his dog. Now, she said that to say this: we do the heavy work and get beat whether we do it well or not. But the white woman is closer to the master and he pats them on the head and lets them sleep in the house, but he ain' gon' treat neither one like he was dealing with a person. Now, if you was to tell a white woman that, the first thing she would do is to call you a nigger and then she'd be real nice to her husband so he would come out here and beat you for telling his wife the truth.

No, my mother beat me for my own good and I was a child then. But let me tell you one thing that you can believe if everything down here turns out to be a lie: Nancy Sawyer Tucker White is not going to have no man beating on her after she is out from under her parents' rule! That is my law and I live by that law first! Now, I have been married two times and both of my husbands were nice men, but they had one thing wrong—no man don't go to bed with no child. If you gon' treat me like I was old enough to *have* children, you cannot treat me like I *was* a child myself! Now, that's it! James Tucker was a fine man! He worked hard, I'll say that for him. But he made the mistake of putting his hands on me like I might have been his child, not his wife. Now, at the time I was carrying his child. I told him that had to be the first and last time that anything like that happened. He was a good man, but he was weak—I mean, he let people outside his home tell him how to run his home. Now, he was lucky because I worked right along with him and we was making a nice home together. We was even saving a little money! All right. Everybody was sorry and we made up a little sweet bread and swore it wouldn't be that way again.

Now, when I swear that I'm gon' do something, I mean that thing! Now, a couple of years later, nothing James Tucker must do but to go out and get drunk and lose everything he and I both had. Well, I knew that he drank when I married him, so I said, "All right, honey, we'll start again." But, you see, he got the devil in him and hit me again. Now, there wasn't any reason for him to do that and when he did it, it sobered him up just like I had poured a bucket of spring water over him. I have not seen him since and don't want to see him! That's why I came up here, because I wanted to put some states between me and my children and James Tucker. That was in nineteen and twenty-two and I have been here ever since.

Now, quiet as it's kept, these white men try to rule their wives like that too. And if they can't beat them, then they toles them with nice things. If my husband had encouraged my children to go out here and treat some woman the way white boys have tried to treat me, I would leave or he would have to leave. But that's because I do not need a man to feed myself. White women don't, either, but they think that they do, so they just put up with all this stuff that they should not stand for. Now, just like I have had to get out here and hit it, they could too.

Now, I understand all these things from living. But you can't lay up on these flowery beds of ease and think that you are running your life, too.

Some women, white women, can run their husbands' lives for a while, but the most of them have to take low when that devil tells them to and they have to see what he tells them there is to see. If he tells them that they ain't seeing what they know they *are* seeing, then they have to just go on like it wasn't there! I have seen this with my own two eyes, so I know what I am talking about. Now, me, I can't live that way. I don't have to live that way. I have always been able to put what I had in a bag, get myself and my children together and put my foot in the path to somewhere else. You hear them saying that thing about living on dirty water being better than being treated like a dog. Well, I mean that thing and most black women can be their own boss, so that's what they be.

I've worked for many white women and most of them did not have the sayso any more than I did. Not as *much* as I did sometimes. If I had been the kind of woman that they might find in bed with their husbands, there wouldn't have been anything that most of them could do about that commonness but maybe get their husbands to fire me. Now, what they *should* do is to fire these worthless white boy-men they married to and get out here and get it just like we have to do. But laziness and all that trash them white men talk to them keeps them running along beside these no-good men of theirs just like little yard dogs. Now, that won't work with black women because black men don't have any more than we do. How I'm gon' boss you if you got just as much as I got?

Now, I might be nice to you and not call you out of your name just because I was raised right, but you can't keep me barefoot if I can buy my own shoes, and I have got a closetful of shoes which Nancy White went downtown and bought for herself. Now, I might even buy you a pair of shoes, or we might buy each other a pair of shoes or something we both need or something one or the other might need. But what I'm trying to say is that there is a very few black women that their husbands can pocketbook to death because we can do for ourselves and will do so in a minute!

There ain't nothing in this world I cannot do for myself. I told that to my second husband one time and he laughed and told me I couldn't get no baby by myself. Well, I told him that I could get just as far as he could with that and he fell out. Now, that is the beautiful truth. Men don't need women and women don't need men for nothing but getting children. Now, most of these men out here are not on strike. They will be evermore glad to give you just as much nature as you need. I used to think that children just got here, but when I found out that they got here because folks went out here and got them, I made up my mind that I was not going to do anything to get any until I could look after them and me. Well, I was a liar. I listened to all that moonlight boogie-joogie and before a hoecake could make a crust, there I was with two children. Well, I promised God that if He would help me through that little tight, that I was going to think about what I did a long time before I done it. Now, that's what I did do.

I have worked for money for more than sixty-four years. I know what is out here and that's what I'm talking about! Now, I wouldn't say what

I just said to everybody. You have to tell some and keep some with white-folks and most blackfolks too. I told a white woman that one time and she just worried me to death trying to get me to act like she was black. Now, if I called her name you might know her. She was no friend of mine, but she thought she was. But if you are not a friend to yourself, you sure God can't be a friend to nobody else. And the changes she went through with that sorry mess of breath and britches she called a man. Well! I wouldn't have believed it if I hadn't been there and seen it myself! Now, I never got into that with her. She was always trying to get me to talk about their business, but that was the last thing I wanted to get mixed up in. I could see that she didn't mean herself much good, so I knew she couldn't mean me any!

Now, her husband was one of these white men that you just couldn't get away from. That devil was always out there in the kitchen pinching you and trying to get as deep into your apron as you was. That whole family was very strange. When the daughter and the two boys were great grown teenagers, they walked around that house with no more clothes on their back than that dog over there. Now, they learned that from their parents. One day that woman told me that she wouldn't be mad if I let her husband treat me the same way he treated her. I told her that *I* would be mad and *damn* mad at that if he tried to treat me like I was just as married to him as she was. I had to threaten that devil with a pot of hot grease to get him to keep his hands to hisself! They taught all that filth to their children and that was a mess. But those children could have been just as nice as you want to see children be if they had been raised like they should have been. I have had to put up with some stuff on jobs, but I can tell you that that comes from letting these white men have the sayso. It's just like they was a snake looking at these white women and telling them more lies than Carter got pills, and they just eating all that mess up. You see, a woman ain't nothing but a woman, but that snake has made so many women think that they ain't able to do this or do that. They supposed to be so delicate that they ain't got sense enough to look after themselves.

I saw my mother do every kind of work my father did and more work than I ever seen any white man do. Now, she was a little woman and it might take her longer to get what she wanted to do done, but she did not really need to have a man to live. Hard work don't have a thing between its legs. I know because there ain't nothing I don't know about real hard work.

My father one time near 'bout beat the black off my brother because he came home and found us fighting. Now, when my mother came in and found out about that, she started 'fendin' and provin' and found out the truth about that thing. She made me give my brother my meat. It wasn't nothing but fatback, but in them days meat was meat. Then she whipped me because she found out what happened. That fight was my fault from start to finish. I didn't think my brother would hit me, so I just kept hitting him, but he got tired of that after a while. He even went out into the little yard garden to get away from me, but I went right out there and started after him again. Now, my father came out there just in time to see him pass the first lick. That's all he had to see, so he made my brother get those switches and he whipped him till *I* cried. Now, if I had not ran to my father crying and made it look like it was all my brother's fault, maybe my father would have done what my mother took the trouble to do—you know, to get to the bottom of that whole mess. But when I saw my father I just started to cry because the devil was in me. I was wrong, but I did not care. My brother was a child just like I was, but my father didn't listen to him. I knew that he wouldn't. Now, that was boogie-joogie too, and my mama knew it. Now, that was whipped out of me, but most white women whip that *into* their daughters.

You see, a person is a meat person. But I have seen so many white women think that they are so much that they might just as well be nothing. They start thinking that that perfume is a part of them and that they are just as fine as them fancy night things they wear. Well, the same thing is under there that is under all them flannel ones. But that man tells them that they are so special that they can't let their little feet—that ain' no smaller than mine—touch the ground. Now, while he is feeding them all that moonlight boogie-joogie, he is out here getting just as deep into black women's underwear as his law and his ropes and his pocketbook will let him. He give them all that "Oh, darlin' " and "Sugar, I love you" stuff, pat them on the head and give 'em another child for me to raise and then wipe his hands and go out here and bother some black woman. Now, he don't bother with all that "Oh, darlin' " stuff with me because he know that I know him and so he wants to talk nothing but business to us. He told hisself, or his wife or mother told him, that I'm common anyway, so all he is supposed to do is snap his fingers and we are supposed to roll over. Well, I'm here to tell you that I have never been any man's yard dog and most of the black women I know do not go that way, either.

When I was just a child, I could just get away with more than my brothers and boy cousins that might be with us. I remember that my cousin that was just a child herself was staying with us because she was going to have some number man's baby. Now, like I say, she was just a little bit older than me. One time she said that my brother was bothering her. You know what I mean, they was both just getting up some size. So I guess he tried to talk to her about getting between the corn rows, on the way home from church I think it was. Now, nothing she must do but go and tell my father, and that led to a whole heap of shooting and cutting, you can believe me! Now, that thing taught me a lesson. She could have said no and he could have had some sense and let her alone. But, you see, this sex thing is not just men and women doing what they feel like doing and then just going on about they business. That's what it should be, but that is not what it is.

You see, people just love to trick each other, but you can trick until you get tricked. Now, I am a woman, so I know that most women tricks themselves. If they didn't, then these men couldn't talk holes in their clothes and treat them like they was children or simple-minded. I know that every trick that was ever pulled on me that worked, worked because I was fool enough to let it work. You know that joke about the gorilla in the ladies' room of the tavern that the drunk white man swore was a black woman? Well, there is a lot of truth in filth. That joke is a parable if people would look at it. You remember that I told you that my mother told me that we was the white man's mule and white women was his yard dogs. Well, that's what it is all about. You know that women ain't nothing but women. Now, you know that no woman is a dog or a mule, but if folks keep making you feel that way, if you don't have a mind of your own, you can start letting them tell you what you are.

Now, women are women, just like I told you and just like you know. Men ain't nothing but meat men too. But these whitefolks plays all these tricks on people and makes the weak-minded think that a woman is better than other women—you know, I mean the white woman and the woman that looks white. These yallas try to play Miss Anne and Miss Anne is just playing the tricks which her brothers and uncles and all them want her to play. The lighter a woman is, the more like a angel she is supposed to be. Now, you know that God is supposed to keep his angels from this sex thing. You remember I told you that when you get under all those fancy bathing suits and nightgowns you will find the same thing under there. But the white man, who knows just as well as I do what's under there, come out here with this angel boogie-joogie. He puts wings on some of these women, but he treats them all the same. You know that thing about "If you white you all right, and if you brown you can hang aroun', but if you black git back"? Well, that's how the white man treats women, but he wants the same thing from them that have to git back that he wants from those he says are all right. Now, to the black woman he acts like a devil and to the white woman he acts like he think she is too good. He treats her like her shit don't stink, as the old foreparents used to say. I have to tell you like I understands. I don't have but a few years of school, but I can hear and there is not a thing wrong with my mind! I understand what's going on out here because it has gone over me!

When they have this Miss America mess on, I never pays any attention to it, and now that they have some brown or yalla fool up there showing everything she should hide, that make me even madder than before. In the country that's just how they buys cows. Well, a woman ain't no cow and if she don't have no more sense than to think she is, then I don't personally give her one bit of credit! I don't know why they don't just bring in the auction block and just sell 'em altogether! I wish I'd catch a child of mind acting that common. I'd miss her America for her! But, you see, all that comes from this man out here telling these white women all that off-the-wall boogie-joogie about some women being angels and some other women being mules. White women believe all that stuff, so they don't want to see that that man is just patting them on the head and doing the same thing to them that he is doing to everybody else out here!

I worked for this family and the oldest girl got married and they had one of these big old weddings, but things got real tight round there because they had this thing about the woman obeying, you know. Well, I think they took that out. Anyway, they got married, but it don't matter what it says on that paper. She had to obey him whether it was written down or not. She didn't have nothing of her own and was too lazy to work, so she had to obey somebody! Now, the bathroom she got was bigger than my kitchen and dining room. But, you see, the difference is that my house is my house because I pay. Ain' nothing of hers really hers. That white boy told her that quicker than a hoecake can make a crust. Now, she had her college and her trips and her car and even a boat, but twan' none of that really hers.

People can do things together, they can even marry. You can work with people if those people will work together. Now, my second husband, being human, had his faults. He was sickly—now, that's something you can't help in this world. When he was working he made good money and he could hold on to his money. We worked together and it was not *my* money and *his* money, we worked together. Now, all I ask is that you do right when you can and that's just what he did. Anybody who knew Rupert White would give that to him. When he would get sick, there was no ifs, ands and buts about it. Like the Bible says, "Faithful servant, take your rest." Now, we was both faithful servants to the other. But by then I had got some sense in my head. I knew better than to marry color or hair or big car. Rupert was about the darkest man I know of. There was a time when nobody his color could do a thing for me. Now, that shows you how dumb I was. I learned the hard way that you can't make it on looks. If you are good you look good to Nancy White.

Rupert went down there to his people when he got real sick and didn't say a word. I knew where he had gone because he didn't have no place to go but there. I grabbed me a armload of airplane, I want you to know, and brought Rupert Alexander White right back here to this house and he stayed here with me until he died. If you do right by Nancy, Nancy will do right by you. It really hurt me that he would think that I would just let him stay down there. I didn't go round here and loud-talk Rupert in the streets, because he never did that to me. He was a man and I was a woman and we could have just done for ourselves, but we decided to do for each other, so we did. Now, if Rupert had aped up—there was nothing that he did for me in his best days that I could not do for myself. Don't get me wrong, I know that thing work two ways. When Rupert was up on his feet, he could do anything for hisself that I could do for him. I have not poisoned anybody yet, but Rupert was a better cook than I am. He could iron a shirt so it would look just like the Chinee had just turned it loose! Now, you know that there are always uku folks right ready and willing to break up any marriage, so either one of us could have got some man or woman to breathe in our face. But we got along nice because we looked after each other.

There was a boy in my home that looked just like Rupert and he really liked me, but I actually got mad when he talked to me. That's how dumb

I was! You know, I got madder at him for being mannerable to me than I did at Donald Wright for inviting me between them corn rows! Sometimes I still can't believe I was so dumb. Now, I was not the only one that was that dumb, but I'm trying to tell you how things really are out here. But, you see, when you are dumb you are too dumb to know how dumb you are. Now, this is the truth. When you are really dumb you think you are smarter than anybody! I know that. You see, just like I said, "Well, so-and-so is black," a white person could say, "Well, Nancy is yellow." All that don't count for nothing except in the mind of a fool. Don't nothing down here make such a big fool of itself about color like people do. Ain' nothing so simple about the male and the female as people, either.

Back in my home, the whitefolks love to tell these stories about colored preachers and bears. Now nobody knows whether these are lady bears or men bears and nobody is fool enough to care. Now, when they put Daniel in this lions' den, do you think he cared whether they was lady lions or men lions? That is because a lion is a lion and a bear is a bear, and that is the way it should be with people. Now, you remember I told you about that fight me and my brother had. Now, my father didn't know it, but I started that fight because I thought I could win it. I thought I could win it because I didn't think he would hit me back. Now, that is wrong. It is wrong to start fights, but it's wronger to think you can win because you ain' gon' git hit. Now, that's how the women think today. That's how white women think. A boy would not have thought he was going to win because the other boy in the fight was not gon' hit him. I have found out that most men don't mind hitting. They just say that they wouldn't hit a woman, but they don't really mean that. They say that they will treat you like a angel, but they don't really mean that. Why should they mean it? That is just that moonlight boogie-joogie. Now, lady and men lions and bears don't break bad with each other because that man lion has not told hisself some lie about the female lion being weak and delicate. Now, you might say, "Well, the women are weaker than the men"—I don't know that you would say that, but you might. But if they weaker they just as wise. Man is weaker than a bear or a lion or lots of things out here, but he is wiser, so those things are afraid of people. I am afraid of people myself.

Now, those Vietnam people are smaller than American women or men, but they are doing all right. Size don't mean nothing nowdays because I can go to the drugstore and make myself strong enough to deal with most people. I can leave people alone if they'll let me, and if they won't, then I can do something about that, too, and have done it! But if I put you on this queen-sized bed and put all this fancy night clothes on you and let you have all this perfume and tell you that your time can't be beat, so you just lay up here and be here whenever I git back, you will make a fool of your own self!

My first husband used to tell me, "Oh, baby, I don't want you in the tavern because that's no place for you." Well, I used to go along with all that boogie-joogie. I scrubbed and cooked and busted suds at home and then went out here and did the same thing for white women. I had two children and kept them just like they should have been kept. Now, I should have done all that, but I was doing all that for James Tucker. We should have been doing that together or not at all, or I should have just gone and done it for myself.

Now, my second husband asked me if I wanted to go to the tavern with him and I was highly insulted! I have never been nowhere near drunk in my life. I love beer, but I would not make a fool of myself with nothing! Now, I haven't been in a tavern since Rupert died, but that's because of the way these streets are out here. If I felt like going to a tavern, I would get myself down those stairs and go to one! I believe in knowing some of everything out here. Rubert said, "Baby, you grown so you do what you want to do, but I enjoy myself as much in the tavern as I do in church. If you don't like it ain' nobody gon' chain you to that stool. You better get out here and see what's happening." Well, I told him that I would go if he wanted me to go, but I had to find out if Lucy would keep the children. He said, "Bring them with you this time if you want to." Well, I couldn't stand that, but I got Lucy to keep them and I went to this tavern. Now, you'da thought that I was crossin' the ocean or something! We went to movies and taverns and churches together. One day Rupert said, "Where are you going to take me?" So I thought about that and I found out about different kinds of restaurants and the circus and music programs.

I know now why he made me do that—because he wanted me to get out here and find out some things for myself. Now, he would help me, but he wanted me to be able to help myself because he knew that I would probably be here when he was gone. Now, that's the kind of man Rupert was. He would not deal in boogie-joogie. I came close to leaving him, although I had had a husband that lied to me all the time. See, the devil was in me and I wanted to hear all that old boogie-joogie. Sometimes you can be mad with people for doing you good. I used to break bad with Rupert just like I did with my brother. He said, "Nancy, you have been raised once and I am not your father! I am not going to hit you and I'm not going to live with anybody who would hit me." I knew he meant that thing and I stopped behaving like that.

You know, I'm a different person than I was the first twenty-seven years of my life. I am lucky too. My son told me when he was eighteen that he didn't like to see me sitting up in the tavern. "Well," I said, "don't come in here when I'm in here, then." I told him that I knew that what he *meant* was he didn't want me to see what he was doing in that tavern. Now, I am sick and tired of seeing these women raise their sons to be their fathers, and Nancy did not do that! If there is something I can do for any child of mine, I might do that thing if it's what I think should be done. They help me and they should because God knows I did what I should for them! But I know that "supposed to" don't get it. I know that I have to look out for myself.

You are right to pay people for helping you. Now, nobody is going to buy no farm that way, but it's a little something for their time, and besides, it shows them that you are trying to do right. Now, I see the ways that you do that. It don't have to be money. I'm not doing days work for you—I'm doing you a favor because you are my color and you are trying to help yourself and us, too. And besides that, I like to talk. I thank you for that fancy beer. Now, that is the way it should be. We'll have this bread and beer and that will be a nice lunch. You know, I just go along, but I like to say what I think. But I don't do that much because most people don't care what I think. I can do all right that way because now I do not need three brass bands playing and a circus to entertain me. These streets are just like a movie and I can read and think, which is what I should have done when I was young. I was glad that I got a chance to help you before I go. I'm going to go south, too. When I was living in the country I just couldn't wait to leave there. Now I got sense enough not to fight the quiet.

Clifford Yancy

One thing about Cal'donia, if she don't want you, you
are out of luck because that thing between her legs is
hers and hers alone.

*My old friend Clifford Yancy is a prudent grandfather in his late fifties. He
is from Michigan. He and his wife Alice and four of their six children still
share the same spacious apartment. Clifford's mother and maternal uncle
also have apartments in the same building. "Yancy City" is a tight unit.
When the eldest of Clifford's brothers died in an industrial accident, the care
of his three younger children was assumed by Clifford.*

*He has worked for wages since well before his fourteenth year, and job
experience informs his view of the world. He has been a sharecropper, an
industrial worker, a chauffeur, a cook and a gardener. He is a keen amateur
naturalist whose desire to understand natural processes impelled him to
apprentice himself to a taxidermist and to make annual pilgrimages to the
countryside to observe the autumnal transfiguration of the foliage.*

Are we different from white people? You know, nobody ever asked me
this question, so I don't know if I can get all my thoughts together on it.
I'll just tell you what I think.

My father used to say that if people wouldn't lie to each other, half of
the problems would be solved right there! I don't know much about it from
the book angle, but I have a lot of J.K. and mother wit on this thing. I will
just tell you what anybody out here would tell you.

I think a lot of it does start with people lying to each other. Now, a lot
of black people will act dumb whenever they are around them. He might
do that because he wants something out of them or because he doesn't want
them to know how much he does know, or he just might be dumb. But they
just put these two things together, dumbness and darkness, and they say,
"All niggers are dumb!" I hate to use the word, but you know that's what
they say when we are not around. A white man will tell a black man his
most private business because he doesn't really think that he is talking to
a man or a woman. You know how people say the walls have ears or how
some people talk to their dogs? Well, that's what we are to them.

Whitefolks love to talk. On my job these paddies talk and talk and they tell me everything. Sometimes they'll stop and ask me some simple question just so they can say the two of us are talking, but they don't really want to hear a word from me, they just want to talk to me. The black man says, "These are some dumb chumps to believe that lie I just told them!" But where it really is, is that we don't pay much attention to anything they say and they don't care about what we have to say. Everybody stands there trying to look like they're interested, but both of these people want to forget it or talk about something that is interesting to them. So each one thinks that the other one is dumb as hell!

My little boy Clifford told his teacher some lie he had seen on television and she really got upset behind that. Well, after I warmed his sit-down-stool for starting all that who-shot-John, I asked him why he did that. He said, "Daddy, everyone tells her stories because she is some dumb!" Now, you see? That's what I'm talking about. I tore him up again and told him, "Fool! *you* are dumb! That white woman has *got* her education and even if she didn't, you will still have to work three times as hard as she does to get half of what she has!" We think they are dumb because they would have to be dumb to be fooled so easy. But what a lot of black people don't stop to think about is the fact that they are playing dumb too. They don't believe every lie we tell them, just like we don't pay much attention to what they say.

White people and black people are both people, so they're alike in most ways, but they don't think the same about some things. Your white man might be a little weaker, but that's just because they generally have easier work. I think they are probably as smart as we are because I have seen them doing any kind of work that any of us can do. Now, some of these young white boys might get a job they can't handle just because they know somebody, but, I mean, an experienced white man can do anything an experienced black man can do. I go by what I see going down out here and that's the way it looks to me. But we are all jiving. If we told each other out loud what we really think, we wouldn't do a thing but fight! So we pretend to be something we are not.

Almost all the white people I talk to tell me they haven't got anything against my color. Well then, a few whitefolks must be raising a lot of hell because it seems to me that I am catching a lot of hell, but none of these white people out here will admit that they have anything to do with this tough time I'm getting. Trouble is not just out there in the air, somebody has to start it. I'm not crazy! I don't just *think* I'm catching hell. Now, that is one big difference between us. I can still talk to you although you have had uku education because we are dealing in reverend things. When I say something to you there is no need to break it down. Now, that's the kind of people we are. Except for some educated fools and some jacklegs out here, when we talk to each other we talk so that we can be understood. We say "shit" when we mean shit. White people have all these ways of saying something else when they really mean shit. They do want to have the reputation for being honest and all that, but they can't do what they are doing and still be honest. So they have to think of all these trick ways to say a thing. They wouldn't tell you, "You can't vote," but they would say, "You can't recite the Constitution backwards," but that *means* you can't vote. They don't say, "You can't have this job," they just say that they don't have any openings and it just goes on like that. Well, they think that way about everything. Now, they have forgotten how to think straight because they have invented all this trick talk to deal with us. People are much happier with some lies they appreciate than with some truth they don't appreciate.

There's a young black boy on my job and those white cats have made him tell them so many lies about what they call his love life that he can't tell whether he's coming or going. They want to believe that we screw like dogs or cats—you know, just go out here and get you a piece, just like they might scratch their backs or get a glass of water. So they are ready to believe any lie he tells them that makes them think that they are right about us being like dogs. So he tells them all these lies and they believe them. Now, he wants people to think that he is bad. Every man wants other men to think that they are the baddest cats in bed, so telling them that heap of lies makes him feel better. But if he was to tell them the truth about slipping around with a certain young lady in that office, you can believe they wouldn't want to hear that and it would be out-the-door for him so fast it would make your head swim. It might be worse than that because all those white guys are shooting at her, but Old Country is making it and that would get to them if they knew about it. They want to believe that he is tearing up much black pussy because they want to believe that there are all these black women out here just dying to go with anything with pants—even them! Another thing, if we were just like dogs, then all the rotten things they have done and are doing to us would be okay! You see what I mean?

In my home white men were always running after colored girls. Many times a family would just have to send their daughter up here to keep her away from those crackers. But you have never heard of a white girl being sent away from her home to keep some black man off of her! Down in my home a lot of white women would slip around and chase young black boys and men. But you don't hear much about that, do you? I'm telling you what I know because I saw these things happening. I saw plenty of it going on and I see more of it now than ever before.

It is really a dumb way for white men to behave—you know, telling all these lies about how tough we are in bed. People are curious and women are more curious than men because the average woman is smarter than the average man, and all those lies just makes these white women want to see if there is something better than what they are supposed to have. One thing about Cal'donia, if she don't want you, you are out of luck because that thing between her legs is hers and hers alone. But Miss Anne tries to deal with hers. Cal'donia will tell you in a minute, "Yes, I did thus-and-so! What do you think you can do about it?" But Miss Anne, well, she'll hem and haw because she thinks she's cute. White men have spoiled white women rotten.

It's like that thing I told you, about saying what a thing really is. Well, like this sex thing or love life or whatever you might want to call it—it is not what people say they think it is. I mean, it is no big thing, really! There's a white fellow on my job and he told me that he has to go through some tough changes to get next to his own wife. She actually makes him pay for it. Now, if that is a lie, it is his. I could not make it like that! To me, he might as well say he's living with a whore. Now, this sex thing is sometimes a favor that a man might do a woman or a woman might do a man—now, that's sometimes. Generally it's a favor they do each other at the same time, but it doesn't always work that way. But I would have to be damn sick not to do my duty when I feel that certain little tap on my back at night and that goes for anybody that I have any business being in bed with. Sex is something I can take care of in all sorts of ways and in all types of places, but I try to be cool about it. Now, if I slip around I don't have kick one coming if my old lady decides to do the same. Now, that's how that is whether we want to say it or not. So when these white cats tell their sisters and wives and daughters and mothers too that we are hung like Brahma bulls, the first thing a lot of people that heard these lies will do is to try to get themselves under one of these tough studs as soon as possible!

People's eyes are always bigger than their bellies. It's natural for men and women to want everything they see. Just count the number of times in a day you think to yourself, "I sure would like to get a little of that." Now, every woman knows that that is just what we mean. We can't deal with all that stuff! We only want a *little* of it. All that stuff about everlasting hammers is just bull. Now, everybody knows that, but you won't find many people saying that. I saw that when I lived in the country. I have seen roosters wear themselves to a frazzle and those hens will be there, Jim, just steady waiting. Any cow can take ten times as much hammer as any bull can throw and still do ten others just as much good. Now, that's really the way it is with people too because they are just the smartest animals and they have this hang-up too.

No one man is really going to satisfy any woman by making it the way he wants to. You have to take care of that business just like you take care of any other kind of business. But people do not want to deal with that. Men don't because they hate not being able to hang in like they are supposed to do in all that junk you read or see on TV. Women don't want to tell the truth because it might hurt some cat they like or it might make them look like there was something wrong with them. So everybody just keeps on lying about it.

The average black woman is dealing for herself, just like we are. Now, a country girl, you can get over with her before some other woman hips her, but when she finds out what it's all about you are going to have to do her some good too. You can't do no Speedy Gonzales thing with Cal'donia when she knows the score. She'll tell you in a minute, "All right, you had your fun. Now how about me?" When my cousin first came up here he was used to that corn row quicky stuff, and he got together with this young lady and she told him that a lame dude with a boiled Slim Jim could raise twice as much hell as he could. So that got to him. He started to go up beside her head, but she told him that she stayed ready for anything, so he just took it easy. But all that is nature. It isn't anybody's fault. So, what you have to do is to help each other, not lie to each other. You can't help how you feel, but you can try to do the best you can for everybody.

It's just natural for people to feel certain ways, though. If you are sitting in the barbershop and you hear men talking about a really stacked woman going by there, the first thing you want to do is get next to her. Now, you can't see this woman, but you still feel the same way as the men who can see her because that is the natural way to feel. You don't have to say a word because I know how it has to be. I'm not saying you would lie about it, but a lot of people would. How many men will admit that they throw their nature down the toilet? I never knew one who would admit that, but you and I both know that most men do. See, people are always making rep, but sometimes—as a matter of fact, a lot of time—they have to do something to make rep that is not natural for them to do. Like I say, without seeing her, you would still want to get into a built woman and you wouldn't care what color she was. She could be green or blue, but if she had everything put together you would still want to get next to her. And, you know, another thing, she would just have to be a woman for you to like her because all that stuff about this woman being the sharpest woman in the country or the universe is just bullshit. I mean, men don't really think like that in their minds. You can't just go around here jooging everything you see, but that is what we do in our minds. In our minds we are on it all the time! In his mind a man does not respect a single thing out here. I know and I am man enough to admit it. Women are the same way in their minds too.

If you say that to most people who are thinking precisely the same things you are thinking, they will call you all kinds of names and say that you are dirty-minded. Now, I think the dirty-minded folks out here are those who are thinking these same things and doing dirty things about it and denying that they are into anything wrong. I know that nothing is safe in my mind. I mean that thing! So I know I have to control myself and I generally do. Nothing anybody thinks is dirty; it's when you start doing things that dirts come into it.

I wanted to marry my cousin. Now, some people might say that was dirty, but I don't think so. We really liked each other and there was no slipping around or anything like that. I was a man about it. I told them how we felt, but they said that the blood was too close and I could see that they might be right. So we didn't get married. I have heard about people who married their own sisters or brothers without knowing that their blood was so close. Now, those people didn't know what they were doing, so you can't say that what they did was wrong or dirty or anything like that. Like I say, they were ignorant to the fact, but generally most people know what they are doing is something they should or should not do. It's just a matter of being strong enough not to do something that you know you should not do.

I used to work in that place Clint was talking about, so I know that a lot of crazy people have got sense enough not to do something wrong if they know that you will shake them up for it. The same way with people in prison. I have worked in jails, and let me tell you, those cats will push you as far as they think they can. But everybody figures on what they can git over with. Like I was saying to Clint, everybody is a fool sometimes because they do things they know they have no business doing. It is not that they don't think about these things, it is that they want to do whatever it is they feel like doing when they feel like doing it, and it wouldn't make a damn bit of difference how long they thought about it, they would still do what they wanted to do, right or wrong, when the deal goes down. Now, one sure way to make almost anybody want almost anything is to tell them that they can't have it. I can remember when they called themselves cutting off the whiskey and beer and wine and all that. Do you know that when they did that, old ladies and all kinds of folks who never even thought about anything but persimmon beer and lemonade just had to get drunk then? Now, most of the people who were supposed to be stopping people from getting liquor were selling it, and those top men didn't care what the law said, they were going to drink whatever they wanted to anyhow because the law don't mean nothing to them. Because they *are* the law.

I can tell you one thing right now. That dude Nixon is not going to do a day and he is going to leave his job with more money than you or me will ever see. I got a bet with this white boy on my job. He says that if Nixon is guilty he will go to jail just like any other guilty man. I tell him that is just not going to happen. Did Agnew go to jail? Why didn't he go to jail? Because Nixon covered for him just like somebody is going to cover for Nixon. They are all in it together and if one of them went he might blow the whistle on all the others. So you can believe me when I tell you that Nixon might quit, they might run a contract on him, but he is not going to do day one. Now, you know that Nixon just did what I think most people would do. He tried to be too big, but he is big not for himself but because the big shots sold him to all these little crackers out here who put him in. Now, you think those dudes are going to admit that they did wrong to put him in there? Everybody wants to make it like that, just do what they want to do, but there are just a few people who can really do that. Most white people say they think they can do what they want to, but that big shot has got his thumb on them, too.

I used to be a chauffeur and a butler, too, so I can tell you that that big shot gets whatever he wants. And if he is not happy it is because he generally does not have sense enough to know what he wants, but getting what he *thinks* he might want is not a problem for him like it is with you or me. Now, we know what we want, we just need a way to get it. I used to work for this white man and his liquor cabinets were always stone full and every time he would go somewhere he would come back with more! Whatever that dude wanted he bought or took. One day he asked me, "Clifford," he said, "what is it like with a colored woman?" I said, "I don't know, sir." He said, "Clifford, you're a damned liar, but I give you credit for it. But that's all right, I'll find out for myself." Now, a few days later he was leaving in the morning, so I brought him his suitcases and there were two of the finest women you would ever want to see in his bed. One of those women was white and the other one was colored. Now, he wasn't what you would call a hot person; he wanted to know what the difference was, so he just went on and found out. Now, he was a married man and he was nice to me, but he didn't let a damn thing come between him and having his way. I saw that with my own eyes—didn't anybody tell me about this, I saw it. He was nice to me, though, but he was always trying to find out what I was thinking about. Some white people know that we want the same things they do, and he was one of these people who want to know everything about everybody. You know, one day he told me that I treated him like he was a fool. I knew I was supposed to ask him what he meant, so I did. "You treat me as if I didn't have any more sense than a postman or a milkman!" That's what he said.

I never got along too well with those little crackers that lived around there, but I fed them all with a long-handled spoon, as they used to say. But you know that your ordinary, average poor white person is always harder on black people than the big shots. See, a big shot don't have to worry about nothing in this world. But these little ordinary white people got the same things to worry about that we do, but, you see, they don't know that. Those big shots treat them just like little children. You know how you get a child to think about something else if something is going down that you don't want him to see? Well, that's just how the man treats old Chahlie. His big shots are into every opening Chahlie got. Whenever he wants to hit on the poor dude, he tells him, "Look! look over there! I believe that nigger is after your grandmama!" Well, old Chahlie rushes out there to hang some black girl baby for raping his dead grandmother, while the big shot gets a little piece from his wife and daughters. Then when Chahlie gets back the big shot slaps him on the back and tells him that he might have made a little mistake hanging that little black gal for rape, but you can't be too careful. Then the little guy goes out there and kills the best chickens he has and makes his wife and daughter cook them for the big shot, and he's so proud because Mr. Big Shot is eating his chicken. Now, he don't know and don't *want* to know that Mr. Big Shot has made a fool of him in his own bed.

I can understand why some black people think that some white people are very dumb. That big shot is steady sticking it to these average poor white folks, but they act like they love it just as long as they can give me a hard time. Now, will you tell me what good it's going to do me if I'm poor to keep you poor? I could see it if they got what the big shots get out of keeping everybody poor, but I can't see what they get out of this segregation thing. Now, that poor sucker knows that we are tricking him and he must know deep in his heart and soul that his own big shots are making a fool of him.

He'll tell you right away that there is no such thing as a honest politician! But he won't stop putting those same dudes back in there. If Jesus Christ came down here and was black, those fools would still put Nixon back in there and send the Lord back!

I don't know whether this man is just stupid or whether he is shamming like everybody else out here. I mean, it seem to me that everybody is ducking and dodging. People are always trying to get you. Like when that guy I told you about asked me what it was like with a colored girl. See, I had to think real fast because I wanted that job, but I am not going to pimp for nobody, white or black! If I had said, "They are the best," then he might have said, "Here's a couple of bills. Can you fix me up?" He could also have said, "How the hell do you know, Clifford? How do you know they are better than white women?" He could have said, or thought, "Have you ever gone with a white woman? Have you ever gone with one of *my* women?" Now, you know where *that* could lead to. Even telling him that I didn't know could have got me in trouble. He might think that I was a cherry boy or that I went with every woman except my own kind. He could have thought anything! See, I didn't know what he was after. If he had been a Southern cracker, then I would know what he was probably trying to get me into. They like to get us to lie to them, and the filthier the lie the better they like it. The daughter in one family I worked for brought a little cracker girl home on her vacation. Now, that filthy-minded Georgia cracker told everybody that she had grown up with colored people and that she knew for a fact that colored boys went with their sisters and mothers. Now, those two girls, who were just as grown as they ever had to be, used to walk around that house in practically nothing and they were just as common as they could lay in their spoiled, lazy hides! But they had the nerve to look down on our women!

One thing about big shots—they say everybody is somebody's fool, and they are the fools of their own children. I have known fifteen- and sixteen-year-old girls to slap their fathers' faces and get a hundred dollars out of them in the same day! Hell! in the same hour! I have known people who could and would tell a chief of police or a mayor or a governor, "Look, I want this done and I want it done pretty damned quick." Now, you better believe that that thing got done and done soon! But a girl can slap his face, call him so far out of his name that it made *me* feel bad, and still get anything she might think she might want out of him. Now, I still cannot understand that, although I have seen it happen many a time!

Now, that is one big difference between us and them. I don't have any kind of respect for a person who will put up with that and even less for a person who would do that. You know, in most of the families I worked for, the children showed me more respect than they did to their own parents. Now, that wasn't all that much respect because they didn't respect anything much, theirselves included. I don't know any black people who would put up with that! I know that I couldn't stand that. I never raised my voice to my parents and they generally treated me the same way. When I couldn't see things their way I had to make it for myself. Now, if I had raised my hand to them I would not be here talking about it now. Now, that's the way I think it should be.

Your child is your responsibility when he is under your care. You have no business arguing with a child like you would a grown person. Tell that child how it is and let him do what a child can do! Now, if you raised a child right you won't have to treat that child like a mule, but you might have to start that way because the child has got to know that it is a child and that it cannot do anything and everything that comes into his mind. You can't do this do-as-I-say-do thing, either. Raising a child is the hardest thing anybody can do. I know because I have raised nine. It's easy to go out here and get one, but raising them holds your feet to the fire, Jack! All of my children are getting a good education and none of them have ever spent a dishonorable minute in jail. But it was not easy for them or me.

The first thing you have to do is to fight that great enemy out there, the street. That is tough because you have to learn to live with it and pass some of it by and still take some of it in. You have to learn to think for yourself and you have to learn to do that *before* it is too late, not *after* the bad deal goes down. There is nothing in the drugstore that will mess you up quicker than you can yourself if you are not cool!

Mabel Johns

He was a man and I was a woman, so we didn't neither
of us have to raise the other.

*Mrs. Johns is a mystical seer and dreamer of prophetic dreams. She is a
widow of sixty-four from the Georgia Sea Islands. Her pretty granddaughter
is her principal link with this world. She gives advice, "but not for money."*

*Her dedication to otherworldly expectations is impressive. At times her
small frame is unable to contain her "spiritual energy," and she jumps
convulsively, shouts or lapses into long trancelike silences. But for all her
otherworldly absorption, she has a keen sense of the workings of this world.
A young Jehovah's Witness missionary hastily deposited a tract with Mrs.
Johns and practically fled to avoid disputation with her. Commenting on this
incident, she observed, "His heart is not in his business. He would much
rather talk to my granddaughter."*

*Mrs. Johns has done domestic work all her working life and still does
occasional days work. She longs to "set my foot on soft earth in God's green
space before I go down to my grave."*

I have some illness. My heart is not strong, but it is clean, so I am not
bothered. I have sugar, but I eat well. Honey is the only sweet I have. I make
everything that calls for sugar with that because it is cleaner than sugar
because it comes directly from nature. I make these sweet things for my
children, but I do not eat them because it is against me.

You asked me if I would help a white person to do what you are doing.
I don't think that we could help them because they would help themselves
if they could, and if they can't help themselves, how could we help them?
Can you help a dying man? I learned when I was no higher than that child
that you can't help most black people and *no* white people. White people
are ungodly and they are withering like all ungodly things. Look around
you. The children of Shem have chased them. Africans with spears and
good hearts have run them and their machines out of Africa. Nothing they
do does them any good and everything they get is dry and bitter to them.
They carry their filth to the very planets. They spew piss and corruption

upon the revern' moon, and still you can see them growing weaker each and every day! There is nothing on the face of this earth that is more discontented than a white man. All the things they have snatched from all of us gives them no joy in their hearts.

If one of us goes in the street with dry eyes, they say, "Why is that black fool merry when we have taken everything he had and rained down death and corruption upon him?" They want to know why *they* are sad when they have tried to take everything that would make people joyful away from *us.* Now, if our hearts are cast down and they know it, they say, "What has that black fool got that he is afraid we will take away from him?"

When I was a little child my uncle, who was father and mother to me, showed me seven buzzards fighting in a field for one dead eye. He told me that that was the way they were and I never forgot that thing he told me. He was right, you know. My uncle was a slave in slavery-time and he told me how the righteous used to make a wingless buzzard when they wanted to show that the white people were somewhere they shouldn't be, or they would make a sound like a buzzard. Such filth is not from the hand of God, so you mark the word of God, it will fail. That which God hates must go down to hell and what righteousness could love such as them? Their names will be blotted out and the punishment of Sodom was nothing compared to the way heaven will deal with them. I know white people much better than they know themselves. I have worked with them and for them for more than fifty years.

I have cooked and done what you might call general housework. When I was young I worked on the farm. I tell you, I know them. Filth is to them just what water is to a fish or air to a bird. It look like to me that they do not know what they want. They want whatever they don' have or whatever they see some black person with. I work for a woman who has a good husband; the devil is good to her, anyway. Now, that woman could be a good person if she didn't think she could just do everything and have everything. In this world whatsoever you get you will pay for. Now, she's a grown woman, but she won't know that simple thing. I don't think there's anything wrong with her mind, but she is greedy and she don't believe in admitting that she is greedy. Now, you may say what you willormay about people being good to you, but there just ain' a living soul in this world that thinks more of you than you do of yourself. She's a grown woman, but she have to keep accounts and her husband tells her whether or not he will let her do thus-and-so or buy this or that.

Now, I just couldn't be so bothered with all that. I am a grown woman, so I buy what I think I should. I don't mean selfish buying. I know more about these things than my husband did. Now, if you can't pull together, then you best to pull apart. I was lucky and unlucky in marriage. I will tell anyone I had a good husband. He was a man and I was a woman, so we didn't neither of us have to raise the other. We put our money together and bought this barn. It may not be the best in the world, but it will do for me. Now, I can stir up a little collation when one of our scholars comes to see the old lady and I don't have to be ashamed to put foot in the street and I don't have to work each and every day, but that's because we did pull together. What I knew best I did and what he knew best Thomas did. Now, what we both didn't know anything about, we got together and found out about that thing and did that together. I'm not going to tell you that we didn't disagree about some things, but there was never any of this whooping and hollering and fighting that I see some people doing. I wonder why some people get married if they can't make it together no better than that.

Now, my madam and—well, as I might say, the woman I work for sometimes has to act like a child to get her husband to do anything for her. He'll do mostly anything she'll ask him to do, but she has to act like a child to get him to do these things. Now, she's not playing when she puts on this act. If she don't do that, he might not do whatever it is she wants him to do. Now, this might be—the fact is, it probably is—something that should be done. She ain' fool enough to tell him about the things she want to do that she knows she ain' got no business doing. But if she don't behave like she wasn't a grown woman, he just might say no anyway. This woman has got two good eyes and feet and hands and everything else she need to take care of herself, but she would rather sit on her do-nothing-stool and take all that what-I-might-say rather than tell that devil what somebody should'a been done tol' him long ago. It's like she's just too weak to use her strength.

When I first started to work there, they had the mother, her mother, staying there for a while. Well, I always figure that you don' know what you got to come to or what will come to you, so I always try to treat the sick and afflicted like they would like to be able to treat theyself. I didn't do that for money, but when the grandmother left she told me that she had left something for me. Well, I knew what that meant. I figure nobody has to give me anything, so if anybody is nice enough to give you something you should thank them. So, I did thank her for the five dollars, but it turned out that she had left me fifteen dollars and her daughter had just took that ten-dollar bill and left me the five. Now, that's how they are. She felt ashamed, but that didn't stop her from robbing a blind person and me, and she couldn't see that she put herself in the gutter. Now, I am poor, but you couldn't pay me or any black person I know to do something as low as that. I'm talking about people with good minds, now. The only people I see out here who would do something that low are these fools that are putting that poison in their arms. Now, even these dope fiends will not stand up and tell you that they are right to do what they do. And they tell me that they really have to mug and do like that because when the pain gets them they have to get some more dope to conquer it.

But this woman's dope is money and she already got more money than she know what to do with. If *I* had that money I would help my son do something he ought to do and I would help my grandniece, who is afflicted in her feet and legs. I would rent a car and a driver for you so you could do your work easier. I would start a city where blackfolks could live like they want to live, and I would buy a lot of dope so that any fool that wanted to could kill themselves without going out here knocking working people in the head for the few pennies this man don't take away from us.

May Anna Madison

I can handle black men; what I can't handle is this prejudice.

In spite of the fact that Miss Madison doesn't look as if she had entered the fifth decade of her life, she is regarded as a person of unusually mature judgment. The presence of dozens of people at a surprise farewell party for her before her departure for her native Kentucky is evidence of the regard and affection her neighbors have for her. She is essentially a self-taught person of genuine good will and insight. The lessons of her own life have led her to agnosticism, but she is still known as a devoted church worker. She does not see any inconsistency between her very private agnosticism and her active church work. "If doubt is as close to the truth as I can honestly get, that will have to do for me, but I'm not a missionary."

My mother named every child she had for her or for my grandmother. Even my brother Mason is really named for my grandmother May. I don't remember her too well, but I do remember that she came to see us once or twice and brought a lot of food and presents. I can remember one Thursday —it was my mother's birthday and they brought my grandmother up here as a surprise.

Thursdays I remember even better than the Sundays. That's when all of us would have our day-off get-togethers. That was really nice. People would come to one house and cook all the special things that we liked to eat. We would play games and they would make banana-blackberry ice cream or chocolate-banana ice cream. And each person would have a thing that they were called the boss of. My Aunt Ocie was the boss of buttermilk-custard pies. My Aunt May was the boss of apple puppies and hoecakes and simon cakes and anything cooked on top of the stove like that. My mother's friend Mrs. Miller was the boss of fried chicken and my father was the boss of chiddlins and maws. He used to fry them and bake them and boil them with noodles or dumplings, which he and I used to make together. They used to have fresh beans cooked with hocks and lots of different kinds of bread. That was the best times we ever had! They would spread pallets on the floor if there were too many people for beds and the children would sleep on them. That Thursday get-together was what we all looked forward to then!

My mother and father both worked in service. My mother always did that kind of work, off and on—I mean, that was really the only kind of work she did while she was working. My father finally got out of that kind of work, but he used to cook and I can remember when he chauffeured for some white people. But his thing was really gardening! He always kept a lot of plants and he liked to try to grow things that you wouldn't expect to see growing here. He really loved the country. Every time they would go home to visit my mother's people he would bring something up with him to try to grow it. He was really good at that! That didn't come down to me, though. I try, but I don't have too much luck with plants now. The windows to your left have got what's left of my plants in them. I was doing pretty good there for a while. The plants once covered those windows.

The police came here looking for somebody we had never heard of and they got mad because they couldn't find this person, so they tore down the plants and knocked holes in my bedroom and kitchen walls. They wouldn't say what they were looking for. They didn't find anything, anyway. I asked them, "What about the damage?" and they said, "What goddamned damage?" So I knew they were not going to do anything about it. There were four of them and the leading one asked all the others if they saw any damage, and they all laughed and said no. There was one black one with them and I know he felt like a penny with a hole in it, but he couldn't do anything with the others standing right there. They tried to make me sign a paper that they wouldn't let me read, so I told them that I couldn't write. They argued about it for a while, but when they saw that I wasn't going to sign it, they left.

Now, you asked me what the difference between us and them is and that's it—they don't have to put up with that. Those cops came here and wrecked my house, ate my food and used my telephone and took the church envelope with the money, but there was nothing I could do about that because I am black. Now, if I had been a white woman, they wouldn't have done that. My life is different from theirs because they don't have to respect anything I have.

The TV is full of people talking about women's lib. Well, I can handle black men; what I can't handle is this prejudice. White women have done more bad things to me than black men ever thought of doing. Black men will make a fool out of me if I let them, but it was a white woman who had me crawling around her apartment before I was thirteen years old, cleaning places she would never think of cleaning with a toothbrush and toothpick! It was a female chauvinist sow that worked me a full day for seventy-five cents! When I was nothing but a child myself, white women looked the other way when their fresh little male chauvinist pigs were trying to make a fool out of me! That's why I don't pay any attention to all that stuff. A black man can't do any more to me than I will let him do because I can and have taken care of myself. But I do have to work to be able to do that and that means that I have to be able to deal with white people. White men and women are the people who make life hard for me.

I never got married, but if I did my husband and I would have to agree on things and if we couldn't, then we would just have to separate. My Aunt May's second husband always used to argue with her about money. When she got down, he said he would leave her if she didn't spend some of the money for what he wanted. They say she said, "Go on about your business if you feel that way." Now, that's why she saved her money and kept it apart from his.

I don't know any black woman who is too proud to get out here and work. That's why I can't stand this welfare thing. I don't mean that people should not be helped if they are too sick to work. But this business of paying somebody to lay up here and have children that they can't support makes the welfare mother the only black woman who has to depend on some man to get what she has to have. I know that a lot of people are not going to want to hear that, but it is the truth. Mrs. Miller's grandniece got into that. She is a really beautiful girl, but she let some nigger make a fool out of her and so she got on welfare. She has two children for one welfare worker and one for another one! Welfare gives her enough to get over and get pregnant, but that is all it does for her.

Now, in my day she would have had to work, just like I did. You owe children more than just food and clothes, though. This girl I'm telling you about has a little UN. All those children look different from each other and none of them look like their mother and the fathers are long gone because they got what they wanted in a few minutes. Now, white men and black men have both taken advantage of her, but the black men couldn't *make* her do anything. But she put herself in a position by joining welfare, so that white men could say, "Do what I tell you to or you won't get the first red cent!" She told me herself that her first welfare worker tried to rape her! Well, she said no to that one, I guess, but she don't seem to say no to the others. Now, me, I have to work, but I don't have to put up with that. White women don't have to put up with it, either, but black women on welfare do. All these pigs out here, if you want to call them that, had to have mothers. Most of them must have had sisters and aunts and daughters. Now, I would not raise any son of mine to oppress me. If you raise your children to kick you in the behind, then who do you have to blame if they do that?

I have worked for white people almost all my working days. I know them. I worked for a lady for five years, and do you know that woman always called me Anna May? She used to say that she depended on me for everything and that I was just like one of the family, but she didn't want to call me by my name. After I had been working for them for about three years I asked her why she did that, and she said it was just easier for her to call me Anna May. So that's what she did. That's what I was there for—to make things easier for her. Now, that's what a lot of white people think we are here for. The women think that just as much as the men do. I could see that she was mad because I asked her about that. She said she had a headache.

Well, I had a headache and a bill-ache and a child-ache and I had to deal with them and take care of little things like her laundry and her cooking and her kids. Now, all she had to do was to have her headaches whenever it was time to do anything. Now, she could lay around like that and bug people about nothing because I was out there in her kitchen. I had to be out there so that I can say no to anybody.

Now, there are certain things I will not do just to keep a job. I don't know what would happen if all my jobs were the same. I mean, if I was asked to do some of the things I don't want to do to keep a job on every job I went to, I don't really know what I would do. I would try to find some other work, I guess. But I haven't had that to worry me. I have always been able to find a job that was as good as my kind of work can be. Working for other people can't be but so good for you because you are working for them and not yourself. See, the best work is work that you want to do that you do for yourself. Now, work can be fun. Remember what I told you about the Thursday get-togethers? That was hard work, but people didn't mind because they wanted to do that and they were working for themselves. They were working with people they liked and at the end they made this grand meal. Now, they didn't work any harder for the white woman. As a matter of fact, they didn't work as hard for white people as they did for themselves. But when we worked for ourselves, everybody did what he could do best and nobody bothered you. It is not only the hard work that I mind when I have to work for somebody else, but I just don't like people hanging overtop of me all day long. I wish the people I work for would just say, "I want this and this and this done," and then leave me alone to do what they are paying me to do. But, you see, they are afraid that I don't know how to do what they are paying me to do or that I won't do it. They don't know that I can get done as much as I want to get done, no matter how many people are watching me. It's just easier if they leave me alone.

Now, if I tell you that I am going to do it if life lasts me, I will get that thing done! Now, I know a lot of women who don't feel like I do about that. Some women say, "All right, I'll do just what you must think I'm going to do." Now, what I can't figure out about that is why anybody wants people like that to work for them! I am able to do this kind of work. There is nothing wrong with this work. People eat and they don't like to eat in filthy rooms or to wear dirty clothes or walk on filthy floors. Now, I can do all that kind of work and people want it done. But not everyone can do this kind of work and not everybody wants to do it. If I will do it and do it well, then pay me what you would ask if you came to me and said, "May Anna, I will clean and dust and cook for you if you will give me what I need to live on."

Now, I don't do nothing for white women or men that they couldn't do for themselves. They don't do anything that I couldn't learn to do every bit as well as they do it. But, you see, that goes right back to the life that you have to live. If that was the life I had been raised up in, I could be the President or any other thing I got a chance to be. One very important difference between white people and black people is that white people think that you *are* your work. I mean, if a white person comes to a house where I'm working and I'm the only one there, he talks to me in a different way than he would to even a white child. Now, he does that because he thinks that how he see me then is how I am all the time! Now, a black person has more sense than that because he knows that what I am doing doesn't have anything to do with what I want to do or what I do when I am doing for myself. Now, black people think that my work is just what I have to do to get what I want.

You have a good education and I don't, but we know how to talk to each other. Now, if you were one of those educated fools that would say, "Well, I don't wish to converse with her because she is just a domestic worker," then I could tell you a few things about yourself that you might not like. I'm a person just like you are and that's what is important. Now, if I had made myself I would change some things, and if I had made my life I would have changed a lot of things. If I had made myself I would be taller and I would not have sugar. I don't know about being a man. You see, you get so used to being whatever you are that it's hard to think about being something else. If your life is all right it's just about whiddledycut, as they used to say. I don't want to answer too quick. You see, I never have been a man and so I really can't say whether I would like that better. A lot depends on the kind of man you would be or the kind of woman you would be. It really depends on the kind of life you have. There are some lives that people just shouldn't have to live. I have learned that almost anything can be a curse.

The girl I told you about, Mrs. Miller's grandniece, she was blessed, but because she didn't respect herself her blessings just turned against her. She was beautiful, so they spoiled her when she was young. Now, that wasn't her fault, but it was her cross. She really stood out in a crowd and men noted her more and gave her a lot of attention that a plainer girl would not have had to deal with. Because she was spoiled she was selfish and never thought of anybody but herself. She was the baby, so she didn't have to work as hard as the others. She didn't have to do much for anybody or give up anything for anybody. She didn't care what her mother or her brothers thought about what she did with her life because she only lived for herself. Now, it wasn't any harder for her to carry herself right than it was for most women. She didn't do anything that I didn't want to do. I always cared what my brothers would have to put up with if I didn't carry myself right. But men and women and everything in the world that's living has the same interest—I mean, every creature feels its nature. But people are supposed to watch what they do about feeling their nature. You see, going out here and getting these mouths to feed is the easiest thing in the world. But you will be a long time paying for that little fun, so you better make sure you know what you are doing before you do anything.

Remember the old folks used to tell us, "Don't let your heart start nothing that your head can't stand"? Well, that was one of my Aunt May's

parables and she knew what she was talking about! When I was a girl there
was this man they used to call Breeder because he got so many young girls
pregnant. Now, he didn't hit anybody over the head; those girls just should
have not let him put his hands on them and then they would have been all
right. That's all my mother told me about birth control and that was all I
really needed to know then. I found out later that that was just about all
she really *knew* to tell me to do. Now, I did that and later I found out *why*
I was doing it. You see, from the beginning they showed you how to help
yourself. A lot of the places I work in, well, it seems to me that they are
just begging their children to do wrong. Grown people parade around
practically naked in front of their children! They make their girls and boys
take baths together! Now, that to me is just plain common! When they used
to put those pallets down they always matched up those children right.
They didn't spell out things, they just said, "You boys here and you girls
here." They didn't really say that, but they just arranged it so when you
were making up your pallet you were in one group or the other. They did
not mix those children up!

Ever since I was a little girl I have thought about how I would change
things if I could. I get headaches thinking about that. I remember that I
told my mother that if I was the Lord she wouldn't have to work so hard.
My father heard me and gave me a beating. That was the only beating he
ever gave me. He got very religious after he was sick for a long time. He
liked people to call him Reverend Madison. My mother said that he was
wrong to beat me for saying that and I remember there was a big argument
about that and I can remember being sorry that I told my mother about
it. My father said that God drove people out of the garden because He
thought they might live forever. I never could understand why He wouldn't
want us to live forever. My mother didn't want me to die and yet and still
she was just another person, just like me. I told my father that I didn't think
that was right and he told me that whatever God did had to be right. Now,
that makes sense in a way, but in another way it doesn't make any sense.
When I take care of children I am responsible for those children. I can't
just let them do whatever they want to and then let them die. You know,
some people have done me pretty dirty, but I never wanted any of them to
die if they could be better. If I was the Lord I could make them better or
even make them right to begin with, so why should I want anybody to die
or get old or be poor or selfish or blind or lame? Well, if you get to anything
about that, we could just behave better down here. These white people are
not really running things right, and that's the fault of the white men mostly
and the white women go along with that. I would get color out of it
altogether. I just wouldn't let nobody get but so rich and I wouldn't let
nobody get but so poor.

Life just seemed so unfair to me. It still does look that way to me. I have
worked hard and tried to carry myself right, but I don't have very much
to show for it. If I was the Lord, I wouldn't let things be like they are now.
There wouldn't be any of this some-people-with-money and some-people-

with-nothing. There wouldn't be any of this white-first or black-first. People would just do what they should do. If I could just touch people and give them their sight or new legs, that is what I would do. No! I'd just fix it so there wouldn't be anything bad or sad or mean in the world. I mean, if I had the sayso I'd just make things right; then they wouldn't get bad or wear out or die.

TURN

I'm twenty-four, but sometimes I feel much older because the things I believe in are the old ways.

Margaret Lawson

Now, I like children, but I like a child in a child's place. That means I have to see that I'm always in a man's place. Some people want to be kids along with their kids. A man or a woman cannot do that and still help the child.

Hasten Clifton

Miss Lawson is a very traditional young lady. Many persons within her wide circle of kinship and friendship contributed substantially to this project out of deference to her.

Mr. Clifton is a spare, merry man who likes people and things in the places traditionally assigned them by core black culture. Although not yet forty-five, he is all but retired after a long military career. "I live to leave the city or the country when I want to," he told me. His decision to assist me was especially gracious as it required the donation of several hours of his precious urban vacation time.

Yula Moses

Christ warned us by his life and death, so who am I
that I should not warn my daughter by my life?

---

*The essential inadequacy of street-corner ethnology is manifest in the contrast
between the exterior and interior of the house of Mrs. Moses. There are almost
as many beer cans, stray papers and undomesticated cats and dogs in front
of the building she lives in as anywhere else. But once beyond her trebly
locked street doors and up the steep, clean, creaking stairs that lead to her
home, you enter another world. The smells of urban decay yield to those of
fresh, damp earth, herbs and fragrant plants. There are bottles of "holy oils"
and incenses that she makes herself and stores in large gourd bowls. She will
not sell them, but will give them to people she thinks "will let them work."*

*If it were not for the all but universal local belief in her sincerity and the
quiet way she tries to do good with very little, people would fear her. Her
speech, her intensity and her extreme personal maintenance of the "old-time
religion" and the traits associated with it make her an uncommon member
of even her own very senior generation. The Bible and things biblical are the
ridgepoles of her existence, and thinking and talking about them at great
length are enough to make her slip in and out of a world of trance, where
most of her friends cannot accompany her. But for all her otherworldliness,
I do not know anyone with a keener grasp of the admonition to watch as well
as pray, and all her neighbors know that "Miss Yula is not nobody to mess
with."*

There is a woman's understanding and there is a man's understanding.
And there is wisdom. You go up and down and in and out and you will
not find one wise person in ten thousand. Those that come into this world
with a still spirit might grow to be wise. But howsoever their spirit is turned
by those who have care of them, that is how they shall be when they have
put away childhood.

But now, that child is the shadow of the woman or man that it will grow
to be if it is spared to live so long. Everybody living came here wanting to
go a certain way. When you breathe your first on this earth, you have a will.
I have given milk to all kinds of children, white ones and black ones. I never

saw a living child that did not tell you by its actions what kind of person it was. This is so when they are just from their mother's bellies. I think it is true even before they breathe their first. Some are born curious, some are born lazy, some are born angry and some are born of a still spirit. And so they have their different dispositions from the first minute of their lives, but there are none which this world cannot tame. I have known children that came into this world with strong and angry spirits who have been made mild. I have known children born of a mild disposition who have been made proud and mean with much spoiling. Those who keep a child can make that child anything a child can be. They can puff it up with pride. They can fill it with wisdom. They can make it a woman among wise women or they can make it drylongso. All that depends on how the will you came here with matches the wills of those who keep you.

You will not find one parent in ten thousand who bring up their children for their children's sake! I have heard more mothers and fathers than I have power to count say, "Lord, let my child be wise and good." But what they mean in their hearts is, "Lord, let this child have more power and money than I have had so that my name shall be written in riches and power, so that my child's strength shall be blackness in my gray hair and firmness in my feeble steps and a monument to my name." Now, that is why the earth is troubled. That is why the world remains the same. It don't never change, as our foreparents said. Every parent's mistakes are born again with their children. Most folks are weak and wisdom is harder to *do* than it is to know. The robber wants his child to be a successful robber. And there you have most whitefolks, right there. You know that a robber can no more train his child to be just than he can restore what he has taken and punish himself. If he raises his child to be just, he may be training up the very judge that will take his life! So he can in nowise do that! The child of the harlot will condemn her mother if she grows to righteous womanliness. It is not in the color or the size or the sex of the child but in the desires of the parents and the wills that the children come here with that the differences are rooted. No matter what the plant is, you can make it grow in this way or that. You can let it murder its fellow plants, you can have it achieve a great size or keep it low for its kind, but you cannot alter its kind. Mankind is one kind of creature. In the same way you can train people toward meanness or goodness or ordinariness. So that whatsoever I shall say about these differences, you know that they are the same kind of creature.

Now, you have understanding from God and the sons and daughters of God and the creatures of His holy hand, so you know that I have spoken a deep parable and that there is no lie in it. You know that white children follow the ways of their mothers and fathers, which are far from justice and wisdom and righteousness. These things are far from most of us, white or black, but black people do not shun or despise them as white people must to do as they love to do. A black mother or father would have their children do justice and be wise so that the evils of this world might be brought to dust. For any child to be righteous it must have a love and knowledge of righteousness and wisdom from its first breath. It is not enough to tell such a child what is right. To know what is right is not to do that thing.

I worked for a judge. He was wise in the law, but his wisdom was a stumbling stone for justice. Now, that father taught his son to make the law even more of a snare to the righteous! The unjust son of that unjust father would tell you that I was like a mother to him, and in that he would not tell a bit of lie. The truth is that I was more of a mother to him than the white woman who brought him into the world and then gave him to me to feed and teach. But that boy and his brothers and sisters were not taught by me for long. I would have taught them to love the things I love and to hate those things I hate. Now, that would have made every one of them a trial to their parents and an enemy to their people! Their mother was too lazy and weak-willed to do anything but have them. Oh, but that woman loved her ease! She trained her children and had other whites train them to give another white woman ease. That's all she could do for them. Justice and right were enemies of that ease she loved, so much so she treated them like poison. They were merciful to me and a few other blackfolks, but they hate justice and real righteousness out of respect for their parents. They love that lying law and the shame and filth they have been taught to live by.

My sister's daughter gave me a child which she *should* have given a father! I trained that child in the ways she should live, and her mother thanked God and me upon her dying bed that she had lived to see her daughter being the kind of woman she wished she had been herself. Now, it was not easy to do that. The street is a pit and there are ten thousand hands ready to undo what you have done. You can only do so much and then it is with the child you are trying to help whether they will go your way or follow the street ways. I am not so big a fool that I imagine that I can stand between my daughter and evil, which is everywhere. I know that the right I have meant to do is greater than the wrong I have meant to do. It is not in our power to do more here. I do not know how many people have justly cursed my name for things I did which I thought were right. The innocent who were brought to unjust sorrow by the children I raised would not be liars if they called me wicked. I knew that the children of the wicked learn yet more wickedness, but still I gave them my milk and I did not take their lives, not any of their lives, and I might have done that. If the young men of the street curse me because my daughter cares more for her soul than she does for her body's joy, then their curse is wickedness and nothing to me. But the other thing is upon my soul.

I told you that I did not stand between my daughter and evil. Evil is everywhere good is and I can only be in one place at a time. I would not lie to my daughter, and people do a foolish thing to tell their children that there is no joy in doing wrong. Then the children will know that we have lied to them and they will have an excuse not to put any trust in anything we tell them. If sin was bitter, who but a fool would taste it twice? The drunkard loves his wine because it can do something for a little while for him that life has not done for him. The junkies love their filth because their marrow aches when they cannot find it.

I gave my daughter—most people call her my granddaughter—a little rule: never do anything the first time you think of doing it. I showed her with hot soup and penny candy and things a child could understand how that little rule made sense. All she had to do was what I showed her to do. Now, when she could understand things better, I showed her more. I showed her what could happen if you waited too long before you ate your soup. But I also showed her that you could heat it up again if it got too cold, but if you ate it when it was too hot, you would suffer more. I showed her what happened to penny candy if you left it too long too. I told her about my mistakes and my sins, and that was not an easy thing to do. But that was so she would not do those things which I have done that I should not have done. Christ warned us by his life and death, so who am I that I should not warn my daughter by my life? If there is something in my life that I am ashamed of, it is more sin to hide it if it will spare someone else. If I didn't want to tell it, then I should not have done it!

All people suffer, whether they do right or wrong. If more people did more right, we would all suffer less. Most white people do wrong because goodness is the enemy of the life their parents have chosen for them to live. Most black people do wrong because white men have burdened them down with wine and dope and toil and lying law and every kind of vain and vile thing that you can see on a TV screen. White men have much to answer for. I have lived north and south and I know that what I have told you is the truth. Walk in these streets and hear the vain filth on the lips of young men and women who might as well be dead. White men have done this crime and it is worse than slavery. If these young men and women wore chains they could see, then they could never love them. But white men have dug a pit for the body and the mind. Their greed pinched the faces of my brothers and sisters, and when I was twenty I had not one left to me! They have given a child a beast's portion and meted out a child's portion to the gray-haired! They have robbed the poor and then come shamefaced to beg for that that their fathers missed! Their iniquities are past all reckoning, and when time shall be no more one roach will be accounted more worthy than all of them! And this judgment shall surely fall upon all of the children of white men for their fathers' sake. It is not given to me to know how it shall come, whether from the left hand of Holiness or from the anger of His just children, but I know that it will come. I live for that day, but I would be a liar if I said I did not dread its coming. I shall stand in that judgment, as you shall, but many we love shall fall. Is there pity in your heart even for the wicked as there is in mine? I cannot help myself, I still don't know anyone I would not rather love than hate. If it please my savior, I shall see my fourth-score year this May the sixth and this is the first time I have spoken my mind to a living soul on these matters. Many see much, but know little. You see nothing, but you know much. I can see it. God has opened your heart, though he closed your eyes. I know that you were born of a still spirit. I can see that, too.

Joseph Langstaff

If you teach your children to be fair and honest only
some of the time and only to some people, you are
really telling them that the truth is unimportant.

*There is something about Mr. Langstaff's general bearing which discourages
excessive flippancy. He is a lively, dispassionate observer of domestic and
international politics. Virginia-born, he has seen much of the world and has
come to some cogently reasoned conclusions about the varieties of human
nature. If integrity and personal merit were of greater account, he might very
well be dispensing his perspective-restoring, unconventional wisdom at the
human-nature desk of some just administration. Unpretentious decorum is
his due and his neighbors are pleased to give it to him.*

I was a placid child, everyone said, and I am a quiet man because that
is the kind of life that pleases me the most. I am seventy-three years old.
I never have believed in doing anything to death, as they say. I have worked
hard all my life and I have taken good care of myself. I never wanted to
waste myself on foolishness, but always tried to stay clear of rash men. I
take a little strong drink, but I would not make myself a fool with anything.
I do not want to be a slave to anything, and I have learned that if I have
to take so much of anything to enjoy it that I risk my capacity to enjoy
everything else, then it's not worth taking that chance. When I was a young
man I depended upon my hands and feet and good companions to keep me
in good health and safety. A man lives but so long and he has limitations
upon his strength of mind and body, so now I lean on steel as well as my
own power.

A thing or a man cannot break out of the natural limitations of things
and people. In the white man's mind, hoping and thinking are more mixed
up than they are in ours. Moses got water from the rock in the weary land,
but white men would want wine and they would want a strong wine which
would not weaken them. They want that which in the nature of things is
impossible. They believe that there must be a man who is more manly than
a good man can be, and that there is a beautiful woman who is more
beautiful than all the other beautiful women. They really think that every-

thing and every people, except us, can be whatever they would like it to be. Children read about super men and wonder women, but that's not just a story. White men think that there are super things everywhere. They want Miss America and Mr. Universe, super eggs and super bacon and super-sweet honey that isn't too sweet and the Sunday papers on Saturday. Now, only a child can really think like this without doing great damage to his mind. It doesn't matter so much if a child doesn't know the difference between what he would like to be true and what is true, because children are learning to think and their mistakes do not hurt everyone. Good advice, mistakes and the good sense to learn from their mistakes are what make children into women and men. So the mistakes of children are part of the natural way they learn not to be children. Hard-grown men can think about childhood and recall it pleasantly, but they must think as grown men or they cannot fail to hurt themselves. If they think for other people, then they can do even more harm.

At this moment I am plainly aware of the fact that I am doing you a favor. You need me more than I need you. I don't mean to be offensive and I like being able to do this if it is of any use to you. I didn't think I would like talking to you because, as you know, I do not generally speak for very long. Your offer to pay me indicated to me that you know that I would just as soon be doing something else.

We want to know how things really are, but white men are more interested in making things be what they would like them to be. They are so interested in that that they despise things for not being more than they are. They are never contented with anything. If they win at anything they can be sure that the victory is not theirs but their group's victory. If they lose, then their group tells them that the loss was their own doing, and they have to care for the opinion of their group. They are never contented because they are always looking for a happiness which is greater than happiness. They want to find love where they have sown only hate and selfishness. They want to run and never tire, to satisfy their thirsts and hungers and not be full. They cannot see that the sickness which they all suffer from comes from greed, a kind of childish believing that when they close their minds, the world is not what it always was and always will be. Children cover their eyes and are astounded to find that they can still be seen, though they see no one. We say, "You may say you saw no one, but you cannot say you were not seen."

When I was just getting to be a very young man, I worked for a white farmer. I did a man's work and when it was time for my dinner, this farmer's wife gave me a little dog bread and a little thin sorghum syrup. Each day she would put a little more water in that syrup and each day that piece of poor bread would be a little smaller, and she would never give me this poor meal warm. She had dogs which she fed much better. She gave them meat and biscuits from her table, but she gave me cold dog bread and syrup that was little more than sweetened water. She would come to the kitchen and ask me how I liked this meal, which a black person would not give to a dog.

I knew that I was supposed to praise this slop, so I did. She always praised this meal, even when she started to give me moldy dog bread and syrup that wasn't even good switchy. She would always tell me how lucky I was to have a good dinner, and make me say a blasphemous blessing. One day I was full of the devil, so I let her catch me giving that fine dinner to one of her dogs. She told my mother that she was sure that I had been raised to know better than to waste good food. My mother said that since I didn't have sense enough to appreciate the dinner she had gone to the trouble to make for me, I should be punished by being obliged to bring a cold lunch. Now, that's how I got out of having my throat scratched every day, but none of us could really say the truth about that business. We all go around lying to each other. That woman kept taking from that little poor meal she gave me, and the more she took, the more she wanted to be praised for her generosity. This cheapness is driven out of us when we are children, but it is driven *into* most white people.

In my home we always had plenty of milk, but we never made cheese. I was a fool about cheese when I was a youngster. One day my elder sister, Dorothy, and I put our money together and bought some "snappy cheese." That's what we called it then—it was a kind of sharp cheddar and it was a great treat to have it with gingersnaps. It was mostly Dorothy's money, but she was a young lady then, so most of the selfishness had been trained out of her. But to tell you the truth, I didn't have much turn then. So, although she had more money, she still said, as she should have, that we would divide the cheese evenly. Doglike, I ate my portion instantly and a little later begged Dorothy for some of hers. She gave me half of her portion. At night when Dorothy was washing our supper dishes, I took a large part of the rest of her cheese. My mother saw me do this and said, "Isn't that your sister's share, and haven't you had all of your share and most of hers already?" Dorothy came and said that I had asked her for the cheese and that she had given me permission to take it. My mother could not stand a thief or a liar, and Dorothy was tender-hearted and did not want to see me beaten for taking the cheese or for lying about it. But my mother whipped Dot for lying to her, and then she took the piece of cheese and put it on the floor and called our dog. She let the dog bite the cheese and then she made me get on my knees. She said, "You have made yourself a dog about this cheese. I give you this choice: eat like a dog or I will give you ten times what I just gave your sister!" I couldn't eat that piece of cheese and she was true to her word. I still remember what those peach switches were supposed to teach me.

That was many more years ago than you have lived. You know, those old people hated a liar and a thief. My mother pinched off the little money we had and sent me to the store to buy more cheese. She made us share it as people should share things. I have never forgotten that. That is how most of us get to be the kind of men and women we are, because we are taught by peach switches and good example not to do every greedy thing we feel like doing. Most white people are taught that dishonesty and theft are honorable, so they get to be the kind of men and women most of them are. If you teach your children to be fair and honest only some of the time and only to some people, you are really telling them that the truth is unimportant. If you live so that your children see that you think it is all right to lie and cheat, then who can correct them? If I had seen my mother giving food to people which was not fit for dogs and lying about the quality of that food, then I could not have believed her about anything else. Children don't just listen to you, they watch you, too, and if your life is not a good example, you are certain to fail to make them the kind of adult you want them to be.

It is more complicated to live a lie than the truth. If God gives me thirty more years to live and you are so favored and we should meet, I will not have to think, "Well, what did I tell that man?" You see, if you build a country on lies, then all of the successful men in that country will have to be liars before they are anything else. Keeping the lie going is almost all they can do. The truth about anything is the truth of its making. The rightness of anything is in the first step you take in building it. If you make a poor cake you will have poor cake to eat. And you know—because your mother told you—that good bread is better than poor cake. It is just like white men to build a bad building higher than they used to build good buildings. Nothing anyone can ever say or do can make a bad job good. Every time I turn on my television set or look at a wall or listen to a radio, I hear somebody trying to convince me that that thing or this thing just can't be done without, or that thing or this thing will make me a young man that young ladies just cannot resist. All that is vain and foolish because I buy what I need or want and I don't want anything to be anything but what it is. I hear much talk about truth in the packaging of things. Well, to me that means not lying about what you are selling. There is just too much lying, there always has been, but there has never been as much as there is now. Try to find one thing that is true as you go through the day. That's much worse than being unable to get through the day without having to tell a lie or finding that you have been lied to at least once. That's how it used to be. My mother would say, for instance, that there was at least one lie in every hour, but now there are whole weeks in which there is no real truth at all.

You know that people can tell you the truth and make it have the same effect as a lie. People can tell you a lie and have it affect you like the truth. It depends on what you mean to do with the truth whether it comes out to be a bad thing or a good thing. There is much spite in some people's frankness and much sympathy in some people's untruthfulness. You must have found this out very early in life. It depends on how you are in your heart. If you mean well, the right you do will not be against your own nature, and it is death to live against your own nature.

It is easier for some people to do right when they know what it is than it is for other people. Some people like peace and others despise it. Some people are happiest when it is quiet and some people are never happy unless there is some kind of fighting. If you know what kind of person you are, you can watch yourself. If you like quiet and you know it, you will watch yourself to make sure that you do not do something dishonorable just so things will be quiet. If you are the kind of person who must have a circus going on all the time to be happy, you can watch yourself to see that your love of noise and jumping up and down is not making a fool out of you. But you can do nothing for yourself if you don't know what kind of person you are. You should make sure that you are controlling your feelings and that you are doing what you think is right, not just what you want to do. You must not do anything to death.

Edith Baker

I feel like something heavy just rolled off my chest.

Mrs. Baker is fifty-six, but she says she looks "twenty years older than I am."
She is from Massachusetts. If you talk to her for any appreciable length of
time, she is certain to tell you with an air of bitter resolution that "there is
nothing in this world I can't do without." Mrs. Baker is a desperate woman
who feels no responsibility for her circumstances. She does not inveigh against
the cosmic circumstance which widowed her, but her hatred of officialdom
and the street, which she feels interfered disastrously in her domestic affairs,
is boundless. Her neighbors respect her as a virtuous but unlucky woman.
Like many, her lot is hard, but she takes it harder than most. Many politely
avoid her, not because they have troubles of their own but because she is past
comforting.

After everything I tried to do for my children, they can't stand me and
I don't want to have anything to do with but one of them. My oldest boy
is—everybody knows it—in jail, where he ought to be. I had a daughter in
there, too, but she died in there. My youngest girl was on her way there,
but she sees what happened to the others, so she's trying to straighten
herself up and do halfway right. It's hard for the young these days because
the parents don't have any sayso.

I can tell my child to do something, but that white woman can come into
my home and tell me all kinds of junk. I worked hard and got us a good
apartment. You hear me when I say that I worked to pay for this apartment,
and my daughter wanted to keep it like a pig sty and the counselor said,
"It is not your room, it is her room, so the only way she will feel like it is
hers is if she can do anything she wants in it." Well, by then I had learned
my lesson. I tried that with the other children and all I got was more
mouthing and dreaming. So I said, "Lady, if I had a woman to clean my
house while I'm out cleaning somebody else's, I could do what you say, but
I am not living in filth for nobody, least of all a child which I have birthed
and taught right from wrong."

Mildred said that she was unhappy with me, so I said, "All right. You
go and see if you get any happier by yourself," and she went. Well, she found

out that it wasn't so easy that way. Food don't just jump on no table. Sheets don't iron themselves, and don't think you are going to be able to go out here and have everybody stand back every time you break bad. She got cut in that little home they have for the children. Now, I took her to the emergency myself and when she got out she come talking about coming home with me. I told her that she could if she would clean herself and the house while I was at work and help me to help both of us. She said, "Oh, Mama, I'm really going to do my share." We took this cab home, and before we had gone six blocks she started cussing and showing out, so I told that taxi driver to turn right around and take her back to those people who don't mind being talked to like they might be dogs and who think it's all right to wallow in your own filth.

She keeps calling me, but I have got to the point where I like living without all that mess and I am not working to have a child of mine call me out of my name. I did the best I could and it wasn't enough for her. I did what I think I should have done and worked like a dog to do it and they say I have to do things that I know don't make any sense. Well, I think I have done enough. Even if I haven't, I have done all I am going to do. I feel like something heavy just rolled off my chest. I am really through helping anybody who will not help herself.

Avis Briar

In high school they told me that it was the wonderful
world of work and my father told me, "Shug, it's a
bitch out there."

*Both the Briars and the Lawsons take a great deal of pride in the "sit-down"
jobs of the daughters of their working-class families. Twenty-year-old Miss
Avis Briar and twenty-four-year-old Miss Margaret Lawson are known as
"young ladies with turn." Both young women have their own apartments but
maintain close ties with their large, ramified families. They were frequently
described as "decent," "attractive," "sensible" young women. Despite the
restrictions of life in minuscule apartments, Miss Briar and Miss Lawson
admirably observed the traditional civilities of core black culture, especially
those centering around hospitality. They are the kind of young ladies their
community is proud to call "our girls."*

You know, when I was fifteen my uncle made me a birthday cake and
they gave me a party. My little brother asked me how it felt to be a big lady.
I could see him looking at me the same way he sometimes looks at my
mother. And I knew that a part of what he was asking was, how does it
feel to be made like a big lady, and how does it feel to cut the cake for the
rest to eat? That question really got to me and I started to thinking about
it for a long while. He wasn't quite five then, but he noticed everything. I
guess I generally think of myself as a kind of complete person, and when
somebody asks me something that makes me think about a particular part
of my person, then I'm always a little surprised and, you know, our people
hate surprises, as a rule. I mean that when Orlando asked me about my
womanliness, or my grown-upness, or you ask me about my blackness, it
sort of shakes me up a little bit because I think of all of those parts as just
pieces of the complete me.

I think it's just unnatural to be thinking about anything all the time. I
mean, you don't say, "I live by breathing, so I will now think about taking
a breath." I know that a lot of black people think a lot about color, but that's
because they think they have to and they do. But really, it is not important
unless someone makes it important, and the people who do that are white.

I'm not sure how to say this, but that reminds me of what I think is one of the greatest differences between white and black people. Black people seem to me to be more natural. Maybe that's because being black, I mean, thinking in the ways I do, is more natural than any other ways. We can look at each other and somehow we will know that we are going to do something together at about the same time. We move the same. We think the same and we don't have to spell things out like white people do. I mean, it doesn't seem to me that black women need cookbooks very much, and black girls just keep them around for moral support. Black boys don't seem to need books to make cars run or to play sports. Black people have very strong personalities. They are better at saying what they think than they are at doing something someone else thinks they should. White people seem generally to need strong leaders or leadership more than we do. They like books because the books are just the words of their leaders and they don't like doing anything just as one person. They are really group people and we are individuals. Now, that's good sometimes and sometimes it's bad. I'm sure some white people are not like this, but most I have to deal with are better followers than leaders. They become excited when their leaders are excited, and they would not ever help a member of their own family who they thought was right if their leaders told them not to do it. I don't think they have the same kind of sympathies we have.

There's a girl on my job whose aunt raised her and sent her to secretarial school and treated her as if she might have been her own daughter—that's what she herself says. But this lady is very sick and all you hear is how tough it is. I don't think she thinks how tough it must be for her aunt. You can see by what she says that she is just waiting for this aunt to die. Now, if that were an aunt of mine who had done so much for me, I don't think that I would feel that way about her if she were sick. Black people might do horrible things because they were afraid for themselves, but they would never do these things you read about and see on the television about Vietnam, you know, if they had a choice.

My uncle was born in Mississippi and he used to tell us how white people would do to black people many of these things you read about Nazis doing to prisoners. He told us that he and four other boys were swimming and some white men came and shot at them and wouldn't let them get out of the water. They hit two of the black boys and all of them almost drowned because those white men wouldn't let them come out of the water. Now, I can't think of a single black man who would do a thing like that. I really don't know of any black person who would do that and I can't imagine a group of black people doing that. My father's best friend drowned and people who were having a picnic just let that boy drown. They were white and he was black, so they just rowed away from him when he got cramps and let him drown. In plain sight of dozens of families, he drowned. Now, that's the kind of thing I would call unnatural. I don't want to be that hard. If I had a child who was going to grow up like that, I would kill him myself because that is not human.

We're not such good followers because we all think we are as good as any leader. I have seen this happen with black people ever since I was a little girl. We get more done when we just go on and do a thing than we do when people map out everything. I like to play the violin and I guess that's not as rough on the neighbors as it used to be. I like to play with my cousins and my uncle, but they just play. They seem to know what they want to do and they can read the music, but they don't have to. But I do. I don't have the freedom to just sort of blend in with them as long as that page is in front of me. They can play anything anyone else can, but they find the written score inhibiting after they know it. I guess it's like the cookbook thing. I need to see the score just as a kind of moral support, but they don't. That's the way most of us feel. This is good in a way and it's bad in a way. It's good because it's good to be able to think for yourself, especially when people might not be dealing honestly with you. But it's bad because you can just become too overconfident.

I have an uncle who is a chef and a baker, and he really amazes me because if he doesn't have something that I would say he *had* to have to make something, he can think of something instantly which will do just as well as the thing he hasn't got! I can't do that and it scares me to see him do it, but he never misses. Even when he looks like he has really goofed, he just blends his failures into something that is really good. Sometimes he cooks for a lot of people, but it never bothers him—anyway, it doesn't seem to bother him. I guess that's the thing that black people pride themselves on the most—you know, maintaining our cool. Just don't let anyone think they can rattle you.

We used to live on this main street that was really a part of the highway and these trucks used to go by and backfire. They really made a lot of noise! I would always be scared when they would do that, and my father and my brothers would always say, "No cool, no cool!" And that would really bother me. I was about five when I learned not to lose my cool when the trucks backfired. I remember the day that happened. I had asked my father for some money for something and he had said no. But when the trucks came by and backfired, I just sat there like nothing had happened. He said, "Girl! let me shake your hand!" And he gave me some money and I felt just as tall as he was. My brother Harry, who is three years older than I am, without even looking at me said, "No cool." Then everybody teased him for running off at the mouth without knowing what he was talking about and he felt very bad, I think. You see, you can think you know what's going to happen, but people don't always do the same things all the time and you might wind up looking pretty bad.

We don't like to show out, but if you guess wrong you might be, well, you might be out there all by your lonesome. But we don't really have a choice out in the world. We have to stay as many steps ahead of the white man as we can because life isn't something like a musical score which is written and then you can read it or not. I mean, nobody is going to come along and add three more pages for me to play or take five pages away from somebody because they are a certain color. In life white men change things to suit them, so there is never a rule which means anything in itself. Those rules mean whatever the person making them up wants them to mean at any particular time. You see, white men don't want to be bound by anything, especially their own laws or rules or whatever. So we have to be ready to move when they change the meanings of all these rules and laws. The rules don't mean what they say, that is the truth. They mean what the rule-maker feels like having them mean.

I wouldn't mind that so much if these rule-makers knew something about what they are supposed to be getting me to do. But they generally don't. But if I tell them that, I'm finished. Maybe I had it too soft. In high school they told me that it was the wonderful world of work and my father told me, "Shug, it's a bitch out there!" I always knew he was right, but, you know, when you actually experience the weight yourself it's different than just knowing a thing in your mind. I can remember my father patting me on the head and telling my little nieces stories and reading his newspaper at the same time. Each one of us thought that we were getting all his attention, but I now think that he was probably concentrating most on the paper. But he made us all think that we were more important. He just did this sometimes. Sometimes we were most important, and sometimes he would actually come and find us and take us with him to places or just sit with us. But sometimes he was busy with his own concerns, but he could always make us think that we were number one. That wasn't too hard to do because we all wanted to think that. Now I have to do the same thing with grown people on my job and I just don't like it.

I've been out here hitting it for three years now, but I guess I'm still the only golden baby daughter and I know I'm still watched more than I like to be sometimes. But I always try to remember that my family means me nothing but the best. They expect a great deal of me and I've always tried not to disappoint them in any really big thing.

Margaret Lawson

A junkie generally has to mess up the people he can—
that means his mother or his sisters or his brothers.

*Miss Lawson has had to become skilled in the use of handguns, with which
she has successfully defended herself and others at least four times. Her
decision to become her own minister of defense was forced upon her by a
number of outrageous and perilous affronts to her person. Her determination
to survive on terms of her own traditional core black way of being human is
manifest in her life style. Her wonderfully flexible alto voice is devoted as
much to the spiritual as to the gospel idiom. Her command of the traditional
cuisine is laudable. Her sense of the easy, reciprocal deference that the culture
insists upon between generations is flawless. In a core black word, Miss
Lawson has "turn" if anyone ever possessed that silver element.*

I guess I know that I can cook some things well. When Mrs. Margaret
Sampson Lawson brings you up in her kitchen, you will know how to cook
and to do a lot of other things that you better know how to do! My mother
was a fantastic cook and she did not waste much patience on the stubborn,
let me tell you! She put that chair in front of the sink when I wasn't even
thinking about going to school and said, "Now, Shug, you help Mama by
washing these dishes. Don't play with them, Shug. You wash them and be
careful because they are pretty and we had to work very hard to get them."

Well, that was the way she was about everything. She would start you
out right. I don't just mean you would have what you had to have to do
the thing she told you to do, but she would tell you exactly what you had
to do and why doing it exactly as she told you to do it was so important.
I really felt important. You would have thought that I was taking a message
to the king of Jalapa! She told my father that I had washed those plates
when he came home. Tired as he was, he went out and bought me some
peanut bars. If there was anything I could be bribed with—to this day—
it is those peanut bars, which they don't even make anymore. They make
things that are supposed to be peanut bars, but a real peanut bar nut is not
deceived. Anyway, I can't find them anymore. I remember that very well.
I also remember what happened when I didn't do what I was supposed to

do, and that was not pleasant. She would hear you out, but if you were wrong you were wrong and you paid the penalty. That's how it was and that's how it should be now.

I remember this one occasion: When I got home from school—I was just starting second grade—I got home and my mother sat me down and gave me one peanut bar and said, "All right. now you have one and that is all you get until after dinner. Now you wash those few dishes in the sink and do your schoolwork and then you can play until supper." Well, that one tasted so good that supper seemed ages away. When she went outside to work in our little yard garden, the devil told me to be greedy. Those peanut bars in a dish on top of our china cabinet got to be the most important things in the world. I took that very chair which I *should* have pulled up to the sink to wash those dishes, and eased it up against that china cabinet and helped my little fresh self to those three peanut bars. I ate all three, and while I was up there I saw a whole bag of them. So me and the devil decided to take four more. I was going to put three in the dish to replace those I had eaten, and the fourth one was just to kind of taper off with.

The big bag of peanut bars was in a big fancy cut-glass bowl in the back of the china closet. I had to tip the big bowl to get the bag of peanut bars and it just kept right on tipping. Now, that big bowl had belonged to my mother's grandmother and I just knew that I couldn't allow it to break, and in my concentration on saving it I knocked the little dish which had the three peanut bars off the china closet. It just flipped up when the big bowl tipped against it and flipped right off. I have never known anything to make so much noise! I cut my hands trying to get the pieces up. I had a wild plan to hide the pieces, put another little dish up to replace the broken one and wash the dishes in that sink faster and better than dishes had ever been washed before! I was so busy cleaning up that broken glass that I didn't even hear my mother walk into the room.

She bandaged my hands and took me to the doctor. I can remember hoping that it would be really bad so that my mother would take pity on me. But the doctor looked at it and in a very short time he just said it looked worse than it really was. It just seemed like a couple of seconds and we were going home! I was praying that my father would be there, just to take some of the heat off. He wasn't there and my mother just swept up the mess and set the table—I remember that as if it were yesterday! When my father finally came home, she served him and herself—lima beans, sausage, green gumbo and sour corn bread. When she had put their food on the table, she went to the china closet, took that whole bag of peanut bars down and dumped every last one of them into my plate! "Eat them," she said. "You are going to earn them and many more before I'm finished with those two little fresh grains of coffee of yours, Missy!" Then she told my father what I had done. My father said that I should pay for the dish and I really wanted to do that. I ran to get my pennies and said that I didn't want any supper. My father said it would make me sick to eat all that candy. But my mother said, "She will eat every one of them or sprout wings!" So I tried to eat them, but I got sick. Then my father put me to bed. I felt really bad that next day, but my mother said, "You were big enough to do something you had no business doing, so you just get your fresh self out of that bed and do something you know you ought to do!" When I got home from school, my mother said, "You wash those dishes. If I hear nothing but good about you from school and everywhere else, I won't warm that fresh backside of yours but once." Well, that was the way she taught me and my younger brothers. You really learn that way!

I think that's one of the biggest differences between white people—anyway, most white people I know—and most black people I know, although I must say that a lot of young black people are bringing up their children in some very strange ways! I'm twenty-four, but sometimes I feel much older because the things I believe in are the old ways. I believe they are the best. I really don't understand some of these people. These young, flashy, revolutionary dude types are filling baby carriages faster than they can make them. They used to say that a dark child born of a dark woman would see dark times, and I know that's true. So I'm going to be cool—I mean, before I get into this motherhood thing myself! You can believe that Margaret Muriel Lawson is going to have a husband long before she needs a baby carriage! I am not going to kill myself with any pill, either. When they give me that beautiful-black-sister-please-let-me-mess-you-up-for-life stuff, I tell them right away that they are wasting their time and mine! You know, I can still remember when everybody your color or mine was too black for a lot of these people that are going around screaming that black is beautiful! Some of those same people who thought I was too black for anything except a little fun far from Mama are changing their names and wearing all sorts of outlandish clothes and letting their hair grow long. I tell them in the beginning that they are wasting my time and theirs because I am just as black now as I was then and I think just as much of myself now as I did then.

I have a cousin who is only fifteen, but she talks and acts like a grown woman, as long as she doesn't have to back up her crazy plays. She doesn't really know the first thing about taking care of herself and she's talking about having a baby. I told her not to come to my house talking that way. I told her not to bring that lazy junkie boyfriend to my house anymore, either. You know, she just has lost all touch with reality! She thinks everything, even my house, belongs to her! She told me that she would come to my house whenever she felt like it and that she would bring anybody with her that she felt like bringing. She told me that I should be careful because she didn't want to have to hurt me! She said, "If you want to deny your blackness and try to put us out, just come on and try if you think you are woman enough!" Now, *that* really tore it! So I threw her and her Muslim boyfriend out of my house! She called me late that night and asked to borrow money to get home. But by then I had had it up to here! I told her to keep the money she had already stolen and borrowed and leave me alone. They came here the last time and started to act like they were on their honeymoon. I told them to take that stuff somewhere else and they both told me to mind my own damned business—in my own house now! Carol really should be ashamed of herself. She has no reason in this world to carry herself like that because my Aunt Muriel was no tramp! She would turn over in her grave if she could see what a mess her baby daughter is. I used to try to help Carol, but I'm just as through with her now as Lincoln is with life!

These young men out here have got a lot to answer for. It's getting to be that black people are more afraid to see a young black man walking behind them than they are to see a white person! I have been robbed three times! Each time I was robbed it was young black men who took my money and scared me to death! I have a gun now and I know how to use it and the next person who tries to rob me, purple or green, is either going to have to kill me or get killed. I mean that! The last time they tried to make me take off my clothes. I said no. As luck would have it, they just took my money that time. They robbed my father too! They took his pants so that he could not chase them, or maybe so they could sell them. Every time you turn around there's some young thief trying to sell you something he has stolen from somebody like you or me or my father. Don't think they would hesitate to rob or beat someone in your condition. You should have a gun if you don't. It's this dope and this revolutionary jive every one of these hoods are talking that is messing up our young black men. You know, it is a shame to have to say it, but our own young men are becoming our worst enemies! As my father says, there are a few who would not work in a pie shop. They live for dope and these freakish white mod styles. Every time I see one of these lazy, stupid boys in their silly-looking long leather coats and that whole crazy getup, I almost get sick!

I told you, I am just an ordinary dark girl. I don't want to be anything else. I am not an African and I really don't understand why these young hoods are so strong for Africa. After all, the Africans obviously have less sense than we do. I mean, they sold the only ancestors both of us should be proud of to the white man! Now, that was really brilliant of them! And what did they get out of it? Some rum, some beads and trinkets and some white women. Now, what reason does any of us have to thank them for that? Some of our people are so easily led. These boys are putting a knife to their own parents' throats—for what? Some dope, some freakish clothes and a big car! People like that should be stood up beside the nearest wall and blown away. If my own brother turned out to be like that, the best thing I could do for him would be to blow his brains out. White people don't have to do a thing as long as these young black hoods are willing to mug honest people for money to fight for a place in line to buy the white man's dope, wear his crazy clothes and drive his big cars. It only takes a few people like that to make these streets the way they are. Those few are the same ones who make the most noise about revolution and black awareness. I don't know what it will take for most of us to see it, but those few must go!

One difference between us and white people which I'm not very proud of is that we are just too good at putting up with things. I mean, black people have had to put up with so much for so long that some of us just can't seem to see that some things are just too hard to bear! Things can just get too bad! I know it's hard to tell, but that point does come and sometimes not saying a mumbling word, no matter how much courage or selflessness it might take, is just plain stupid! I know we are not cowards, but some of us are just too patient. My father, for example—I know that he would have lived his life much differently if it had not been for us kids, and I know he had to take a lot because he wasn't just on his own. I love and respect him for what he put up with for us, but things are a little different now. I have a job that my mother knew better than to train for. Things are by no means perfect, but so much of the things we have to fear are coming from our own young people now. They have a better chance than I had when I got out of high school and I probably had it better than you did when you graduated, but that's because the people fought every step of the way.

Now, I'm really not bragging on myself, but so far things are pretty good for me, but I could blow it tomorrow, I know that. I guess what I'm trying to say is that we have come a long way and I just hate to see even a very few people messing it up for all the others. I hate to see decent people sacrificing and keeping quiet for people who aren't worth their spit! My father knew those young hoods who robbed him the last time. They have eaten at our table many times when we were just a little less hungry than they were! My father helped them and they robbed and shamed him in the street! You see what I mean, he just should not have to put up with that! If they are stupid and selfish enough to put something in their bodies that makes them behave worse than animals, then they do not deserve a dog's chance. They are much worse than roaches! Everyone really feels the same way I do. I work very hard for whatever I get, like almost every black person I ever heard of. I always used to be afraid of white people. If I had thought about carrying a gun in the streets I would have thought of it as protection from white men, but now I'm afraid of black teenagers! A lot of people would probably put me down for saying that, but they can't say I'm lying —not and tell the truth themselves. I promised to tell you the truth and the whole truth, and you know that that is the truth. You know that most people think exactly as I do. Everybody I know has been worried about you. It's like a kind of civil war out here.

I know that you know about a certain lady who killed her own son. That's not a lie. Everybody knows she did that and I don't know anyone who doesn't give her credit for it. The police wouldn't keep him in jail and he wasn't human anymore! So she did him and everybody else a big favor. He pawned everything he could steal from friends and relatives even. He stole his own mother's sewing machine and TV set and clothes. She had to take her stuff into one room of their house and lock it all up to keep him from stealing it! With that stuff in him he did whatever filthy thing that came into his mind. He even molested his own cousin and she was a baby. She was too young to walk. Can you imagine such a thing? He is dead now and that's how he would have wanted to be if he had any control over himself. Every time he got caught they'd just give him a little time and then send him back here to worry and rob and cut and shoot us! I went to school with that boy. I can remember when he had much more sense than most people. I certainly can remember when he had more sense than I had. He used to be the finest person you would ever want to meet, but that poison made him into something worse than an animal. I'm not talking about something I heard! I'm talking about something I know and something which really hurt me a great deal.

We used to do our homework together and I guess he was the first so-called boyfriend I ever had. He was like a son to my mother and sometimes he thought more of me than I did of myself. If he hadn't respected our house I might have been pushing a baby carriage before I was as old as Carol. I was lucky, but I learned fast the easy way. I mean, I could see what happened to other girls, and even now I break out in a cold sweat when I think how close I came to messing up my own life! If anybody had told me that he would rob and cut an old lady who had saved his life, I just wouldn't have believed that! Then, nobody would have believed that he would have made his mother's life hell after all she tried to do for him.

When my father came home from the hospital, I stayed with him for a couple of weeks. I slept on that little couch because every sister he had came to help out. I woke up one night and saw Marvin taking my father's hi-fi set right out of our living room! I didn't say a word, but I don't think he was convinced that I was asleep. He came to the couch and looked right down in my face and said, "Girl, I wish you would offer to do me that good you promised me when we were kids." He told me where he pawned the set, so I got it back. He told me where the set was about two weeks before he died. We had the first long talk we had had in years. He said he knew he was going to get killed by someone and that everybody would be better off when that happened. Two weeks later it happened and he was right. When I think of what he could have done with his life, it really gets to me. He was like somebody who was crazy most of the time, but every now and then he would be a little like the boy everybody liked and respected. That's why I hate the whole drug scene. If I ever got into that, I would hope that someone would do me and everybody else a favor and stop me from messing up myself and so many other people.

What people don't seem to understand is that a junkie generally has to mess up the people he can—that means his mother or his sisters or his brothers. It means his own people. If they robbed the mothers and sisters of those judges who keep sending them out here for you and me to deal with, they would never see the street again. If you write anything about this, though, please be very careful.

Ellen Saunders

My daughter listens to me sometimes, but I listened to
my mother *all* the time.

*During the dozen years I have known the Saunders family, I have always been
impressed by their striving to be honorable in one another's sight. Ellen and
Janice Saunders still display in their customary attitudes and behavior all any
people can expect of valor and integrity. At twenty Janice was assured admis-
sion to a fine graduate school, while Ellen, her mother, has completed at
forty-two her high school education and has begun undergraduate life. Decent, principled, profound Mark Saunders did not live to see his daughter well
and truly graduated from college.*

I have a few friends and they are really all I need. The common run of
people can't mean me much good since they don't do themselves much
good. I'm like most black people in that respect. We don't have but so many
friends, but those we have are real friends. I always told my daughter that
she should make all the friends that there were to make and if there weren't
any she should forget it, and so far she is doing that thing. It's very hard
for the young ones coming along now because these young people generally
don't think like we do. My daughter listens to me sometimes, but I listened
to my mother *all* the time. But, you see, my mother would tell me if she
knew something or if she *thought* she knew something or if she didn't know
that thing. And with my mother or my aunt it wasn't any of this "Do what
I tell you, but don't tell what I do." Those women were straight, so they
could expect you to be straight too.

I came up here when I was just fourteen with my aunt and she was strict
and fair, but she was strict first. Fool-like, I wanted to spend all my money,
and then, too, there was a set of young men who didn't respect age or right
or nothing. My Aunt Clara told me just what was going to happen when
I got up here. I was always big for my age, but I was not smart for my age
until I was almost twenty. Now, that's very bad for a young girl because
if you won't look out for yourself, nobody else will be able to. But I knew
what I didn't know, and that is what you really have to start with. Then,

too, I would hear folks that I respected. Now, that's why my head kept from being turned and how I managed to put a few pennies away. I asked my aunt to save for me. She told me that she would do that until I was sixteen and then I should save my own money. Now, that's why a colored woman can have a nice home though she doesn't have much money. I was lucky in finally meeting a man who felt like I had been taught to feel about money and decency and, well, you know, the really important things.

Mark is the kind of man that a fool would think was a fool. He doesn't say much, but he does what he is supposed to do and then some! He's in the V.A. hospital and we go to see him as often as we can. He doesn't stay there all the time. I've had to work hard to get what we decided we really should have. Mark has worked hard too—we all have. I have done many kinds of work. I worked in service until Jan got up to school age. Then we moved. We didn't want her being the poor little black girl. You see, my daughter means just as much to me as anybody else's daughter means to them. I didn't want to do that kind of work and raise her in it. I used to live in and Mark used to do that before we got married and then we worked together. But we were hard-grown people and what they did didn't mean anything to us by then. But you know how children are.

I was married five years before I had a child, so when one got here I really appreciated that and I wanted to give her the best chance I could. I didn't want her being a little clown or getting away with murder or having people be nice-nasty to her or crying over her or any of that. You know, at first I couldn't see that. Mark said we should stop working in service when she was born, but I really couldn't see it and that was as close to really falling out over anything that we ever came to.

I guess I couldn't see it because I didn't want to. I really didn't mind that kind of work and, besides, I liked the woman I worked for. As a matter of fact, I liked the whole family. Mark liked them too. They liked us and they should have because we did what we were supposed to do and then some because they were straight with us. They offered us more money and were very nice. We stayed there for a little more than five years—no, I guess it was closer to four years after Jan was born. But Mark never liked that. He would want to send her down south to his parents and that always made me mad because I wanted her to stay with us all the time. People would invite her to parties, but Mark didn't want her to go. His nephew came to stay with us and I guess that's what made me see that Mark was right.

You see, Jan was—well, she had lots of friends—well, playmates, anyway —and Mark's nephew Mark was new and you know how kids will tease any new kids. One day I was helping to do some canning and Mark came in the back there and said he wanted me to see something. So I went out there in the back and there was my daughter and some white children, all yelling "Black nigger" at little Mark. Well, as they used to say, that was the lick that did poor Dick! I know that was the first time and I think it was the last time that Mark ever put his hands on Jan, and I mean he warmed her two grains of coffee till I felt sorry for her. I believe Jan was too surprised to hollah much, but little Mark screamed his head off and tried to make Mark stop beating Jan. Those little white children must have thought he was crazy. Anyway, they ran and got Mrs. Bates and she tried to find out what was going on, but Mark just finished what he was doing.

Well, I knew that that was wrong—I mean, that Jan should do that—but I didn't really know what *we* should do. Then I thought about it and I could see that he was right. I just thought that maybe he was making too much of it. He wouldn't call Jan by her name, but always called her by some name of one of those children who were with her when they were teasing little Mark. You know, a child can sense when you are really mad—I mean not just, you know, what I might say annoyed. Jan and Mark were very close. She always used to bring him ice water; that was her little kind of personal thing she would do for both of us. For a couple of days Mark would not drink water if she brought it. Well, that used to make her feel very bad and it used to make me mad with him. I felt that he should tell the child how he felt and what she should do, and let that be the end of the whole thing. I knew what he was doing. I knew that he was a grown man and that he wasn't really angry with the child and was trying to teach her something that he thought she had to learn. When Jan dreamed about what she had done in that little garden that day, Mark took her into our bed and tried to tell her what she had done really meant. Well, we stayed up almost all that night talking about that thing. Mark said, "All this talking has parched my windpipe clean dry. I wonder if somebody would get me a good cold drink." Jan has never moved that fast again! We sat there like three fools drinking ice water at three o'clock in the morning. He said, "Shug, I didn't raise you to be no cracker. You do like you see us do and don't be doing every simple thing you see white people doing." Now, that was the last of that, but Jan remembers that thing.

Well, things like that made me see that we would do better to live where there were some other black people—I mean "better" not in a better house but better in other ways. We couldn't have asked for a better apartment than the one we had. You know, that is a very funny thing. I knew that Jan was being invited to too many parties and I know that a lot of times they didn't really want her around, but I didn't want to see it that way. And sometimes I felt, "Well, I don't care. Yes, I'm going to stick my little black child under your noses." But I could see that kind of thinking was stupid too. Mark asked me if I would go to a party where I knew I was not wanted. When I said no, he said, "Well, why are you trying to shove Jan down these whitefolks' throats?" As long as we were there, there just wasn't much getting along, so we left. I see some of the children who didn't leave and I'm so glad we did. The people we worked for were really nice, but I don't think that they understood how we felt about it. But now, in a way they understood and didn't want to know that they understood. It's one of those things that would get so messy if you really went into it that people just say, "All right, do what you think you have to do." That's the way white people and black people get along best. Generally they don't even try to half understand each other. There isn't much we can do about that as long as we live like we do.

Janice Saunders

Now, how is having a lot of fatherless children for the
white man to half support going to help us?

*Janice Saunders' awareness of the strong element of deadly fatuousness in
the black nationalist renaissance of her time does not dispose her to nihilism
or despair. Her level of aspiration is subordinate to her very keen sense of
reality. She is diligent and imaginative, but is under no illusion that her
sagacity and meticulousness will automatically produce the appropriate re-
sults. "If I expected it to be fair and right out here, I'd have to learn to make
my own handkerchiefs because I could never afford to buy enough." When
last I talked with her, on the eve of her departure for graduate studies, she
was "awaiting developments" with that same attitude of intelligent resolution
which has characterized her life.*

I'm almost twenty now and I'm trying to stay in books, but it is very hard.
Everything is very hard, not just because of the hardness of the thing you
might be trying to do, but people keep giving you all this extra grief. But
it's the young brothers who are really the most wasted. They are talking
awareness and doing nothing. I mean, they want to play all the time and
that is no way to get anywhere! I mean, they have it down to a system and
if you don't go along with it, then you are wrong. But if you do go along
with it, you will wind up down south all by yourself.

When I went to college I really thought that was a big thing. Nobody in
our family ever did that, so like I say, I really thought that was important
and I was ready to study back! But books were definitely not cool. I didn't
and don't want drugs of any kind and I couldn't see letting anybody talk
any revolutionary holes in my clothes, so I was on the s—— list right away.
Now, those people who put me down knew that they were wrong, but they
didn't care. My girl friend Jeanne went for all that and she is wasted now.
Do you know that her baby was born hooked? Now, how is that going to
help us? To me, black awareness is for unity—you know, so the people can
improve themselves. Now, how is having a lot of fatherless children for the
white man to half support going to help us? Will you tell me that?

I just keep to myself because I don't feel like arguing with anybody when we both know who's right. One time some people tried to get me to boycott a class and I said, you know, "Tell me why we should do this." And they said, "This dude was using racist books in the class." I asked which books and they couldn't tell me, so I went to class. And a black girl told me that she was going to beat my "black ass." It was just a lot of talk, I guess, because I kept on going and nothing happened, but she and some others tried to scare me. Now, these were my own color! None of them had read the books they were mad about. Now, it's not all like that, but a lot of times it is. So I mostly keep to myself.

My mother says, "Don't sit up here under me, get out and get about!" But everywhere I go people who know they are wrong try to give me a hard time, so I just stay home or in my room when I'm in school. You might say that's not much of a life for a person my age, but I don't mind it at all. I can make it on my own and by myself. I really do feel that way now. I tried going along for a while, but that was really no good. I mean, if I had friends like my mother has—you know, people who will try to help you and tell you what they think you should know. I don't mean they boss you around, but if they see you into something wrong, they will find a way to tell you about it in a nice way. I'm not lying when I tell you that I couldn't find anybody who meant any good, so I said, "I have to cut it loose!" I don't care that much. I play my records and do my work. I go to the things they have on campus sometimes. Sometimes people who put me down would tell me that they thought I was right when there was nobody else around. But I don't call that a friend, and I don't have as much respect for somebody like that as I would have for somebody who was wrong all the time!

I know how to be my own friend and that is all I really need. I don't argue with people. My cousin is into some things that we both know she wouldn't want her mother to see her into, and she wouldn't tell you that she thinks that she is right, but the crowd will tell her that she is with it and laugh behind her back. She was trying to hide from me. I told her, "Look, Gwen, I'm not your mother. What you are into is wrong and you know that, but that's strictly your own business. It's all I can do to take care of Jan Saunders. So do your thing, girl, do it to death if you haven't got any more sense than that!"

Estelle O'Connor Kent

> I always wanted my mother to be proud of me, but I
> never really turned out to be nothin'.

I have known Estelle since she was just a little older than her infant son, who sat cradled in his mother's arms, silent and secure during the lengthy interviews. It was a source of very personal pain to me when her school system, contrary to the evidence, stigmatized her as a "slow learner." Her life demonstrates that she has a mind preeminently worthy of much more serious and humane cultivation than it received. Estelle found the courage and wit to reject drugs when many of her contemporaries were nodding their lives away. She has done more than just survive in callous and perilous school and work situations, and she is able to perceive the passing scene, both political and social, with at least as much sagacity and integrity as many a formal leader or social philosopher. Mrs. Kent is a good-hearted young woman with an inextinguishable passion "to be somebody." Those of us who know her feel she's gone as far in that direction as most good people go.

I was *up* until about a couple of months ago. I'm carrying another baby. It's a fine time to be doing it after me and my husband got separated. I'll make it, you know, but I have seen better days. And they sure wasn't in the country!

But about being black and about the community: there are some good things about being black. If I had to do it again, I'd still be black because to me a black person keeps more beauty in himself. He's got more soul, he's got rhythm. Like a black woman—she looks pretty just being herself, you know, I mean without a lot of make-up. I don't wear make-up, I wear wigs and stuff; but as far as a lot of make-up is concerned, she doesn't have to wear that because the pigments of her skin are nice. And when you are black you really have something to be proud of, although sometimes you may not know it. There are so many things you can do to beautify yourself! When you go for that education or something really important, the black person is more outstanding and upright because they look for the white person to come on like that, but they don't expect that of a black person, they don't look for a black person to do that. Even when we have that know-how, it's harder for a black person to get up there and get that substantial job.

I think if I could do it over again, if I could go way back to the time I was a little girl, I would have stayed in school and got all the education I could get. As a matter of fact, I probably would be in college right now. Because I really wanted to be somebody. Even though I feel like I'm somebody in a sense, I don't feel like I'm the somebody that I would like to be. I'm not the real type of mother that I would like to be towards my son. If I could do it—well, just the other day I had this dream plan and I really would like to do it. After I have my baby I'd like to go to modeling school if I could find a good modeling school, and, you know, see what I could do. When I got out of school I would go to an agency and just see what I could do. Regardless to how it comes out, if I fail, if it's six hundred dollars thrown away, at least I can say I did something that I wanted to do in life. I like the idea of being a model. I've wanted to do that for a long time now. I did some modeling a long time ago, but we were just kids then, so we were just git'n over. I say to myself, "Maybe I'm having these dreams just because I'm pregnant." But I don't really want much. I just want enough. You know, I would like to get a job so I could make enough to make me and my two kids happy.

I never really wanted a whole lot of money. I just want a house and a car. I'd like to have a home fixed up real nice the way I would like to have it. I would like to look at me and say, "Estelle, you are somebody!" Oh, boy! If I could afford it. I like two families, but we all get two-family houses. I'd carpet my house all through either in red or black, and all the bedrooms in my house would be upstairs. In my living room I'd have two high-backed chairs, one long sofa, a long stereo and picture-window drapes. My ideals are small. They aren't real fabulous, but to me they're beautiful! My imagination is great! I can be a thousand people that I would love to be! I can think of a thousand different people that I could say I'd really like to be in their shoes, but really, my greatest goal is to be a model. That's really what I want to be. I guess there is a pretty good dollar involved, depending on what agencies you work for, but it's what I would like to do and you have to like what you do—I mean, to keep on doing it.

Lank, you know they say that they don't have no more slavery days? Well, no, no, no, that ain't so! I don't care what nobody say! This last job I work is all the proof you need that all them slavery days ain' gone! I worked two years at Metro. When I first started working out there it was kind of rough. And the more they raised your salary, the worse off you were. The benefits were lousy and you were making three thirty-two and a half, but you were working like a dog! That place is a glass plant, and we had these big boilers down there, and I had to make the containers for the glass, and they cut about 590 pieces of glass every five minutes or whatever. But, you see, you had to keep that line full of boxes because nothing would stop that glass from coming out! The only way it would stop was if they had a lightning storm which cause the power to blow out. Then it took three days to get it going again. This summer, about a month or two months ago, I just could not take it anymore! I was losing weight. I was under pressure because I knew that I had to make them ends meet! I knew that I had to bring that bread for me and my son *now.* I had to see that my son got the proper things that he needed.

There was no air conditioner in this place. There were six windows in this place, but by the time air would hit it would all turn to heat! I worked under a lot of pressure out there. I withered to a little bone! One Sunday my foreman, who was a very prejudiced person, asked me to work on line two. Now, this was a bad line, but I went over there; and all the Spanish and white girls kept going off this line, but I had to stay there! This was a bad line and I was doing two girls' work on this bad line, so I asked my foreman, "Why is it I have been stuck on this line for five days and everybody else is coming and going?" She said, "If you don't like it, you cut your time card and go home." I said, "Listen, I've been here for the last two years and nobody has ever told me to punch my time card and go home, and you have only been foreman for the last six months!" So I went downstairs and told the plant manager what she had said. He's a stone cracker too, but he had to deal with the situation the best way he could, you know, to keep a lot of static down. So he went upstairs and talked to her about it, and then my shop steward came up and said to the foreman, "Listen, if anybody around here punches their card and goes home, it will be you!"

So after that died down the foreman came to me and said, "Estelle, don't you never ever go to anybody over me again!" I said, "Listen, if I feel that I ain' getting my justice, I will go to your foreman and the foreman over him and the foreman over *him* until I feel like I got a piece of the rock, until I feel like I'm satisfied!" I said, "Don't be talking to me like I was no dog. You talk to me like I was a grown woman and I'll talk to you the same way. But when you start getting silly and simple, I can get that way right along with you and do it even better!" She never liked me from the day I came there. Because they feel that we are silly and simple, they feel that they can make us do anything. She felt that she could tell me to do anything and I would just have to do it.

Working in that place was just like having somebody beating you with a whip that you couldn't see. If it was a hundred degrees outside, it felt like two hundred inside. You were always under pressure from people's mouths and people pushing and pushing and pushing! You worked all types of times, four to twelve, twelve to eight, all types of hours. Let me tell you something: we may be black, but we ain't that far back in the background! Nobody should have to work on a job like that under those conditions like that, and nobody does anything about it, and things are continually being pushed to the side and under the rug. Some emigration people came over to the job and took away some of the Spanish people who were working there because they didn't have visas. But they had jobs that black people couldn't get. To get the jobs we had, you had to show drivers' licenses. These people couldn't even speak English, but black people were told, "You can't get any job down here unless you have a driver's license and registration." Now, how come we have to have all that if they will take people from a foreign country who don't have a thing?

We worked seven days a week with one weekend off a month. That was an eight-hour day and a half! We had half an hour for lunch and two ten-minute breaks. I mean, you worked down to the nitty-gritty! I worked so hard that I couldn't do nothing but sleep. I lost a lot of weight because I was sweating so bad. My father said, "Give it up! Girl, you'll be done died at that place!"

I guess in a way being black is what you make it. But the thing which gets to me the most is to see so many pushers out here in the streets. If we had as many people out here in the street doing good things as there are people out here doing bad, we'd really be in good shape! One thing I have found in this world about white people is that they do at least stick together. We don't have no togetherness hardly. But I will say this: I don't care that much about the Muslim religion, but I will say one thing for them, they do stick together! They do have some type of unity about themselves. Every race has this kind of unity, even the Spanish people. If they say *"Mira, mira!"*, the whole building's empty and they are all out there on you. But black people can be knocked down in the street out here and nobody will call the police. Black people don't have less courage, it's that white people are sneaky. They will call the police and then ease back into the house, so that when the police come nobody knows anything about it. They'll be back on their porch again, so you'll never know who called. A black person might do the same thing too, I guess, but blacks are treacherous. You can get killed over a penny out here! You could be killed for nothing out here. You could be walking down the street minding your own business and some nut might come up in a car and blow you away.

I can remember when I could come home at two o'clock and nobody would bother me. I could go anywhere I felt like going. I was never afraid then, but you couldn't beat me out the house now! I'm home before eleven. You know, sometimes I get depressed thinking about all the evil things in the world. Of course, there are just as many good things in the world as there are evil, but you just hear about the evil. That's why I don't bother with this news, because you don't hear nothing but bad things. You never hear that Mrs. Jones just had ten babies or that a child's life has been saved.

I think it's beautiful when a child comes into the world. I remember my son when he was being born to me. I never experienced such a clean and cleanly feeling! I asked my mother if she had ever had that feeling and she said that she had never felt that way. I had a rough time with him; they had to induce labor and he almost strangled to death. But when my son was passing through me I went, like, over to a whole different side. I didn't know where this place was, but I was so clean. Wherever I went there was nobody else there. I knew I was dying, but I didn't want to fight it. I just said to myself, "Well, it's happening, but I'm not going to fight it like I always thought that I would." It was like someone had vacuumed me, because all the dirt was going out of my body and I was going over to another place and looked like there was a whole lot of static in the air. And when my heart started to function right, I begin to feel all the dirt, just like someone was taking watercolor paint and had colored my whole body. And, you know, that was the best feeling in me! When they smacked him and he didn't say anything, I just knew he was dead and I just said to myself, "Well, I don't want to live, either." But they smacked him again and he whined and my heart just flooded. I was ready to go then! Tired as I was then, when he hollered the only thing I wanted to see was my baby! From a woman's womb comes every little boy and they all have something of Mom in them in some kind of way. I love him. He's black and he's mine. I don't know what he's going to turn out to be, but whatever he is he's still gon' be my baby. He could get to be a hundred and twenty, but I guess I'd say he's still my little baby.

I want to go back to school and make a better me so I can make a better him. But I get so undetermined sometimes, you know. My reading's poor and my spelling's poor. I want to really go back because those are the only things that really hold me back. That's why I feel like I'm less than the next person. That's why I feel like I have a handicap. I'd like to go back, but I don' want to sit there, big as I am, looking stupid! Maybe that's the wrong way to look at it, but I think if they asked me to spell some word and I couldn't spell this word, I'd never come back to the class again. Nobody knows everything, but I'll bet you dollars to doughnuts they out-know me.

I always admired people who make it, like Edwina—she has a good job. And some of the other girls—I look at what they are doing and wish that I had jobs like that, but you know where my complex really was and I know where it is now. I was willing to learn in school, but, you know, when you are the clown in class, the clown of the class don't learn a thing. You laugh things off so people don't really know what's going on. You put up a shield against the world. I mean, I'd try really, really hard! I'd study, but I'd get to school and the teacher would mix the words up and I'd get a big, fat F. I wouldn't just get an F, but a big, fat, *red* F! I'd think to myself, "I studied so hard! I mean, I knew these words when I got to school!" When she gave the papers back I just knew I had a C or a B! But there would always be another big, fat F again. After that, when I left Central, I really got a complex because they put me in a school for slow kids. Everybody knew that school as a school for dummies. "Oh, you're a dummy"—that's what they'd say to you if you went to that school. They sent retarded kids there. I wanted to stay with the rest of the girls and graduate with them. I never got to graduate from anything! I just went to another grade. I would have even felt good if I had got a diploma from the grammar school. By the time they were passing out diplomas, they had put me into a school that was slow. Everybody knew that this school was for anybody that couldn't read, write or spell! I used to feel so ashamed because everybody else was going ahead. I was kept back twice and that second time just did me in. The first time I felt that I still might have a chance; I knew that everybody was ahead of me, but I knew that I'd be coming back next year and I thought I might have a chance. But when they kept me back the second go round, that just did it! I've had that complex ever since, and when they put me in that special school, when they said, "Miz O'Connor, we have to put your daughter in this special school because it's for slow kids"—Oh! I just found it very hard to catch on. I have really tried. I have tried to all extent! I mean, I'd be going whole hog at it, but if that lady asked me to spell something, I just couldn't do it.

When I can get by myself, I really like to be alone! I think about these things generally in the bathroom because I know ain' nobody gon' bother me there! I daydream and my imagination really gets built up. I dream mostly, I guess, about being a model. Seeing me up there, you know, everybody wants to be the best. But I have to take what I have to take until I can get what I really want to get. When you become a failure at so many things in life, I know from my own experience, you just feel like there just isn't too much more that can really be done. Regardless to what I do, it never works out! Things never work the way I planned them or the way I want them to. Like I said, when I was in school I really got down to business, but that teacher would knock me every time! They would knock me down and I'd be in the principal's office and everybody would be so much more advanced than me and they were always talking about keeping me back that next year. I would say, "Miss Riley, I'm doing the best that I can and I can't do better than this." But she'd say, "You've got to do better or you're not going to make it." And sure enough, I stayed back twice. I never even graduated from a lousy grammar school!

I used to daydream about being somebody—I mean a real somebody. I guess everyone is somebody, even if they are wanted on the street, but I mean a *real* somebody. I still carry the memories of school now, but I still daydream about really being somebody. I'd like to have, you know, prestige. I'd like to be my own boss, to be able to say, "I know what I'm doing." I'd like to be so people couldn't really do much to me, so far as me being fired is concerned. I got out of school at sixteen—fifteen, as a matter of fact. I got in a fight with this boy and they told my mother, "Well, Miz O'Connor, the only school this girl is allowed to go to is in the next town. She is not allowed to go to any more schools in this town." There this boy was in school, but they put me out and left him in there. The fight was about he wanted to go with me and I didn't want to go with him. I got in one fight in school because a boy threw my baby sister's shoes out into the street and threw her books out there, too. I came to school and found them out there and told him to pick 'em up. He wouldn't pick 'em up, so me and him started fighting. I punched him and knocked him down the stairs. So they put me out. Then they put me in another dummy school, a worse one! That was for slow people; that was for slow people that were halfway criminals.

Now, those girls down there just knew they were rough! They were into some of everything. They were snorting much coke! You know what the big thing was? It was this cleaner they called Carbona. I went into the bathroom there and these girls had this paper up to their nose. They were snortin' like mad. They asked me if I want some, but I said, "*No, no!*" You're supposed to clean floors with this stuff and there they were. They used to come out of there just as high as they could be! That is a good way to mess up your lungs and that's just what they were doing. I knew that stuff was strong. If you smelt the bottle you knew it was strong. And then in school we had bulldaggers, fags, some of everything. I don't know how I managed to save my little life!

Black kids get hung up on drugs because, well, because—I don' know. I can't quite say why so many would. I don' know. I never got hung up with it. I know I've had my ups and downs and felt like I should have jumped off the roof a long time ago and do myself a favor, but I ain' had enough nerve to. You know, sometime I'm very proud of myself. You know, I've gone through my generation and my sister's generation and now I'm going through my baby sister's generation. I sit down and I think about that and I say to myself, "I really have got something to be proud about because I never got on drugs." A lot of girl friends of mine got on it. It looks bad, but they did do it. That never ever appealed to me because I see that as just like when you drink. You can drink because you have a problem, but when you finished drinking you're sitting there with that same problem plus you are hung over. You got another problem, too, because you're sitting there broke because you just drunk up all your money. So you ain't doing a thing but adding on to your problems. Now, I always had enough problems, so I knew I could not afford a habit of twenty-five dollars, forty dollars, eighty-nine dollars a day. I can't afford that unless I go out there and steal it from somebody. I never took a thing that didn't belong to me in my whole life. I don't care what it was, Estelle don't steal a thing. Now, I'm not going to put something in me that's gon' make me go out here and knock somebody's mother or father in the head.

They say, once a dope fiend, always a dope fiend. I can't quite go along with that all the time. With my two brothers, though, I guess it was once a dope fiend, always a dope fiend. I remember when my brother first got on drugs. He was smoking reefer then. Everybody was out the house. I guess he didn't hear me coming upstairs. He had this bag of smoke on the table and he was rolling it up in cigarette paper. I didn't think much of it, but when he saw me coming he grabbed up the stuff and headed to the other room. I then began to feel that whatever it was, it was something wrong. Well, I knew what it was later on. When I asked him about it, he just said, "Oh, shut up, girl, and get out of here." Later on he began getting on drugs. I caught him one time. I didn't know what was wrong with him. It was six o'clock in the morning and he was sitting in a chair just shaking away! He looked like he was having cramps or something like that. I thought maybe he had been drinking. So when I went over there to him, he asked me if he could borrow three dollars. I asked him what he was going to do with the three dollars, but he didn't say anything, so I gave him the money and he left the house and when he came back he was walking just as straight as anyone else! It was just like there had never been anything wrong with him. So then I knew what was wrong and why he had been acting so crazy. I knew why his attitude had changed so much. I asked him why he wanted to throw his life away like that—you know, to wake up every morning confined to something, to depend on something like that. If you don't have it you don't function right that day; I mean, you're just like a slave. It starts off like a monkey that just wants one banana. Then you start doing it so much that it gets to be a gorilla and this gorilla wants *bananas*! You got a bigger habit, a habit you can't support.

I tell you one thing, if I was in charge I'd stop that methadone. I don't feel that taking an addict off one drug and putting him on another drug does any good! Especially when you can go and get your whole week's supply and then return on a Monday and get some more. Half of the people were selling methadone to the kids out here and they were getting high off of that. And then some people had contacts in the centers, and they could always get more methadone than they were supposed to have, and they started to deal methadone out in the streets. The idea should be to get 'em off the drugs, period! What sense does it make for somebody to get high off of somebody's medication? I mean, what is the point of gettin' high off of something you don't even know what it is? The only thing they know is it's a high and they know that if they don't watch themselves, it will kill 'em. But they don't know what it contains. They don't really know how much to use. You're only on a hummel. You don't know how long your high will last. Maybe a hour, two hours, something like that, and then you're right back where you were and you still got the same old problem! So methadone, pills—none of that stuff is the answer. The only real answer is determination —I mean determination in yourself. You just have to say to yourself and mean it, "I'm going to stop using these drugs!"

Pushers are well-dressed people when you see them out here in the street. They are always dressed to the latest. Now, they don't have heart the first. They can't have much of a heart if they are out here selling drugs to babies. In my experience, you know, in seeing 'em out here in the streets, they don't care what they do as long as it gets them that money. As long as it pays for that Cadillac and puts gas in it and puts a three-hundred-dollar suit on their backs, they don't care what they sell to whoever out here will buy it! As long as they can put that thousand-dollar bill on the figure and live that life, they don' care how they do it. There is no limitation to what they will do and if you mess up with their money, then they run a contract on you. They'll run a contract on you to have you beat up so you'll know that they'll kill you if you mess up with that money again. But that's not the thing. These little pushers out here that the police go for are not the ones. If you take one of those little pushers down, he's got five dope fiends out there who will do anything to get drugs. All you have to do is tell a dope fiend, "Look, go and kill that man over there and I'll give you five dollars." Now, if he's in a bad enough position, ain' nobody in the world can tell him that he is not right to go over there and kill that man to get that dope! He doesn't care! He's dead! He's living from day to day on a hummel! He don't know what tomorrow's gon' bring for him. He don't know how he's gon' get that next drug. Like my brother said when he was on drugs—my mother asked him to get his kids some milk and he told her, he said, "No!" My mother said, "Why not? You got money." He said, "You think I'd buy milk before I get me some dope?" Now, that was some kind of choice right there. But he had to have his drugs first, even if it meant seeing his kids starve to death. Now, maybe when he got them drugs he would have done a little something for them, but he would see them die before he would give up his drugs. Now, I have heard him say that.

I don't think that taking the little pushers and dope fiends down is gon' do it. The main way of dealing with this dope thing is to go right to the port! You got to get to the home base! You got to get to those big shots, those people that are so highly respected in those big offices where the big bucks are coming in! These are the main people bringing in drugs. These are the people that run the drug business. I'm not talking about the little five-thousand-dollar chump change-pushers, but I mean the ones that are making the millions.

Lank, how can you knock all these drugs down, anyway, if your police ain't legit? Your police are not legit, not the majority. The first thing they do if they make a raid—say it's a crap game—they take all the money off the table. Then when they get down to the precinct, they got to give the captain something. After they pocket their money, they say, "Listen, the only thing that was there was four hundred dollars. It was a little game." Now, they just divided two thousand dollars and brought the four hundred dollars in. To fight that you got to have a system that is right from the bottom all the way up to the top. You got to have togetherness and dedication to stop this drug thing. So, these little men here ain't nothin'.

I know a fella around here, they had him kidnapped. They had a seventy-five-thousand-dollar ransom out on him. And who didn't know him here? You know, twenty-three-year-old big shot; every year he switched over to a new car! Now, if he had wanted to, I guess he could have switched up twice a year! But now, out of all that money he's made, how much does he really have to show for the life he's lived? Now he's paralyzed! You see, when they run that seventy-five-thousand-dollar contract on him, they just promised to send him back alive if they got the money. They didn't say *how,* I mean, in what condition they were going to send him back. They just said, "Pay us this seventy-five thousand and we'll send him back, but we didn't say which way he was coming." So he "jumped" out of a second-floor window and he broke his spine somehow. He never was able to walk after that. He has killed so many mothers' sons and daughters and now he has to crawl on his belly like a snake. But he's a big shot. All the dope fiends praise him around here. He's going just as strong. He just bought a twenty-thousand-dollar car! It's made to his perfection—you know, everything's on the steering wheel. Some people really admire people like that. These dope fiends make a pusher think he's a big shot. They build him up because the dope fiend worships anybody with big cars and fancy clothes. That is the only thing they care for and these movies aren't doing any good at all! This "Superfly" and all that mess.

I guess so many people dig this big-car scene because for so long the only thing we ever knew was the back of the bus. For a long time we just wasn't supposed to know anything else. Like they say, if you black get in the back! That's why so many of us still go straight to the back of the bus automatically. It's naturally the thing to do. I've been on buses where there was uku room, but some black people will go straight to the back anyway. I guess some people say, "Well, I guess we're so used to the back of the bus, so we might as well make our own habitat there." I guess it's like on the job—you work and get old and tired, and you say to yourself, "Well, I'm going to retire soon, so I just as well to finish my days here."

I don't know what it's like to die and be someplace else, but to me I think it must be beautiful. It's got to be a little better than here. Because I feel like your hell is right here. You're livin' in it. This is it. I don't care what nobody says, you got heaven and earth right here! It's all what you want to make out of it. I always wanted my mother to be proud of me, but I never really turned out to be nothin'—I mean, nothing that she could really be proud of, you know. I always wanted her to be able to say, "This is my daughter and she did this or that"—you know, something nice that she could really be proud of. They're good, my mother and my father, and I never miss an occasion to show my appreciation. I don't care what it was, birthdays, anniversaries, I don't care what, I would try to scrape up that money and do something about it! Like one time their anniversary came up and I bought this bouquet of flowers. That thing cost me three dollars! I remember I bought my father a razor on time and I was wondering how I was going to finish paying for this razor because I wasn't gettin' unemployment, but I managed to pay for it. There are so many things I want to do. I'd like to buy my mother a front-room set so she could say, "This is what my daughter bought me." I never had a chance to do anything really nice. Like I said, ain' none of us turned out to be nothing, you know, nothing she could really be proud of. There are so many things I want to do for him and her to pay them back. But I don't have education! I don't have the job! I didn't turn out to be the kind of person I wanted to be.

MORE THAN MERE SURVIVAL

You got to live it the best you know how.

Cora Sumter

Sometimes I think Aun' Hagi's children were born to lose. We sure have to be better at losing than winning. Since we don't have too much practice at winning, we best to know how to lose right.

Roland Weldon

*Cora Sumter will soon "step into her ninetieth year."
Three years ago she survived the trauma of the amputa-
tion of a leg, but she still volunteers to cheer shut-ins and
others whom she deems less fortunate than herself.*

*Roland Weldon's long-distance truck driving, ama-
teur baking and fine acoustical-guitar playing make
him a welcome member of and link between widely
separated groups of friends.*

Velma Cunningham

All these doctors want to do is cut you or starve you.

Born in Alabama, Mrs. Velma Cunningham is a very traditional senior woman whose amazing vitality was one of the wonders of her neighborhood. She is an unofficial but locally well thought of healer with a very wide knowledge of core black folk-medicine. A week before she was going to tell me some "animal parables," Mrs. Cunningham was robbed of $3.15 and beaten by three young men. She knows that she will be severely crippled when her lengthy hospitalization ends.

I have sugar, but I don't have it bad. Long as I don't eat anything that is against me, I do all right. But I'm makin' that soun' a little easier than it really is! Blackfolks have a lot of trouble with this food business. We all used to eatin' lotsa strong food like yams and rice and grits and 'specially pork. Now, all that is food for hard-workin' people! There just ain't no substance in whitefolks' food. Now, we don't work in the fiel's so much now, but we love that food still because it was the food of our fo'parents. That was the food we growed up on.

Now, you hear people sayin' we gettin' wiser but weaker, and that is so. Pretty soon we gon' be weakened down and sickly, just like whitefolks. We can't eat the food of our fo'parents! They was all mostly slaves, so you know they had to be healthy. All blackfolks used to be strong and smart, but then they commenced to be weakened down from all this mixin' and doin' till some of 'em ain' much better than these crackuhs! Nowdays blackfolks look like whitefolks and whitefolks look like blackfolks! You see as many white children with these dev'lish Afros as black! 'Course, we always did have some peolas, an' everybody know most of these whitefolks is passin'. But this mixin' business is gettin' out of han'!

Now, you know all this mixin' and doin' is not good for our people. Our fo'parents loved pork and all that strong food. Now, they didn't have no high blood pressure nor no diabetis nor no stomach trouble, neither. But they was almost all black and that is why they was not mean like a lot of these nigguhs you see now! Strong people need strong food. Them strong black people ate pig and yam and goat, and it help them. Now! all that strong food is too much for they children. They systems just won' take it! When I was a chile, my mother fed me yam from her own mouth and I was strong! But that weak blood turned my system against that strong black food. So now I can't eat the food of my fo'parents because I just ain't the woman they was!

Our fo'parents had much bettuh sense than we got now. Back when they was slaves they ordained they own ordain and they stole out to the woods and the swamps and did they own business, and the whitefolks didn' know doodleesqua' about it till they done done whatever they wanted to do! Half the time the whites didn't know they was gone! Them ol' blackfolks made they teas and worked they roots and signed they younguns with the blood and the water, and the crackuhs didn't even know what they was seein' even when they was lookin'. To this day whitefolks don' know near as much about our slave fo'parents' business as they do 'bout these Black Pantas and all these other college nigguhs and they business. Nowdays blackfolks just ain' happy 'less they got some bukra peepin' in they what-I-might-say!

Miz Stokes tell me, "Velma, there are three people you simply cannot lie to: God, your doctor and your lawyer." Now, will you tell me how I'm gon' lie to God, who know my thoughts before I do? I ain't got no lawyer an' don' want none. Now, my doctor is white, so I tells him some and keeps some. All these doctors want to do is cut you or starve you. Shoot! I works harder than that little young devil I goes to! These whitefolks don' care nothin' 'bout you and me and they don' want to see us flerishin'. That's why so much of that medicine they always after us 'bout takin' is agains' us. These doctors ain' nothin' but whitefolks too.

Didn't them crackuh doctors take my susta's younges' boy into the army? Now, they knowed he had heart trouble and was sickly, but they didn't like him, so they put him in that army and kep' him there till they thought it was jus' 'bout time for him to die! Then they come tellin' his mama to come an' git 'em. A crackuh is the lowes' thing the devil ever made an' since it's in 'em to be low, ain' nothin' gon' change 'em! They took that boy knowin' he was too sick to work reg'luh or go to school. An', you know, they kep' him in there long as they could without payin' him his benefits. Yeah! That was them Southe'n crackuhs that did that, an' them crackuh doctors jus' went right along with it because God's truth ain't in no crackuhs.

These white doctors ain' nothin' but snakes, jus' like all the res' of they coluh. These ol' noices ain' no bettuh! When they grinnin' in the face of one of these ol' doctors, they tryin' to be biggety with us. One a them little ol' devils—look jus' as much like a woman as she do like a man—come callin' me granny when I was in that hospital las' time! I ask that little devil what my tempriture was and she say, "Granny, let's leave that to the doctor." Now, you know some of these hinkdy black ones treats you wuss than that. Lotta them so busy tryin' to show they 'thority they can't be bothered with you 'less they think they cin git somethin' out of you. When I was a gurl I used to swear I was gon' be a noice. When I got up some size I knowed

I couldn't be no doctor. I thought I could be a healin' missionary and go to Africa, but now I think somebody need to sen' some missionaries ovuh here 'cause we more weaker than anywhere else now! These whitefolks done done so much wrong that it done come back on everybody. They used to say we gettin' weakuh but wisah, but look like to me we gettin' weakuh and dumbuh!

These pecks ain' changed, they ain' never had no sense. An' now, bless Gawd! a lotta blackfolks try to do every fool thing they see these bukras do! These whitefolks ain' had no mo' sense than to turn the nacheral moon into a junkyard and privy! An', do you know, these nigguhs ain' got no mo' sense than to go roun' killin' theyself to watch 'em do it! You couldn'a paid none of them slavery-time fo'parents of ours to watch nothin' that low. My father was born a slave, and he tol' me and he said that one time the bukra preachuhs and they little black jacklegs said the moon was goin' to trickle away into blood. Now, on this night that the moon was suppose' to come down in blood, all these whitefolks was standin' out in the road by they big houses waitin' for the moon to trickle away in blood. But the blackfolks warn't worryin' about that foolishness because they elduhs had done tol' them that the moon wasn't gon' do nothin' no bukra preachuh or his little black jackleg thought it was gon' do. Even them blackfolks who didn't hear the word from they elduhs went in they houses and stayed there. Way back yonduh even, whitefolks had done done so much evil and wickedness that they knowed they didn't have no hidin' place. It says right in the Scriptures that the goats shall be judged wherever they shall be found!

My cousin is one of them Moozlums and she say they elduh say these whitefolks ain' got long. I think he is right 'bout that, but I think they wrong about pork and strong food. Most of them is hypocrites about that, anyhow, far as I can tell. My susta's oldest boy is into that mess, but you know how our folks are—they was raised on strong food and they likes it. You see, they likes that food till they die because that was the food they been eatin' since they mothers birthed 'em. I tol' you my susta's boy been in the Muslims for a long time now, but when he come to my house he eat pork like they done kill the las' hog in creation! An' he say to me, "Aunt Velma! You certainly do know how to cook lamb!" Now, you know they ain' suppose' to eat no corn bread of no kin', nor no yam nor pork nor possum nor anything wuth eatin'! That's what he say they elduh tell them. But when my nephew is in my house, he eat what I put befo' him jus' as he done since he was eatin' yam from my finguh! Now, you know some of these religions out here done gone too far. Turnin' blackfolks 'gains' other blackfolks don't help nobody in this worl' but the devil and his cracker children. An' if anybody tell you anything else, he is a liah and the truth is not in him.

My friend Marthi's daughter done turned Muslim and that girl is doin' some kinduh foolishness where she don' feed her little chile but one time a day. Marthi say to her, "You ate mo' than once a day, why you let somebody make you starve yo' chile?" But she don' give that chile but one meal a day an' she git her what-I-might-say up on her back if anybody else feed that po' little chile. Now, if you wants to mess yourself up, I guess you can do that, but that child ain' tol' nobody that it wanted to eat one meal a day!

I think most of these elduhs now ain' nothin' but jacklegs! They suppose' to help the people, not git 'em to fightin' each other. But ain' nothin' of ours good enough for these preachuhs now. In slavery-time the elduhs and deacons and such like, they ate what everybody else ate and slept on hard boards on the groun' itself! They wasn't too proud to work and they didn't have no big cars nor nothin' like that. They brought blackfolks together. They married them and they cured them and they signed them with the water and the blood and they close they eyes in death. Didn't a one of them slavery-time elduhs have nothin' but the respec' of they people. They didn't do no dirt an' they didn' cloak no dirt. You didn' hear 'bout 'em jumpin' out no winduhs and they didn't do the crackuhs no favuhs by goin' roun' cuttin' each other's heads off! I don't know what's happenin' to black people! So many folks out here tryin' so hard to be anything but what they was born. Some passin' for crackers, some callin' themselves Moozlums, some callin' theyself Jews, but they all really black! I don' need to be nothin' but what I am. I was born black and, praise God, I'll die so! That is how I feel about that.

I don' know if that help you, but I sho' would like to help you because I feel that you are a sign to many. I don' understand it all—what you doin', I mean—but you are my coluh and God is speaking to a lot of sorry folks through you. A lot of these lazy devils and dope fien's out here who ain't got nothing to do but rob workin' folks ought to be ashame' every time they see you. One of them devils who could hardly walk hisself call hisself snatchin' my bags. I cut that devil jus' as long as I could see 'em. If I live to see November the twenty-ninth, I will be seventy-nine years ol'! I does my little days work because I am poor. I needs my few pennies, and they ain't gon' git my pocketbook if they can't carry me with it. I know that God will bless you and I ain' gon' flerish if I take your money! So don' even open your mouth about no money. I'm a ol' lady and I has my way in this house.

Seth Bingham

Right now, every day is just something you got to get through.

I have known Seth Bingham for more than fifteen years. A West Virginian, he is in his late fifties. He has the respect of his neighbors because he has not been daunted by appalling chronic illness. Seth is fully aware of the perilous incongruity of the requirements of a short-order cook and of the health regime of a diabetic with hypertension and heart disease. He earns his bread by shortening his life, so he is preoccupied with the quality of existence. Seth is a rotund, voluble man of great tact and animation. Gordon Etheridge says that Satan would have swallowed his pride and begged for an invitation to the Last Supper if Seth's butterscotch-bread custard had been on the dessert menu.

Mr. Bingham finds the courage and rectitude to be a courteous man whose word is quite literally his bond. He was drafted into extremely rigorous military service by racist physicians who were cognizant of his history of chronic disease. He was discharged from the army very near death just before he would have become eligible for the benefits attendant upon military service. He has endured and prevailed in the face of maddening physical trauma and administrative small-mindedness.

Everybody believes about themselves the things they want to believe. Now, in this world there just ain' many things you can prove and most people cannot dig most of those very few things. Now, that is because they do not want to dig them. Rhythm and Blues is not crazy when she gets on the bus doin' her act. She knows that she stopped being a young stacked stallion uku years ago. She knows it, I know it, you know it. Ain' nobody don' know it. Now, why do everybody and his brother go along with it? Everybody got uku reasons for not blowing her game, right? Now, me, it don' cost me a thing to go along with her thing. Also, I think to myself, "Hell, it's a damn shame she couldn't get a break doing what she is trying to do when she could do her thing. So why not let her have a little soup since the paddies done her out of the meat?" Another thing—her goin' through her changes takes my mind off my own hang-ups.

People would be much better off if they did not dream, but they have to dream and their dreams are their weaknesses. You dream about the things you can' do. Old men dream 'bout pussy they cannot use. Young studs dream 'bout pussy they cannot get. Unless you very cool, you dream about seein'. Now, if you are hung up about something, that thing can be your thing or something the man laid on you. If it's your thing, then that is your thing, but with blackfolks it's mostly something the man throwed on us. Even if it is something that comes from ourselves, we don' have to dig it if we don' want to dig it. Now, who is gon' blame hisself when there is some other rotten cat that do deserve plenty blame that can be blamed? Now, everybody would like their weaknesses treated like we treat Rhythm and Blues' weaknesses—either go 'long with it or forgit it! Now, that is black-folks' thing.

We can stone mind our own business, Jim! When I think of the things I have looked away from, it surprises even me. That's the way I would like people to deal with me. I would like them to say, "Well, my man, I do not care whether you burn my corn muffin or not because I know you got things on your mind." I wish somebody would say, "Seth, my man, you really put some sport on that cathead!" I would like them to say that even if the damn bread was a little burned. Now, you did that with my simon cakes and I really did appreciate that. Now I might burn up somebody else's order trying to lay something cool on you. You see, people like to lay a little extra on everything they do if they feel that their thing is appreciated.

My job is hard! I have to keep a lot of things straight. I got to watch lots of things which I have started at lots of different times. All of these things has their own ways of cookin'. I do everything! Some things I make up the day before, some things I have to warm up slower than some other things. Now, you see that I tries to make this bread puddin' into something. People buy all I can make because they like a bread puddin' that ain' like some leftover cinder block. This is not no simple thing. Mos' people likes their bread puddin' slightly less sweet than cake. They like it to be light and creamy with a crus' that is crisp and buttery and slightly sweeter than the rest of the puddin'. Everybody wants it that way. Now, they don' ask where I'm gon' get all that crus' from or how I'm gon' get that crus' to be a little sweeter than the inside of the puddin'. When they get it they eats it fast, and mos' don' care how much work go into it. After all, what it mean to them? Bread puddin' ain' no big thing, and if it was all to go to hell this afternoon, it wouldn't get to them.

They don' know or care that I got to make this puddin' and this cake and this pie and all the other things I have to make whether this diabetis is down on me or not. I have heard more than one person say that Africans don' have no suguh, so maybe this is just one more thing that the man laid on us. I don' know. I do know that it is very hard to do my job with sugar diabetis. It is very hard for me that sweets are against me because I love them. But that's my hang-up. I should be able to have some job that has nothing to do with sweets or eatin'. Now, if you cook you must eat. Sometimes I hate food just because there is so damn much of it. Sometimes I slap the shit out of food, but I generally treats it nice because I like it. You know, food make people happy or sad. You can make food say anything you want. I can say "Go to hell" or "Come back again" with my food. You can do that with a lot of things.

When I was in the hospital behind this sugar thing, there was a girl that worked there and she would empty them bedpans with real class. She didn't make nobody feel like dirt. She would get you things like she really knew how bad you needed them things and how you wished you could get them for yourself if you could. And if she couldn't do something right away, she would tell you that she still remembered and was going to do that thing as soon as she could. Now, that's the kind of person who should be the President. I'd vote for her in a minute, Jim! If you can't empty a bedpan without making the patient feel like what you just sent down the drain, then how could you run the country? Once a nurse tried to give me a hard time because I asked her what my temperature was. Mind now, I said my *own* temperature. So I told her the next time that if I couldn't know what my temperature was, she wasn't gon' know, either. So she said I had to do it and I said I didn' have to do a damn thing but die! She went away from there and came back faster than she had ever answered my light with a whole passel of doctors and male nurses. She told them that I had threatened her and that I had tried to get fresh with her and put on a real good act.

Now, these doctors was framin' up on gettin' several armfuls of law when my girl walked in there and said, "Mr. Seth, what is wrong?" I told her what had gone down and she asked me if I would have my temperature taken if she would tell me what it was. I said "cool," but the bitch that started all the hell to begin with told her to mind her own business. But these doctors could see what was happening, you know, but they didn't want to sound this bitch in front of me, so they said it wasn't important and that they could take my temperature in the morning. One of the big doctors was making it with this bitch who was giving everybody a hard time, but from then on she really laid it on Miss Donnelly. The dude who was joogin' her was married, so he had to come on like she wanted him to. I still say that Miss Donnelly was one of the best people of any color that I have ever met. She was straight and she carried herself so that you had to respect her if you had any sense at all. I seen her slap a doctor *and* a patient, and they both knew that they asked for it. I thought about the same number they did, but when I saw how she carried herself, I said, "More power to you, chick."

I have been in the hospital a lot. Generally I just lay dead because you can get yourself in a lot of trouble in hospitals. They got their way and they gon' do their way no matter how you think about it, and if you get in their way they will try to waste you. I used to work in a hospital, but me and this cat that was the cook could not make it. I used to pick up some change barberin'. I didn' have no papers, I just know how to cut hair, but, you know, ain' no barber making no money these days. This wig number is causin' our barbers to starve, and you know that our people used to depend on that barberin' and hair dressin'. But that's gone, Jack! If I was not able to handle my liquor, I would not work in a bar. I used to be a bartender and I was a good one, but I started drinking too much. But, you know, that liquor don' move me that much now.

But to do this job I do really have to taste food of all kinds. Now, I wouldn't lie to you, I don' *have* to have sweets, but I do have to have this job. I have to have this job or something mighty like it. It seem to me that I ain' going anywhere. I used to think that I would be a doctor—well, I didn't really think that. I guess I just daydreamed that thing. Sometimes now when I'm into something I don' have to think too much about, I think about finding something that would help everybody—you know, like a real cure for sugar or something like that. Sometimes I think that things would be better if I could just get somewhere else.

Right now, every day is just something you got to get through. I work. I work hard—you can ask anybody out here—but I don' seem to get nowhere. I can do a whole lot of things well, but the only way that I can prove that I can do them is to get a job. Ask Mac or Red. They'll tell you that I am as good at barberin' as any barber they know. Now, they are barbers and good ones, too, so they should know. You know, I can cook as well as them dudes in those fancy places. I know a lot about machines and I can do anything with a car that any of your mechanics out here can. But what good do that do me? Kids with papers ain' workin', so you know I better stay here as long as I can. But it is a natural drag.

Johnetta Ray

I'm no respecter of churches in the same way that the
Lord is no respecter of persons.

---

*Miss Ray is a well-read, well-traveled lady on the threshold of her sixties. She
has a fine mind of her own. Her approach to everything from Jeremiah
Clark's "Trumpet Voluntary" to almond- and watermelon-sweetmeat–filled
fried pies is tastefully personal. During a teaching career of close to forty
years, she introduced thousands of boys and girls to everything from human
biology to the* Odyssey. *Many of those former students still remember with
gratitude her patient, considerate, humane and thorough dedication to their
learning. She is an amateur historian and vintner of commendable depth and
subtlety who is "looking forward to seeing more of those places I've been
talking about for so long." She is loved and respected by people of sense for
the learning and wisdom she has acquired and shared and her quiet refusal
to flaunt it.*

I was born in Virginia in Southampton County, but I grew to womanhood
in the North. I've been a teacher in the South and in the North. I'm a
Baptist, but, like most of our people, I'm no respecter of churches in the
same way that the Lord is no respecter of persons. I believe there is some
good in all. I have thought about devil worshipers and, you know, I have
concluded that there must be some good even in Satan! I think everything
must have in it its own imperfections. The worship of god is marred by evil,
so the adoration of Satan must be marred by good, so I would personally
love the good in both kinds of worship.

When I was a girl in the country, the Negroes used to speak of the devil
as Old Sam or the King Yukka or Kwashi. Now, I've heard white people
say that, to the Negroes, God and the devil are very much alike. Now, the
truth about that is that to the blacks I was born among and any blacks I
have ever lived among, both God and the devil are differently thought of
than they are among whites. Our people don't think of God so much as a
Triune but as a dual divinity. Jesus is a kind of suffering servant, like we
are, and God is a triumphant tryer in whose sight our time is as nothing.
But when it shall please Him to cut down the wicked that flourish, no man,

especially *the* man, can hinder Him! To us, Jesus and King Jesus are really different gods, I think. I think we depend upon the devil much less than we used to during slavery-time, but even now we depend upon him more than we do upon King Jesus. I don't think we depend upon either King Jesus or the devil nearly so much as we rely on Jesus lynched, who is in nowise just Christ crucified! It is the Lord wronged, the good 'buked and scorned we sing of mostly. It is not so much that we are healed by His stripes as it is that by keeping alive by singing and shouting and raging the memory of His scourging, we incline the ear of Jesus, the conquering king, to our own fresh scars. Jesus is the suffering servant whose precious bleeding side is an alarm and an affront to his all-conquering Father to move this race and raise up a nation to obey.

You know, our people and white people do agree on one thing—both of them see heaven as an essentially segregated place. Remember, "In dat Rumshumkrushafu ain' nobody but me and you." I can't think of any European artistic representation of heaven in which Negroes are really among the blessed.

Our people are unashamed gluttons for almost any pleasure imaginable, perhaps because daily diplomacy of an interracial kind is so exasperating. I don't really know why any group of Negroes can extract ten times the humor or pathos from any situation than white people can, but they can. I know the more merriment we extract the simpler whites imagine us to be. But we are a very provincial people on one level. We are not concerned enough with other people's opinions of what we eat or how we think. A sorority sister of mine has been ashamed to eat watermelon publicly ever since I've known her and that's been a good twenty years, so you know how she secrets her chiddlins! But she will not give up the chiddlin or the maw. She knows a dozen dozen ways to cook them divinely and will consume them as if Pharaoh's army is rapidly approaching when she is among blackfolk. But if you were a white anthropologist or psychologist questioning her, she would deny all knowledge of maws or chiddlins, assure you that she had indeed heard tell of folks who had heard tell of such things and apologize profusely for not being able to enlighten you any further.

No matter how hard we try, I don't think black people will ever develop much of a herd instinct. We are profound individualists with a passion for self-expression and yet we are generally governed by an ill-defined code. My friend Ida is a Jew and she lives her way of life, especially her religion, according to very strictly prescribed, often written, instructions. She thinks of these instructions as almost eternal. In her family her husband pours honey on an apple to sweeten their New Year, yet their written tradition has it that the new year is already inscribed in a book of life. We eat pork and peas at New Year's time for luck, but no one has time to write about it. The people who cling so desperately and often secretly to their traditions understand very little about the reasons why they believe what they believe. That is why I am glad to see that at least one black person is a professional anthropologist. Perhaps you could help our people to know itself better.

Any way I can help you I would certainly be glad to try. I know some people you should speak with. Many people I know would be very pleased to help you with money or transportation. My part of Virginia is Prophet Nat's country, and there are still people there who revere him and fear him with a clean fear. They would never tell any white man anything of importance. There is one man from my home whom we used to call Pa Mojo. You should really speak to him if you want to know about carving and slavery sermons. His father was an elder in slavery-time and he knows a great deal about that. I'm sure he would want to talk to you about the religion of the slaves. He made some ox-bone crosses and this pendant for me. He has a number of walking sticks which he makes himself. There is not a trace of the jackleg in him! Prophet Nat and all those slavery-time elders followed King Jesus, but they had very little for the suffering servant to do.

Gordon Etheridge

God is the baddest ass in the firmament!

His neighbors see Mr. Etheridge as being just on the right side of the line which divides the prudent majority from the exotic marginals. He is generally thought of as "doing the cheap wine number to death." His personal cleanliness, his refusal to rob or steal from his neighbors and the general view that "Gordon is not freakish" conspire to make him "just straight enough." Most people think that Mr. Etheridge will probably become a full-time member of his local chapter of the ubiquitous "standing and leaning society," that sad assembly of human beings reduced by cheap wine and other drugs to aimlessness. But when I last had the pleasure of his company, I found that the people who called him crazy just meant that he would, when asked, tell you what he was really thinking in so many cogent, original words.

I has but one difficulty in this world and that is the lack of bucks! Money, honey! That is my hang-up! If I had money I would have it made! I could tell whitefolks and spooks to lovingly embrace my rusty hind parts! But without money I have to go through some changes, Jack! which are tough enough.

Now, you understand that I just told you a lie. These changes I must go through to get my weekly wine are not really tough! Not when you considers how some—no, I'll say most—blackfolks have to make it. Now, you probably go through more than I do in two months! 'Cause, Jim, let me assure you that Gordon E. stone don't sweat no causes! No! Not even the only cause that means very much to his well-soaked heart, that is to say me, Gordon E., or whatever else I might be known as! Now, when I tell you I don't sweat no causes, you can believe that thing, Jack!

You understand I ain't got nothing but time an' I lie so often that it is a pleasure to be able to tell the truth if I want to. Some cat out here was a wise enough fool to write in a book so that every living ass that could read could read the stone truth about this life. You just can't fool with the golden rule in a crowd that won't play fair. Now, he was wise to dig that, but he was a fool to put it in the street. Success in this world and all them others means digging that the rules are for honkies! It is the sign of the power and the trick that gits it every time! Now, I am a stone believer in the sign of the power and the trick because that is what is out here and up there! But I fall short of the glory because I am too soft to run some games. But I do many of the standard brands of bullshit, and every now and den I do a number which I really feel bad about! But I ain't goin' tell you about that here; besides, you probably know already. But I never tried to kill nobody who wasn't messin' with me. And I ain't never took nothing, neither pussy nor wine nor scoff nor money nor anything else, that I didn't have a cryin' need for. Now, I hear that the wolverine is mean and that the eagle hunts for pleasure. Now, I find that very hard to git to. Anyhow, I would have found that hard to believe before I understood how life works. I now do believe that them animals do them things, but I still do not think that they mean the same kind of meanness that people are into. The eagle got to practice his food coppin' or he may lose his skill, but most of the shit people do messes up them and somebody else too! It genally cost several people time and money!

One day me and the last woman in this world I had any business with my hands on was talking about wine, and she was stone against it! She always asked me what I see in it and I told her, "Anything I want to see." She begged me to tell her what I see, so I told her the truth, which is I see whatever I want to. Jack! then, I was seeing all types of things: money, no worries, pussy, understanding and anything I want but have a hard time getting. So she said that was like dope and she told me I should work for what I want and learn to live with what I could get because with wine I don't have anything. She said sometime she think wine mean more to me than anything else. And I told her the truth, which is that wine *done* more for me than anything, so I naturally love it more. Then she said she would do anything for me that a poor woman could do. And I said that everybody said that, but most folks don't mean that. They will do whatever *they* want to do for you, never mind about what *you* want done. But she said she wasn't that kind of person and begged me to tell her how she really could help me. So I told her straight out then what I really needed was some tiddy squeezin' and pussy teasin' and, you know, that woman hit me with a chicken frier—with two chickens in it at the time! She wouldn't even go with me to the emergency! Now, I ain't seen that woman since and I still don't know why she asked me what I wanted if she did not want to know! Now, she could have said "You gets nothin' here!" or she could have said yes or she could have let me have a little of what I needed. But no, she had to kiss me with that hot, heavy pan!

Now, I said that to say this: You see all these spooks jumpin' up and down talkin' about "come sweet Savior!" Now, you know as well as me that there will never be anything in this world as empty as the first church on the Sunday that Jesus gets here. I was once into that holiness bag an' I know *that trick!* All them jackleg elders and deacons know that when you dead you done! Now, they say that Jesus died. That mean he just as done as anybody else that died! Now, if the Lord didn't die, the whole entire deal ain' nothin' but a lie! They told me that He gave His life for ransom just because He loved me so. My mother was a stone kwistion, and when I came home from work one day and told her this old Jew I work for told me that they used to have TVs and toasters way back when, she say right away she don't believe that 'cause nobody never found any of these things and she know that these heavy science numbers had not been done way back then. So then I asked her if she really think Jesus died for her, and she say she *know* that He died for her. So I said, "Now, Mama, how He gon' die for you if you born after He died? Before your great grandmama's great grandmama was dreamed of, He died!" So then she said Jesus knowed everything and He knowed she would be born a sinner and that His blood would wash her sin clean away! So I asked her why Jesus didn't fix it so she wouldn't be born a sinner and she said that Jesus don't want no slaves and he give her her free-will choice. So I ask her why she don't let us have our free-will choice and if us kids want to kill our fool selves, why she don't let us 'cause that's what the Lord done for His children. "Behold, I put before you life and death, choose ye life," that's what it say. Now, with children you got to make the choice till they can make it with grown folks' sense and we all supposed to be the children of God. Now I say, "Mama, now, what would you think of me if I was to take that little gold grandchild of yours down to the water and rare back like them jacklegs do and say, 'Now, Bubba, this is the land and that is the sea. Now I know you ain't but four years old and I also know you cannot swim a stroke, but you choose which of these elements you want to live in.' " Well, she knew I was right, so she told me to hush.

In heaven, when the deal go down it's the blackest and the baddest ass that makes the others deuce out. They say that Satan the devil was the brightest angel and he fell and the Boss hurled his ass down to low stones! My mama used to say, "Everybody would be beautiful if they made themselves." So now, God made everything and if it ain't beautiful it ain't that ugly thing's fault!

Now, this Mad Dog is messin' up heaps of folks. The fault is with the people that made it and the folks like me who are fool enough to make these Jews rich by messin' ourselves up! Now, suppose I make this Mad Dog when I don't have to make it, and suppose I make you buy it and then turn around and send you to hell for drinking this shit which you wouldn'a known nothin' about if it had not been for me! That's like these cats runnin' after these young girls out here and then the minute they give 'em a little piece they start soundin' on 'em, callin' 'em biffas and whores just for doin' what they begged 'em to do! I sure Gawd ain't the best man I know, but if I was runnin' things they would be better than they are now.

Now, nobody but a fool would say there ain't no God 'cause all this stuff out here stone did not make itself, and since it is here, somebody had to put it here. Now, am I right or wrong? So God is the baddest ass in the firmament! He spare who He want to and He strike who He want to and there ain't nothin' you or me can do about that. I fear God and God got sense enough to know that, so He must know what I'm thinking and if He decided to kick my ass, He might do it just as quick for what I think as for what I say, so I says what I think when I want to.

Now, all my people died and their bones done rotted and wasn't but few of them fools, so they had to know anything I know and then some, but all of them died God-fearing and God-respecting folks. Now, I'll tell anybody I fear the Lord, but I do not tell people that I respect the Lord because I don't lie no more than I have to. If I went round punishin' people three generations after the crime their great grandpeople did, I would not respect myself for doing that. A lotta times I do something just because I'm bad enough to do it and I don' give a damn whether I should do these things or not! I just want to do them, so I do them. I know I'm wrong from de git and ain' nobody in his right min' gon' think I think I'm right! But they know they gon' git a stone stompin' if they ain' badduh than me. That's the way it is anywhere I know anything about on earth or in heaven.

Now, you know God told us He was a jealous God. Not me! I wouldn't tell people I was jealous because I ain' bad enough to do nothin' about it most of the time. I was messin' around with a little ol' girl. She tol' me she had to stop comin' around here because her mama was watchin' huh too close. Now, I know she got some young stud going up beside huh head because she come round here sometime and give me a little. But I *said,* "All right, baby, don' git yo'self in no trouble." I got hot with *everybody* that day, but since I don' know who the young cat is and since I couldn' do anything about it that would make any sense to do if I did know, I just play dumb and wait. If I was bad enough I might kill huh and huh mama! An' I *know* I would waste that young stud, not because I had any business whatsoever in that young girl's draws but because I liked feelin' huh and did not like anybody to stop me from doin' this thing which I know I ain' had no business doin'. She young, but she a woman! I don' mess with no children! An' if I have all I need to tas', I don' rilly need nothing! But if I don' take my tas' I need everything anybody else need!

Now, I would like it if I could have what I need. If you got money or if you bad, you can have what you really need. Truth is, I don' need nothing freakish. I just need what everybody else need—a wawm place to live in, something clean and good to eat, some pussy, some clothes to wear and a way to wash them, an' some time for me to think or play or lay back or do anything that cross my min'. Now, if I had money enough for them things I would not bother anybody for anything else. Now, I would work for that money, but nobody won' pay me to do what I can do! Now, I can whiddle *some* an' I ain't poisoned nobody yet. I can preach and I can sing an' I can rub pain out of folks an' I can make plants grow and I can make wine—I mean *good* wine, not this Mad Dog out here. I could do these things if somebody would pay me to do them. But nobody don' want me to do anything but just be quiet over here. An' that's what I genally tries to do because I do not want to go to no jails or hospiddles or homes or any of them places where crackuhs mess you up and call it helpin' you. I don' need nothin' but some steady money and I can help myself. I ain' no chile! I done had all that whitefolks' help I can use! An' let me tell you, a whole heap of blackfolks ain' a hell of a lot bettuh! Like that time I went to the emergency behin' that chicken-fryer number I tol' you about. I'm sittin' there bleedin', but they got to know who my father was and where my mama was bawn before they even thought about stoppin' me from bleedin' to death! A lot of these black ones ain' worth shit, either. One time when I was in the place all these little fresh-ass white nurses who didn't know me from Adam started callin' me Gawdy, and don't you know, mos' of the black ones started doin' that too. But there was a sustuh there that straightened their asses out! I heard the whole thing. She tol' a couple of them black nurses, she said, "That man is old enough to be your father and you call him Mr. Etheridge." She tol' 'em right down front! She said she didn't care what the whitefolks did, she was gon' remember huh bringin' up and put a handle on everybody's name and she wanted to see them do the same. But some nigguhs try to be so shitty you'd think they people was all crackuhs.

Now, you take Duke! That nigguh ain' got nothin' but time an' money! Duke could help you if he wanted to help you. Now, the truth is, he want to talk with you or anybody else he can fin'. That joogie was bawn with diarrhea of the upper and lower lip! He done been through every change you and me ever thought of and then some! He got, right in his house! more money than you ever gon' see. So why he give you that song and dance? I'll tell you why: because he want you to beg him and because if he can, he will git every cent you have. Now, I'll tell you what any of these people out here will tell you. I'll do anything I can to help another coluhed man. I was so glad when you didn't beg that dude, I decided to help you out myself! I was gon' to hip you not to give him your numbuh, but I see you still got your street sense. You know, he been aroun' lookin' fo' you twice! You know, he gon' have a shit fit if you don't talk to him too!—I should say, if you don' let 'em tell you how great he is. He could have talked to you Wednesday an' he wanted to, but he jus' played pussy till he got fucked. I don' believe you gon' run up on too many of them "important nigguhs." Mos' people will go out of they way to help you because they proud to see you tryin' to git somewhere. But you know there are some educated fools out here. Some of them been to college and some of them done educated theyself. I think what you are doin' is all right. Ain' nothing gon' change these whitefolks' min's. Ain' nothing you could tell 'em gon' make 'em do right! But I like to see some of our people doin' these things too. You know what I mean.

I would not talk to any joogie who comes over here and bothers me. There was a gray chick that used to come over here askin' me all kinds of simple-assed questions. She would answer most of them her ownt self! I put up with huh for a while because she always used to have a tas' on her and naturally I wanted to git nax' to huh if I could. She said she'd gi' me some, but I want you to know I'm careful where I put my peduh! Like all these damn refugee kids, she didn't have nothin' for soap and water to do! I jus' jive aroun' with huh. You can' talk nothing heavy with that woman. She all right—I mean, she mean good, I guess. But she just don' know how to talk to people! She like mos' whitefolks, she ain' got no min' of huh ownt. She come here to get me to talk to huh, but the way the deal go down, she done spill huh in-gut to me. Now, I'll tell you what I think is goin' down out here, but I can't be talkin' about nobody else! She tell me huh business! huh mama's business! huh sustuh's business! I know how much huh mama drink! I know how much huh ol' man got swingin'! I know that huh brother ain' suppose to be the father of a one of his kids! I know she done got ridda three babies and huh sistuh done got ridda two! Now, she don' know a damn thing about me an' ain' gon' know no more! But, you know, that's how these whitefolks do. They so busy tryin' to mess us up they messin' up everybody. An' you can' tell 'em that they shit stink, too, because they are too simple to get to that.

Now, this las' fool they put in the White House!—he is a stone white dude and that is why all them others are gon' go 'long with him no madduh how bad and simple he git! Now if G. Etheridge had done jus' one skosh of what he did, they would have put his black ass *under* the jail and sent the key to the moon! Whitefolks are simple, but they ain' that simple. They musta known that cat was wrong as two rabbits when he got in there and raised his pay even before his ass had wawmed the White House throne! Then he tell me to eat less meat and I ain' eatin' none now! They know he wrong, but he ain' no worse than them and he their color, so they gon' hang in there with him. If it hada been any black man from Jesus Christ to you or me, they'da impeached his ass for thinkin' 'bout half of these dirty deals that Nixon done done. He bad, so every one of them little dudes look at him and say, "Well, maybe I ain' bad, but there's somebody up there look like me an' he is *very* bad." They would rather see a cracker do wrong than give a black man a chance to do right. They know damn well that when it come to fuckin' up, they done already done bedduh than anybody else could do. Shit, I rathuh see my dog be the President.

Ella Turner Surry

Some people are the horse shit of the earth.

"They don't come no better than Mrs. Surry." Estelle Kent said it and there is nothing of any consequence in the way of local dissenting opinion. Mrs. Surry's excellent table, discreet counsel and measureless humanity have benefited countless friends and acquaintances. Her selfless devotion to others is all the more remarkable as she is not now, nor has she ever been, blessed with very much more than the scores of people she has helped to help themselves.

Mrs. Surry read me the first novel I ever heard, Robert Louis Stevenson's Treasure Island. *She held school after school and taught "slow learners" without making them feel subhuman. She and Mrs. Melton, Sr., pooled their meager resources and organized a boys' club. Those ladies fought the worst effects of street life with cake and ice cream and wholesome company.*

If life were a matter of rich recompense for noble service, Mrs. Surry's wealth and happiness would defy estimation. But in this world as it actually is, for all her gallantry she has lost the battle against the street. She has been mugged, her possessions have been stolen and the house she strove so mightily to purchase is a crumbling, beleaguered island in a sea of urban decay. She lives in a bombed-out city and has had to take cover in her own house from the fire of her own army in her own country, but she is still clinging to sanity somehow.

Have I encountered discrimination?! I was told by my adviser in high school when I wanted to take the secretarial course, "You cannot take it. Who's going to employ you? You people don't have any businessmen who are going to employ you and the white businesses are not going to employ you. You're a nice girl, but this is not the course for you. You're not going to be able to go to college and there's just no future in it for you." I can see that little thin lady right now and I remember her name, too. She gave me the facts.

Now, I'll tell you another thing that I was just discussing with my children: when I was coming along looking for a job, if they would employ a Negro they would specify in the paper whether they wanted a light-colored one or not. I can remember an incident with another lady. I can call her name, I remember it as well as if it had happened yesterday. Mrs. Peters! She had a store on Main Street. I answered this ad because I was desperate. I wanted a summer job. She wanted a waitress and she asked me over the phone, "Are you light?" I tried to ignore the question because I wanted the job, but she asked me again, "Are you light?" It wasn't this black or white thing then, because black was a fighting word then for some people. So I said to her, "I am colored." So I went up and she gave me the job. But this is the way it was. It was put right out in the papers. I tried to tell my girls about that. No bones about it—they specified when they wanted light-colored or fair-skinned.

There was one other black girl working at this place, in the kitchen. She was dark and she was washing dishes. Now, I quit that job because of that girl. I was in the dining room and there were two white girls working there with me. I called my orders to the kitchen and this girl in the kitchen would bring them to the serving window when she wasn't busy washing dishes; then I would take them from there. Well, you see, I was very busy because I worked one half of the dining room by myself and the two white girls worked the other half together. I had a habit of never writing down my orders; I liked to try to keep them in my mind. I used to pride myself on my memory and I never used a pad or pencil. Now, this girl that was working in the kitchen was rather slow. She had been told by Mrs. Peters never to come into the dining room. Now, this was just a luncheonette on Main Street. Well, this black girl—I think her name was Tina—could see that I was really busy, so she came into the dining room to bring two orders. Well! Mrs. Peters saw her and stamped her feet and said, "You black nigger, I told you never to enter this dining room!" Tina ducked back in the kitchen, and after I came out of shock I came out of that dining room taking off my apron! Now, at the time the dining room was full. It was so busy that Mrs. Peters didn't notice me at first. But when she looked around I had on my street dress and was ready to go. She said, "Where are you going? Are you sick?" I said, "Yes, I'm sick." I said, "Because if you'll think that way of her, you'll think that way of me." She said, "Think what way of who?" By that time she had forgotten all about what she had said. So I reminded her and she said, "You can't leave like this. The dining room is full." I said, "Watch me!" I said I would come back on payday for my money, and went home. When I told my mother what had happened, she said, "You did absolutely right." Now, Mrs. Peters herself evidently had to get out there on that floor and hold those customers that lunch hour I left. She came to my house, and while she was sitting in my living room she raised my salary three times! I knew I was good at what I was doing, you see. But I wouldn't go back there. When I went there to get my salary, however, I saw that the other black girl was still working there.

I have always been conscious of a kind of pride—not this kind of pride they got in the streets now. It was that real pride from knowing who you were. My grandfather made me feel that way before I was a teenager. It had something to do with knowing where you had come from and knowing your family's history. He made me conscious of the fact that I was black and that I had a history like everybody else. That was something different than the garbage they handed out in school that kept telling us how much we owed Lincoln. Every time you heard his name mentioned you were supposed to bump your head on the floor five times. He said, "Read and see behind this Lincoln business so you will see what the whites are trying to do." He got me to read about a lot of people. He introduced me to Harriet Tubman. Now, there was a person I really admired! I've read that she was supposed to have these dizzy spells, but I believe that this was an act that this woman had to get her point across. I don't think she could really have been sick and did all the things that she got done. I think she had an act which made people do what she wanted to do. She had to play the game to get her point across. We have always been the best actors in the world because we have always had to live at least two lives and we have done that successfully.

I remember another incident. This lady was in her eighties and she had never been married and she put this ad in the paper for a girl to come in and do her little washing and cleaning. So one day I took a girl up to her apartment—I was the elevator operator. Now, this girl wasn't up there but a hot minute. When I brought her down she didn't look but so happy, so I just said to myself, "I see you didn't get the job." She was a very neat and clean, heavy-set dark girl. I had no sooner got this girl out of the building when I was called to the seventh floor again. The old lady who put the ad in the paper asked to see me. She asked me, "What was the idea of bringing that girl up there?" I said, "Well, she said that she wanted to see you." She said, "Well, don't you ever bring anybody as black as that up to see me again, because I'm not going to hire anybody that black." I said to her, "I've never seen a black person in my life!" She said, "Well, you should have taken a good look at that one!"

You ask me if I ever encountered discrimination! It was right up to your nose. I worked half of Mrs. Peters' dining room—that's right, it was sectioned off in thirds, well, supposedly in thirds, but my third was the entire back half of the room. You see, I had the biggest third. Now, these two blondes worked the front, but I had the whole back of the room and the sides, too. That's the way it was and if you wanted to work you had to accept it. We had to work.

Now, we were talking about how white people expect more of black people. I just thought of an incident that will show you what I mean: I was in the hospital and I was sharing this room with a white woman. Now, we had both had operations and we were just laying there together. Now, I had had serious surgery. I was a diabetic, 240 blood pressure. Now, I got up at night when the doctors and nurses weren't watching me and washed out my nightgown because my husband was working, all my children were small and I didn't have anybody at home to do for me. Now, this white woman, who was evidently quite well-off, she said to me, "Sweetheart, would you mind if I asked you a question?" Now, I knew when I heard that "Sweetheart" that I was going to get hit with something. Oh, I knew that! This was the approach—"Sweetheart" or "Darling." Her incision was draining very copiously and this was messing up her beautiful silk pajamas. She said, "I don't want to ask my daughter-in-law to wash these because they are so messy, but would you mind washing them out for me?" I simply told her that I was doing my own but I wasn't going to do anybody else's. I told her that I didn't think that her daughter-in-law would mind doing that for her because a little blood wouldn't hurt her any more than it would me. She turned her back to the wall and cried. She was quite upset. Said she didn't know that this would offend me. Now, she didn't want to ask her daughter-in-law, but she felt no qualms at all about asking a total stranger because I was black! I shouldn't mind this blood and drainage! Now, I was dealing with my drainage, but she didn't feel that it was necessary for her to deal with hers. Now, she hadn't had the extensive kind of surgery that I had had. You see, when they look at a black person they see someone who is supposed to be able to stand much more heat than they can. I'm supposed to be able to stand much more work than they can without getting tired. These lazy Negroes are the ones who dig ditches and build roads and lift heavy pots and things.

Yes, heavy pots! When I worked in the kitchen of St. Mary's Hospital I was supposed to be able to grab one of those big pots and run right 'cross the floor with it! Now, white girls who were older than I was weren't supposed to be able to do that. I've actually been asked how I could stand the heat by white girls who were going outside because they said it was too hot for them to stay in the kitchen. But, you see, if I had decided that it was too hot for me and gone out back to cool off, when I got back I wouldn't have had a job. We fought that plantation thing because we had to, not because we were any more able to fight it than anybody else. You can believe me, when it comes to steam tables, it's just as hot for me as it is for anybody else!

Finally I got away from those heavy pots and went up on the floor. Well, this lady patient was lying there very hung up by arthritis in her hands, so I started to crack her eggs for her. Well, I thought she was going to jump out of her bed. "No, no, no!" she said, so I put the egg back and stood there looking at her, and she said, "Eggs are very personal." At first I didn't get it because I couldn't figure out what was personal about these eggs. So I went down and I told one of the Sisters. The Sister said, "Oh, they are, are they?" I still hadn't figured it out, so the Sister said, "She just doesn't want you to fix the eggs. Just leave them there." So I left them there and the patient rang. So the nun went there and the patient said she wanted the eggs cracked. The nun said, "We're extremely busy, but the young lady will fix the eggs if you want them, and if you don't, just leave them there." Well, evidently she just left them there. But by lunchtime she was a little bit hungrier. The food had gotten a little less personal. So I went in with her tray. She picked the whole piece of meat up with her hands and tried to bite it rather than have me cut it for her. But by the next morning when those personal eggs came, you'd be surprised at how friendly they had got. I cracked them, she ate them and it did not kill her. As a matter of fact, she lived to walk out of the hospital.

I don't know about that woman's mind, but when I understood what her problem was, I said to myself, "You silly fool. Those people down there in the kitchen, who are just as black as I am, have practically washed their hands down your throat, and they cooked these eggs!" Now, all I was going to do was crack it open and put it in a little dish so she could spoon it up and put it in her mouth. This piece of meat that she would rather pick up with her arthritic hand and bite than have me cut for her had been thrown on the stove by a black cook. I mean, it seems so stupid to me to think that way. It's just not reasonable! Who did she think was down there in the kitchen? The kitchen was as black as coal! I can't understand that. Remember how when you'd get on the bus some white people would sort of draw themselves up into a knot rather than risk touching a black person? Now, the same people would go home where a black cook was washing his hands down their throats three times a day. Those same people would go on vacation to places which boasted, "We still have the mammy."

I think black people are more reasonable than white people. I don't know, maybe the word is not "reasonable," but I think that we are much more clever than they are because we know that we have to play the game. We've always had to live two lives—you know, one for them and one for ourselves. Now, the average white person doesn't know this, but, of course, the average black person does. If you sit on any bus coming from the suburbs and hear black people laughing about the fool things they have done at work, you'll know how many of us are playing this game.

I used to work for this Jewish lady. It was one of the first jobs I got. Now, this lady had all these old hats that looked like something from a Slabtown convention. You see, I had to get there at seven and then I would clean until twelve or twelve-thirty for fifty cents. To ease her conscience she would take a shopping bag and clean out her refrigerator and her closet. There was always one or two of these ridiculous hats and some little dabs of salmon cakes or something else which she would have thrown out. Well, I just transported her garbage to my house, where I threw it out. I wouldn't have eaten any of her food because she was a nasty cook. She just didn't wash her hands. It wasn't a racial thing, it's just that she was one of these people who would set up all day picking their corns and then go right into the kitchen without washing her hands and start cooking! With us, even if you had just gotten out of the bathtub you washed hands before you started messing with anybody's food! And when she cleaned her closet she would fill up a shopping bag with all these old hats and dresses, and say, "Give these to your mother." We'd sit around the table at home and laugh at this stuff and sometimes the kids would play with it and then my mother would say, "When you get finished with that stuff, put it in the garbage." But that lady just *knew* it was good enough for us. She could see my mother going to church in that junk. She always stressed the fact that it was a nice hat.

You know that old saying that so-and-so's behind would make somebody a Sunday face? Well, that's how she felt. Her garbage was supposed to be something special because it was *her* garbage. Her garbage would be Sunday best for my mother because my mother was black and she wasn't supposed to know about any value but the value this white woman put on this old stuff. If that old hat had Rosendorf's label in it, that was supposed to be it for you in them days.

I'll tell you another incident. My grandmother sewed. She didn't just pick it up, she took domestic science in college and was very good at it. She used to make me all types of clothing, really beautiful things. I had this Southern white teacher and she asked me where did my mother work? I said, "My mother doesn't work." So when I went back to school my mother went back with me. This was one of two times that my mother ever went to school. My mother asked the teacher what she meant by asking where she worked. It turned out that the teacher really wanted to know where I had gotten the clothes that my grandmother made for me. My mother told her that she did not work and that my grandmother made the clothes. Now, this white Southerner automatically assumed that if I were a black child and dressed well that somebody—some white person my mother worked for—had to have given me these clothes.

You know that there are two things that all blacks are supposed to be able to do. If you're black you are automatically able to hum a fine tune and do a fine tap. Singing and dancing is our thing! Now, I have two left legs and couldn't carry a tune in a bucket! I found that out in school. White people are terribly shocked if we cannot sing or dance. That was the one thing that was set aside for us. In junior high the spirituals choir was something else and it was taken everywhere! I just couldn't make it, though, because I'm very unmusical. I was a nice kid and minded my own business, so the man just kept trying to make me sing, but I just couldn't get to it! But there were other things that we were not allowed to do for no really good reason. We couldn't get into the modern dance classes, for example. There were very few of us into puppetry. I loved that and I considered myself good at it. There were very few of us in that. I didn't realize how much discrimination there was until I was grown up. It's a lot easier to be white and make it. To be black and make it, you have got to put forth a double effort.

I'm not just talking about these days but when I was coming along or when any generation of black people was coming along. If you find a black doctor, you know that took blood, sweat and tears. Most black people think that they are mentally and physically better than white people, and I think that they are physically superior to white people. I think it goes back to slavery-time. I think that only the strongest of us were able to survive, so that gave us better stock to start with. In those days ninety-nine-pound weaklings just couldn't make it. Those fields separated the strong from the weak and only the strong were permitted to breed, generally, and they tried to inbreed the strong. We fought their battle while they sat on their verandas drinking their dern mint juleps! We were out there making it. Our bodies were conditioned by all that hard work and living in those huts. Only the strong could survive. We lost the weak by the wayside. So, therefore we are superior! As a race we are sturdier and made out of better material. Now, in the Depression we weren t jumping out of windows because we didn't have a steak. We simply boiled a pot of beans and kept on get'n up. If we lose a million dollars they won't be putting us away in mental hospitals. We can cope with adversity much better than they can. We've had our trial by fire, still are having it.

Even that stuff about all babies are the same—it has been my observation that that is not true. Black babies are born looking more like people. They say all Negroes look the same. They just turned that thing around. Now, the truth is that all white people look pretty much the same when they are babies. Almost all of them have big heads full of veins and they don't take on character nearly as quickly as a black baby. You see, a black baby looks like a person when it's born, whereas white babies don't. And a black child out here is much better able to take care of itself than a white child of the same age, because it has had to learn to do that because its mother might have had to go out here and take care of somebody else's child. So it might have to be home taking care of itself at a much earlier age.

Black people feel that white people will do anything to succeed, more so than Negroes. They feel that there is nothing too dirty for a white man to do to himself or anybody else in order to get that almighty dollar. He is very dollar-conscious and to get the dollar he will do anything! This is the way most black people feel about white people. Now, a perfect example of that I've seen in the hospital. Now, I have never seen black people out in the hall dividing up the loot while the patient is still breathing! I can tell you, Ruth could tell you, of cases where they force a pen into the mother's hand so she can sign the will, you know, or write the checks. Now, they know this person is breathing their last breath. Now, I can't think of a single black person that I know that would stand there with that kind of thought in their heads. Now, I don't know about the younger generation, but in my generation they wouldn't think of doing that. Sure, they've got more to divide up than we have, but what we've got left is just as important to us as what they've got left is to them! But, I mean, these people are standing around in the hall like a bunch of vultures dividing up the loot, and the patient is still breathing!

Now, this isn't one or two cases! When I was in the hospital the last time, there was this family there. This woman had ten children! Now, evidently they were quite well-off, you know. And they were talking about who was going to get this and who was going to get that, and the poor lady had been laying there for about two weeks in a coma. She was in a diabetic coma and she was going. She was ninety-some years old. But everybody was arguing about the silver and the crystal—in the little waiting room. All these daughters were in there, and some of them said, "Well, she's just a daughter-in-law. Where the hell does she come in at?" "After all, that's Tony's wife and he's older, you know." They ignored us completely. There were two black men and a black woman in her eighties. We just sat there looking at one another. We were shocked. The only thing they were worrying about was the loot and getting the priest there on time. The fact that the lady was dying didn't bother them at all. Nobody shed a tear about that. But they were steadily worrying about the loot and this silver and this daughter-in-law who had evidently put in a claim. Well, they figured since she was just a daughter-in-law it was up to Tony to take care of this claim.

I think that the average black person thinks that the average white person is much more callous than we are. They don't have the tenderness that we have. I don't know if they thought they were right to act that way. It's just greed, John. They figured this woman had outlived her usefulness! They just wanted to get on with living. Blacks wouldn't feel this way, not to the same extent. These people just wanted to get on with their living. You could hear them down there arguing, "You gonna stay here tonight?" "I got to stay here tonight." I got to, they said. You know, it's really going to hurt me, but if I got to I'll do it.

Yes, I've heard that saying about the only free people are the white man and the black woman. I contend that only one of them is free. I know that the black female is not free. I don't think being female has been much of a disadvantage to me personally. My disadvantage has come from the fact that I was black. When I was younger, among black men, anyway, being female was an advantage. I remember when I first went to work in the tray room of the hospital, if there was something heavy and a black male was there, there was no problem because everybody would bend over backwards to help me with this situation. Or if I went to the store then, if I met any of the fellows I went to school with, if I had a lot of groceries, they would automatically take the packages out of my hands and bring them home. I was at an advantage among my own black males. I never resented that help. I *welcomed* that help! I didn't want to carry that twenty-four-pound bag of flour. I wanted to be female. I would want equal pay doing an equal job. I would certainly want that! But there are certain jobs that I don't feel that I am capable of doing and certain jobs that I don't want to do. I don't want to climb telephone poles. I wouldn't want to do that even if I were sixteen or seventeen again. That's not my thing. I figure that there are certain things that women ought to do and certain things that men ought to do. I enjoy being female.

I don't see any kind of union coming about between black and white females. No, I don't think anything like that is ever going to come about. I really don't think so and I really don't want it. I really don't see that because as I listen to what's going down in the ladies' rooms and in the library and on the buses and in the little political scenes there, I see that the white female is beginning to get jealous of the black female because they figure that we are moving them out. They figured they had these little secretarial jobs and these little clerk jobs covered. Now the black female is moving in on them, see. For an instance, take city hall. You didn't use to see any black girls sitting around there, but now that's all you see. Black women are moving them out of these little jobs. Now, the white women who had those jobs were not all that much for brains; they just sat there and said, "Oh, you want to see Mr. So-and-so, he's in room five." They were sitting at this little desk directing you to room 5 or 10, but we couldn't get those jobs. They were receptionists to this councilman or that councilman. Now we have those jobs. No, I don't see any closeness. The fact is, they are going to be even further apart. For instance, this one girl that I met, she felt that she was qualified for this job, but they promoted a black girl over her. Now, it was pointed out to her in this little session that we had that she wasn't qualified. The black girl was very qualified, but still there was this office tension. The white girl never accepted it. She was in tears and said they just put her there because she was black. She said, "I was discriminated against because I was white." So, you see, this thing is doing a little reversal.

I didn't finish high school and that's made it harder for me. But I was bogged down, I was half sick, trying to work after school until twelve and one o'clock at night and then coming home and trying to do my homework. Mama would find me asleep at the kitchen table when she got up to fix my father's breakfast. But maybe I could have done better; I didn't have to work those hours. I just barely made it to class and then I started falling down the stairs. They wanted to get me out then because I was sick. I had already lost two years and all the kids were younger than I was. I didn't have enough sense at the time to go ahead and push on through. I had to live for these kids and everyone in my class was younger than I was, so that made me feel odd too. Then, too, every time I came home somebody's shoes were flapping, somebody needed this or that. I felt like a dog. Here I was over there in high school and Pop was always saying, "I'm the only one working. I'm standing outside like a tree!"

One morning I just went there and threw the books up on the table and told them, "I want out!" I didn't even come home. I went back to Mr. Sawyer and asked him if he could give me a job. Full-time. He said, "Ella, I'll be glad to have you, but you should make arrangements to go to night school." I had this job which was twenty-one hours a month, which just wasn't enough money for me. So I had to go to St. Mary's full-time and they gave me all the overtime I could stand up under and all the old pot roasts I could take home. They liked me. I knew how to mind my own business. That was my greatest thing. I didn't get in any trouble. When I saw those gangs clustering, I just eased on out of the way.

I was seventeen then, but my God! I had been working ever since we were on Barrington Street! That's when I met Mrs. Reese. I worked for a Mrs. Nelson and there was one named Canning or Canling. I worked for my father's boss. I went and washed her draws and socks. Her name was Fillmore. Then there was another one, named Vaughn, I think. You see, I came in nice and neat-looking and I didn't pilfer anything, so they were always happy to have me wash their draws. There was a Jewish lady—she would always leave money and things around to see if I would take them.

Oh, she was great for that. She would leave money, you know, just peeping out from under the rugs she expected me to clean and all kinds of nonsense like that. Mama told me how to deal with her. Mama told me to take her money to her and tell her that the reason I was working was that I wasn't a thief, but I wasn't responsible for any money she lost up the vacuum cleaner. Now, after that little talk no more money was ever left just lying around like that.

Then there was a Mrs. Nelson. I worked for her when we were still on Barrington Street. I had to wash for her. I would hang out the wash, wash up the breakfast dishes and then get the kids ready and take them to the park. I brought them back, fixed their lunch and then I put them down for a nap while I did the cleaning. When the cleaning was done I got the kids ready and took them outside in the yard to play and then I would help her prepare for supper and when supper was over I would wash those dishes and clean the kitchen. Now, I got one dollar a day for doing all this! Now, that was more than a seven-hour day and I got one dollar for that time and hard work. She gave me lunch. The first day I was there she took the two ends of the bread and made me a jelly sandwich and gave me a glass of water. Now, they had chops, potatoes and some kind of vegetable, I don't remember. When I went home and told Mama about it, she said, "That's not right. You should eat what they eat."

I told Mama that she was going to have some people for Mah-Jongg and that she had ordered a lot of fancy things, but just enough for the guests and her. Mama said, "When you go in there tomorrow you eat one of everything that everyone else is supposed to eat." Mama told me about correct serving. I was about thirteen, I guess. Well, John, I laid out these fancy meat pies. I guess there must have been seven or eight of them, but when it came to her place I had already eaten her meat pie. But Mama had told me just what to do when she rang. So when she rang to find out about her missing meat pie, I came in and told her that my mother had done domestic work, and she said that I should always eat what my employer ate because I had prepared that food and that I shouldn't have to eat a lunch which was nothing but the two hard crusts of bread with a little jelly while other people ate chops and potatoes and vegetables which I had prepared. I said this very politely, but I said it in front of the whole Mah-Jongg crowd. So she said, "Oh, that's perfectly all right. Just make me a jelly sandwich." Oh, she was a diplomat! She ate a jelly sandwich and when it came time for dessert, I brought on all these cream puffs, but, of course, I had eaten hers. Now, you know when you're thirteen and you're living in the "ghetto," those things taste like manna, and they were covered with chocolate and loaded with whipped cream, too. So you know I swish-boomed one of them down! So she told me to go to the cellar and bring her an apple. I brought it out on a saucer with a little knife so she could peel it. So when the Mah-Jongg crowd left, she told me I had done very well. She said, "But, Ella, hereafter if we have anything to discuss, we will discuss it privately."

I'm not just saying this because it's me, but I was a good, neat worker.

A lot of girls probably did just as good work as I did, but they didn't always look as neat. I had worked for black people long before my first job for a white lady. I worked for Mrs. Dodge for pay. I scrubbed her kitchen floor. It wasn't a set job. She paid me whatever she wanted to pay me. I did her floors and grocery shopping, cleaning and ironing. I worked for Mr. and Mrs. Burns, too. Now, she more than paid me because Mrs. Burns was a generous soul. I was lent out to do labor for some friends. There was a certain lady who kept having kids. Now, every time she had one I had to go down there and take care of these babies. Now, they didn't give me nothing, not one thing. They would give me all the criticism I could use and then some. I went because Mama told me to go. Now, then, they didn't *ask* you, they *told* you to go over there and do thus-and-so, and you went. Now, Mrs. Burns stayed in on her job and she would ask me to water her flowers or do something like that. She would give me two or three dollars. She would bring me a new dress or a skirt or a blouse—that's how I started to get a few clothes. Now, Mrs. Dodge was not that generous, plus I didn't like her husband. He was all hands, but you couldn't tell anybody because this would break up the friendship.

The job with Miss Reese I got through school. I had to go in Thursday after school and all day Saturday, and I got a dollar and a half for that. I was about thirteen then, but I was doing the same kind of work in sixth grade. Miss Reese was a heavily built Jewish lady. She just sat and studied the Mah-Jongg books until Thursday, when the Mah-Jongg professor came. All these fat ladies sat around while he told them how to do this Mah-Jongg thing. I served and cleaned up the Mah-Jongg mess. I prepared their supper, but I was never offered anything to eat there. I came Saturday mornings at eight o'clock. She would still be in bed. She would tell me to do the bathroom. Then she would say, "Wash your hands good and make me a cup of coffee and a couple of eggs." She wasn't a kosher Jew—she'd have toast and jelly or sweet buns that had to be put in the oven or anything she felt like having. After she had read the paper in bed, she would struggle to the living room and sit in her easy chair in her red robes. She was always wearing some kind of red satin Japanese kind of thing. They were all too small for her. Then I had to go into her room and change her bed and turn the mattress over by myself. She had a little thing that she kept in her closet for beating her mattress and fluffing it up. I had to brush the drapes down and do the woodwork. The woodwork was a famous responsibility in any Jewish home I ever worked in. You had to go around baseboards with rag and toothbrush, and every so often it had to be washed with many a pail of water. But you had to get in those creases in the woodwork or between the molding and the wall with that toothbrush. Then I would roll up this floor rug and drag it downstairs, hang it on the fence and beat it.

There was a man there and he saw me beating this rug, and he said, "Little girl, where'd you get that from?" So I told him and he went straight to Miss Reese and told her that if he ever caught me out there again beating or hauling this rug, there was going to be lots of trouble. You see, I was a small kid for my age. I got into the movies until I was sixteen for ten cents, the children's price. This man lived in the apartment house. He said when he had seen it the first time he didn't believe it. But when he saw it again he did something about it. She got very angry, but he told her to shut up and told her just what he was going to do if he found this situation again. She never asked me to do it again. I was glad because I had to carry that thing down from the third floor.

Sometimes she would give me these old hats which, I'm sure, she would not even think of wearing. They must have been her mother's, I guess. She'd give you these unbelievable dresses and she'd clean out her refrigerator, and everything in there she didn't want, that she couldn't imagine herself eating, she would give to me. Now, these hard, hard, moldy cheese fragments were supposed to convince me that I was in the lap of luxury, but I got paid a dollar and a half for working all day Saturday and more than three hours on Thursday. I got fifty cents for Thursday and a dollar for Saturday. A dollar was your Jewish limit. Most of them gave you seventy-five cents, but I was such a good kid that they generally gave me a dollar. Now, I was supposed to make waves with that dollar. Now, grown-ups were getting four dollars and carfare, but it was generally seventy-five cents for a day's work for a kid. Now, if they only had "their girl" in every two weeks they would save all the ironing for her.

I was about fourteen years old when I was working for this family. They had a son whom, I guess, must have been a midget. But I didn't know this. I just thought he was a little boy until he tried to get fresh. I told him that I would slap his head off if he didn't stay away from me. He wasn't much bigger than Fred, but I guess he had been used to some terrible things with his mama. I guess the girls in his class certainly were not going to have much to do with him, so they had to introduce him to sex with their own thing. It's all with the person. Sometimes you would meet some very nice people.

There was another lady I met, I think she was English. I'll tell you how they were—they did everything right in front of you. The child would be in the next room, but this lady and her gentleman friend would hug and kiss and go through all kinds of motions just as if she wasn't there and as if I wasn't a person. One New Year's she went to this party and I was sitting with her daughter. It came up a really terrible storm! There was so much snow and sleet you could hardly walk. Well, when they finally got home from the party, her boyfriend was so disgusted with her because she had gotten so drunk that he just left her at the door. I guess he forgot that I was even in there waiting for this ride home. I said, "I can go home by myself." But she said, "No, no! Your mother would never forgive me!" I tried to tell the lady in a nice way that she was in no condition to walk me home. But that just made her more determined. So in nothing but her evening dress she insisted on going with me. So we slipped and slid down Hawley Street in all this snow. Well! I had to hold her up and I just couldn't make it. There was a drugstore on the corner and it had a little cement platform which was about a foot high. I set her down there and told her that I was going to go on because I couldn't hold her up any longer. She said, "Well, I'll see you." I went on and left her sitting up there in the sleet and hail. As luck would have it, that was one of the few times that Mama didn't hear me come in. So I went right to bed. Next morning when I got up I told Mama where I'd left her. Mama said, "Fool, run out there and see if she's still there!" So I went out there and I could see that there was nobody sitting in front of the drugstore, so I came on home. But, you know, when I went back she never mentioned it.

When the war came I took a job in defense. I had been out of high school for three years and it was a kind of toss-up, but I didn't want to go back to school because I had been out for so long. I did go back to high school and finally got my diploma when I was thirty-eight. I'd like to do some college work. I like going to school and learning about things that interest me, but I would really like to become a registered nurse. But they told me that I was too old to register in that program. They told me that they only take people below fifty and I'm fifty-one. It really hurt me, you know. Here I was trying to go to school and they tell me I'm too damned old. I really don't think that this is a program that should throw people out just because they are fifty. Some people at fifty can still do useful things. But I couldn't even get past the receptionist. She wouldn't refer me to anybody and I don't know how they run that system. I called down there till I'm tired of calling. When I first called they told me to go to the office, where they gave me such a hard time I didn't know what to do.

I don't feel that my life has had any high spots—no, not too high, I guess —because, well, after all, what in the world was I doing? Just living there, we didn't think of it as a ghetto. We didn't have that word. I thought I was doing pretty good. I knew I was poor, but I wasn't as poor as some of the people I knew. There were two sisters who used to steal my money. Now, *they* were really poor. They were what folks call no-good people. Now, we just weren't that kind of people. Like most people, we were proud poor. My Aunt Sarah had property and money, and my grandfather had property and money in four or five banks. My aunt could write a check in four figures and the first one didn't have to be a one, two, three or four. In those times that was a good thing. I remember that when this lady took a job she told them what she wanted to be paid. Now, she got what she was worth or she didn't work for you! She was a cook and she told them that she did not leave her kitchen for nothing! That was Aunt Sarah, and she didn't allow certain people in "her" kitchen. Now, you understand that this frequently included the lady who owned that kitchen! She didn't allow anybody to get out of hand.

I can remember when she would come on Thursdays, that meant a good time! We would sit around and talk, and in the summertime we would freeze big freezers of ice cream. We would make cakes and sweet-potato pie. It was like a feast day every one of those Thursdays off. That was a very important consideration to us. The people who were working arranged their jobs so that they would all have the same Thursdays off. Very often they would refuse to take a job if they couldn't get the right Thursday off. These people were good, experienced domestics and they knew what it was all about, so they could demand a good price. The Thursday feast was a way of keeping alive the community spirit they had when they lived in rural Kentucky. Mama had come up here when she was seventeen to earn money to pay the taxes on the little farms. But she tricked them because she never went back. Those Thursdays were proper meat feasts. There would be huge pots of greens and chiddlins. They would fry fish and cook corn breads and there would be sweet-potato pie. Whoever got off first would come and help Mama with the cooking. Mama would get up very early and begin picking the greens, and she would be humming because it was a happy time for her. She was happy because all her people were together again. We had a big tin tub which stood almost as high as this table. We would get a big piece of ice and make that whole tub full of lemonade! That would be sitting out on the back porch covered over with a cloth. Everybody would come and each person would give something to make this feast. Aunt Sarah would leave money every Thursday for the next feast. There would be much flying back and forth to the store, and I did most of it because there were no other kids around. Miz Flora was here, but her children were still in the South. When Cousin Hardy stayed with us, he would be working. He was a young man, so when he was around they would flag him down and send him to the store, but he was generally working, so I had to go most of the time. I can remember flying down those stairs if somebody had forgotten the nutmeg to make the sweet-potato pies. You see, you didn't have this huge stockpile of stuff in your house like I have now. If somebody forgot something, then somebody had to fly back to the store and get it. And then, with a houseful of people, my sister May would be very excited and somebody would have to look after her. A lot of times people would insist on holding her. She didn't like to be held and this would upset her very much. I used to wonder why people didn't just leave her alone.

Nobody knew what mongolism was. I didn't know what it was until years and years later. They just stuffed her full of food and she ate everything! Thursdays and times like that were nice, but other times were pretty sad. I could sense that Mama wasn't happy. That's one thing that made it sad and then May's condition made things sad, too. Then my sister Thelma came along and she was sick. She had a heart condition and double pneumonia—you name it, she had it. And then these babies dying six, nine, ten months apart. I was responsible for May and I was responsible for Thelma to see that she stayed in what they called a pneumonia jacket. It was just cotton wrapped all over her body. Literally, she was so tiny that you couldn't get anything else to stay close enough to her body to keep her warm! They called it a pneumonia jacket, but all it was was cotton, which Mama wrapped all around her arms and legs and everywhere else. Every time you had to change her, you had to unwrap her and clean her and then wrap her again in the cotton and then try to put a shirt or something over the cotton.

I don't remember the ages too well, but I was in school. Thelma was six or seven years younger than I was. I remember quite distinctly when she was born. I remember that Mama went to the hospital after the doctor had come to the house, and in about five or six days she came home with Thelma. I didn't know what was going on. As a matter of fact, I didn't even have enough presence of mind to think, "Well, there's going to be another baby!" You know, each one was a surprise to me. I can remember standing there looking at Thelma and laughing! I had never seen anybody that little! She was pretty, but she was so little her arms were like your fingers. Her little hands and fingernails were so small that I just laughed until Pop said, "What's so funny?" Uncle Pete came to live with us about then. He either came slightly before Thelma was born or right after. Anyway, he gave her her nickname of Lambie, or Lamb, he said, "because you couldn't hear the little thing." He must have just come because I remember he said, "Good God, Ola, if that one is a lamb, the other one must be a lion!" You could hear May screaming all over the house. And I can remember then saying to myself, "Now, if I have me a baby I'm going to name her May." I really did love May very much. She was either very, very happy or very, very sad. She would get fits of laughter! Sometimes I would sit on the floor and play with her. Sometimes I would tickle her. She had a little white animal toy. I think it might have been a lamb. I would pull her legs apart and put my feet to her feet, and we would throw this toy back and forth. She couldn't catch it, but she would get such a kick if it would hit her and I would throw it so it would hit her. She couldn't even throw it back, but by making that small circle with our legs, I could reach and get it. She would just sit there and laugh when it hit her. She had a hearty laugh—I can hear it now! I think that was a little lamb. It was a fuzzy-looking thing with yarn on it.

You know, even though she didn't understand anything, she liked to hear the fluctuations in the voice, so I would read to her. I would read her my schoolbooks and all the fairy stories. She would pay attention for a long time. In the morning when I would leave for school, it would break her heart. She knew just as well when I was getting ready to go to school. She would just fly into a fit. She didn't want me to leave her. And Mama said that something would tell her when it was time for me to come home from school. She'd go to the window and pull herself up so she could see out and just wait there. When she saw me she would start laughing and making noises. Mama said she would not miss me, she would be right there at that window!

One reason I never liked most of the kids much was the way they behaved about May. On my way home from school the other kids would look up and see her in the window and say, "There's your crazy sister up there!" I took a hell of a lot of abuse. Any kid might say this, but they were mostly black kids who did this. Now that I think about it, I don't ever remember a white kid saying that. You see, when she learned to wait at the window we lived in a black neighborhood. We had moved from a white neighborhood. Almost all of the hard times I got was in the black neighborhood.

Now, Boomey, who Mama used to think was such a dear, dear soul, she used to tell the other kids, "She got a crazy sister!"

We were living on King Street then. I was in third or fourth grade, so I guess I must have been eight or nine. I used to think a lot about life then. I used to wonder why it was we had such bad luck. The hard luck of sickness bothered me the most. Then in Sunday School they used to talk about visiting the sins of the fathers upon the third and fourth generations. That never did set well with me. I used to ask Daddy about that. I knew what to say to Mama and what not to say, but I used to ask him these questions. How come we had so much sickness? And why did God punish the fifth generation? Why did we have to be punished for something somebody I hadn't even heard of had done? It wasn't my fault! I didn't do a thing to anybody! Why did it all come to our family? Then for a while there I got mad with them—Mama and Daddy, I mean. I wondered what sneaky thing they had done! I wondered if they were the generation that did this thing for which we were all being punished! I used to say to myself, "Well, Grandpa—he looks all right." I used to think back as far as I could to try to find out who this guy was who had done this bad thing that caused all this trouble for us. I was trying to figure out who had made God mad enough to give us all this trouble—one sister wrapped up in a blanket all the time, the other sister unable to talk. I wondered what went wrong back there. There must have been some really terrible people back there. So I thought I would go to church and see if things got any better. I guess I thought that with all these people in the world, God wouldn't have time to read my mind. But things did not get better. As a matter of fact, they went downhill completely!

I used to talk to Pop about these things, but Mama—well, then I didn't talk to her about these things and she didn't speak to me about much. She just told me to do this or do that and to be quiet and not to question anything. If I would ask why, she would say, "Because I told you to. Now get over there and do it before I knock half your head off." She always had these half-headed children standing around there with mashed mouths. I used to play a little game in my mind about that. I used to visualize different people with only half their heads.

But I was always trying to figure out why we had such bad luck. Then for a while I thought it might have been Grandpa Henderson who acted so bad, going off and leaving his children. I thought that maybe that was what had made God so mad. But then, that didn't make much sense because I couldn't figure out why I should be punished because of what he had done. I wouldn't have done that. That would be like going over there and kicking someone else because I was mad with you. I figured that would be just plain dumb and I figured that God has to have more sense than that! They used to sing, "Be not dismayed what e'er betide, God will take care of you." I used to think to myself, "It's a lie! He ain't taking no care of me!" I would really feel terrible. Then I would think that maybe I was being punished because I had thoughts like that. I used to talk to Reverend Harper about it. He told me that I had to accept things on faith. That was no answer at all for me. I challenged him one day about that cane of Moses' that turned into a snake. I told him that that was a trick. He said I had to believe this on faith. I asked him where I could get the faith from, because I didn't have it. They kept on telling me to shut up and read it, but I couldn't believe half of the stuff. I would go to Sunday School and pray for everybody and then rush home to see if anything had happened. Mama dressed me and my grandfather would come by and take me to Sunday School, but he didn't take anybody but me. May couldn't go. They couldn't handle her in church and Thelma was too young. I would pray as hard as I could, but when I got home Mama was still mad, May was still in the same condition, Thelma was still in the same condition, and nothing would ever be changed! The miracle I needed just never happened, so I decided that I wasn't going to go any more. All these people were in there jumping up and down and talking about how He had touched their souls. All I wanted was for Him to walk over there on King Street and give Thelma what she was entitled to and give May what she was entitled to. If I could have seen any miracle or sign, I would have felt better, but I couldn't see a thing happening.

It's like my grandson here the other day, out on Main Street. Well, you know what Main Street has become. There was a sign that said GOD CAN DO ANYTHING. Well, Fred looked at the sign and then said, "He can't do nothing over here." He didn't say it to anybody in particular. He was just making a sad observation about life. Children are much more free to say things now and I don't believe in shutting them up. You ought to be free to say what you think. His growing up is so different from mine. In a lot of ways he has it much harder than I did. I didn't have an addict for a father.

I knew my mama was as good as anybody. She had so much trouble she didn't have any time to be bad! This lady was good and the only pleasure she had was a fifteen-cent *True Story* magazine. She bought a lot of those and she read them religiously. They were the soap-opera thing of the day, and I'm sure she had a dream world which she escaped to whenever she could. Above all else she wanted her children to be healthy. Then she started doing the miracle thing. She would bring May to tent meetings. One time a healer called Black Herman came to church and he also had a tent meeting. Some people thought he might be of some help. From our window, my cousin Yula and I could look through a hole in the top of his tent. He claimed to be able to turn coal into cherries. We could see how he did this trick because we were looking down on him. Right downstairs there was a restaurant, and we would send down and get sweet-potato pies and watch Black Herman's show through the hole in the top of the tent. I didn't get too much of a chance at that hole. The tent was full every night and he was healing the people. I had a sore leg, so I went, but when I came back upstairs my leg was just the same. I used to say to myself, "You are a nonbeliever and He just dropped you here, and now He doesn't even know you are here!" There was always some little body coming by to pray. Mama kept iron on her person to ward off evil spirits. She used to scare me. I was born with a veil, so I was supposed to "know" things. If somebody lost a ring or something they would ask me because I was supposed to "know." A lot of things that I "knew," I knew them because people had told me. They would forget that they had told me, but I would remember. Like phone numbers and things like that; I would remember those things.

I don't dismiss the supernatural altogether, even now. I remember what Cousin Ruth used to say: "You better say, Jo, 'cause you sure don't know!" Most people believe in these things. You couldn't find a nonbeliever then. Pop used to say that the believers were a big bunch of crazy people. "Believe in yourself," that's what he would say.

Sometimes Mama would scare me—I mean, she'd just be so far away. Sometimes I would be talking to her and she wouldn't even hear me. I guess she must have been thinking about the trouble she was having and the kids. I can see why this would get to her. But I didn't see that then. You don't see that when you are a seven- or eight-year-old. I just thought that she was ignoring me. She would go off to her room and read these books and just leave me out there. She just should have had a better life. And then, I did even dumber things because I had more opportunity than she had. She was off in her room wishing for the health of her children, and if she could have had that, then she would have been perfectly happy. She had a hard life. You better believe it, John. It's one thing when something bad is happening to you, but when something bad is happening to somebody you love and you have to stand by and watch it and can't do a damn thing about it, that is really hard. I think that is far worse. I used to have these terrible combination toothaches and earaches. I would lie down and my legs would just draw up; you could see the knots just coming up in them. And that thing would hurt so bad! She would say, "I wish I could take every bit of the pain for you." I would say, "No, you don't, Mama, because you don't know what it's like. You don't want this." Now I often think about that. At the time I used to say to myself, "She must be crazy because nobody wants this." Now I know that she did mean what she said. She would be sitting by the bed and the tears would be just rolling out of her eyes.

They put pee in my ear. Aunt Rebecca came up here with that idea. She's responsible for that pee bit! It was your own pee that they would use, but I still didn't like it. And then Ma would sit there and blow smoke from a corncob pipe in on top of the pee! That's probably what's seeping around inside my head now! Old pee with corncob-pipe smoke in it. It got to be that you would be afraid to say that you were sick because you could never be sure that they wouldn't give you a cure worse than your sickness. They rubbed you down with mutton tallow and dosed you with sulfur and kerosene and molasses, and I had to carry asafetida around my neck. I had to wear long ribbed stockings up to here with long draws stuffed down in them down to here. I was wearing the asafedita because it was a thing that sickly kids had to do. It kept germs and everything else away from you. It was in a little bag and they seldom washed your little bag, you know. I think it was considered very bad to wash it because you would wash some of the asafedita smell away. I don't remember my first bag, but I do remember the last one. My father saved me from that. He just told them, "No more of that goddamned shit!" and that was the end of that. There was much moaning and weeping and conferences with Aunt Sarah, but he said, "I don't want that kid with any more of that damn shit around her neck!" Hell, I was washing dishes and scrubbing floors; maybe if somebody had let me sit down and rest I would have gotten better!

I was the only one who could help my mother, so I really had to help! I did everything that nobody else wanted to do. On Regent Street I had to lug a white galvanized pee pot down icy stairs to empty it. It was a heavy thing which stood almost as high as that chair seat. And, boy, when it snowed you really caught it! It was a long flight of stairs with an open railing, and I might have fallen and broken a leg. Several times I dropped the pot and got a load of pee all in my high-topped shoes. You only had one pair and then you had to come upstairs and de-pee them. Ma would wash them and stick them in the oven and then they would get too tight for my feet. And there I'd be, with my peed-up shoes, my asafedita around my neck and my silk and wool slip which came from Rosendorf's because my Aunt Sarah always saw that I had the very best! Oh! It was fun. I was dressed like something out of Jane Eyre, but it was not Jane Eyre time— the other kids had on plain cotton slips with a ruffle. But they felt that I should have been grateful for these things because people had paid extra for these things.

Fresh air was not very well thought of. You were supposed to stay inside and let the soot get up your nose from the oil stove, along with the fumes from the pee pot on the back porch when you opened the door. There was no bathroom in that house. Pop never used the pot; no grown man would. They went out to the outdoor outhouse. But Ma always used the pot. I understand why now. She was always pregnant and she might have fallen down those stairs and hurt herself. Then I didn't know that she was pregnant and I used to wonder why she wouldn't go out to the outhouse too. The kids always put a strain on the pot. May always ate everything that didn't eat her. She had a prodigious appetite and it got so we were a three-pot house! And sometimes they would let them get too full. You had to take it out of the bedroom, through the kitchen, out onto the back porch and down the stairs. You took it out in the morning, and then when you got home from school, the first thing you had to do was to empty the pot again. Maybe it wasn't always filled, but you had to get it out of the house. May was very nervous and she went a lot and Thelma's diapers were shaken in the pot and Ma used it quite often. I used to sit there and think to myself, "Oh God, I wonder who's going to go next to the pot!" You watch those pots carefully when you are responsible for them. You noted carefully how long anyone used it, and when Ma would say, "Hand me my pipe," my heart would sink because I knew that she would be there a long time and there was a tough aroma to camouflage with pipe smoke. When I used the pot I was so thin that I had to hold on for dear life to keep from being sucked in. I have actually fallen into the pot! I am even now very narrow through the hips. I imagine Ma must have gotten mad just looking at me. A sniveling little dumb-dumb sitting there trying like mad to keep from falling in the pot.

I would take the pot down and come back and play with May to take her off Ma's hands so she could get dinner ready. While she got supper I'd have to watch Thelma and May. Then we'd eat and I would do the dishes and my homework. I would play with the kids till it was time for them to go to bed, and that was it. Sometimes we would have wood and I would have to go out in the backyard and bring that up. If there was coal in the cellar, I would have to go down there and bring up scuttlesful for our stove. If there wasn't any coal in the cellar, then the coal man could leave the hundred-pound bag on the porch and that was much easier for me. I had to get kerosene. I used to go get the kerosene in two-gallon jugs, but by the time I was seven or eight I used to drag back a five-gallon tin. I had a lot to do and a lot of responsibility. I guess that's why I am the way I am now. I just can't sit around and wait for anyone to do something. This makes me very impatient and I would rather go and do it myself. I have gone downtown and dragged back food with a temperature of 103 degrees. I had to do it because there was nobody else to do it.

Sometimes I want to get away from the whole damn thing. I just can't take any more. Now people still talk about the goodness of God, and I ask myself, "Where in the hell is your God? Don't feed me that bullshit because I have never received no benefit of it!" Damned old whores and prostitutes live to be a hundred, and a woman who lived the kind of life Mama lived dies like she did. No! There is no justice unless you just take it. The only kind of justice you get is the kind you take! And it looks like the nastier you are and the dirtier you are, the better off you are. I have tried to live a decent life and I have been kicked in the ass by every bastard who came along that felt like kicking me! But I'm supposed to sit around and wait for my reward in the sky. I'm supposed to sit around and wait for my reward in the sky when the worms move in and the worms move out. If you have any reward, you better get it right now! If I've got one coming, it better get here within eighteen or twenty-four months if I'm going to enjoy it. But I will never get it because some son of a gun is going to kick me in the ass as long as I live!

Some people are put on this earth like the manure to grow somebody else's peaches. Some people are the horse shit of the earth. And that's my lot in life—to be the horse shit of the earth. I don't care what I do, I will always end up on the messy end of the stick. I think it is a predestined thing —regardless to what I do, I'm going to have to walk through other people's shit. I'm not just saying it because it's me, John, but I have done damn few things in this life that I am ashamed of.

Gloria Melton

A faithful person means more than anything else in the world!

Gloria Melton is a large, good-humored, sensible woman in her thirties. I remember Jonathan's courtship of Gloria, their wedding, the birth of their child and their successful campaign to be a "normal" family in the best sense of that word in the face of daunting chronic illness. Gloria is the great Pearl Bailey's vocal double. Her singing, her inexhaustible fund of jokes, her unfailing hospitality and her manifest good sense and insight make her a great many people's best friend.

I went to grammar school and then when I went to high school, out of a graduating class of about three hundred there were only about twenty-eight blacks. So we went to school in mostly white schools and we got along very well. I took the practical-arts course and we did a lot of things like making leather pocketbooks and wallets and shopwork. Now, in a couple of my classes I was the only girl and the only black person there. I had a lot of fun with the guys—I was the queen! They really liked me and I had fun because I can mix with people, black or white, and get along with them.

Even now that I'm grown and the world is the way it is, on my job I'm the shop steward, and the Puerto Ricans, the whites and the blacks like me because I am fair to everyone because I am the shop steward for *all* the people, not just certain people. I'm not in any clique. I don't segregate myself. I bowl every Thursday night. I'm the only black girl in the bowling league. We have twelve teams. I have friends, but I try not to just get together with my friends. We just had an election January seventh, not in my department but in the back. Now, they had a girl who was shop steward, but she favored her friend. You see, there are some jobs that people don't want to do. Now, when this girl's friend didn't want to do this job, her friend the shop steward said she didn't have to do it; but when another girl in that department said she didn't want to do that same job, that shop steward told her she had to do it. Now, they voted her out because she wasn't fair to everybody. In my department nobody ran against me. They all wanted Gloria because I am the shop steward for *all* the people. Gloria doesn't have any friends that she is going to favor over someone else. Gloria is the shop steward for the whites, the blacks, the Puerto Ricans, everybody. And everybody likes me. As a matter of fact, they nominated me to be chief shop steward, but I declined because I didn't feel that I was ready for that yet. I'm too young. I'll just try a couple of more years of practicing. I've been shop steward for about six years. You have three-year terms and I'm starting my third term. I feel that I can handle ovens seven, eight and nine, but I'm not sure I could handle the whole plant.

My girls are very nice and very understanding people. They know when they are wrong and I will tell you when you're wrong! But some people feel that they are never wrong. And I don't care what you do, if it's not what they want, then *you* just have to be wrong! I can't have that whole plant sitting on my behind just because they are wrong but they don't want to admit it. Nixon is a perfect example of that. Now, wouldn't you resign rather than be impeached? I think the average black person would behave in a different way if they got to be President. It would be just like me in my shop steward's job. You know that the white man is looking at you all the time and you know that he's waiting for you to make just one mistake!

When I got to be shop steward, there was a whole lot of controversy about that. There was nothing really big but something all the time. There was this job up for bid and a white girl who had been in that department wanted that job and a black girl who had worked for the company for twenty years wanted that job. Now, the white women were saying that the white girl should get this job because she had been in that department for fifteen years. Now, I always thought that seniority prevails, and since that black girl had been working there five years before the white girl came in the door, I felt that the black girl should get the job. But now, I didn't say anything because I was waiting for the head of the union to come and settle the thing. He came and he was white, but he told them, "She's not my cousin, she's not my sister-in-law, she's not my sister. She's no kin to me, but the girl that has been working for this company for the longest time is the one who gets the job." Now, that's how it went down, but the white girls were still very disappointed because they lost. But what good does it do to have seniority if you can't flaunt it? You see, there is a difference between the way black people and white people think.

The black girls on my job have more children than the white girls. I only have one, but then, I started so late in life. But we have girls on the third shift who have seven and eight children! One girl out there has nine children; that's why she's working on the third shift, so she won't have to worry about paying a baby sitter. This girl that my brother is going with now, she told me that her mother had seventeen children! It isn't that they are dumb to the pill or don't know about abortion; sometime they are like me, just afraid to take a chance. Now, this white woman, she'll stop by and have an abortion before she goes shopping and think nothing of it! They showed a thing about abortion on TV, you know, the way they do it by suction, and everybody on that program was white! All those that died and were in the paper, they were white too. I'm not saying that they didn't have any, but I haven't seen any black women on the news yet who have had abortions.

I'm not going to have any more children because I think we were lucky and I don't think you should push your luck. My daughter's doctor said that if I had four children, then one might be sick like Jonathan. But he didn't guarantee me that it would be the fourth child. If he had been able to guarantee that it would have been the fourth child, then I would have had two more. I'm too old now. No, I take that back. Even now, if I knew that my children would not be sick, I would have two more. A couple of years earlier and I would have had them, but now I don't want to press my luck.

If I could plan for my daughter, I would like her to finish high school and go to college. But I'm not one of these people who believe in forcing their children to go to college. I would like her to want to go, and then I would do everything I could to help her to go. But I would like her to take up some kind of a business course that would give her some kind of a trade. I'd like her to be able to get herself a good job and not have to go into a factory. I would be really disappointed if she spends four years going to college and then comes out of school and gets married the very next year. You know that most women, if they study to be a nurse or a doctor or whatever they might study for, if they get out of school and start having babies, they will forget about that thing they spent all that time learning to do. Now, a lot of women are not like me. When they start having children they can stop working, so they stop. Maybe she'll have the type of husband who doesn't want her to work. But if she has some kind of profession or if she could be a secretary, if she knows how to type she can always go out and pick up a job. Her chances are good, but if my job closes down I have nothing. I don't know how to type. I can't do hair. I would really be lost!

I don't think my job will close unless the energy crisis gets so bad that they say to heck with everybody. They are putting in new ovens. They are putting in oven number ten right now. The factory across the hall from us moved out and it looks like they're thinking of getting that space for making frozen food. They have a frozen-food plant in Detroit. I hear they are thinking about setting up a frozen-food plant here so the girls would have work all year round. That way, when the girl-scout season is over, they'll still have work to do. It looks good right now. I have twenty-one years seniority and I wouldn't think of changing jobs. As long as the bakery hangs in, I'll hang in with it.

Sometimes I do think that I would like a year off so I could take up something like practical nursing or something like that. But my husband is a sickly fellow and I couldn't afford to take off from work for a year because if he got very sick while I wasn't working, we would really be down the drain! You see, with sickle-cell anemia you can't plan much. We don't plan, we just take it as it comes and play it by ear, as they say. If we want to go on a vacation, we don't say very much about it, and then on the night before his vacation starts, he'll say, "All right. We'll leave tomorrow. I feel good. We could go to South Carolina or Canada or Detroit." Then I'll start washing and ironing and packing, all at the same time. Then we just get going! You remember that I was saying how I would like to go to Bermuda? Well, if I could just go to a travel agent and put down the money and take off that very night, I could go to Bermuda that way. But to say now, in the winter, that we're going to go to Bermuda next July—no, my husband wouldn't like that.

I used to plan things before I got married. I still plan things for myself. I might say, "Let's go to Massachusetts." Now, common sense tells me that I might get sick, but since I hardly have any illness except colds or something like that, I don't mind planning. But my husband always says, "No, I don't want to plan that far ahead because I don't know when I might get sick."

When I was, you know, thinking about getting married, my husband's doctor talked to me about Jonathan's illness. He said that he might not be with me in ten years or maybe he might not be with me in twenty years. I told the doctor that I understood all that. After all, I was twenty-three years old then. I was no kid. That part of life really doesn't bother me. I know somebody might say, "Oh, she's just saying that because she's in a TV attitude." I always felt that I would want somebody to love me if I happened to be sick. I can't see taking advantage of somebody because they are sick. And I really couldn't see taking advantage of somebody when you knew from the beginning that they were sick. Now, if my husband had gotten sick with some incurable illness three days after we got married, I still think I would feel the same way because your marriage vows say "in sickness and in health." And to me you shouldn't stop loving a person just because they are handicapped. He is a good husband and a good father.

My mother never tried to persuade me from marrying Jonathan because he was sick. She never did! My mother was the kind of person who wanted adults to make up their own minds. But if I had gone to her six months after we got married and said, "I can't do nothing because he's always sick," she would have said, "Well now, you knew he was sick before you married him." She wouldn't have said, "Oh, my poor daughter. She can't have anything out of life because this guy is sick." My mother loved Jonathan just like he was her own son and he loved my mother. She was nice to him and she never said anything about his sickness. I've often told my friends that I always respected her for that very much. Have you ever liked a person very much and then one day they say something and that just seems to take something away? You know, you just can't respect them as much as you did. If she had ever said anything about that, I guess I would have felt that way about my mother. But she never did.

You know, this girl said to me on the job one day, "Gloria, you're a good woman, but I couldn't be like that. I would have started out meaning well, but I couldn't keep it up." That took something away from her. She was married and had a daughter, but she was separated from her husband. Now, suppose her boyfriend had said, "You know, you're a really nice person and

I could love you if you would give your daughter away." Well, I think that's almost the same thing. I was surprised when she said that because she was white and usually white women don't even go to the bathroom without their husbands' permission—most of them I know, anyway. A lot of the white girls on my job say, "Oh, that's really something! Your husband lets you go out by yourself." I say, "Why not? I go to work by myself, don't I?" I had been married about seven years when this happened and I still didn't have any children. Now, suppose her boyfriend had told her to give her daughter to her sister. Well, I know people that are giving their children to other people to raise, but I don't think that is right. If a man came to me and said he loved me but wanted me to give my child away, well, my daughter is part of me and if he loved me, then he would have to love my child! I also think that man would lose respect for you if you did what he asked you to do. I think sometimes people just say things like that to see what you will do. Maybe they just want to know if you would really be dumb enough to give your child away. Nobody has ever said that to me, but they do say it to other people.

Looking back on it, if I were, say, twenty-one, I would do the same thing because I do not regret having married Jonathan. Well, you know, Jonathan makes me mad sometimes and I make him mad sometimes and that hasn't anything to do with his sickness. Well, I tell him off and he tells me off. I relate to Jonathan as a well man when he is well. When he's sick he's sick and when he's well he's well. I always say "Jonathan, my husband." I never say "Jonathan, my husband, who has sickle-cell anemia." When he's sick and goes to the hospital, sometimes I tell people and sometimes I don't. I don't want people to feel sorry for me or think I'm looking for a handout. I don't feel sorry for myself. My husband does have sickle-cell anemia, but he does work whenever he can. Now, I have some friends on my job whose husbands have never in their lives been sick. Now, they are rotten men! They are really bad husbands. Now, Jonathan does not smoke. He does not drink excessively. He drinks sociably, and even with his sickle-cell anemia, I couldn't have found a better husband.

I have a friend—she's a nurse—she said it doesn't seem to affect women as severely as it does men. It seems to affect boy children more for some reason. But this young man that Jonathan met in the hospital was not affected until he was almost twenty. There's a girl who has it also. She comes to the same hospital that Jonathan goes to for treatment. She seems to have an alcoholic problem, too. The last time she was in there, it seems she had fallen down the stairs after celebrating a little too much. Of course, anytime they get sick it relates back to sickle-cell anemia. If Jonathan gets a persistent head cold, his legs and arms will begin hurting and that might lead right into a sickle-cell attack. As I said, if I had married a man who was rich or, rather, if I had a boyfriend who was rich and healthy and I decided not to marry him, then I might feel that I had some regrets. But I never had such an opportunity. And as I said before, I have a good husband. Because he is a good husband and a good father, I consider myself lucky.

Living with sickle-cell anemia might be enough to drive a person to drinking or some other kind of bad thing. It takes a lot of courage to have so much pain and still be a good husband and father. I'm not sure I wouldn't be driven to suicide by such pain. I'm not too good with pain. Jonathan has cousins down south who drink a lot, I think because of sickle-cell anemia. And there's that girl I told you that we met in the hospital. I guess they do that just to ease the pain, for a little while, anyway. But I don't think that's much of an answer because after your drink and your hangover wear off, you still have the same problem.

Jonathan is thin, but otherwise he doesn't look sickly. He really takes care of himself. And I think that has a lot to do with it. Like the lady said, "If you take care of your body, your body will take care of you!" When Jonathan is sick he's sick, but when he gets back from the hospital, in a couple of days he's ready to go back to work. Now me, I feel like staying out an extra little time for recuperation, but not him! The minute he thinks he can, Jonathan is ready to go back. One summer Jonathan did not have to go to the hospital for almost three months. That's the longest time I can remember he ever stayed out of the hospital. Sometimes he has to go every three weeks; at others almost two months may go by. I guess he has to go to the hospital averagely every month and a half, but it varies. He says that when he was younger he sometimes used to stay in the hospital for long periods—you know, months and weeks at a time! The doctor told his mother, "Oh, he won't live to be fifteen! He definitely won't live to be twenty-five!" Now here he is at forty-six and still going strong. The nurses in Memorial Hospital say that he is the oldest person they know of with sickle-cell anemia. There was a lady who was fifty-two, she died, but not from sickle-cell anemia; it was some other kind of complication.

I guess one reason why this young fellow who told us about the blood-donor program is so crazy about Jonathan is that when he sees how well Jonathan looks at forty-six, it makes him feel that he might have a chance. Now, he tells Jonathan that he doesn't have girl friends. I think he's a little shy. I think he is afraid of tying anybody down. I know he was surprised to find that Jonathan was married. He was really surprised when Jonathan told him that he had been married sixteen years and had a daughter. After that it really seemed that he became especially friendly with Jonathan.

Well, as I said before, it's a matter of the individual and, you know, just what kind of person you happen to be. Some women figure you are their husband just as long as you're up on your feet! But when you get down sick, that is the end of that! Some women are like that and even worse. Sometimes you are the husband as long as you're looking at them! But when you leave for work, sad on you! Some people are like that—they don't care about a soul but themselves!

I take Mary Ellen to the emergency room when Jonathan gets sick sometimes. At first she used to be very worried when she would see him there tossing and turning. Now she understands that he is sick. Whenever I go up to the hospital without her, she always says, "Please tell Daddy that

I hope he feels better soon and that I love him." A lot of times when he starts to feeling better, I'll call the supervisor and ask permission to take her upstairs. He likes to see her there when he's improving; it gives him a kind of lift. She brings him a little bag of pretzels. Jonathan is very fond of salty things.

He has a very strong will and he just doesn't let some things bother him. He stands it very well. I guess he was that kind of person before I met him. He says he has enough to worry about just dealing with sickle-cell anemia, so he doesn't have any time to be worried about anything else. I guess that's a good way to look at it.

Now, if he hears that somebody else is in the hospital, he'll run up there and see them. You'd think that that would be the last place he would go. Maybe it feels good to walk in there and not have to stay.

What people who have sickle-cell anemia need most is money and medical help. Jonathan would need at least four hundred dollars a month to make ends meet and fix it so he wouldn't have to always be worrying about his being able to work. You see, Jonathan is up and down. He could be sitting here laughing and talking and later on that night he would have to go to the hospital. Things might be going well on his job and then the next thing anybody knew, they'd be short a man on the truck. You know, I think about the kind of work that Jonathan wanted to do—oil-burner installation and maintenance. He couldn't get a job in that line of work because of color prejudice. But no matter what job he gets, he cannot work for a long time because he gets sick. It's not a case of calling in and saying, "Jonathan won't be in tomorrow," every now and then. But, you see, this happens often and you can never tell where or when it is going to happen. I wake up plenty of mornings and find that Jonathan has gone to the hospital! Very often he takes himself there for medication, and if he feels groggy he will stay up there overnight. He's had it so long now, he's a good judge of what he can or cannot do and he is always very careful. Sometimes he'll just lay down in the emergency room for a while. I think they can stay in there forty-eight hours before they have to be admitted. His medicine is very expensive and he never really knows when he is going to need it or how much of it he will need, so he must have some of it on hand at all times. If you can't say when you can work, then the bosses on your job can always say, "Well, we don't have to keep you here," and you have to do whatever they tell you, even if it's more than you should do. Now, Jonathan's foreman, for example, has asked him to take jobs that would pay more, but because Jonathan is sick so often, he would rather just fill in wherever they need somebody than get to be a key man, who would have to be there all the time. Now, Jonathan is very responsible, so they know that when he doesn't come in it is because he is really too sick to work. He can't help it if he is sick. I know he could be doing much more highly paid work if it weren't for his sickness. I think Jonathan and all other people who are willing to work but can't should be given money so that they can at least be free of financial worries.

If I wake up and find Jonathan has gone to the hospital, I have to call the job, and sometimes they have to call in somebody else to take his place. If I were in charge of a line at my job and there was someone on the line who was sick as often as Jonathan, I don't think I could run that line, economically speaking. I understand the problem, but it's really not his fault that he gets sick and he works every single day that he can. It's hard on him, it's hard on the company, it's hard on everybody. I guess there are things he could do that would be easier for him to do in his condition. He could manage a restaurant. Or if we could afford it, he could get a little pickup truck and go around and paint for people and do little odd jobs. That way, if he worked that would be fine and if he didn't he wouldn't be hurting anyone else. He could manage a farm because he knows a great deal about agriculture. He could do that and I think he would have liked to be a farmer if he could have made a living doing that. The only reason something like that can't happen is the lack of money. What people with sickle-cell anemia need most is money so that they can live better and get the medicine and the medical attention they need to make them feel as good as they can. They need money when they need it because you can't be telling that pain to wait until the end of the month! If you are not working, you still have to eat and you might have a family depending on you and they have to eat too. If the doctors didn't have an experimental interest in sickle-cell anemia, it would be even rougher. If I had it I would like for doctors to experiment on me because they might find something that would help somebody else. I have a daughter and so far she's fine.

You remember this fellow I told you about who was in the hospital with Jonathan? Well, he's twenty-two years old and he didn't start having sickle-cell attacks until he was nineteen years old. He's just as fat as he can be! You'd never think that he had it because most people who have sickle-cell anemia are thin like Jonathan. He's a very nice person. Last Monday he called up here. He said, "Miz Melton, is Jonathan home?" I said, "No, he's working." He said, "I wanted to get in touch with him about something. I wanted to ask him about doing something." He said, "This lady from a laboratory comes to me every month and takes a tube of blood, and she is looking for some more sickle-cell donors. If Jonathan gives her this tube of blood, she'll give him twenty dollars! If she takes two tubes, she'll give him forty dollars!" So I said, "You call Jonathan after seven. I'm sure he will do it." So, sure enough, he did call. Jonathan made arrangements for that lady to come that Wednesday night, and she came and took a tube of blood and gave him twenty dollars. She said that she is trying to get more money for the people, maybe thirty dollars or twenty-five dollars. She was a very nice black woman. I said to Jonathan, "That was the fastest twenty dollars you ever made!" Jonathan said, "I would do this for nothing. After all, this may help me or someone else with sickle-cell anemia." The lady said, "If my lab wants to give my people this money, you take it." So Jonathan took the money. I tried to con him out of ten dollars, which I never got, of course. Seriously, though, I was for him. At that time, I wished that they needed some good blood and would have taken some of mine for twenty dollars.

I thought it was nice of that fellow to share that with Jonathan.

As long as the experimenting doesn't seem to hurt Jonathan, I think it is a good thing. Now, if they were to say to him, "We'd like to cut you open to see what makes you tick; you might die, but maybe we will find something that would help someone else," I would say no to that. A lot of the interns who are interested in sickle-cell anemia like to look at Jonathan because they just can't believe that someone has lived to be forty-six years old with that sickness. Well, that's all right. Like they say, "Look, but don't touch!" When this new medicine came out, one doctor wanted to try it on Jonathan. He told him he could try it on him. So the doctor cut a gash in Jonathan's arm and ran a tube right up from his arm to his heart! He put Jonathan in intensive care for a couple of days so that he could be watched. The medicine made Jonathan very sick. When the liquid form didn't work, they decided to try it in a powder, but that made him sick too. So Jonathan said, "You can forget that!" Now, that was nothing but an experiment, but Jonathan wanted to do that. If Jonathan thinks it's all right, then it's all right with me and I really mean that from the bottom of my heart.

When the lady who took the blood was here, Jonathan asked her if they were making any progress. She said that it was confidential. I guess when these laboratories are doing this kind of work they don't want some rival laboratory to beat them to the punch.

Most of the difficulty comes from not being able to work like other people. Now, one young fellow we know doesn't work at all and he gets $265 a month. I don't know where he gets this money from. He lives with his mother and father, so things are not so bad for him. He has no dependents, but that wouldn't take care of Jonathan's bills. I think the government should give people who are afflicted and unable to work enough money so that they can live decently. We send money across the seas to help people we don't know, so why can't we help citizens of the country? Somebody like Jonathan, for example, who does the best he can, should be helped, I think. People who are striving and trying to make it need a pat on the back. A lot of people come to this country and get help because they can't speak English. Then as soon as they can say a few words of English they go on to earn more money and get more advantages than we do, and we were born right here! If I was in charge of some sickle-cell helping program, I would know that the first thing I would need was lots of money. I would spend some to find out how sickle-cell anemia is caused and how to prevent and cure it. I would spend some of the money to add to the salaries of people who could just work off and on. I would spend some of the money to give people with this and other sicknesses enough money so that they could live like any person should live. I think that if you are sick, you should not be worrying about how you are going to pay for something you need to live or ease your pain. I would have my program print a little book in ordinary, plain English which would explain just what my program would do for you so that anybody with any sense could understand it without going to a lawyer or somebody else. Right now, if Jonathan was to be sick for six or eight months, I wouldn't even know where to go to apply for help. I wouldn't even know the first place to start or even if there is anyplace to go to.

You know, that lady I told you about who came and took the blood sample, she said that she called Memorial Hospital and General to see if she could find some people who had sickle-cell anemia; but even in Memorial they said they had had two people with the trait, but they told her they hadn't had any active cases in years. I asked Jonathan about that and he said that they couldn't give out that kind of information. But I thought that because she is from a laboratory and because she was doing *research,* they would tell her. But they wouldn't give her Jonathan's name and address, and you know that everybody at Memorial knows Jonathan.

But it's the same way with our sex life. You didn't ask me; I'm telling you anyway. You know, Jonathan went into the hospital the day after Christmas and he didn't come home for two weeks! I was teasing him; I kept saying, "You better hurry up and come home." But by the time Jonathan came home, my period come down! But this is the story of my life. I don't have any boyfriend; I never have. I tell Jonathan that the Lord has sent me the comforter and I'll wait for him to come home and comfort me. I really am not looking for anybody else. That is the furthest thing from my mind. I've been married sixteen years to the same man. Maybe if I had married a man who was well all the time, we'd be separated by now. Also, you have to consider that some people who are perfectly well won't work. Or he might work but not bring his money home. Or maybe he would be beating me up every Friday night just because it was Friday night! I have a couple of girl friends whose husbands are really rotten. They are running around with girls on the same job! Now, those men have never been sick. So I mean it when I say I have no regrets.

Sometimes sickle-cell anemia does influence his thinking and feeling. I can always tell when Jonathan is getting sick. He comes in here just as evil as he can be. Then, two or three days later, he has to go to the hospital. I don't pay too much attention to this. Now, he goes to the hospital averagely every month and a half. He seems to get sick more often than he used to when he was younger, but he doesn't stay in the hospital as long as he did when he was younger. I think the treatment is better than it used to be. They used to depend a lot on blood transfusions, but Jonathan hasn't had a transfusion in years. They give him medications which I don't know much about but they seem to be better for him. This going in and out of your arm with needles is very painful.

We've been married for sixteen years and I go to the hospital every time he is in there. I bowl on Thursdays at six, and it's almost impossible for me to go home and feed my daughter and go to the hospital before six, so he knows that on Thursdays I'm not coming. But every day after that, I'm there. I couldn't ask for more than that if I was sickly, and I often wonder if he would treat me as well as I treat him. Knowing Jonathan as a person, I believe that he probably would. I'm doing what I want to do and I'm not looking for any gold stars. I don't think that men would generally be as good to women as women are to men, though. I can't see trying to make him unhappy when I knew he was sickly when I married him. I sometimes agree with some of my friends who say that it's me and his job that keep him going. A faithful person means more than anything else in the world!

If I were sick and somebody pretended to love me, if I were sick and my husband had another woman but he kept it hidden from me, sometimes I think that would be all right. As long as he didn't bring it in my face, I would feel good just for that. As long as he didn't torture me or make me unhappy. I know that if Jonathan had that kind of wife—you know, one who would neglect him—I know that his heart couldn't stand it. He might be sick, but he stone be looking for me when I walk in that door! We thought about it a great deal before having a child. Jonathan's parents didn't have it, but Jonathan did, so Jonathan's children's children will probably have it. My daughter probably has got the trait. We thought about it a long time. I believe in taking a chance and just leaving things in the hands of the Lord. As I said, we were lucky.

Jonathan Melton

I have learned to stop feeling sorry for myself, I think.

I have known Jonathan Melton most of my life. His tranquil perseverance in the face of the pain that has been an integral part of his life from its beginning is monumental evidence of the heights of dignity the human spirit can attain. Neither severest sickle-cell anemia and its attendant physical ills nor the studied and entirely unmerited social abuse which a castelike social order has assailed him with have been sufficient to madden or cheapen him. Racist doctors and a racist draft board, knowing of his illness, inducted him and sent him to paratrooper training because he looked them in the eye during the sham physical examination. He has been obliged to do the work of several men for substandard wages and to pay sweetheart union dues into the bargain. His house has been broken into three times and many of his most treasured possessions stolen. But the same lively interest in the natural world, good clothes and quality in everything, which earned him the youthful nicknames of the Rich Young Ruler and Fashion Plate, still is abundantly in evidence now that he has attained what is, for him, the advanced age of forty-six. His integrity of person, his devotion to family, his impeccable sense of reciprocity and his incredible resilience are sources of admiration for a number of black communities in the North and the South.

I was born in North Carolina in 1926. My parents came up here when I was four months old. I was the oldest grandchild on my mother's side, so I was raised back and forth during school age. My grandfather and grandmother still lived down south, so I was raised back and forth. I was down south for a year or so and then with my mother for a while and back down south. I was a very sickly child. I still am.

I'm not a child anymore, but I still have the same sickness—sickle-cell anemia. At that time they didn't know of sickle-cell anemia as a sickness or what it was. All they knew was that most children that had it died in infancy age. Most of the people who had it didn't live beyond infancy. They died in three or four months; most of them died within the period of a year. The doctors down there just diagnosed it as the cramps, like rheumatism or something like that, not knowing what sickle-cell was. And then when I was up here I also had that problem. I was hospitalized with it quite frequently. The doctors up here also didn't know it as sickle-cell anemia at that time or anything about it. I was treated for yellow jaundice, which I did have. I would hemorrhage quite a bit and I would have to get a lot of blood transfusions. When I was a baby—I was born with it—I used to cry a lot. I inherit this from my father's side of the family. It was quite deadly, especially in childbirth. Most of his brothers and sisters gave birth to children who died within the first year of infancy, and most of them was in pain from the time they was born to the time they died! They were crippled, a lot of those babies, and they didn't grow like a normal child should grow. They cried all the time and most people called it the colic. They thought they was just full of gas, but they could never find any way of quieting them except for a very short time when they was sleeping. Of course, now we know why a child like that cries all the time.

Most of the time when I was down there they didn't believe so much in doctors. We stayed way back in the woods in the country, about six or seven miles from town on my grandfather and grandmother's farm. When they took you to the doctor, they took you to the doctor once! That was supposed to last you maybe all week when the doctor gave you something for the pain. They had a tendency down south to be able to bear pain and they frown upon people who can't. Most people down there, when they feel bad, don't say anything; they just, you know, bear it. They say, "What good is it going to do to say anything, anyhow?" But you'll find a lot of people cannot do that and I am one who—well, I have beared a lot of pain, but I bear it with expression.

For instance, I've seen my grandfather—now, he was kicked in the chest by a mule. We had been out working and brought the mule home to feed him at twelve o'clock. Now, this was a female mule, which most people seem to prefer. They seem to hold up better in the hot weather, and this mule was named Rhody and she was a very frisky mule and she couldn't stand men. She was a twin. Her twin, which I don't remember but my grandfather told me was in another town, they had to break them up because no one man could handle them together. They would just run away and jump and buck. They were just too terrible when they were together. But because of her temperamental ways, men always had a habit of trying to beat on her all the time! Now, a woman could go up to her and pet her and she'd stand right there, but a man she couldn't stand! So this day after we had finished working and plowing and came home at twelve to feed her, my grandfather turned her loose in the lot to go to water and eat, and just as he took the bridle off of her, she turned around and whirled around and kicked him dead in the chest with her feet and flattened him! And then she trotted on off. You could see her hoofprint right up in his chest! She had caved his ribs in and he started throwing up. We couldn't get him to go to the doctor. So he would just take and rub some Sloan's liniment on it, and he was in the bed all the time with his chest swollen up, and I believe to this day that his ribs was cracked. But still he would never go to the doctor. He never complained or nothing. He'd just get sick to the stomach and throw up. He just stayed there in bed. He'd still try to get up to go to work. Right away he'd get sickly and couldn't make it. Then he'd go back and lay down for a little while and then come on back again.

And I've seen his daughter, which is my aunt, have some terrific headaches! I mean really terrific. She'd be really sick, but she'd just lay down in bed and never say a mumblin' word! Never complain! My grandmother the same way. Don't care how sick they got, they never said nothing! They just laid there. They'd take a little home remedy, a little turpentine or sugar or a little Sloan's liniment, and rub with it—a little camphor ointment or something like that—until they felt better, and when they felt better they'd go on to work. And I've seen many women down there that have worked in the fields up until time for the baby to come. They just stop, go home, have the baby, stay in the bed maybe a day or so and in the next couple of days they be back out in the fields working again! And none the worse for it. And like I've heard women up here say how painful it was for them to give birth and how they screamed and hollered—I was in the kitchen when my aunt gave birth to one of my cousins and I never even knew that the baby had came. I was right in the next room when she was giving birth and she never said a mumbling word, and she had to deliver the baby herself because it came quick, before the midwife, because I had to go and get the midwife to cut the cord and the baby was here! But now, you'd never have known it because she didn't say a word, no expression of pain whatsoever. I guess they think it's kind of bad to express pain; you should be able to bear a little pain. They have had it so bad in other parts of life that they didn't complain, they just accept it. You know, I never did. Well, I had to accept it because I had no choice, but not because I wanted to.

Down south I couldn't get any medical aid. I had no way of getting needles or pain-killing medicines; it cost so much money that most of the time they just didn't have it. The doctors would give you a needle and it would last maybe an hour or so, but they didn't realize what sickle-cell pain really is. Now, I have had headaches and stumped my toe, but let me tell you, that is nothing like that sickle-cell pain! And when that hits you all over your body, it really takes it away from you. You are in pain! You ache all over. I ain' one of those types of people. I'd like to be like that, I guess. I have seen people who have had just about as much pain as I have had and never say a mumbling word. I admire that, yes, I do. I ain't lying. I think it's great if you can bear pain like that. But that is not my stick! If there is any way to get medical help or aid, I seeks it! Immediately! Ahead of time if possible. They tell me in the hospital that I am good with pain, but I don't think so, I mean, compared to some people.

I've heard my mother tell about those babies suffering. My aunt on my father's side, her first child cried and cried a lot. My father's older sister has two children who have sickle-cell anemia. They suffer very much. My father's older sister and her husband kept their children in the South, and they suffer very much from it because the South just was not far advanced for this type of disease. The doctor always called it the cramp. Now, my cousin is just a little older than I am, but if you were to see him, John, you'd swear he was fifty-five or sixty years old! The disease has really left its mark on him. It has really taken its toll. Now, I have another aunt on my father's side, and I guess she must have had about five or six children who died in infancy. Within a year's time they usually died. But they suffered all that little time they had! They would just cry. They couldn't manipulate themselves, they couldn't use their arms or legs, they were just completely helpless.

They didn't know what was causing this and they didn't have any sexual training or knowledge of how to prevent having children. I wouldn't want to say that the men were selfish, but—well, I don't know when condoms were invented, but they didn't know anything much about them, and women, well, if you had sexual relations, you wound up pregnant, that was it. And you just did that until you weren't able to have any more. They didn't know too much about getting rid of babies. Well, those that did know would do the necessary things to do to get rid of babies. I have heard people talking about these things, but as for actually knowing about these things, I don't. I know some people who have butchered up people trying. You know, a lot of people think they know when they jest think they know.

People used to try to cure crabs with gasoline, back there in those old days when gasoline was really powerful, instead of going to the drugstore and getting some blue ointment. Most people who caught syphilis or gonorrhea were afraid to go to the doctor. I have seen many people crippled behind many diseases which they could have gotten medical attention for. I guess they figured it was bad enough to have it and they just didn't want anyone to know about it.

There were no black doctors; in the larger towns there were. I was told that there was once one down in Rockville, but this white lady had him deliver her baby, so he was driven out of town. Nobody said that there was anything between them or anything like that, but the white man was furious because he just should not have delivered that baby, being a black man. So they made him leave town. This I was told. I did not know of it actually myself. I heard my grandmother talk about it and that was the only colored doctor I ever heard of around there. Even if there had been one, I believe the Negroes would go to the white doctor before they would go to the black one, I guess because they would be afraid to antagonize the white man. When they—the babies, I mean—would be sick, they would give them a little paregoric or put a little bicarbonate of soda in some warm water or in their milk if they took the bottle, but most people breast-fed their children.

These people didn't know what sickle-cell anemia was. They would call it the cramp or rheumatism. We used to go round visiting on Christmas; one Christmas I was at my aunt's house and while I was over there I got sick. My legs were affected by sickle-cell, so I couldn't walk. My aunt stayed up all night rubbing my legs with Ben Gay and Sloan's liniment, and then she tried a remedy of taking salt and putting it in a bag and heating it in the fireplace and then laying it on the leg to draw out some of the pain. It didn't help any, though, but she was trying. I don't know where she got it from. That was the first time I ever experienced that.

The doctor prophesied, my mother told me, that I would not live to be a year old. Then after I lived to be a year old, they said I would never live to be five, which you see I did! I had a pretty rough time in school, though. I really wanted to be up there with my brothers and other friends of my age that I was in school with. But being sick, I would fall back a lot. I couldn't keep up with the work. That did bother me a bit. I would really try, but even in trying I was not one of the best students at my very best —with book knowledge, anyhow. I mean, there were just some subjects that were hard for me to grasp. I went to school in a one-room schoolhouse down south. It was a one-room schoolhouse that went from first to seventh grade, and one teacher taught all those seven grades. It was about a five-mile walk to school one way. It didn't take me that long to get there. The teachers often boarded at my grandmother's house, so they would help me with my work. The school was frequently closed very early in the spring because they had to get the young black kids out there to help get the crops ready. The white schools were never closed because of that, only the Negro schools. The Negro schools opened late and closed early to make sure that the white man's crop was planted and that it was fully gathered, you know, in the fall of the year. Of course, it's not like that anymore. Down in my state of North Carolina it's not like that anymore. In South Carolina and Georgia I don't think it's that way.

When I was a kid the thing I hated most about sickle-cell was it kept me from doing things that I would like to have done—you know, participating with other boys and girls of my age in sports and other things I wanted to do. Then, you see, I didn't really know what it was. You see, I was raised in a Baptist home in the Baptist Church to believe in God, and I really did. I believed very strongly, but I got to the point where I was getting resentful after a while because I couldn't understand why I was being punished. I mean, why was I always being sick all the time? There were others who were carefree and didn't give a damn about anything and they just never got sick. The more they drank and the more hell they raised, the better they were. I had never did anything to anyone. I couldn't see any reason why I should be, as I considered it, punished like this. Why was I always the one being sick all the time? What did I do? They said, "Pray and the good Lord will help you," but I was wondering "When?" and "How come?" Oh, I prayed a lot. I used to pray a lot and cry a lot. I never really talked about that to anyone. There was no one that I really had. I used to try to talk to my mother about it. She said, "God does things in a mysterious way and maybe in the end He will explain it to you." But I guess it was something that she could never explain herself, but she'd explain the best way she could. I felt that I was religious. I used to go to church quite regularly. I still go to church fairly regularly. Maybe I'm still hoping, John. Maybe I'm still hoping for a better day somehow, somewhere. I don't think the church can give it to me. I don't see how it could. It has never given it to me so far. I don't really get anything out of it; actually, it gets something out of me. I used to want to go outside and play ball in the summertime, you know. I knew that my mother would make me stay upstairs. It seemed to me that she was being hard on me, but I knew I really couldn't do it. If I went outside, it would just be a matter of minutes before I'd be back sick. If I could sneak outside, I would. I used to love to ride bicycles, but I wasn't supposed to do anything strenuous. I was excused from gym. I wasn't even allowed to go up and down the stairs in school. I have paid for a lot of things that I wasn't supposed to do. When you're young like that, it's just like a child two years old—rather than take his time and walk, he wants to run. He can't understand why he must walk. It's hard to really penetrate to a person like that. There might be something physically wrong with him that means that he really shouldn't run because he might damage his legs or something like that. It's hard to get a person like that to understand that what you're saying is for their own benefit, and I was no exception to the rule. I figured I was ordinary—I mean, I was devilish at times, too. When I got sick in school they'd have someone send me home by car or the police, something like that. A couple of times they had to take me to the hospital. They took me once by the ambulance. I felt shame, you know, that the students had to see me like this. I wanted so much to be like the rest when they were out there playing soccer. I could just imagine myself out there doing it too, and doing it just a little bit better, but it was never like that with me.

I used to daydream a lot then. I always wanted to be a doctor, I guess because I was sick myself. I always figured I could get help for myself and even do better than that, help someone else. I always wanted to be a doctor. I never did feel that I could ever really be a doctor. I never did finish high school and I had a hard time through grammar school, so I knew I could never make it through medical college. Money wasn't even the thing; it was just my physical health. I worked when I was in grammar school and I worked when I was in high school. When I was in high school I used to work in that drugstore which used to be on the corner of Main Street and Third. I used to work in that drugstore after school and on Saturdays. As I was cleaning up in there I used to imagine myself being a doctor. I used to imagine myself being a doctor and writing out these prescriptions. I used to watch him filling the prescriptions, how he took powders and made salves out of them. I had to clean these bottles, so I used to practice pouring water from one bottle to the other without spilling a drop. I would imagine that the water was some precious serum and you couldn't spill a drop. I used to daydream like that. Those were just things I kept to myself. I didn't confide in anyone about them. Those were just things I kept to myself.

When I went back down south after I got in high school, I was about sixteen or seventeen. I was having a hard time with the physical deal. The doctors said maybe if I went back down south the change of the climate might help my health. So I went back and I was working on my grandfather's farm, helping him out, you know. When I was younger all the land was owned by Negroes in that community where I lived before they all migrated up here. I mean, for hundreds of hundreds of miles around, Negroes owned hundreds and hundreds of acres! My grandfather used to tell me that it was once all woods and how the people had to cut down the trees and how their wives worked right side by side with them when they were trying to clear the land. They used to have a community schoolhouse. They used to have cookouts and fish fries down by the river. They tried to have something. My grandfather could have had a very rich farm if he had used his head, and the Negroes themselves could have been if they had united. They had land, they made crops, but they worked as individuals. In other words, when I say they worked as individuals, when cultivators and tractors came out the people couldn't afford them; but if two or three farmers had gotten together and bought a large tractor, what that one tractor could have done for all three farmers would have been twice what they could have done for themselves as individuals. But this is something no one could see. They didn't *want* to see it, I think. They were Negroes who had their own place and were satisfied with making a decent living, or scratching out a living, as I would say. But they were afraid to really get too far ahead. I think they were afraid of the white man. They thought the white people would take their increase or resent their progress through one way or another.

There were the Cobs, white farmers. They had tractors, and as the Negroes got old and couldn't farm the land and their children left and went up north and didn't pay the taxes on it, the white man would just continually buy the land back just for the taxes, for a little or nothing, you might as well say. And he kept buying more tractors and hiring. This sharecropping, it did all right for a lot of poor people, but it kept the white man on top all the time. In other words, when you sharecrop, if you were a farmer with four or five kids, maybe six or seven, the more the merrier, as far as they were concerned—the more there was, the more there were to work in the fields, and you could have a bigger farm. Well, the man that was farming on shares might go to the white man and say, "I need fifty dollars to get my kids some shoes." So he would give you fifty dollars, but he might put seventy-five on his book. Whatever he want to put down, that's what he put down. You didn't argue with him because you didn't have any book. If you did you wouldn't win because whatever he said, that is what it was. There was no need for courts because if the man said that you owed him, then the man's sheriff then and there proceeded to take you to jail, and that was just it. There was no court, you didn't have any lawyer. If he said you did this and you denied it, you got even more time.

I had a cousin who got over a year in the chain gang for swiping a five-cent Baby Ruth bar. No trial. The lady said he swiped it. He didn't deny it. She said he took the little five-cent candy bar. Maybe he was a little hungry. Anyway, he went to the chain gang for more than a year behind that. They didn't want restitution; the only restitution they wanted was seeing someone go to the chain gang, because that was some mighty cheap labor. I've never known them to work for the farmers. They only worked for the county and state on the road gang. They worked on the roads and bridges and all like that. I've never known them to work on the farms. I have sat on the road many times and watched them. They had to go down into waist-deep water and chest-deep water in dead wintertime and put back bridge supports. I never was afraid of them. They never seemed vicious or criminal to me. In fact, I never knew what it was to be criminal, never having seen what it was they were supposed to have done. I always felt sorry for them. I used to resent that guard with the shotgun very much. He would be standing over there screaming and hollering with his little bullwhip, snapping it and hustling them if they didn't move fast enough for him. The only thing they ever got to eat, look like, was black-eyed peas and corn bread.

People were afraid of the Klan, white and colored, because they dealt very unjustly, rode around in sheets, and did practically whatever they wanted to do and you couldn't get redress through the law because the law was leading them. It was a small community; people knew who they were. The poor whites were afraid of them too. If there was one of them who was known to beat his wife, they would take him out into the field and thrash him. Without any trial, without any reason at all, people have had to leave for standing up for what was rightfully theirs. I have a cousin. The white man who owned this farm he was working on liked his wife. She did not want to go for the program that he wanted to put down. She told her husband how she felt, so my cousin went there and asked this white man to cool his son. But the white man wanted to feel like whatever his son wanted to do was all right, regardless. So my cousin had to persuade the young man in more unfriendly ways. But after that he had to flee for his life. After he had thrashed that white man kind of severely, well, after that, they went to get the Ku Klux Klan. They were going to lynch the boy, you know, shoot him. But the word had got back, so the parents had to sneak him out at night to a far town by car. They all got away and came up here to New York.

There is nothing Christian or very moral about them. They are only interested in what they want to achieve for themselves. On Saturdays they used to ride through town. They had some hick-town sheriffs and these police would lead the Klan through town in their police car. The sirens would be screaming and the lights would be flashing and these police would be at the head of twenty-five or thirty cars. They'd be sitting in their cars and pickups with their hoods over their heads, holding their shotguns. Now, no one would know what they had in mind. All of a sudden, if they got a little bored they would make a little sport at somebody's expense. They might go to somebody's farm and maybe burn it down. I had an uncle. He had a son who was killed in the service and his son had willed him his allotment. Now, after he had died—this was their only child—my uncle and his wife worked very hard and built themselves a beautiful brick home— on his own property, now. It was brick and a lot of the whites didn't have brick, just the very rich. But he built him a nice brick home. Now, every time he built this home it got burned down while he was at church. No one knew why. They had not left any fire. But three times he built it up and three times they burned it down to the ground. Then after that he built a wooden one and it stayed—no one bothered it. You see, the white community was the Klan. Nobody ever told him that his house was too grand; they figured he should have sense enough to know that. It's like those farmers —they didn't want to get too far ahead.

What the black people did when the Klan came to town was *leave,* in a hurry. Each one would get in his little car or his horse and wagon and make it! They would take the back roads. If the Klan was going south, they would go the other way around. If they were walking and they saw the Klan approaching, they would run across the field and lay down. If they didn't they would stop you or maybe shoot at you. I've never seen that, though.

I guess the white people didn't want the black people to have anything that showed prosperity because a lot of them didn't have it themselves. They had the best of what was available for themselves and their kids, but still they wanted someone to lord it over. I guess they wanted to keep them down. They wanted to be able to say that they still controlled the black man completely, even though he was supposed to be a free person. If the white man wanted this particular girl or woman, he would give you the message that you were supposed to stay away, and if you didn't you might end up dead. Segregation just is a way to see that the white man gets whatever he might want.

I think that the black man up here feels that he wants the same thing for his child that the white man has for his. Black men in the South want a decent education and respect for their children and from their children. They want the child to have respect for themselves and their elders and their own equals. That is something that really isn't taught here. I have known students from up here who have really resented the way our schools are run down there because you really do have to show respect. When you're down there you must maintain your grades, you must really try. It all goes back to the point that for an education down south, you had to work and your parents had to sacrifice. When you got it you really earned it! It wasn't a matter of you sitting down and it was handed to you on a silver platter. It wasn't one of these numbers where you walk to school and after you finish with your first class, you could lay down on your bed until the next class. You had a job to go to. You had to study, you had to work and you had to help put yourself through school. And your parents didn't hesitate to let you know that they were making this effort for you. They didn't look for nothing in return. They wanted you to do the best you could for yourself and after you did for yourself, you were expected to help your brother or sister if they were trying also.

I really don't consider myself a Southerner and I don't consider myself a full Northerner. I guess I could say I consider myself a Northerner. I did like the South. In fact, if I could have agreed with my grandfather—we couldn't see eye to eye on the farming bit, but I liked farming, within reason, as long as you modernized it. My grandfather had capabilities and limitations as a farmer. He always overplanted. He believed in buying the cheapest fertilizer and so forth. He didn't believe in cultivating right and keeping his land—in other words, he really got everything he could get out of the land without putting anything back into it. He didn't know any better and no one could tell him any better! He figured he knew how to farm. You see, when he started off you really didn't need a lot of fertilizer because the land was rich because it was newly cleared then. It produced quite a bit and he seemed to think that it should continue to do that. He didn't understand about field erosion and he would continue to plant without rotating the crops. I used to work with him, right? I mean, we worked hard! At the end of the year when we got through we didn't have a thing. There was nothing to last over to next year. It was just disgusting. He could have took a little and still made a lot if he would have rested and replenished his land. The agriculture people would come by and try to help you if you wanted to be helped. A lot of them wouldn't even take advantage of that and I couldn't get him to take advantage of it. My grandmother had a large farm which she inherited from her father, and she said, "Jonathan, while he is living he will take care of all the farming. But stay here, and when I die I'll will it all to you." I tried, but I just couldn't cut it.

When he would plant cotton, he'd overplant; and then when he'd take it to market and the man would be figuring up twenty-five for this and the cents due for one-quarter pounds, this white man would tell him it come to so much and so much. My grandfather was named Wellington, but they called him Willy. I'd be right there by him, figuring it up. The white man would say, "Well, look, this is what it comes to, Willy: two seventy-five for this bale, six seventy-five for the full bale." I said, "Didn't you make a mistake in figuring?" He looked at me and said, "What did you say?" I said, "Didn't you make a mistake in figuring?" So he said, "What did you say?" I thought I would speak a little louder; I thought he might have been hard of hearing or something. So then he looked at me and said, "You're not from down here, are you?" I told him, "No, I'm not from down here. I was born here, but I went to school up north." So he looked at me and said, "Willy, who is this?" My grandfather said, "That's my grandson." He looked at me again and my grandfather said, "Shug, you step outside. I'll take care of this business." I said, "Pa, he's gypping you." And he looked at me and turned almost red! He looked like he was almost ready to choke. I said, "He's making a mistake and he knows he's wrong." He looked at me and said, "What did you say?" I said, "You are not adding or figuring right and you know it!" And my grandfather stepped outside. He wouldn't change his figures and my grandfather, after hearing me say it, would not make him change. He accepted what that white man was willing to give him anyhow. That would burn me up. I couldn't see giving the labor away like that. He didn't have to sell; he could have said, "Well, I changed my mind." If he didn't sell, well, he could take it back home and put it in storage. He could borrow. Probably the other whites wouldn't have loaned to him, but at least he could have tried. It might have condemned people to go hungry, but, well, a number of people have done that.

You know, one time after this time I'm talking about, I went down south in my car. And when I drove up to my grandfather's house they were selling some timber. My grandmother said, "Jonathan, come here a minute." My grandmother and grandfather were out in front talking to this white man who was buying this timber. She said, "I just sold the timber off the Holly place. He's offering us over eight hundred dollars for it. What do you think of that?" I said, "Did he tell you approximately how many feet of timber he thinks is on there?" My grandfather said that the white man said he had checked it out and found out that a lot of the trees were not fully developed and that a lot of the pines had hollow rot. I said, "He offered you eight hundred dollars for it?" And my grandmother said, "Yes, and Wellington wants to sell it for that." I said, "It's worth over three times that amount!" He said, "What do you mean?" I said, "I haven't even been there and seen it, but I know it's worth over three times that amount. If he's offering you eight hundred dollars, Ma, it's worth many more times eight hundred dollars." Then Pa said, "Now, Shug, you don't know what you're talking about." I said, "Oh, yes, I do." So Ma said, "If you say it's worth more than eight hundred dollars, I won't sell for eight hundred dollars." I said, "No, don't sell for that." My grandfather was furious with me! I said, "Now, if you want me to, Ma, I'll take you someplace tomorrow and I'll get another man to come out here and appraise it for you and you let the two of them decide between them." So then that white man sat right there and said, "I'll write you out a check for twenty-four hundred." Just like that! My grandmother said, "I'm glad you came when you did. It's better than eight hundred dollars!" The man had told my grandfather that he was taking a beating to offer eight hundred dollars. My grandfather never did say "Thank you" or nothing. He just acted like he had accomplished a great deal himself. I just felt that I had done my grandmother a service.

Because my grandfather was kind of a hard taskmaster, I only stayed as long as I did because of my grandmother. I used to ask my grandfather for some money to go to town. He'd give me a quarter. Now, I'm eighteen years old. I was supposed to go to town and spend fifteen cents and save ten cents for church the next day. We could never really sit down and talk. I have actually really, really tried, you know, to really help. When I worked the farm with him I had cleared almost two acres of land by cutting down trees on a Saturday. I had to work six days a week from sunup to sundown when I was able to. And then if I told him I wanted a plot of my own, a little crop of my own so I could have a little change of my own, I had to work after I worked on his to take care of mine on Saturday. I had to do all of his work during the week, but if I wanted to do anything for myself, I had to do it on a Saturday—I mean, on my free part of Saturday, after twelve o'clock. This meant no town. So I did that. Not bragging, but nine times out of ten I came out ahead of the deal because I had watermelons. And that year, you talking about some beautiful large watermelons. I had 'em! Those were some beautiful watermelons! I took my two acres, man, and made more than he made on over half of his thirty-five acres. I had two acres!

When I was young I used to think I would like to be a farmer, but my grandfather turned me against farming. When I came up here I got the idea that I would like to be a doctor. You know, when I left the South to come up here for the last time, I told them that I could not cut it anymore because there just had to be a better way. Well, my grandmother said if I stayed down there and farmed she would will all her land to me. She owned about six or seven hundred acres that her grandfather had left her from way back in slavery time. I told her in spite of all that and as much as I liked the land, I just couldn't see it. I left it all. I considered myself to be a pretty good farmer because I could make things grow. I just got tired of having nothing year after year, so I told my grandmother, "I'm going home. It's just a waste of time." She said, "Well, you tried." I could sit down and talk to my grandmother, but with him I just couldn't get through. I tried, I really did. We would always end up arguing or disagreeing. He thought he was right. My grandmother used to say, "Well, you know how he is and he won't ever change." She felt pretty bad about that. My grandmother was a pretty straight person. Very straight!

I never associated with the whites. My grandparents never let me have too much to do with them because I had a resentment against them. I am the type of person that didn't believe in taking no stuff! I would never say "Yessir" and "No, sir" to them, never. They kept me away from them because they thought I was heading for trouble. The first time I went down there I almost gave them a heart attack! There was a young white boy sitting in a car eating peanuts. I had just got off the train and was crossing the street to my grandfather and grandmother, who were there waiting on me. And this young white boy had nothing to do but wait till I was right in front of him and take two handfuls of peanut hulls and throw them in my face. I had just stepped by and when he threw them in my face, I reached round and grabbed him. He started to holler, "Mama! Mama! Nigger gettin' me!" Boy, he took out and I was right behind him and my grandfather was right behind me! He ran me down and grabbed me. But I was really angry. I remember saying, "I'll kill him! I'll kill him. He don't know who he's messing with." My grandfather said, "You're fixing to get lynched!" But, you see, that didn't worry me at the time. I just couldn't see taking that, especially from a white person. My grandfather ran me down, but I kind of shook them up there a little bit. It didn't bother me, though. Fortunately, there were no other white people around, or if they were, they were too astounded. I always maintained the Northern-style relationship from the gitgo. In other words, I never did accept the Southern-style relationships for myself. I could accept Southern-style relationships among the Negroes, but as far as the whites were concerned, you know, all that knuckling down and backing up from the white point of view, I couldn't take that.

I'll tell you, down there I was very happy in a way. I learned to make myself contented. I was the only young person on the farm after my Uncle Thomas left. But after I was in high school, I went back down there the second time because the doctor said that the change of climate might help me with the sickle-cell anemia. It didn't. But then, I was plowing, helping with the watermelons, cutting wood and doing anything that any other grown person might do. On Saturdays I would go to the fields for a half a day plowing or picking cotton, you know, doing whatever it was we had to do, but then the rest of the day was mine to do with whatever I pleased. Sometimes I'd go into town. Sometime I'd just pick up my rifle and go hunting. In the winter I would hunt for squirrels or rabbits. If it were summer, I'd go fishing by myself. I liked that. I liked the woods. I wasn't afraid, although I knew I'd have to watch out for snakes. I wasn't afraid of anything attacking me. Fishing, the same way. I always carried my rifle with me, a .22, just in case I came across a rattlesnake or a moccasin or something like that. I was quite contented just going hunting or fishing.

There were white farmers living near us, but we never had very much to do with them and my grandfather would never let me work for the white man. I seemed to have a certain hatred and resentment of them because of the way they treated colored folks in general—they treated us like dirt most of the time. I knew this man that was a sharecropper, and his wife was sick, but the white man came and said, "I want my cantaloupes hoed." My friend told the white man, "I'm hoeing, so I can't get to it right now and my wife is sick." The white man told him, "Damn your wife. You tell her to get out of that bed and go to the field. I want my cantaloupes hoed!" And, you know, that white man took a stick and whipped that woman to the field, and the colored man did nothing about it! He should have killed him!

You know, one time we were going into town and this white fellow was coming down the road with his family in his wagon, so our wagons drew abreast and this white man said, "Willy, how're you doing?" My grandfather said, "I'm doing fine." So when they got ready to go on, this white man leaned forward and said to this jet-black mule, "Come on, nigger, get along here, nigger." I had these two red mules, so I said, "Come on, cracker, let's go. Get up here, cracker!" The white man turned around and gave me that evil, evil eye! I just hit the mule and said "Come on, cracker!" My grandfather sat and told me, "Shh, shh, shh." A thing like that irked me. I don't know why, it just does.

One time my grandfather was picking up some fertilizer and this white man said, "Willy"—his name was Wellington, but they never called him that; they always called him Willy—anyway, this white man said, "Willy, you know something? You are a good old darkie. You are one of the best niggers around here. We ain't never had any trouble out of you. That's one thing I like about you, Willy, and if all these niggers round here were like you, Willy, everything would be all right." Now, the more that white man talked, the hotter I got. Meanwhile, my grandfather is givin' him nothing but "Yessir, yessir." Then the white man said, looking at me, "Is that your grandson?" So my grandfather said, "Yes, sir, that's my grandson. He's from up north." Then the white man said, "How're you doing?" I said, "I'm doing fine. How are you doing?" Then he asked me, "Do you like staying down here with your grandfather?" I said, "I like it fine." He kept on asking me questions. I knew what he wanted me to say, but I would not "Yessir" him. My grandfather said, "Come on, Shug." He knew that white man was getting pretty hot.

I went on a trip down there once with my brother. We pulled up to this little one-pump storefront gas place. This white man came out and said, "Can I help you there?" So I said, "Check the oil and fill it up, please." He said, "What did you say?" I repeated what I had said. "What did you say?" My brother said, "He wants you to say 'sir.'" So I said, "Shit." I said, "Check the oil and fill it up, damn it, and if you don't want to, go back in your store! We'll go to another filling station." I'm not saying "Yessir" to no damn cracker. My grandfather would never let me work for them. Sometime they would come by in the fall, wanting someone to pick some peas or something, but my grandfather would never let me work for them.

My grandfather was hard, but I learned a lot about life and people through him, too. Living there taught me many things. I had made up my mind for a long time that I would never get married. I couldn't see burdening down anyone with my sickness. Then I met a person who gave me a kind of change of thought about it. Gloria has stuck by me all the way. When I first got married I tried not to have children because of that. That was for the first couple of years. The doctor wanted me to have an operation to make sure that I would never have children. This I didn't go along with. I really didn't approve of that type of operation for myself. I mean, if it hadn't been for my mother and father, I wouldn't be here. Well, after a couple of years nothing ever happened anyhow, so I thought that being sick so long and taking so much medication had made me sterile. I thought I would never have any children, so I never worried about it. We were married nine years before Mary Ellen was born. One day it just happened.

They say that sickness makes people think. You know, there was a time when I used to sit up there in that third-floor window watching other boys and girls, my sister and my brothers playing when I had to stay in the house by myself. Couldn't go out, couldn't hardly walk, sick most of the time. I used to wonder what was the purpose of even trying to live if this was what life was going to be for me. I used to sit in that window many a time when I was sick and figure, you know, "If I jump out, I won't hurt no more. Then it would be all over!" Then I used to think, "Well now, is it? If I do jump, maybe I don't hurt no more, but how do I know whether or not it is really any different? If I did, would it really be any different or would I be doing the same thing, only somewhere else? How do I know that the other side would be any different from here?" You don't, so I'm afraid to leave here and afraid to trust what the other side might be. Yes, I thought of it many times. When I go to the hospital and I'm really feeling bad, sometimes I ask Him to just take me away from it all! No more, please! And then, when I feel like it really might be no more, I scuffle like mad to get back!

I owe a great deal to my mother. Oh, I do! I owe her a lot! Don't care what hour of the day or night I got sick, she was there! If she couldn't get a taxi she'd put me in a carriage and wheel me to the hospital. Then I used to stay in the hospital two and three months at a time! I couldn't walk and I contracted yellow jaundice. I still have traces of that because when I get real sick my eyes become very jaundiced. You know, my first blood transfusion was what they call a direct blood transfusion. They would take a needle of blood from my mother's veins and inject it into mine. Now, when you get blood like that, back and forth, back and forth, it takes about an hour or an hour and a half and it is very, very painful because each time they have to re-stick you. Man, you talk about screaming and hollering—I'll never forget that! After they got through giving me the blood transfusion they had stuck me so much in the vein that they had to take a stitch in it. They told my mother, "Now, when you get through here, go home after you lay down awhile here and get right in the bed." They made her lay down there for a while, but when she left she went straight to work, to the laundry.

I remember one day a couple of years ago I was at Memorial Hospital and a nurse had just called me when a doctor turned around and stared at me and said, "Jonathan! Jonathan Melton! Are you still alive?" Then he said, "Excuse me!" He couldn't believe it. It is unusual, I guess, and I guess I owe that to my mother. She sacrificed a lot in life and gave up a lot. I know how hard she worked. One year she wanted to buy a house. She had saved five dollars here and ten dollars or fifteen dollars there, and she had managed to save about five hundred dollars and she was thinking about putting it down on a house. I got very sick and they had to rush me to the hospital. They gave me some transfusions, and that was when ATCH first came out and they wanted to try it on me. They told my mother that they had to have two hundred dollars before they would send this medicine out. That was way back there and two hundred dollars was a lot of money, but she went and got that money! We got the medicine. It didn't do me any good at all. As a matter of fact, it almost killed me. I had a bad reaction to it from the first time they started to give it to me. They gave me 1 cc of ATCH and a pint of blood every day, a Dr. Tisdale and his wife. I told the doctor that the medicine was making me sick. He told me that sometimes a medicine would make you feel worse before it started to make you feel better. He wanted to keep on trying. And finally the doctor said, "Everything I do seems to be working against you."

In the hospital now they just give me liquids intravenously, dextrose or something else with vitamins in it. They don't give me blood transfusions anymore unless my blood drops really low. I don't know, but I think they've found that my body will build itself back up. I don't know. At times they have given me a blood transfusion and at night I would be down just as sick as I could be! Sometimes in spite of the transfusion my blood would still drop down very quickly because those cells would have destroyed the cells in the new blood just that quick. So they found out that without the transfusion, I'd still do just as well.

When I was down south I never got a blood transfusion. It didn't matter how sick I got, they'd give me a needle and some pills for the pain and that would only last a couple of hours. When that wore off you would be home with no kind of help whatever and then you just screamed and hollered from daytime to nighttime. That pain would make you roll and turn and twist, but the people at home couldn't do anything for you. You just had to lay there until it wore off. You would get to the point where you couldn't hardly walk, you couldn't use your arms or your legs. They'd just sit there and listen to you because there wouldn't be anything else they could do for you. They'd rub you with a little liniment, but that didn't help any. It would be like you were watching a person being crushed by a car and you knew you couldn't lift it off him, so all you could do is just stand there and watch. There was nothing they could really do for me.

Racism played a part in the treatment down there. I have found doctors who were really trying to do their best in both places, but it was there. Then too, like I said, in the South they didn't have the knowledge or the technology. I never went to the hospital down there, you know, to stay. I know people who did and it was not too good. Their families had to go take care of them and feed them. The nurses just wouldn't do anything for the colored patients. People were afraid to go because you heard all these stories about hospitals and you could see that there were plenty of things wrong with them. Most of them didn't go to the hospital. They stayed home and suffered and died!

I think the government should take care of people who are unable to take care of themselves. Why shouldn't it do that? After all, the government can take care of millions of people overseas who do not contribute anything whatsoever to this country. They're always contributing to those people's welfare and benefit, so why shouldn't they contribute to the people who were born here? I feel that I have just as much right to expect help from my government as people who only want what they can get out of it. There are people who are being helped who care nothing at all about this country. I figure that anyone who has sickle-cell anemia should receive this help. Now, I know that this might mean lifetime support, but, John, I feel like this: if a parent is out there working and all they can make is, say, two hundred dollars a week or a hundred and seventy-five a week and he has two or three kids to take care of, there is nothing in this world that will take your money faster than a hospital bill! And there is no way a man can work forty hours and pay even one week's hospital bill because there is just no way to do it! John! when I go to the hospital and just stay in there for seven days, I get a bill of from seven to eight hundred dollars for one week! Now, I have union insurance, but you just can't make that kind of money out there and you got your rent and all these other things to keep up with. Now, you just cannot meet that kind of bill—you just can't do it! Now, I am not rich, so if they were to give me back every cent I pay in taxes, I still could not make it. I feel that I am obligated to contribute, just like you or anyone else, if I'm able to hold a job. I don't resent the tax they take out of my salary when I work, because I like to feel independent, too. I don't mind that, but I don't think that I should be deprived by the government, either. It's just like Gloria was telling me last night: an Internal Revenue man came out to her job to confiscate this fellow's check. They said he owed about five or seven hundred in back taxes. Now, you see, something like that burns me up! Now, here's a working man, right? He owes maybe seven hundred and they're right dead on his behind for that money! Now, they are going to get it! They are going to take his whole check until he pays up that seven hundred dollars. Every week they are going to be on him and they are going to be charging him interest. Now, here's somebody like Nixon with thousands and thousands of dollars who pays practically nothing and all these corporations that owe millions and millions of dollars and don't pay one dime, and they just sit back and nobody bothers them. Yet they will jump right down the poor man's throat for a little fifty or a hundred dollars! Now, they will get that money and they will spend six hundred to get that fifty if they have to. Oh, they will collect from the poor man! Now, that irks me! It really does. Now, what type of government do we have if it allows this kind of thing to go on? But, believe me, they do get away with it. I don't think it's right, but they sure do get away with it.

If I were the director of a program—well, I'll tell you, I have done without so long that I have become accustomed to doing with less and less. You know what I mean. I've learned that if I don't have something, to make the best of what I do have. I learned that a long time ago. When I didn't have a job and I knew my mother didn't have the money because I knew she was trying to feed and clothe us, if I wanted to go to the movies and couldn't go, well, I just didn't go. I didn't sit around and sulk because I couldn't go. So, if I had that kind of job I wouldn't think that I would have to be paid fifty thousand dollars a year or seventy-five thousand or forty thousand dollars a year; all I'd want would be a decent salary. I wouldn't mind making ten thousand a year, and that is not raising much cane. Even fifteen or anything within reason. I don't think that just because I'm the head of something I have to have the biggest portion of it. I would like to live comfortably, you know what I mean. For example, I would like to buy a front-room set. I would like for Mary Ellen to have a brand new bedroom set. She needs one. You know what I mean. These are things I would like to have that I just don't have the money to get.

Right now I don't see any hope for any kind of future. But I would have liked to own my own home. I would like to have owned a nice home and I would have liked to have had it paid for so that, well, you know, when I do kick the bucket my wife would not have to worry about it—so she wouldn't have to worry about bills or anything like that. I think that as a man and as a husband you should feel obligated. You should try to provide not only while you're living but even after you're gone. I know some people say, "Well, let the next person worry about it." Well, that philosophy is all right if you have plenty. I mean, if a person has stuck by you all these years, I can't see being so selfish that you don't want them to have something just because you're not going to be here to enjoy it with them. That is not my philosophy.

I still have occasional daydreams, you know, of just providing a home. Just an ordinary home, a comfortable living place, nothing real fancy. I don't know what keeps me going, John. It's just going to work and coming back home. I just keep on going each day as it comes, that's all. It doesn't bother me anymore like it used to. It did bother me. I just kept it to myself more or less, but it really bothered me that I couldn't do the things I really wanted to do. I always wanted to travel some. I've never been to Florida. I wouldn't mind going there. I'd like to go to Bermuda or someplace like that. I'd like to go to some of the places I have heard of but have never seen for just once in my life, but my money is not long and I'm afraid that I might get sick. I made up my mind when I was a child that I would never get married. I was thirty when I got married, and looking back on it, I really don't think early marriage is such a good idea. I wish I had been able to save more money, of course, and I wish we had had children earlier. As it was, I didn't have a child until I was married nine years. If we had had children when we were first married, Mary Ellen would be almost grown now. But now she's still a baby and I'm up in age, forty-six now. You know that's not exactly ancient, but it's a long way from being young. But, Bruh' John, it is advanced age for a person with sickle-cell anemia; the doctors and nurses tell me that.

I'd like for Mary Ellen to grow up to be healthy. The most important thing is to be healthy. So far, the doctors say she has a one-hundred-percent chance. She seems to be all right. I don't especially want her to be a doctor. I have never made any plans like that. I figure I want her to do what she would like to do. But I would like for her to have an education and be able to take care of herself and be able to think for herself. I would like her to be able to take care of her own self and do her own number, whatever she decides that is. I want her to earn her own living honestly. I'd like for her to want to go to college. I want her to be independent, though. I would like for her to grow up and choose a profession that will give her the ability to earn enough to support herself and her family if she has to. I would like her to be independent so she wouldn't be laying back on welfare or some other program. I would like her to be able to provide for herself rather than depending on some program that will support her for doing nothing.

I think that not being able to be independent and having to depend on these programs has ruined a lot of American Negroes. It keeps them from bettering their condition if they can halfway make it for nothing. I know a young girl who has four children. The only thing she can do is get on welfare. I hear some pregnant women in the tavern say, "Well, this will be another increase in my welfare check." I mean, what kind of attitude is that to have? They just give you enough to get over. It's only for today, there is no provision for tomorrow. They give you enough to buy food stamps and to pay your rent and to buy a few rags to send your children to school. You can't put a dime in the bank. They know that you're getting too much if you get enough to save some. A lot of Negroes are accepting this and I think it's wrong! Now, if you *can't* do any better, all right. But, I mean, John, you should at least try.

I see so many of the younger girls on welfare. They don't want to work and they won't work. I would like for my daughter to be willing to work for what she wants in life. But I would like her to have it without having to sacrifice too much to get it. I don't want her to go to school so she won't have to work. I want her to go to school so she won't have to work so hard to make it. I want her to work so she can achieve something in life if she possibly can. I don't care who you are, husband, wife, whoever you may be, there is nothing like having your own. That's why I want her to be independent. I want her to be able to make it for herself because you can never tell when somebody who you may think is the greatest will turn their back on you. And then, if you have nothing to fall back on, you are lost. You need something or some way of achieving something for yourself in your lifetime. When you sink down to the lowest degree so that you just don't know what to do and then you start thinking that this welfare thing is the easiest way out, it might be the one way out for you, then. Now, if you have an education and some training in something that is needed that you can rely upon—you know, in some field that's needed—that's good. Then if you don't make it, it won't be because you're not able to; it will be because you just don't *want* to make it. John, you know there are so many of us who want to and just can't! There are some who could do better and won't because they don't want to because they are getting something for nothing. Every time I got the opportunity I tried. Even when I was single I just wanted to be independent. I have never—the only thing I have ever drawn since I've been out here has been unemployment. I wanted to be able to stand on my own feet.

I learned how to be alone down south. Sick people have to learn to be alone. So I could take company or leave it alone pretty well. When you first get sick, people come around to see you. But when it gets to be one of those continuous deals, you just have to learn to be alone because you will be alone many days. That's why I used to read a lot and go to the library. I used to read about adventurous people like Daniel Boone. I used to day-dream about what I would do if I could get well. I really wanted to go to college, I wanted to be a doctor. Maybe if I hadn't been sick I never would have thought of anything like that. I thought I would like to be either a doctor or a lawyer because I liked talking, also, at times. I never really knew any doctors or lawyers personally.

I've had two great doctors. Dr. Pine was very good before he decided to be a gynecologist and Dr. Stanovsky was the second. Dr. Stanovsky was an intern when I was going to the clinic at Memorial, and when he set up private practice he told me to come to his office and he would take care of me. He was the second private doctor I had ever seen in my life. I always went to the clinic because I could not afford a private doctor. He was really great. He did all he could. He would try out all kinds of medicines on me. No matter what time of the night I called him and told him that I needed him, he was there! When the house call had gotten to be a thing of the past, he would come here if I needed him. One year there was so much snow out here I couldn't get to him. He shoveled out his driveway, got in his car and came over here! I don't think he has a special interest in sickle-cell anemia. He's moved now to where I don't think he has many sickle-cell patients. But at that time he did all the research on sickle-cell anemia that he could. He would ask other doctors that might have had sickle-cell patients what they were doing for it. And if he read of a new approach in a medical journal, he might try that.

I don't know many people with sickle-cell anemia. There's a man I met in the hospital and a lady I know of, but I don't know many people with it. As a matter of fact, until I met this fellow in the hospital, I didn't know anyone outside my own family who had it. In fact, until I was drafted into the army in North Carolina, you see, I did not know that I had sickle-cell anemia. I found that out in the army as I was almost dead. Now, those doctors down there knew that I was chronically ill with something and they knew I had a heart condition, but they drafted me anyway. I was drafted and sent to Fort Dix, New Jersey. I stayed there for a couple of weeks and then they sent me for paratrooper training. That was during the Korean War and they were drafting people as fast as they could get their hands on them. I wound up in the tank corps. They had drafted so many people so fast that they didn't even have sufficient winter clothes for us! All we had was just regular overalls and pants and shirts and short underwear. Out there in those mountains it was below zero and we had no winter clothes at all! We had to be out there marching and drilling without coats in that cold! No hats, either. They kept telling us they didn't have winter clothes. I was out there in formation one day and I passed out. It was so cold out there that I just fell out. So they sent me back to the barracks. I got in the bed and one of my sickle-cell attacks came on. I was laying up there screaming because I was hurting so bad! You couldn't just go to the doctor. You had to report to the sergeant and then put your name down on the list; then they had to send the list over to the doctors and then the doctors would say how many sick people could come over. In the meantime I was back in this barracks dying!

Now, they said that I was just goldbricking because I didn't want to get out there in the cold. One of the sergeants said, "Let him lay there." So I just layed there all that morning, all that afternoon. That night they could see that I was getting worse and worse. So finally they called an ambulance to come and pick me up. Then they took me over there to the hospital and started giving me blood transfusions right away. My blood had dropped down very low and I was going into a coma then. Then they sent a telegram to my mother to tell her that I was on the critical list and that they didn't think I was going to make it. I was very sick there for quite a while, and they sent all the way to Johns Hopkins for a doctor and flew him to the base. He is the one who took this blood test and told them that I had sickle-cell anemia. And then they kicked my tail out of the army, right quick. I wasn't in there ninety days and you had to be in there ninety days before you would be eligible for any benefits. I was in there a little more than two months. When my mother got that telegram it was just another thing for her to worry about. She had the others to take care of and no husband to help her. If I had been there less than a month more, I would have been eligible for the benefits, but they got me out of the army in quick time. I told them when they asked for my medical records, but they refused to accept it and they would not write to the hospital. I had never seen these men before. They were army doctors. They took a blood test, but all they were testing for was V.D. and that was all! I wrote the name of the hospital on my medical record which I filled out, but they didn't pay any attention to that. When I asked them about that, they just seemed to think that I was trying to get out of the army; that seemed to make them that much more determined to get me in there. They refused to check or write to find out about anything! If they had written to Memorial Hospital or General or checked my school records, it might have been a different story. But they refused to do any of that, although I did ask them to do these things! If I had been white, I don't believe they would have drafted me and I'm sure that they would have checked it out. That was in 1952, and I never wrote to the army about it because I didn't think it would do any good.

I would like to consider myself a cautious person. Although there are times when I would feel like rushing right in there, I don't do that. Now, that time when I whipped up my grandfather's mules and said, "Come on, cracker," I don't feel that was cool. No, I don't, but I am not sorry I did it. I guess I thought I was right, you see, like that time I told you about when that white man was cheating my grandfather on his cotton. They were both very angry at me for different reasons. But I felt I was right, so I wouldn't back up. Now I am a little more rational than I was in my younger days. I guess I was just a little hotheaded then.

At least there are times when I can do what everybody else does. Yes, there are times and I do appreciate those times, although I never know how long they will last. I have learned to stop feeling sorry for myself, I think. I used to be very bitter about it. I tried not to show it, but when I was alone I thought a lot about it. I used to sit around and think about it. It got to the point where I even hated the word "God"! Why me? What did I ever do to deserve this? I would look at the other boys and girls out there running and playing baseball. I would want to do it so bad and I couldn't do it! And I would ask, "What did I ever do to anyone to deserve this?" And I could never find an answer that would satisfy me. I haven't found that answer yet.

AUTHOR'S AFTERWORD

Almost two decades have elapsed since the completion of the ensemble research which culminated in *Drylongso: A Self-Portrait of Black America*. The hundreds of black people who organized and participated in scores of folk seminars did so out of a sense of civic duty and the desire to assist a native career they deemed worthy. For most of the people I worked with, life is even harder now than it was in the early seventies. The siege lines of racism are tightening and deepening.

In terms of the daily existence of the prudent mass of black people, this campaign against us consists of innumerable gratuitous affronts, irrational impediments and inane frustrations of reasonable human expectations. Most of the black people I know are painfully aware that any one of them might find themselves in Rodney King's unfortunate position. Duly constituted authority remains far more dedicated to its role of agent of Euro-American interests than it is to the just and reasonable maintenance of general law.

The core black view of the history of race relations is permeated by a generally justified wry pessimism. Save for brief historical moments when the conspiratorial Euro-American caste consensus has been threatened, either by internal dissension or external foes, we are still a conquered people living under a regime characterized by transgenerational conquest. For us, history has been, and shows most lamentable signs of continuing to be, a series of dreary variations on the same caste-imperial theme. In 1974 Othman Sullivan, that indefatigable organizer of seminars and prince of seafood cooks, considered the future and declared himself braced for "somewhat more of the same old same old." One of the more vernacular terms for the weekly paycheck is still "these few pennies." There are far fewer pennies in black towns since this book first saw the light of print. Clifford Yancey and Howard Roundtree agree that the economy is near that proverbial degree of constriction they and their fathers have described as "tight as Dick's hatband." Clifford and a number of like-minded Yanceys have managed, through cooperative efforts, to keep "Yancey City" an agreeable oasis in a vast warren of malevolent neglect. Nancy White is saddened but hardly surprised by insurrection in South Central Los Angeles, or in any other Casbah. Sadly, wise, kind, resolute Jackson Jordan, Jr., is no longer among the excellent hosts of this world, but his civil passion for a good dinner and reasonable dialogue remained undiminished for the vast bulk of his exemplary days. The satisfaction of those indispensable conditions of the good life became increasingly arduous for him as it did for most other black people. The habit of rating valued objects according to the difficulty of extracting them from the reluctant grasp of caste is even more common now than it was when I began my research.

Over half a century ago, when I was a child musing on crossing the great Junior High School divide, I wrote this bit of doggerel, which I knew better than to submit to Caucasion pedagogical appraisal.

In Jim Crow's bizzare dominion
Certain sacrosanct opinions
Render absolute reliance
On the pure precepts of science
Rather dangerous defiance.
Two and two are never four
When Mose and Mona go to store.
As to what the sum may be,
Whitefolk often disagree.
There is hardly any rule at all,
Except that Negro twos are small.

African American "twos" are still small, difficult to obtain, and generally inferior. Native shoppers are limited in price, choice and quality in terms of meat and produce available to them in Casbah supermarkets. When I asked Mrs. Margaret Lawson Avery why she referred to her favorite Danish dessert wine as a "number four," she explained that to secure it she had to cross four distinctly hostile suburban neighborhoods. Similarly, Mrs. Wakefield in Florida and Mrs. Nelson in New Jersey refer to their shortwave receivers as "nines" and "sixes" respectively. Miz Moses and her grandniece were often obliged to overcook the meat most readily available to them, "to be on the safe side." The proliferation of "Grease Alleys" and the flight of the already inadequate number of supermarkets in black towns still impose a formidable caste levy which is nothing less than the reimposition of sumptuary law. We pay more for less.

Core black culture is immeasurably the poorer for the death of Mrs. Ruth Shays. At the last seminar she organized and conducted for this research, we met to consider, among other things, the nature and profundity of reform in the United States. My research assistant, Miss Harriet Jones, and Mrs. Shays's agile companions did the actual marketing and food preparation at Mrs. Shays's easy but meticulous direction. That afternoon gathering broke up very late that night, after which Mrs. Shays observed that the seminar had been fruitful because we had wanted it to be and had the power to make it so. "Now when it comes down to this business of reform, the lesson is, if you do not mean well, you are not likely to distinguish yourself!"

Self-vitiating reform has generally meant the cosmetic rearrangement of the formidable mess which the avarice and arrogance of the Euro-American Founding Fathers left on the national plate. Such reform is, of course, self-perverting. African Americans are aware that the current hypocritical concern about quotas is calculated to serve the same caste ends for the national economy that "grandfather clauses" were designed to promote for the electoral process.

The dozen or so years between the initial publication of *Drylongso* and this reissue have witnessed a massive increase in the mean peril of our streets. Many more of those streets have become free fire zones in the "war on drugs." A popular public service announcement warns that "dope is slavery." It is certain that profit is and was the prime factor in the transgenerational booming of both those enterprises.

It is very difficult for a reasonable black American to see the great antidrug crusade as much more than a deadly Euro-American blunt instrument employed by the same forces which have traditionally conspired to suppress our human rights. The refusal of Euro-American caste management to evolve into disinterested guardians of truly public peace means that extractive conquest rather than justice remains the prime business of "duly constituted" *de facto* law and order. The regressive tone seems set by the rogue right Supreme Court, which diminishes human rights whether it affirms or denies them. If, in defense of the cross-burning set, bigotry may flout, on the grounds of freedom of speech, the statutes protecting privacy, property and human dignity, how much longer will it be before the entire Bill of Rights sinks even further into insubstantial generality?

Glorious exceptions notwithstanding, the Euro-American monopoly of real power has occasioned transgenerational hurt, harm and danger to all people reckoned as nonwhite in this caste-like commonwealth. When it comes to gratuitous inhumanity, the Euro-American case makes the former Yugoslavia look like the Swiss Confederation. That we are a nation deep in unnecessary decline is not a question for serious debate. Booker T. Washington's warning aboût the perils of keeping people in an underclass ditch was never more relevant than now. Just as Euro-American social science provided sophistic grist for the Nazi mill, the white American record of forced removal and segregation is profoundly etched upon the maps and minds of the whole nation. Every tribal reservation, every inner city Casbah, every human being lost and gone in the "hood" is an example of "ethnic cleansing" American style.

There have always been Euro-Americans who desire to see this caste-like imperial commonwealth become a more perfect union. Some advocate this transformation because they can see that, given human nature, a perpetually extractive social order is self-liquidating. Some feel the moral weight of unatoned transgenerational, ongoing wrongs. Whether they are moved by the promptings of their better angels or stirred by a prudent wish to avoid impending social and political disaster, these Americans must act to generalize the benefits of citizenship, and they must do it soon. If the time-honored policy of malevolent delay and Pyrrhic postponement continue to vitiate genuine attempts at reform, our national fate is ignominiously sealed.

There is nothing impossible about the terrestrial attainment of a more perfect union. It is within the range of human social capabilities, but the prudent mass of core black people who have shared their reflections with me over the years have sustained enough grievous, gratuitous assault to mind and body to know that we are in imminent danger of perishing from a surfeit of ethnocentric greed and racist parochialism. In the meantime, however, we could all do with a bit of Jackson Jordan, Jr.'s active equanimity: "I am not a hopeless man, or a hopeful man. I just go along drylongso."

ABOUT THE AUTHOR

JOHN LANGSTON GWALTNEY was born in Orange, New Jersey, and holds a B.A. from Upsala College, an M.A. in political science and sociology from the New School for Social Research, a Ph.D. in anthropology from Columbia University and an honorary D.Sc. from Bucknell University. As a student of the late Dr. Margaret Mead, he wrote a dissertation on river blindness among the Yolox Chinantec of Oaxaca, Mexico, that won the prestigious Ansley Dissertation Award at Columbia and was later published as *The Thrice Shy*. He is currently a professor of anthropology at the Maxwell Graduate School of Citizenship and Public Affairs at Syracuse University, and divides his time between teaching and research.

CPSIA information can be obtained
at www.ICGtesting.com
Printed in the USA
JSHW031158030421
13235JS00008B/96